Shojo Beat

The Magic Touch

Oyayubi kara Romance

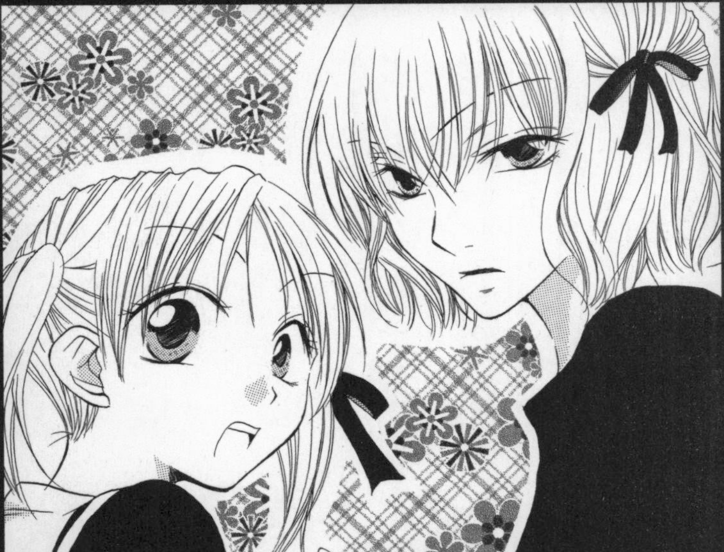

Vol. 2

Story & Art by Izumi Tsubaki

CONTENTS

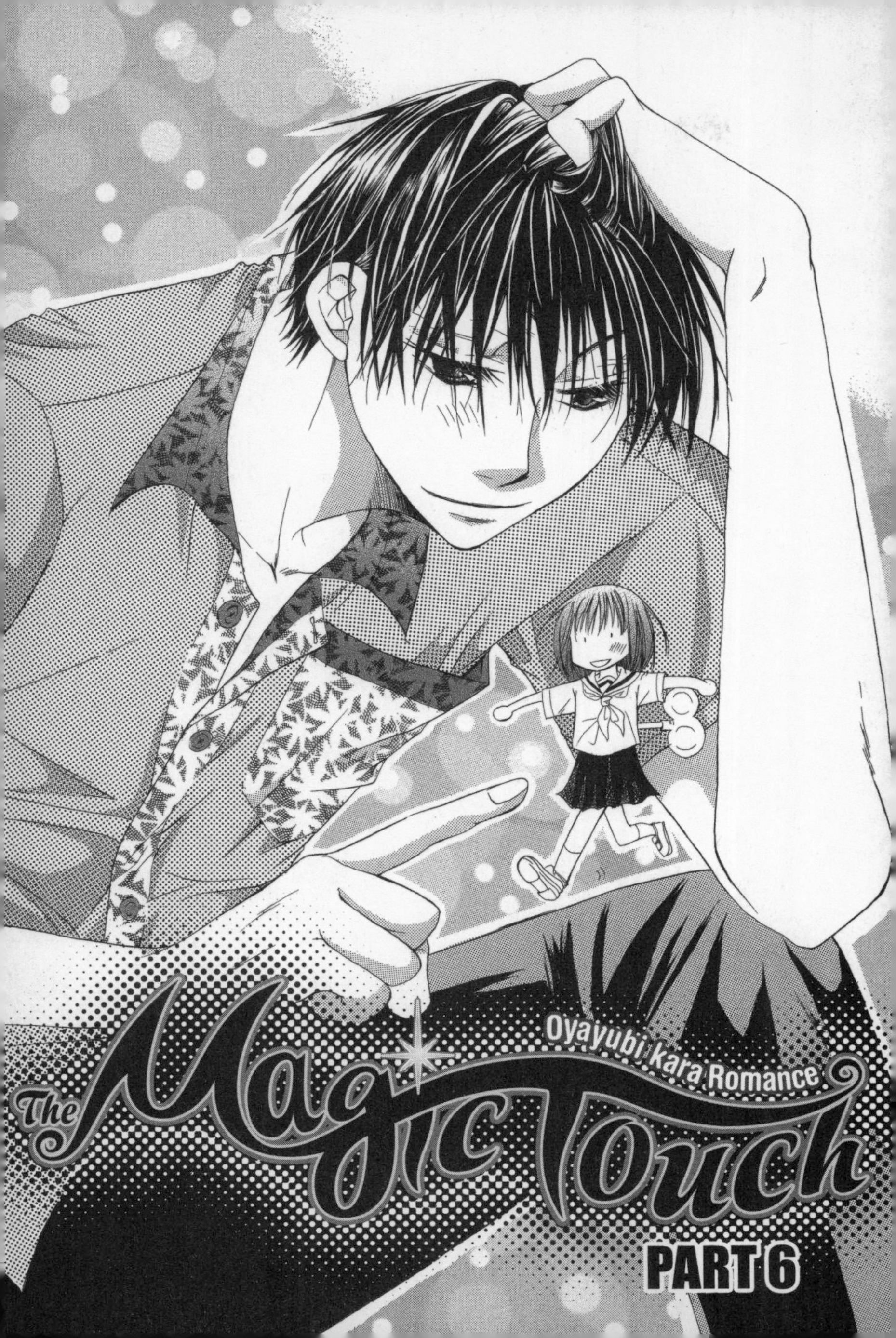
The Magic Touch
Oyayubi kara Romance
PART 6

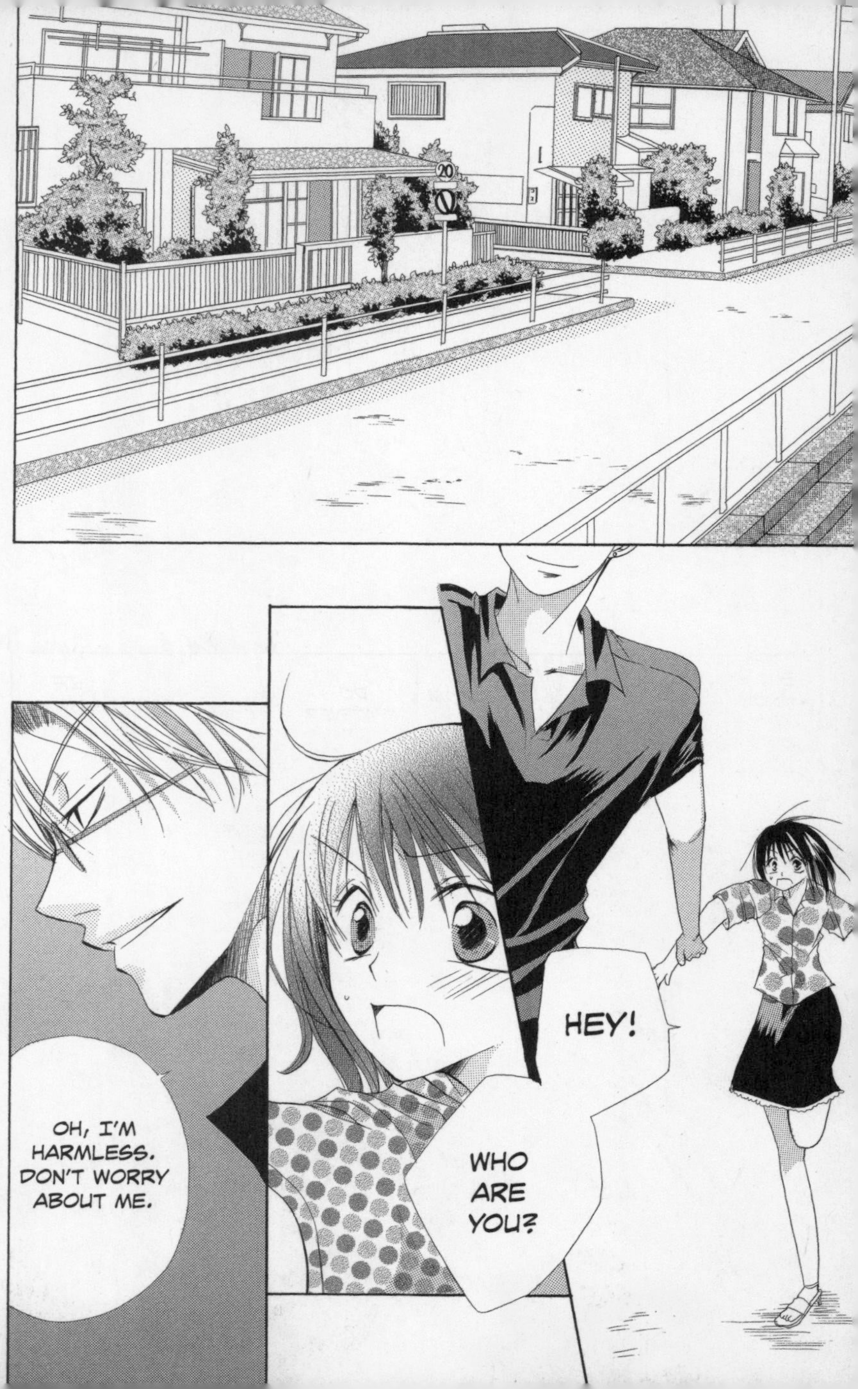
HEY!
WHO ARE YOU?
OH, I'M HARMLESS. DON'T WORRY ABOUT ME.

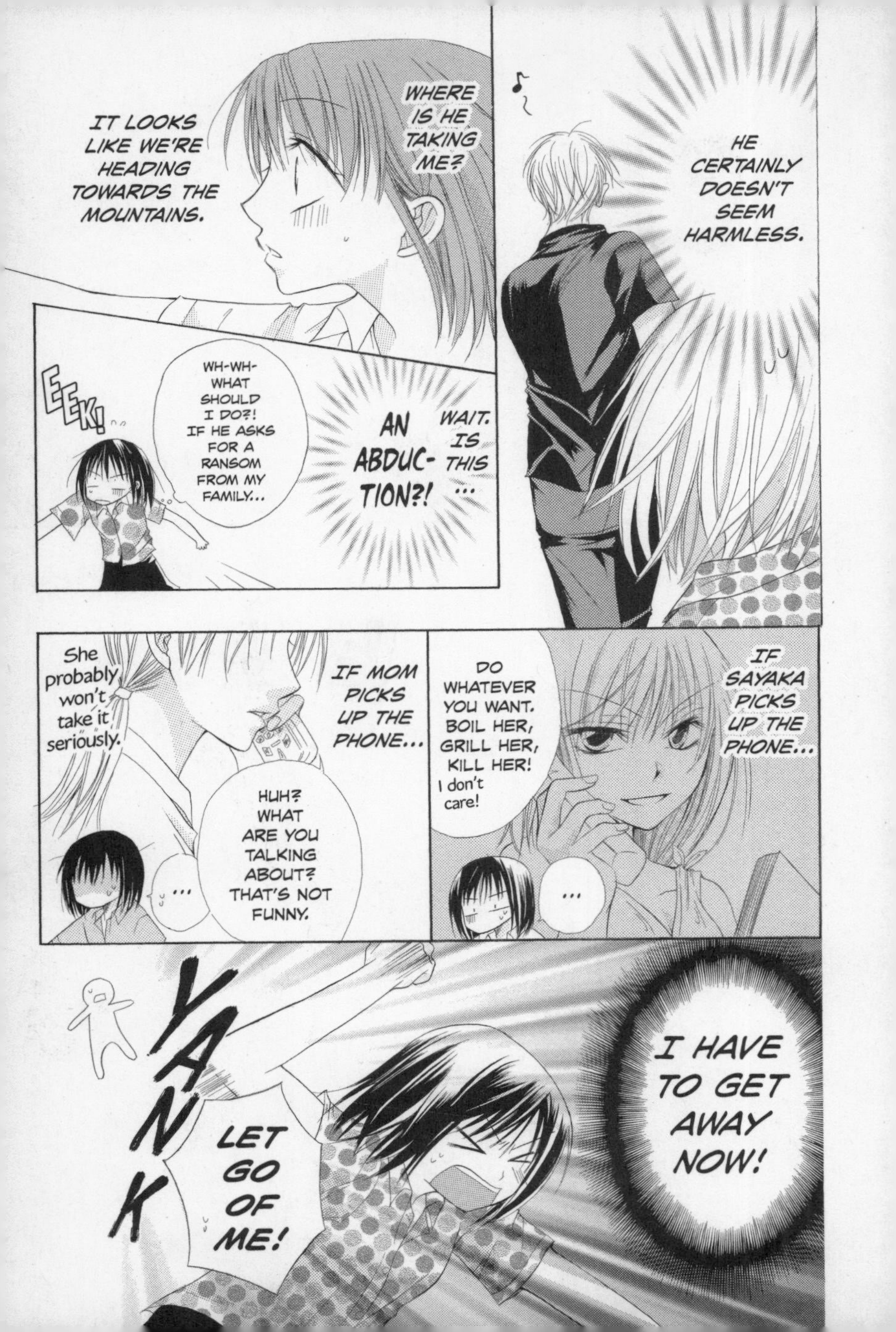
HE CERTAINLY DOESN'T SEEM HARMLESS.
WHERE IS HE TAKING ME?
IT LOOKS LIKE WE'RE HEADING TOWARDS THE MOUNTAINS.
WAIT. IS THIS ...
AN ABDUC-TION?!
WH-WH-WHAT SHOULD I DO?! IF HE ASKS FOR A RANSOM FROM MY FAMILY...
EEK!
IF SAYAKA PICKS UP THE PHONE...
DO WHATEVER YOU WANT. BOIL HER, GRILL HER, KILL HER! I don't care!
...
IF MOM PICKS UP THE PHONE...
She probably won't take it seriously.
HUH? WHAT ARE YOU TALKING ABOUT? THAT'S NOT FUNNY.
...
I HAVE TO GET AWAY NOW!
LET GO OF ME!
YANK

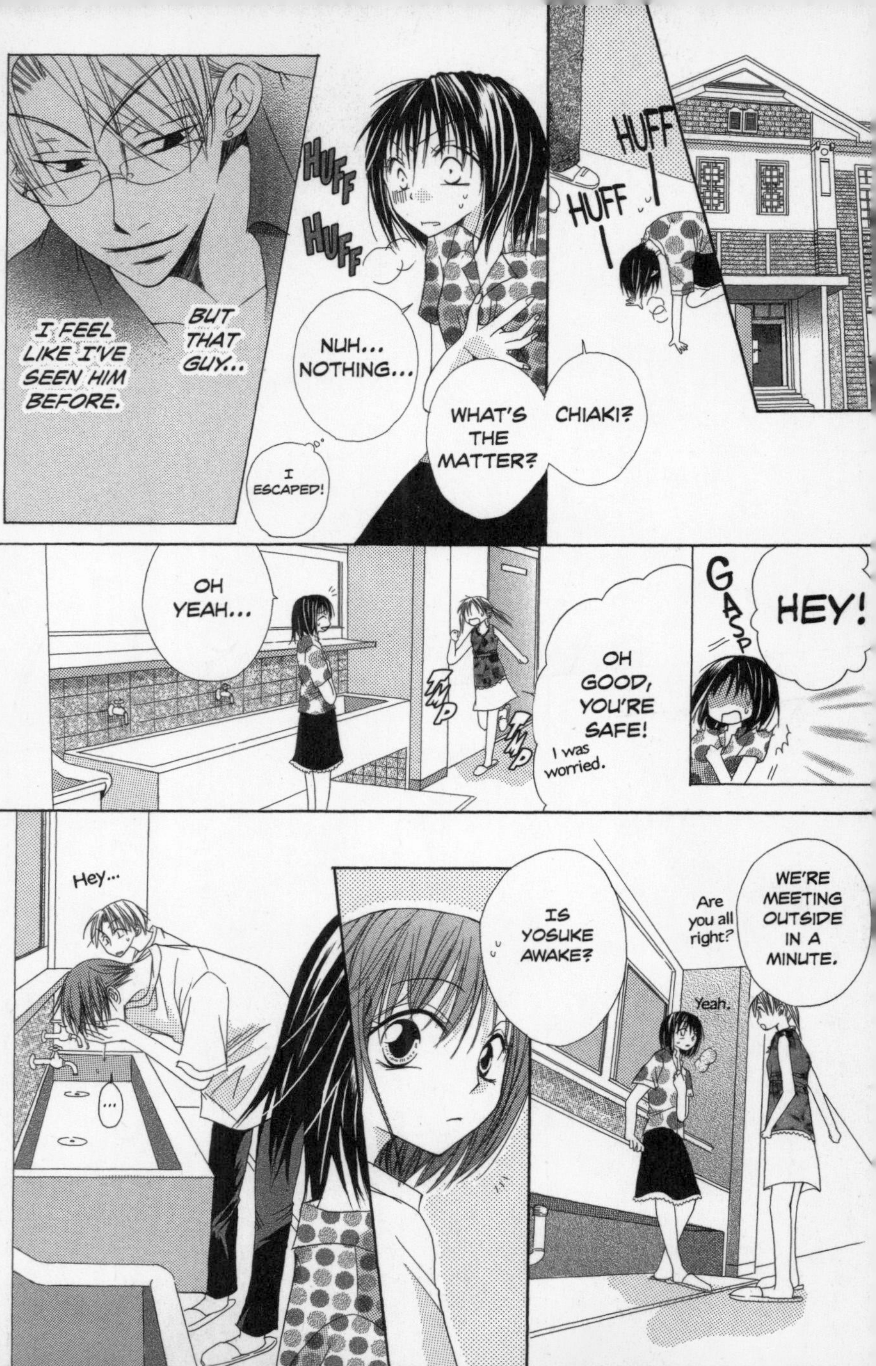
HUFF
HUFF
CHIAKI?
WHAT'S THE MATTER?
HUFF
HUFF
NUH... NOTHING...
I ESCAPED!
BUT THAT GUY...
I FEEL LIKE I'VE SEEN HIM BEFORE.
HEY!
GASP
OH GOOD, YOU'RE SAFE!
I was worried.
TMP
TMP
OH YEAH...
WE'RE MEETING OUTSIDE IN A MINUTE.
Are you all right?
Yeah.
IS YOSUKE AWAKE?
Hey...
...

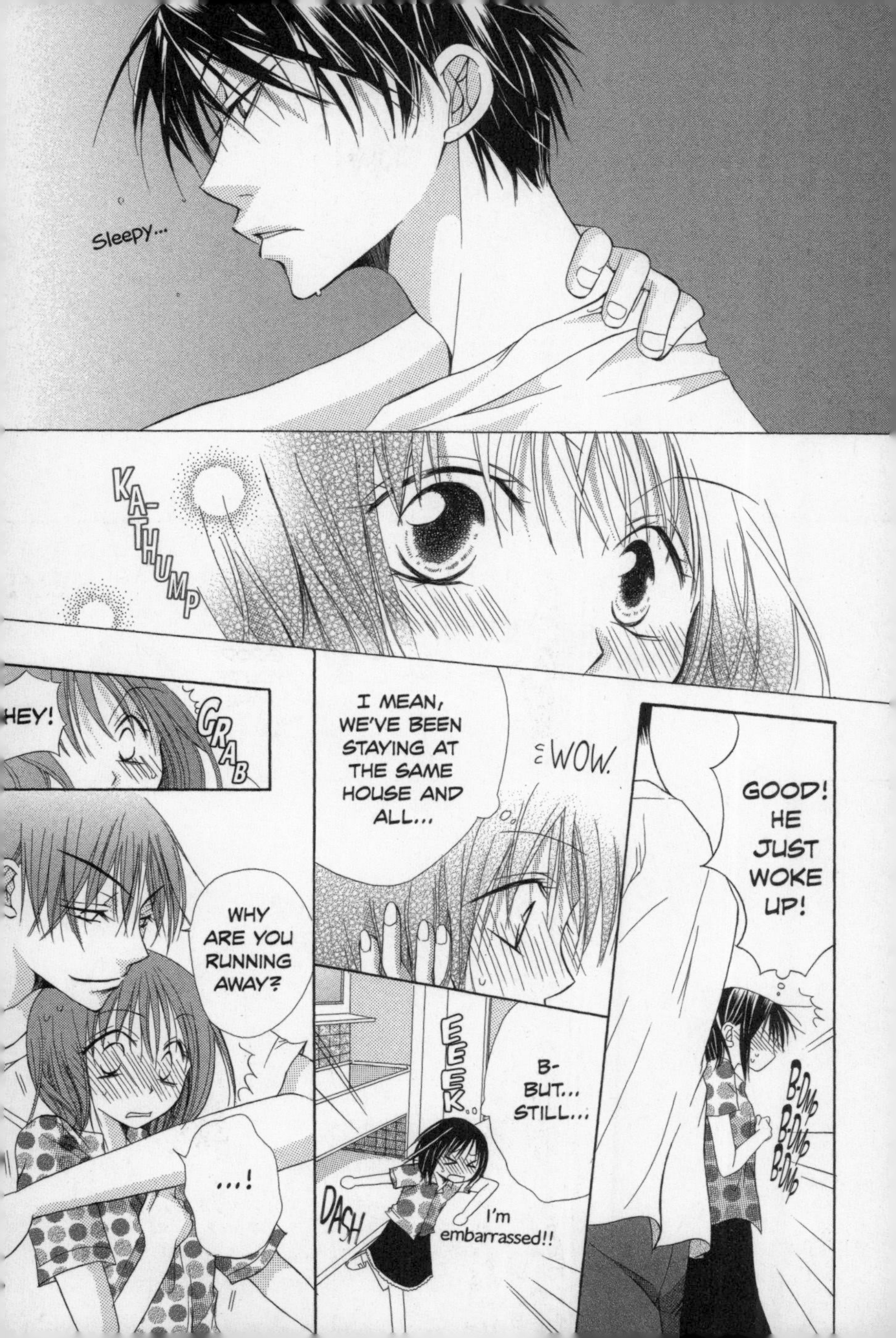
Sleepy...
KA-THUMP
GOOD! HE JUST WOKE UP!
B-DMP B-DMP B-DMP
I MEAN, WE'VE BEEN STAYING AT THE SAME HOUSE AND ALL...
WOW.
B-BUT... STILL...
EEEK..
I'm embarrassed!!
DASH
HEY!
GRAB
WHY ARE YOU RUNNING AWAY?
...!

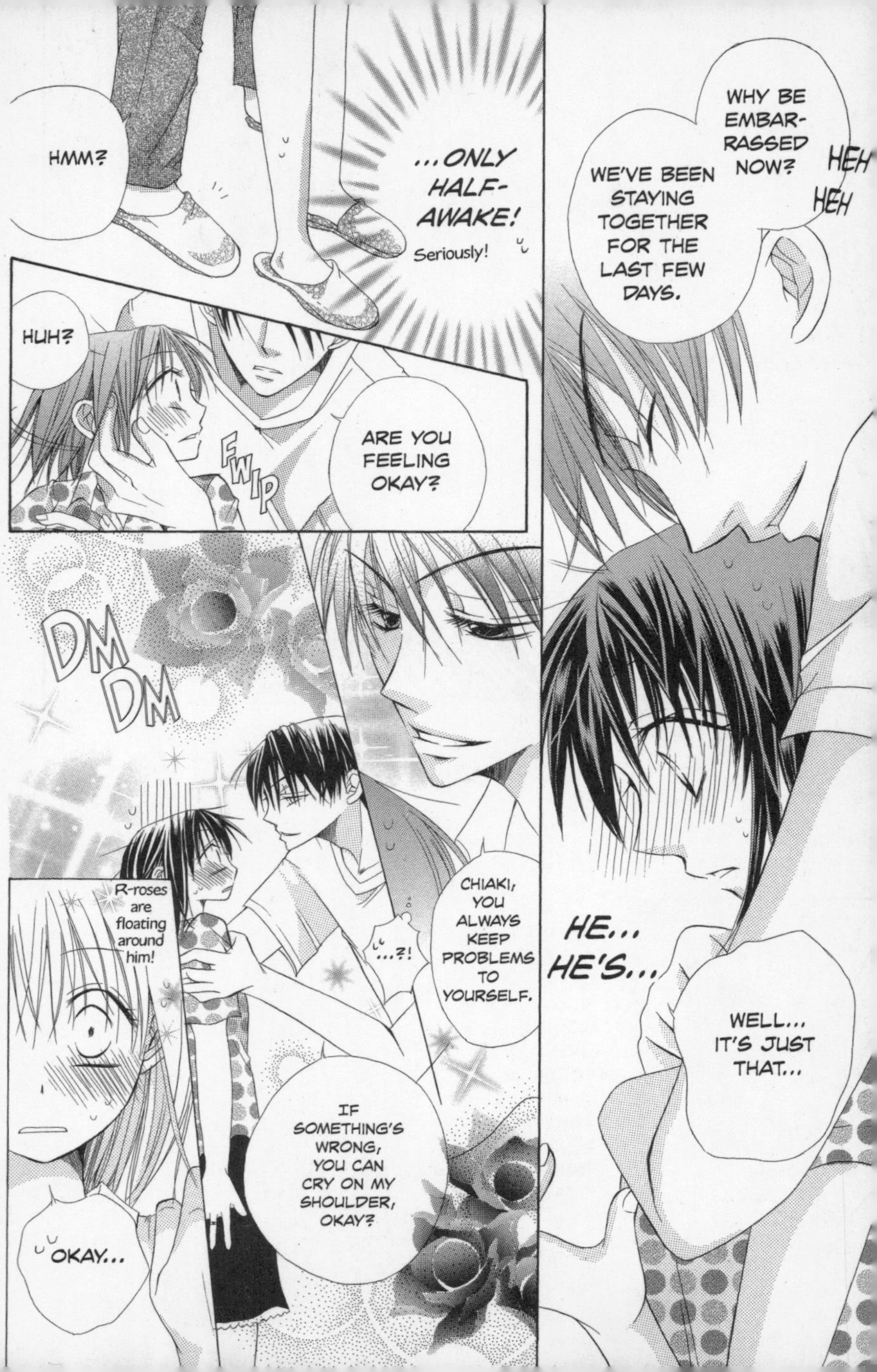
WHY BE EMBARRASSED NOW?
HEH HEH
WE'VE BEEN STAYING TOGETHER FOR THE LAST FEW DAYS.
WELL... IT'S JUST THAT...
HE... HE'S...
...ONLY HALF-AWAKE!
Seriously!
HMM?
ARE YOU FEELING OKAY?
FWIP
HUH?
CHIAKI, YOU ALWAYS KEEP PROBLEMS TO YOURSELF.
IF SOMETHING'S WRONG, YOU CAN CRY ON MY SHOULDER, OKAY?
...?!
DM DM
R-roses are floating around him!
OKAY...

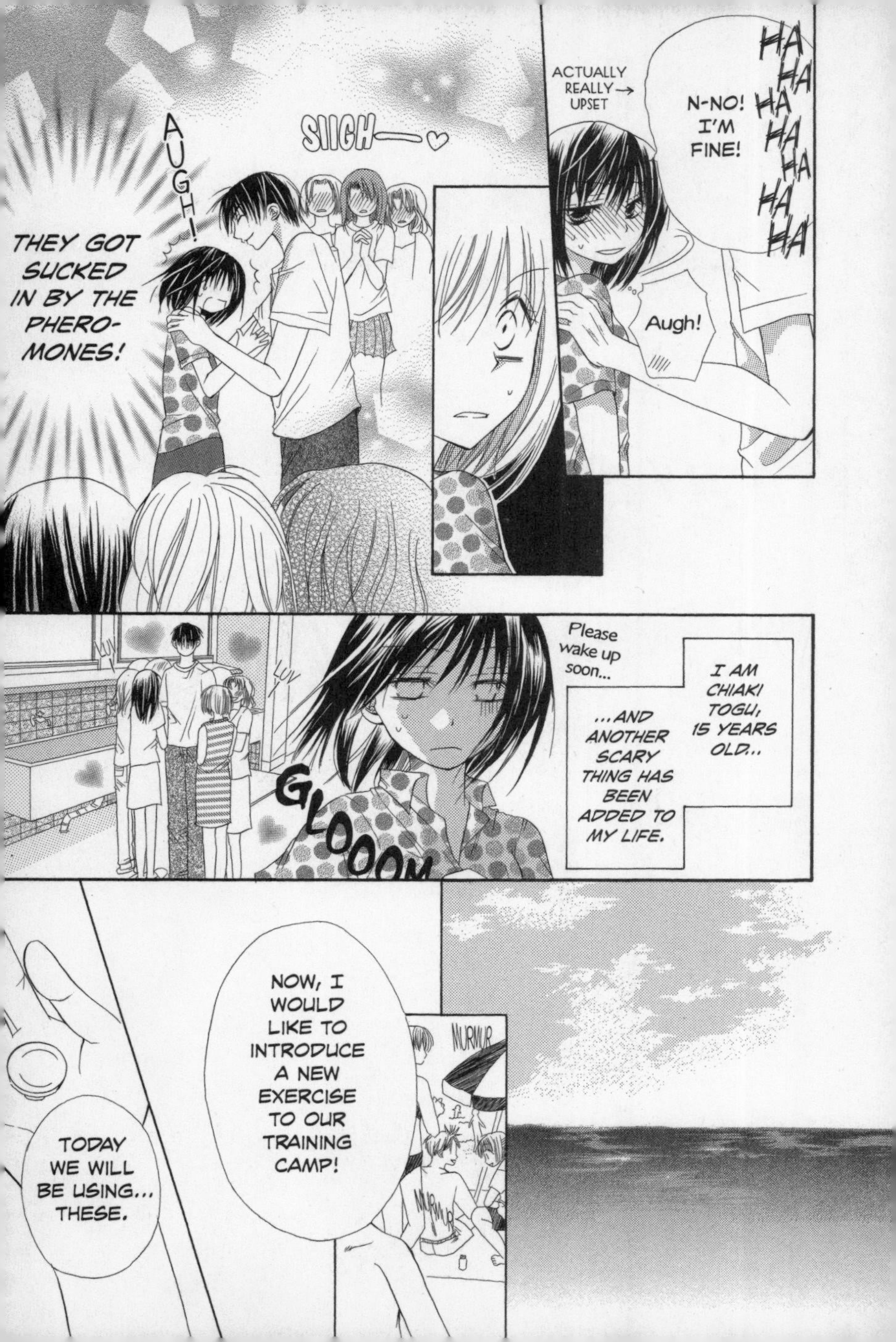
HA HA HA HA HA HA HA HA
N-NO! I'M FINE!
ACTUALLY REALLY UPSET →
Augh!
SIIGH—♡
AUGH!
THEY GOT SUCKED IN BY THE PHERO-MONES!
I AM CHIAKI TOGU, 15 YEARS OLD...
...AND ANOTHER SCARY THING HAS BEEN ADDED TO MY LIFE.
Please wake up soon...
LUV
LUV
GLOOOM
MURMUR
MURMUR
NOW, I WOULD LIKE TO INTRODUCE A NEW EXERCISE TO OUR TRAINING CAMP!
TODAY WE WILL BE USING... THESE.

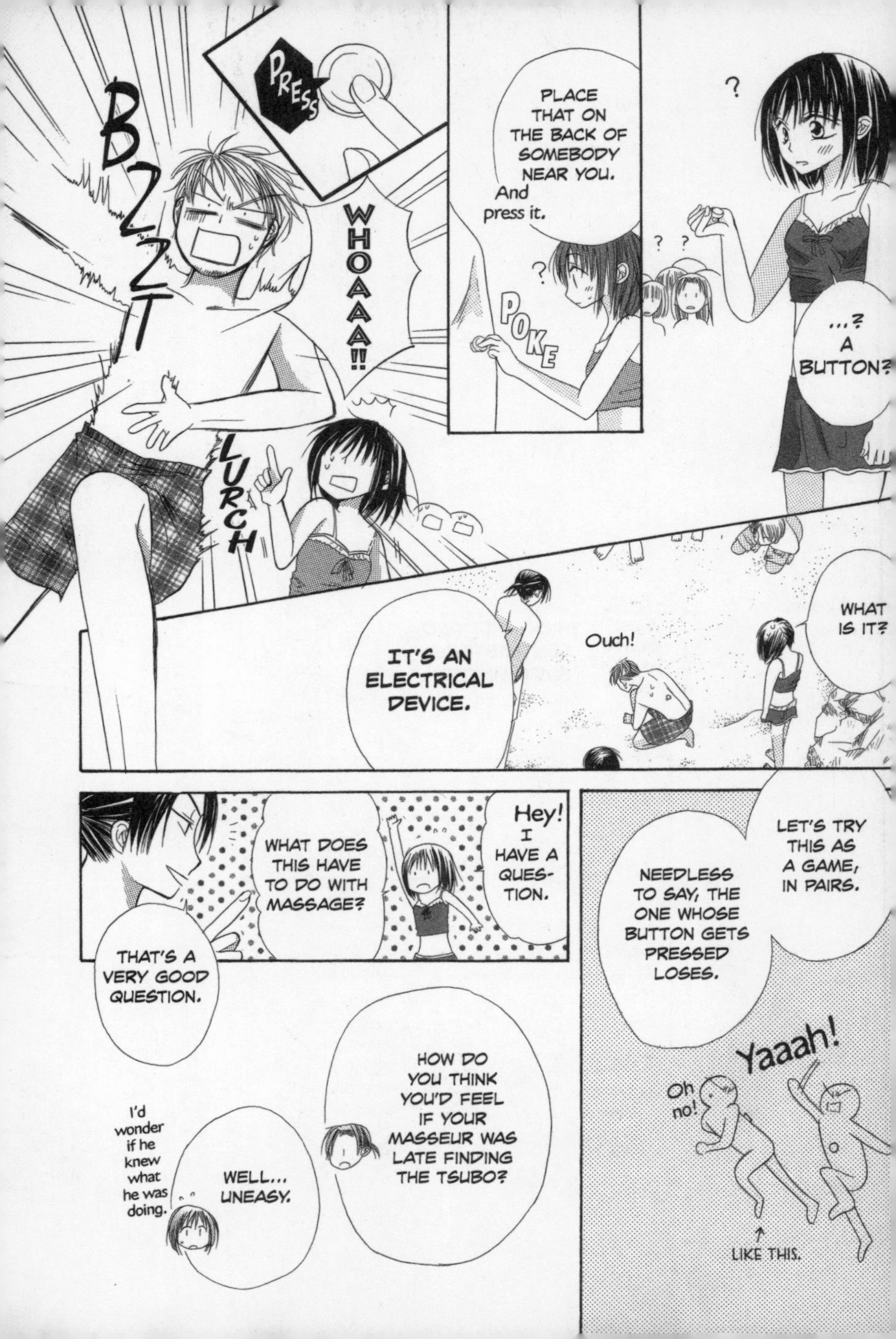
...? A BUTTON?
PLACE THAT ON THE BACK OF SOMEBODY NEAR YOU.
And press it.
POKE
PRESS
BZZT
WHOAAA!!
LURCH
WHAT IS IT?
Ouch!
IT'S AN ELECTRICAL DEVICE.
LET'S TRY THIS AS A GAME, IN PAIRS.
NEEDLESS TO SAY, THE ONE WHOSE BUTTON GETS PRESSED LOSES.
Yaaah!
Oh no!
LIKE THIS.
Hey! I HAVE A QUES-TION.
WHAT DOES THIS HAVE TO DO WITH MASSAGE?
THAT'S A VERY GOOD QUESTION.
HOW DO YOU THINK YOU'D FEEL IF YOUR MASSEUR WAS LATE FINDING THE TSUBO?
WELL... UNEASY.
I'd wonder if he knew what he was doing.

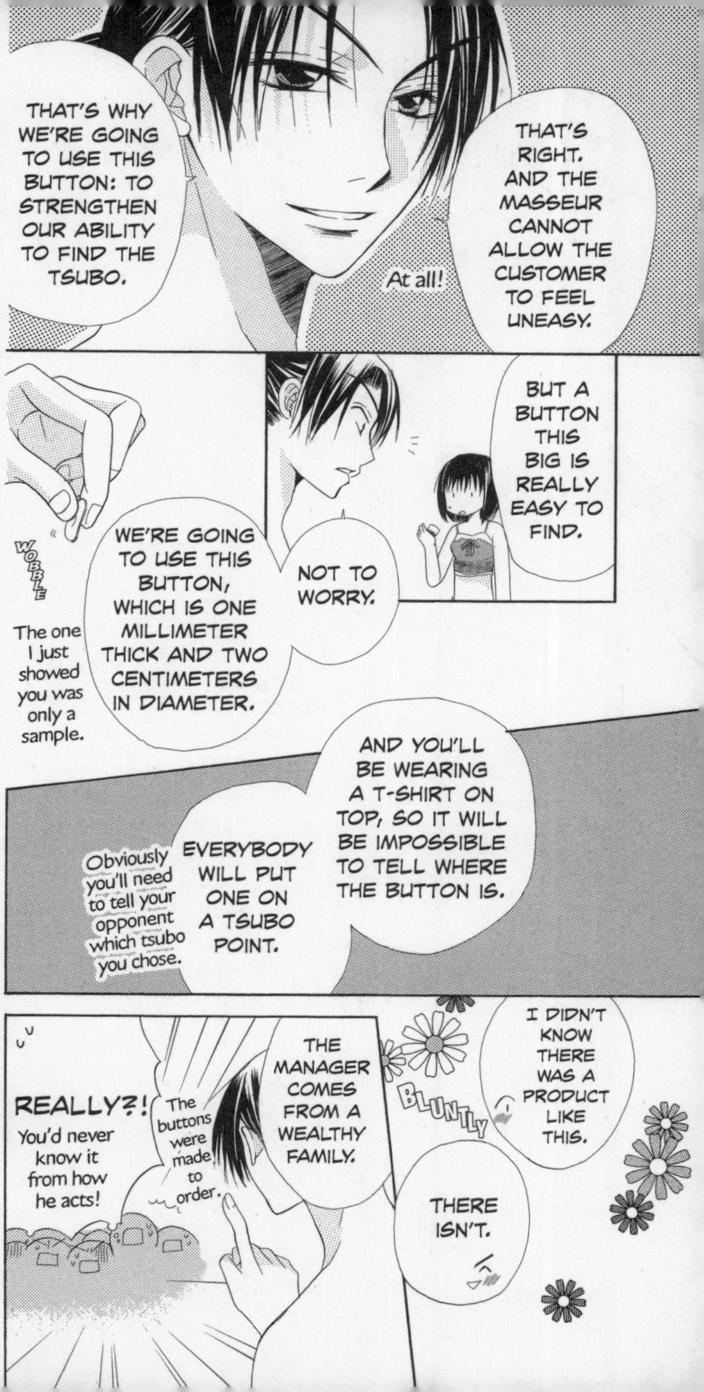
THAT'S RIGHT. AND THE MASSEUR CANNOT ALLOW THE CUSTOMER TO FEEL UNEASY.
At all!
THAT'S WHY WE'RE GOING TO USE THIS BUTTON: TO STRENGTHEN OUR ABILITY TO FIND THE TSUBO.
BUT A BUTTON THIS BIG IS REALLY EASY TO FIND.
NOT TO WORRY.
WE'RE GOING TO USE THIS BUTTON, WHICH IS ONE MILLIMETER THICK AND TWO CENTIMETERS IN DIAMETER.
The one I just showed you was only a sample.
WOBBLE
AND YOU'LL BE WEARING A T-SHIRT ON TOP, SO IT WILL BE IMPOSSIBLE TO TELL WHERE THE BUTTON IS.
EVERYBODY WILL PUT ONE ON A TSUBO POINT.
Obviously you'll need to tell your opponent which tsubo you chose.
I DIDN'T KNOW THERE WAS A PRODUCT LIKE THIS.
BLUNTLY
THERE ISN'T.
THE MANAGER COMES FROM A WEALTHY FAMILY.
The buttons were made to order.
REALLY?! You'd never know it from how he acts!

Hello again... or nice to meet you for the first time!

This is Volume 2 of *The Magic Touch*. People around me keep asking whether the series will continue, and yes, it's still going. And it will keep going! Yay!!

I hope you can keep reading it without getting bored.

Because I've received letters saying I should write more about my life, in my next few columns I'll write a bit about what's been happening with me lately.

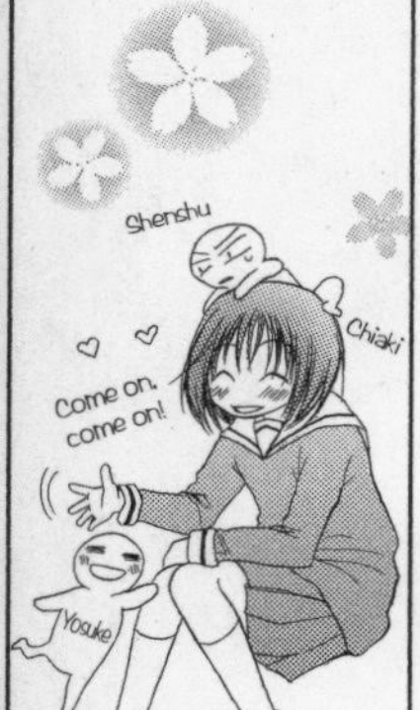
Shenshu
Chiaki
Come on, come on!
Yosuke

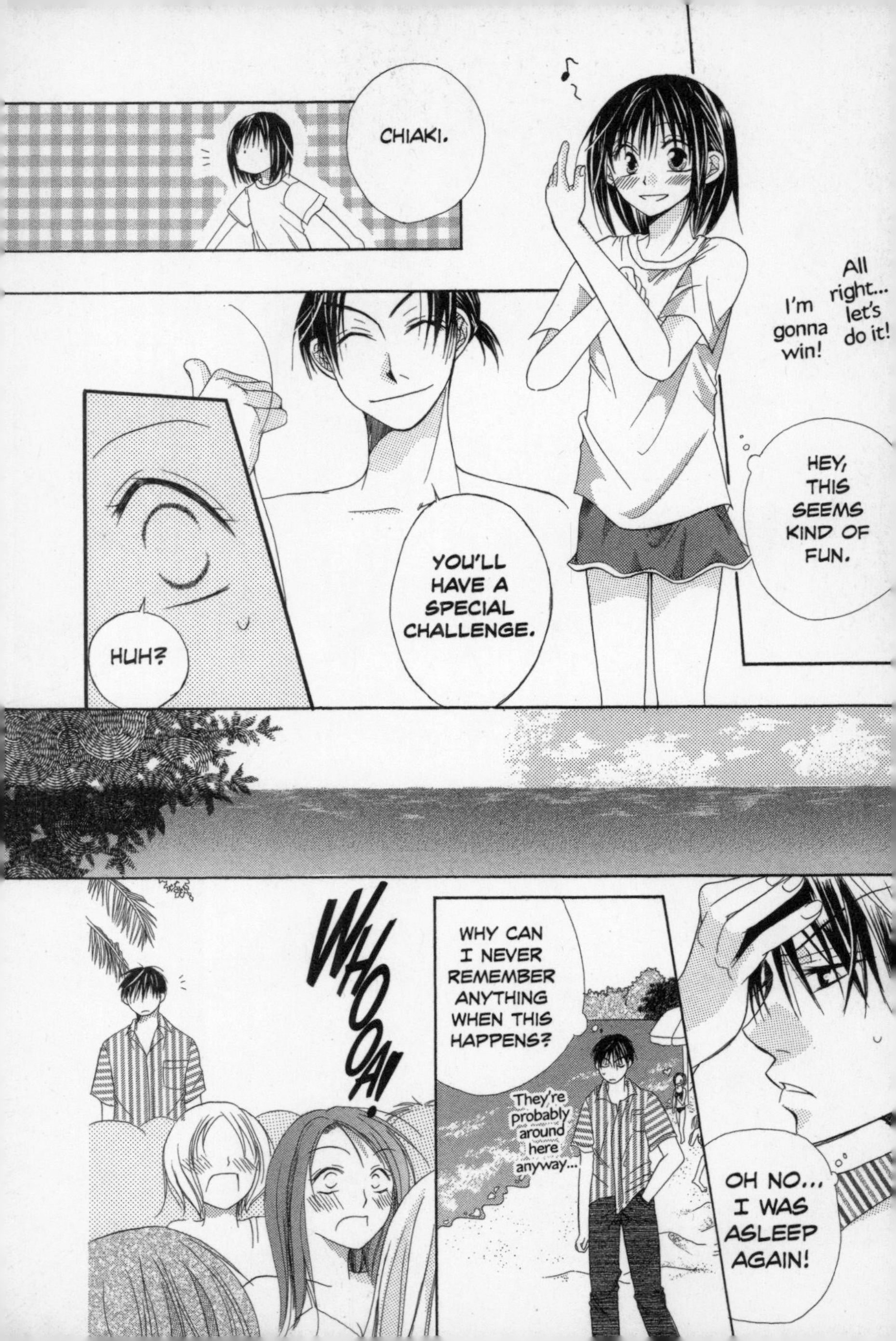
All right... let's do it!
I'm gonna win!
HEY, THIS SEEMS KIND OF FUN.
CHIAKI.
YOU'LL HAVE A SPECIAL CHALLENGE.
HUH?
OH NO... I WAS ASLEEP AGAIN!
WHY CAN I NEVER REMEMBER ANYTHING WHEN THIS HAPPENS?
They're probably around here anyway...
WHOOOA!

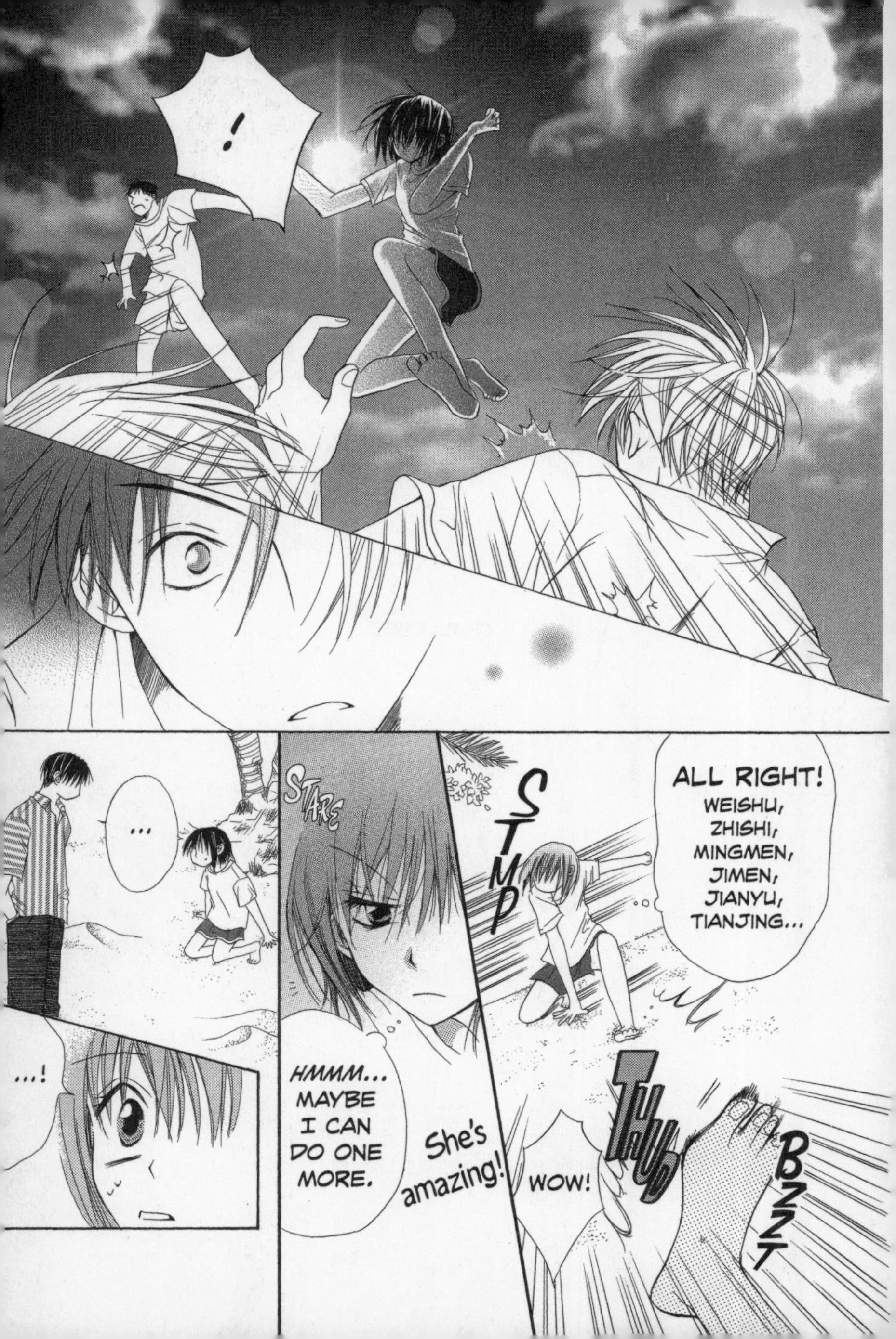
!
ALL RIGHT! WEISHU, ZHISHI, MINGMEN, JIMEN, JIANYU, TIANJING...
STMP
BZZT
THUD
WOW!
STARE
She's amazing!
HMMM... MAYBE I CAN DO ONE MORE.
...
...!

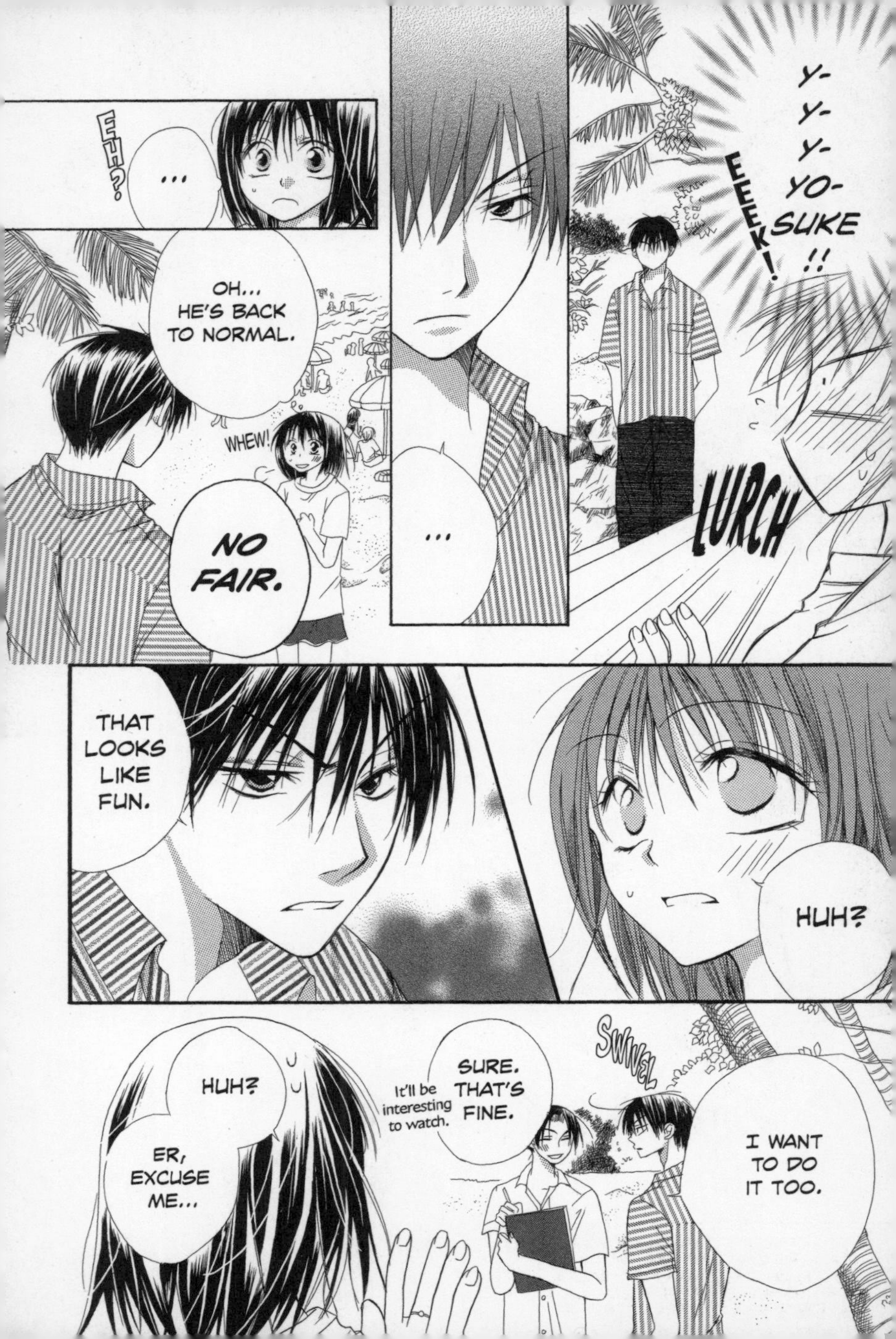
Y-Y-Y-YO-SUKE!!
EEEK!
LURCH
...
EH?
...
OH... HE'S BACK TO NORMAL.
WHEW!
NO FAIR.
HUH?
THAT LOOKS LIKE FUN.
I WANT TO DO IT TOO.
SWIVEL
SURE. THAT'S FINE.
It'll be interesting to watch.
HUH?
ER, EXCUSE ME...

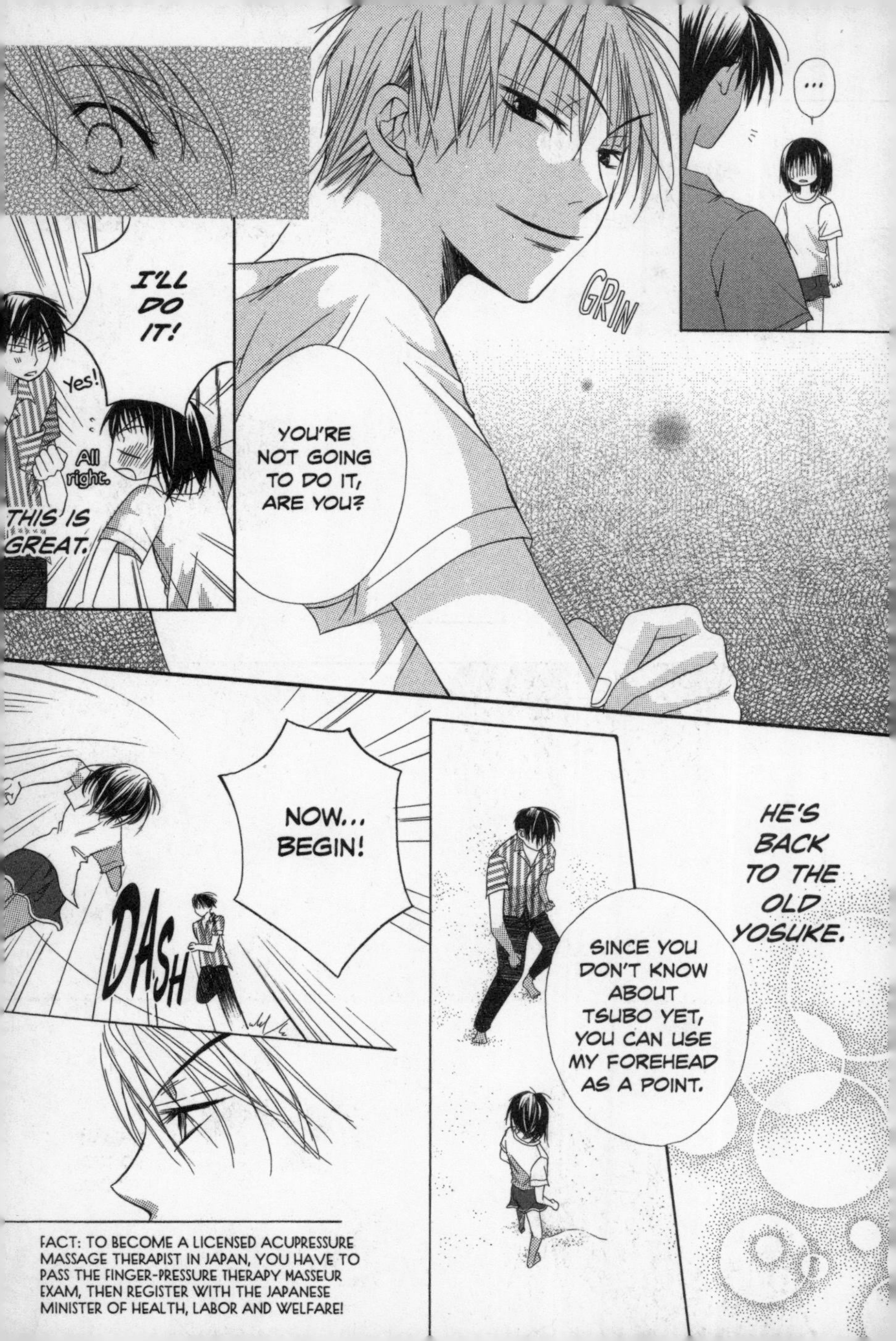
...
GRIN
YOU'RE NOT GOING TO DO IT, ARE YOU?
I'LL DO IT!
Yes!
All right.
THIS IS GREAT.
HE'S BACK TO THE OLD YOSUKE.
SINCE YOU DON'T KNOW ABOUT TSUBO YET, YOU CAN USE MY FOREHEAD AS A POINT.
NOW... BEGIN!
DASH

FACT: TO BECOME A LICENSED ACUPRESSURE MASSAGE THERAPIST IN JAPAN, YOU HAVE TO PASS THE FINGER-PRESSURE THERAPY MASSEUR EXAM, THEN REGISTER WITH THE JAPANESE MINISTER OF HEALTH, LABOR AND WELFARE!

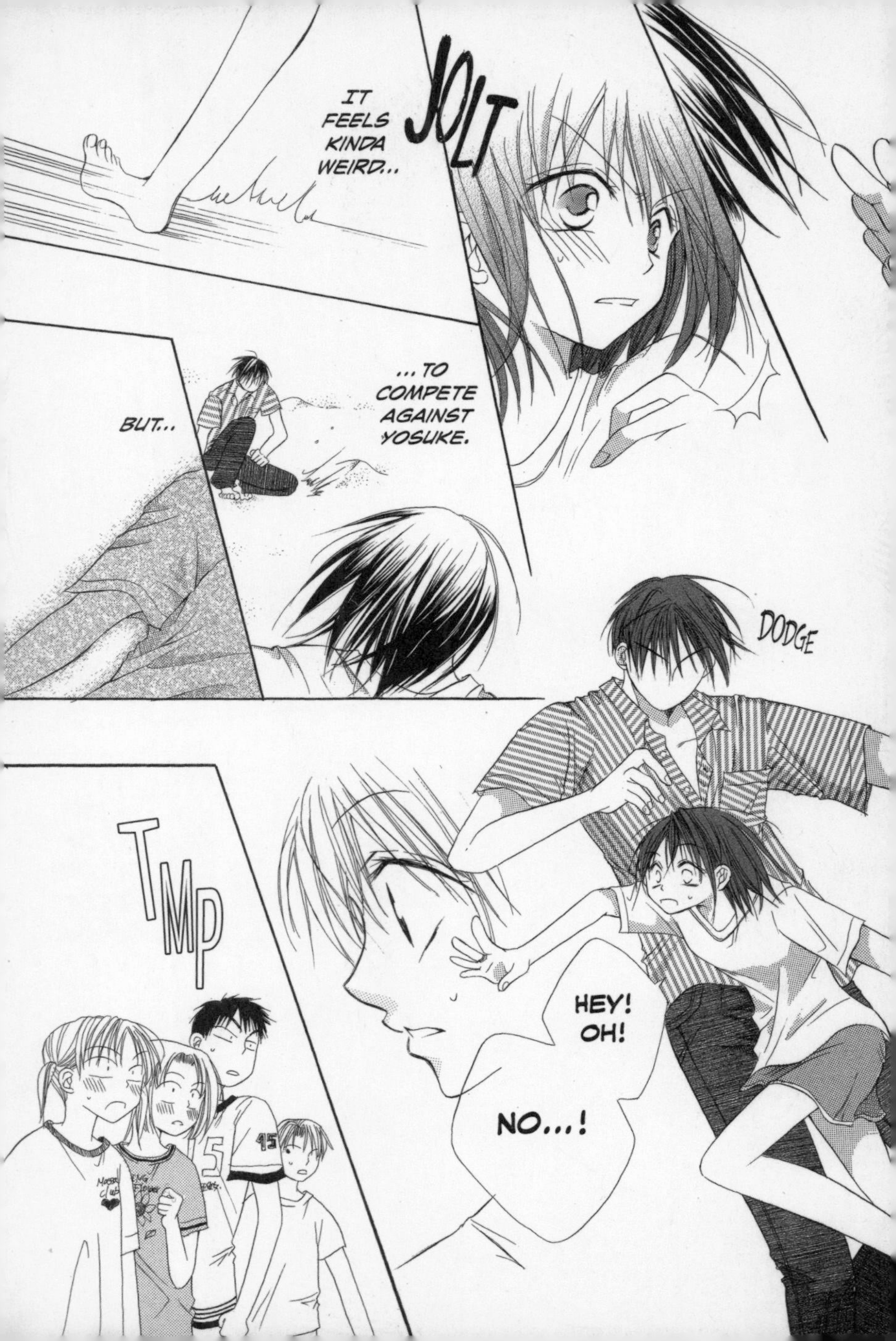
JOLT
IT FEELS KINDA WEIRD...
...TO COMPETE AGAINST YOSUKE.
BUT...
DODGE
HEY! OH!
NO...!
TMP

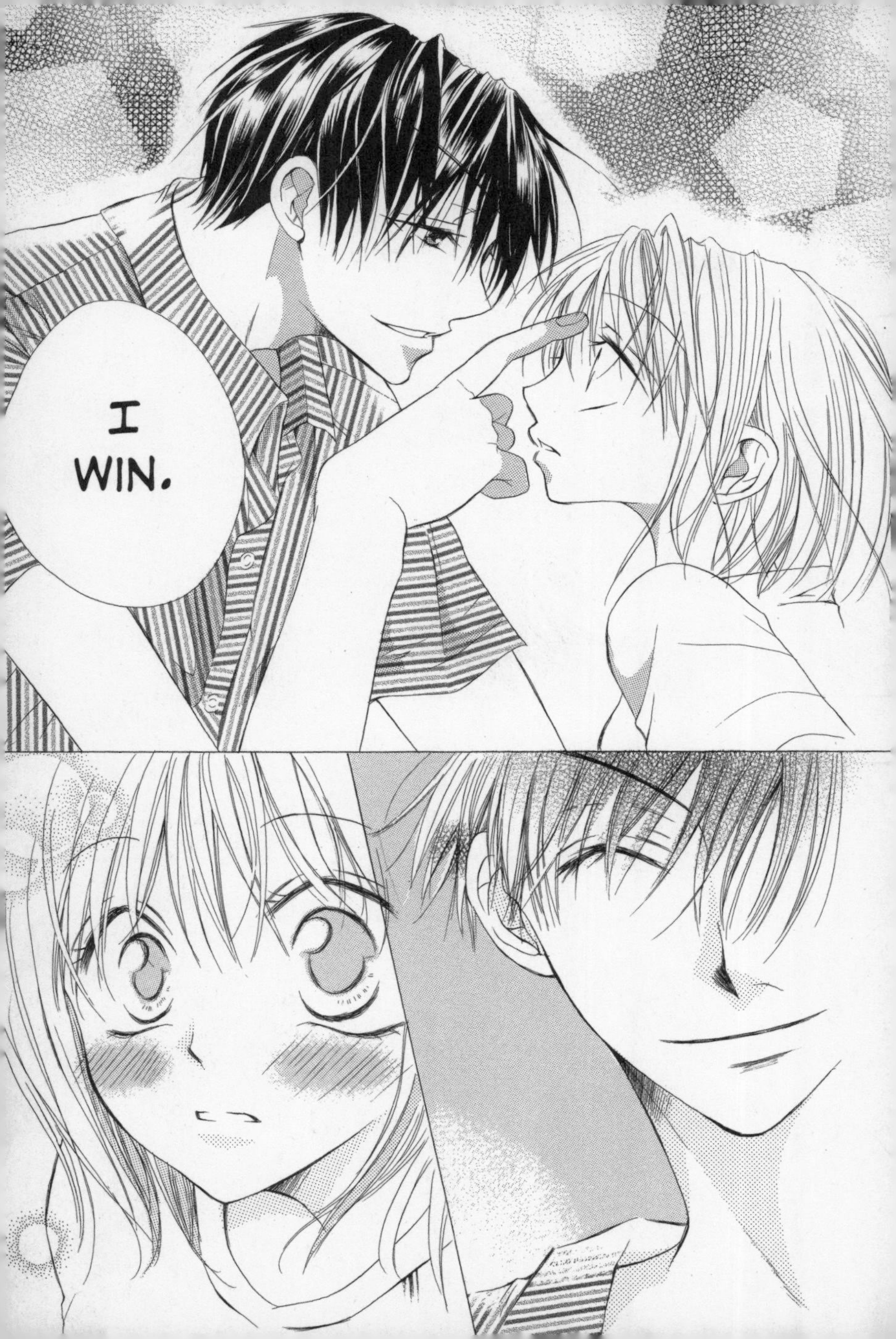
I WIN.

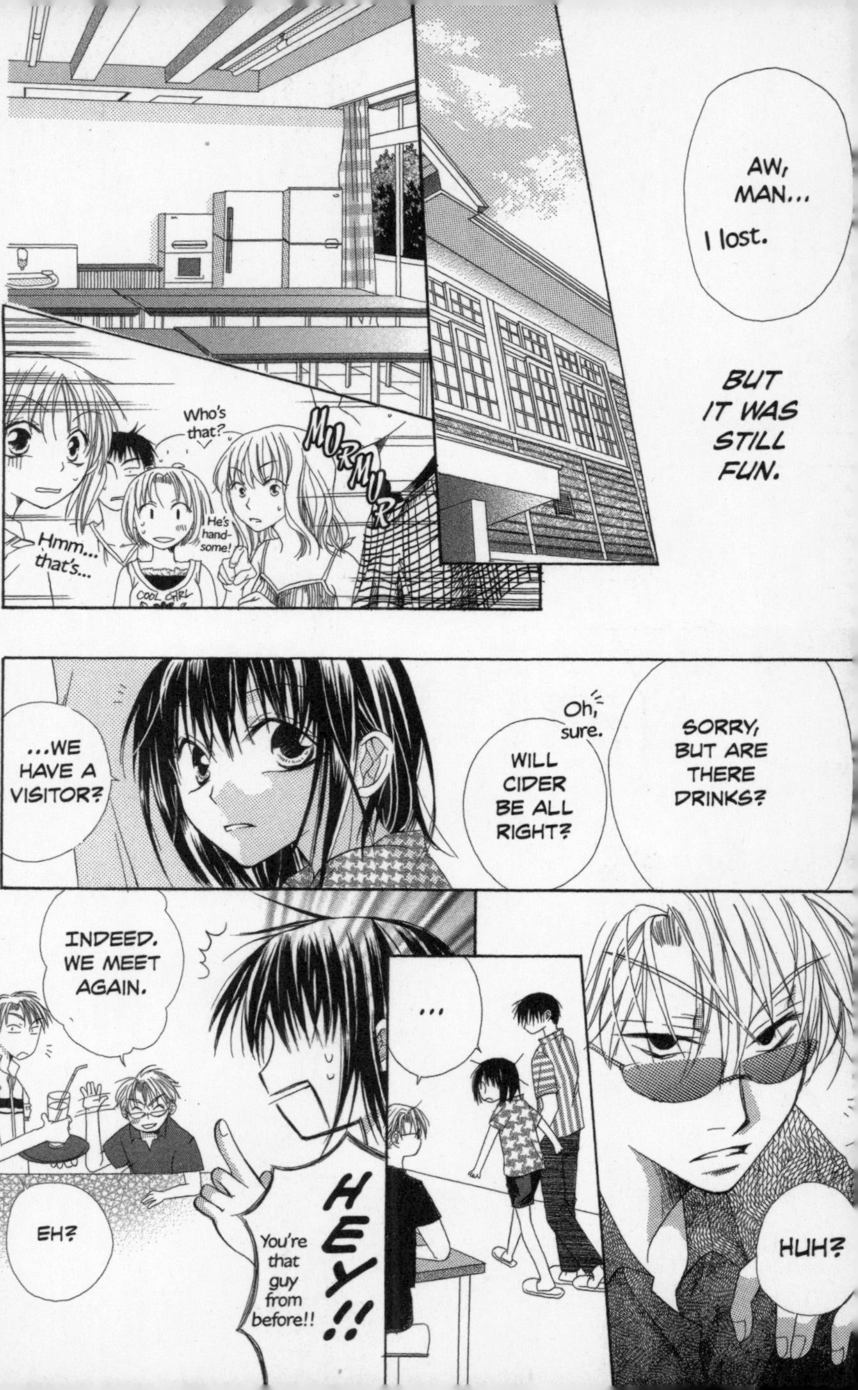
AW, MAN...
I lost.
BUT IT WAS STILL FUN.
MURMUR
He's handsome!
Who's that?
Hmm... that's...
COOL GIRL
SORRY, BUT ARE THERE DRINKS?
Oh, sure.
WILL CIDER BE ALL RIGHT?
...WE HAVE A VISITOR?
HUH?
...
HEY!!
You're that guy from before!!
INDEED. WE MEET AGAIN.
EH?

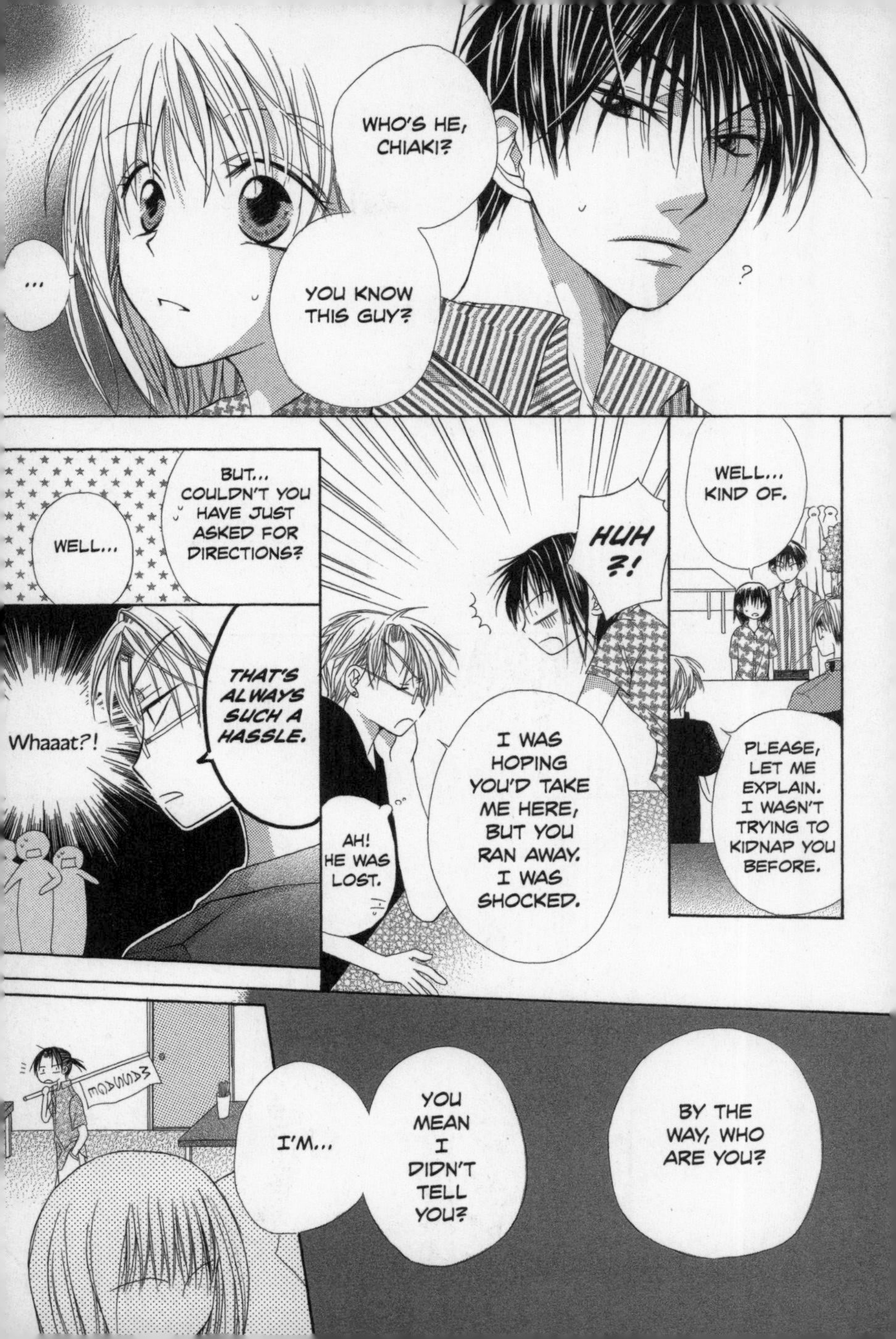
WHO'S HE, CHIAKI?
YOU KNOW THIS GUY?
...
?
WELL... KIND OF.
PLEASE, LET ME EXPLAIN. I WASN'T TRYING TO KIDNAP YOU BEFORE.
HUH ?!
I WAS HOPING YOU'D TAKE ME HERE, BUT YOU RAN AWAY. I WAS SHOCKED.
AH! HE WAS LOST.
BUT... COULDN'T YOU HAVE JUST ASKED FOR DIRECTIONS?
WELL...
THAT'S ALWAYS SUCH A HASSLE.
Whaaat?!
BY THE WAY, WHO ARE YOU?
YOU MEAN I DIDN'T TELL YOU?
I'M...

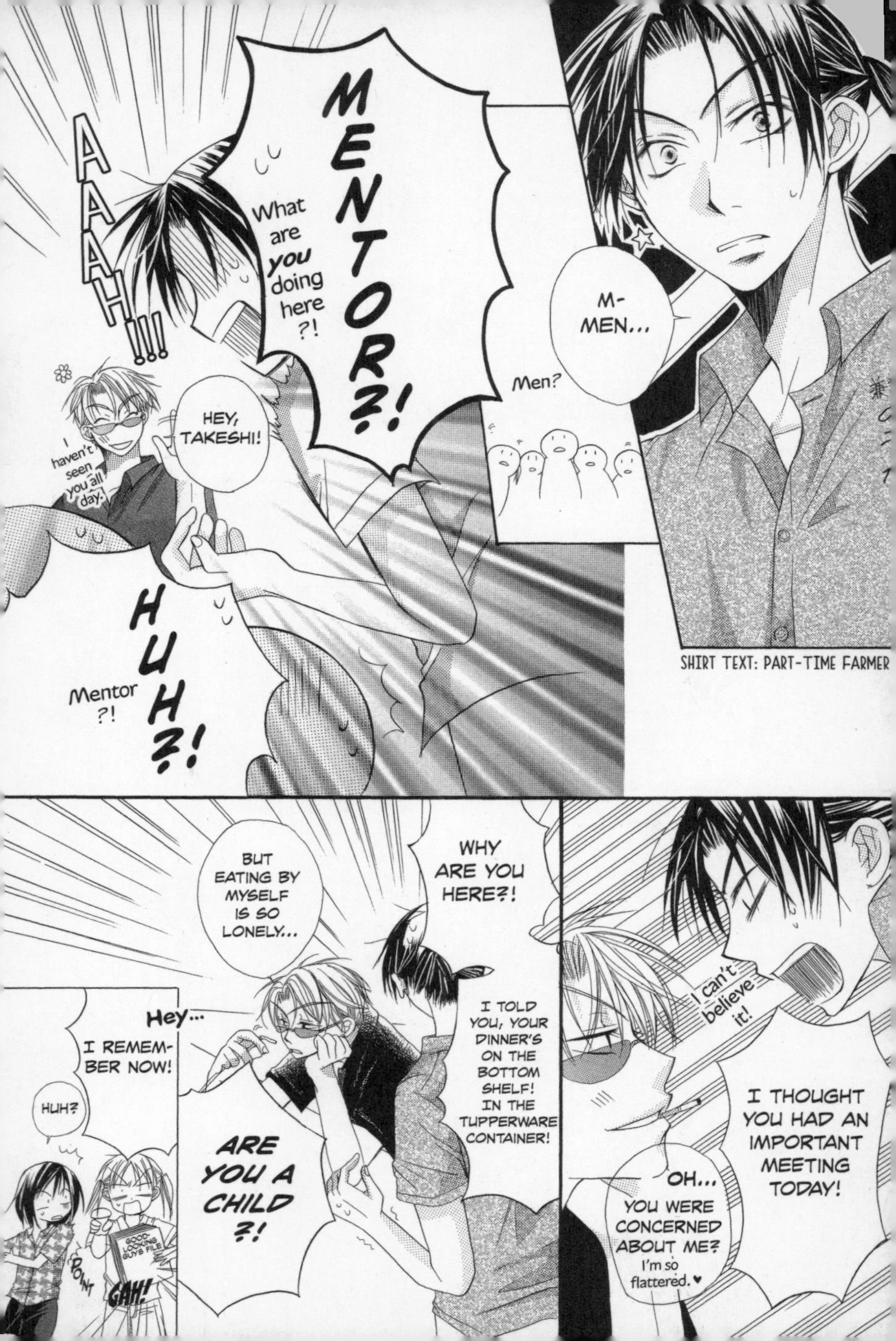
M-MEN...
Men?
SHIRT TEXT: PART-TIME FARMER
MENTOR?!
What are you doing here?!
AAAAH!!!
HEY, TAKESHI!
I haven't seen you all day.
HUH?!
Mentor?!
I can't believe it!
I THOUGHT YOU HAD AN IMPORTANT MEETING TODAY!
OH... YOU WERE CONCERNED ABOUT ME? I'm so flattered.♥
WHY ARE YOU HERE?!
BUT EATING BY MYSELF IS SO LONELY...
I TOLD YOU, YOUR DINNER'S ON THE BOTTOM SHELF! IN THE TUPPERWARE CONTAINER!
ARE YOU A CHILD?!
Hey... I REMEMBER NOW!
HUH?
GOOD-LOOKING GUYS FILE
POINT
GAH!

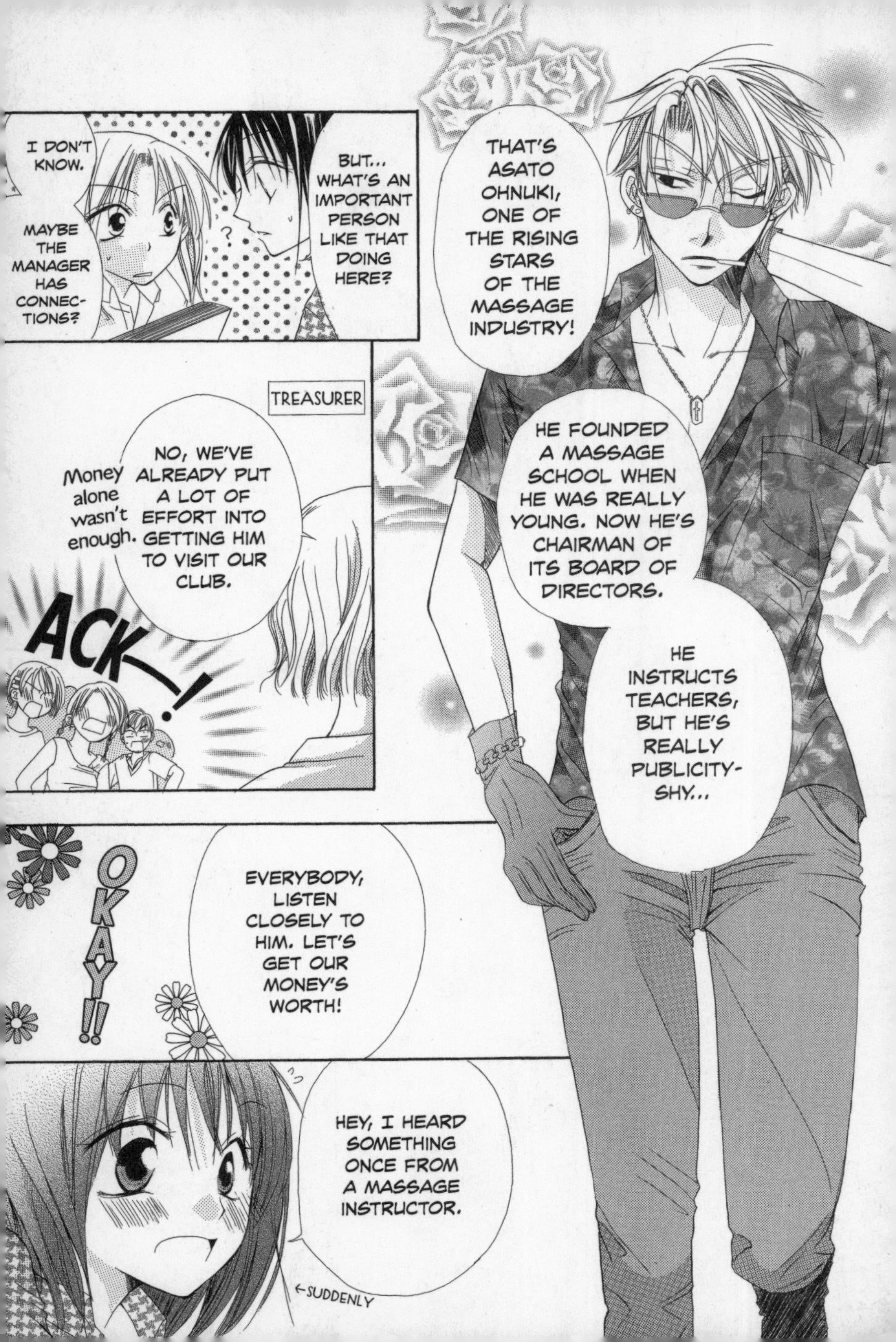
THAT'S ASATO OHNUKI, ONE OF THE RISING STARS OF THE MASSAGE INDUSTRY!
HE FOUNDED A MASSAGE SCHOOL WHEN HE WAS REALLY YOUNG. NOW HE'S CHAIRMAN OF ITS BOARD OF DIRECTORS.
HE INSTRUCTS TEACHERS, BUT HE'S REALLY PUBLICITY-SHY...
BUT... WHAT'S AN IMPORTANT PERSON LIKE THAT DOING HERE?
I DON'T KNOW.
MAYBE THE MANAGER HAS CONNECTIONS?
TREASURER
NO, WE'VE ALREADY PUT A LOT OF EFFORT INTO GETTING HIM TO VISIT OUR CLUB.
Money alone wasn't enough.
ACK—!
EVERYBODY, LISTEN CLOSELY TO HIM. LET'S GET OUR MONEY'S WORTH!
OKAY!!
HEY, I HEARD SOMETHING ONCE FROM A MASSAGE INSTRUCTOR.
←SUDDENLY

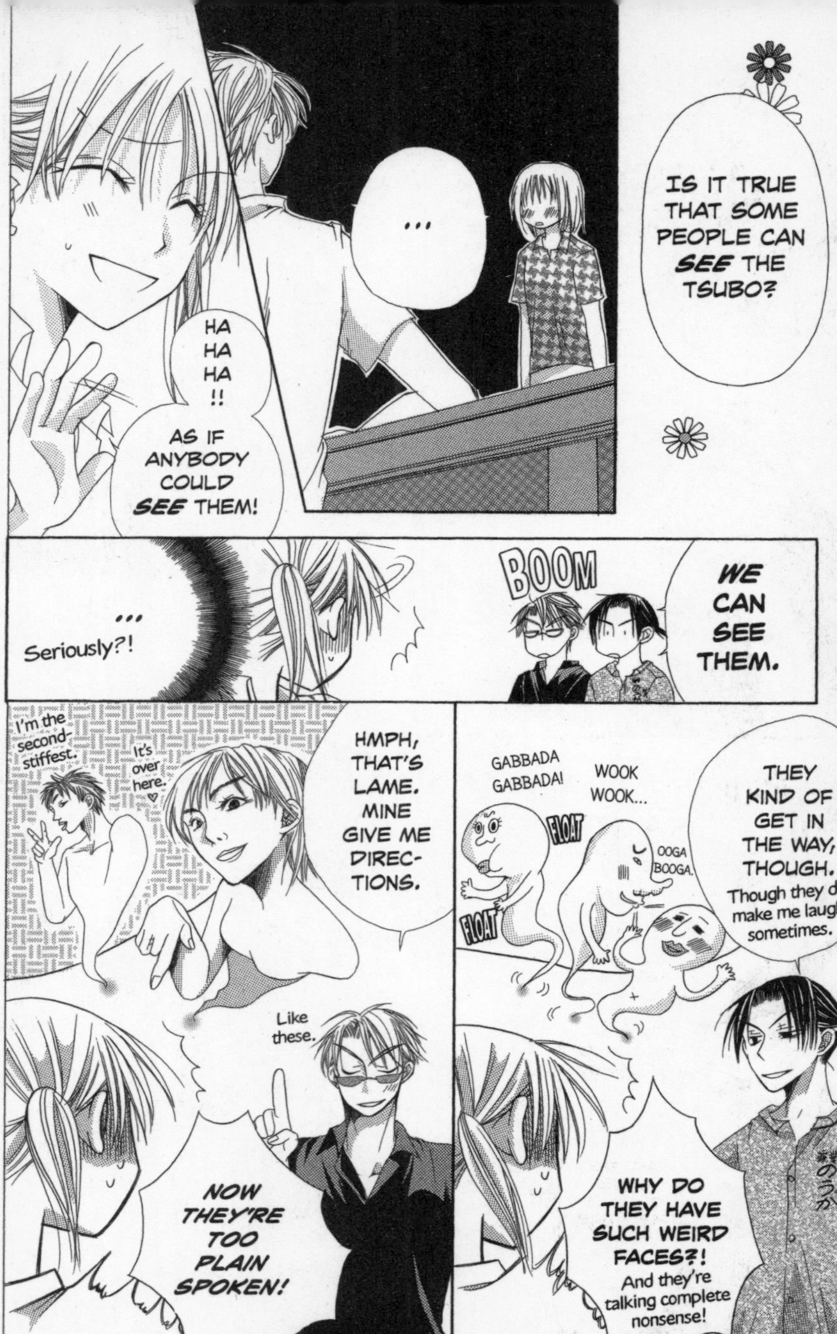
IS IT TRUE THAT SOME PEOPLE CAN *SEE* THE TSUBO?
...
HA HA HA!!
AS IF ANYBODY COULD *SEE* THEM!
BOOM
WE CAN SEE THEM.
...
Seriously?!
THEY KIND OF GET IN THE WAY, THOUGH.
Though they do make me laugh sometimes.
GABBADA GABBADA!
WOOK WOOK...
FLOAT
FLOAT
OOGA BOOGA.
HMPH, THAT'S LAME. MINE GIVE ME DIREC-TIONS.
I'm the second-stiffest.
It's over here. ♡
WHY DO THEY HAVE SUCH WEIRD FACES?!
And they're talking complete nonsense!
Like these.
NOW THEY'RE TOO PLAIN SPOKEN!

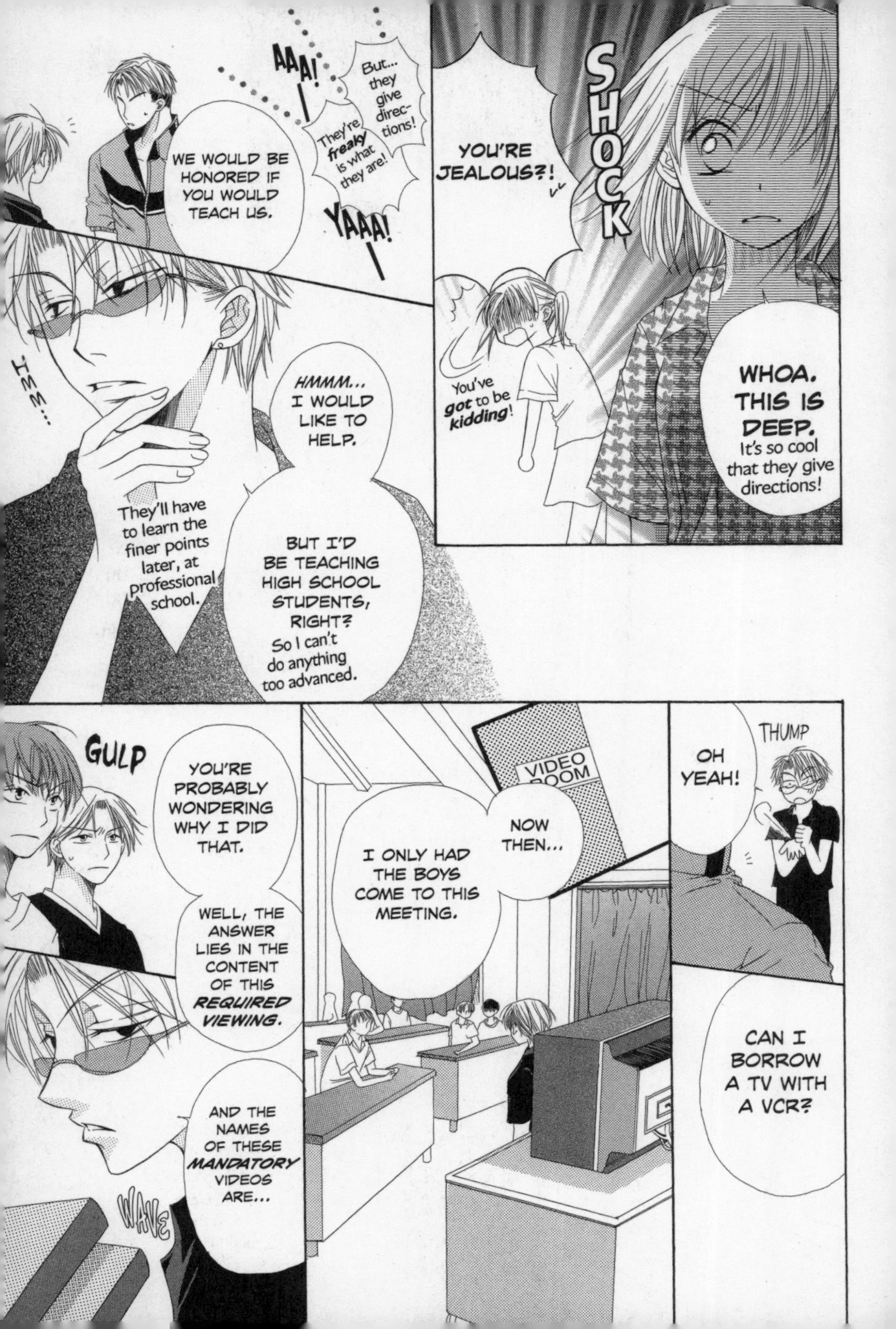
SHOCK
WHOA. THIS IS DEEP. It's so cool that they give directions!
YOU'RE JEALOUS?!
You've got to be kidding!
But... they give directions!
They're freaky is what they are!
AAA!
YAAA!
WE WOULD BE HONORED IF YOU WOULD TEACH US.
HMMM... I WOULD LIKE TO HELP.
BUT I'D BE TEACHING HIGH SCHOOL STUDENTS, RIGHT? So I can't do anything too advanced.
They'll have to learn the finer points later, at professional school.
HMM...
THUMP
OH YEAH!
CAN I BORROW A TV WITH A VCR?
VIDEO ROOM
NOW THEN...
I ONLY HAD THE BOYS COME TO THIS MEETING.
YOU'RE PROBABLY WONDERING WHY I DID THAT.
GULP
WELL, THE ANSWER LIES IN THE CONTENT OF THIS REQUIRED VIEWING.
AND THE NAMES OF THESE MANDATORY VIDEOS ARE...
WAVE

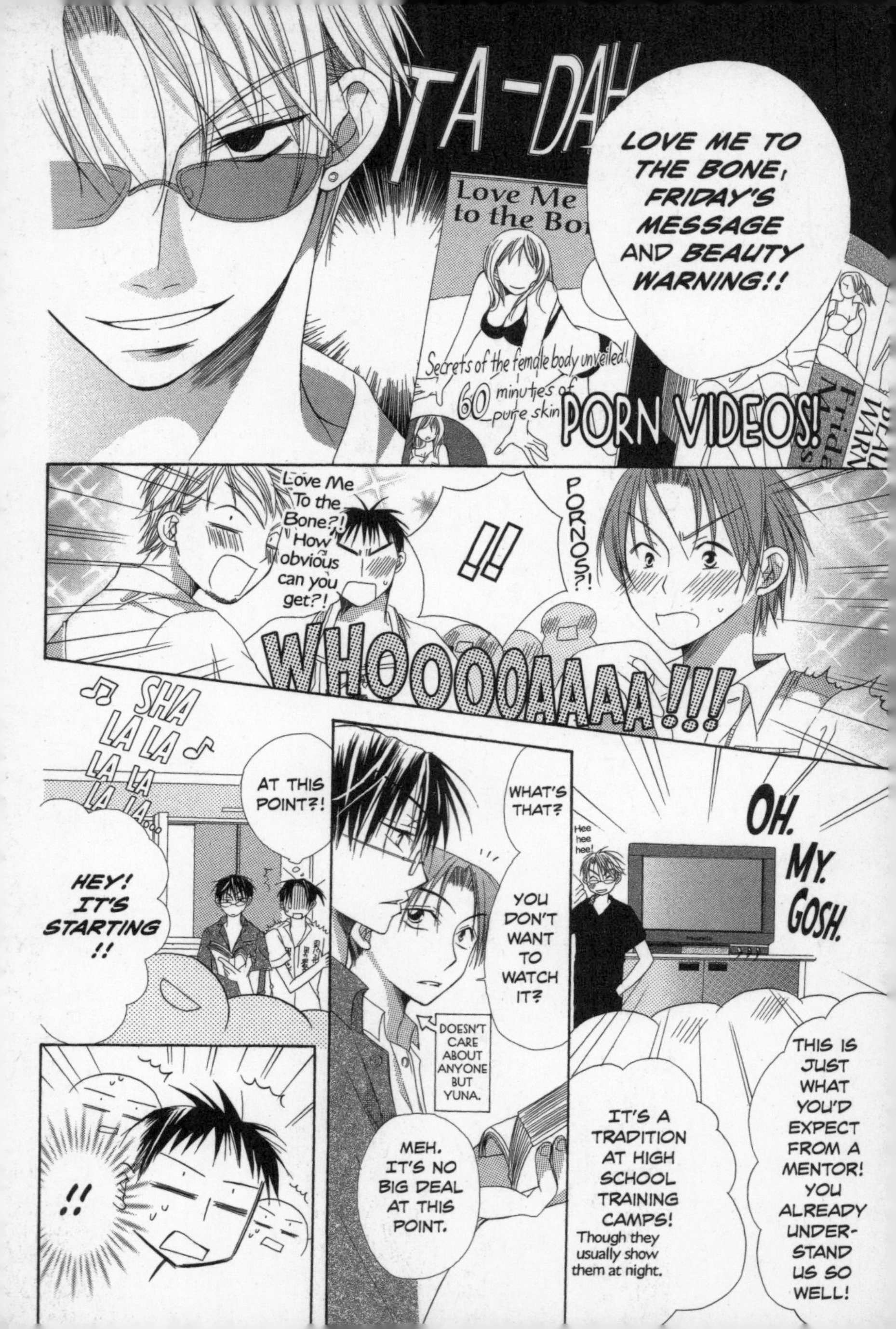
TA-DAH
LOVE ME TO THE BONE, FRIDAY'S MESSAGE AND BEAUTY WARNING!!
Love Me to the Bo
Secrets of the female body unveiled! 60 minutes of pure skin
PORN VIDEOS!
PORNOS?!
!!
Love Me To the Bone?! How obvious can you get?!
WHOOOOAAAA!!!
OH. MY. GOSH.
Hee hee hee!
THIS IS JUST WHAT YOU'D EXPECT FROM A MENTOR! YOU ALREADY UNDERSTAND US SO WELL!
IT'S A TRADITION AT HIGH SCHOOL TRAINING CAMPS!
Though they usually show them at night.
WHAT'S THAT?
YOU DON'T WANT TO WATCH IT?
DOESN'T CARE ABOUT ANYONE BUT YUNA.
MEH. IT'S NO BIG DEAL AT THIS POINT.
AT THIS POINT?!
SHA LA LA LA LA LA LA...
HEY! IT'S STARTING!!
!!

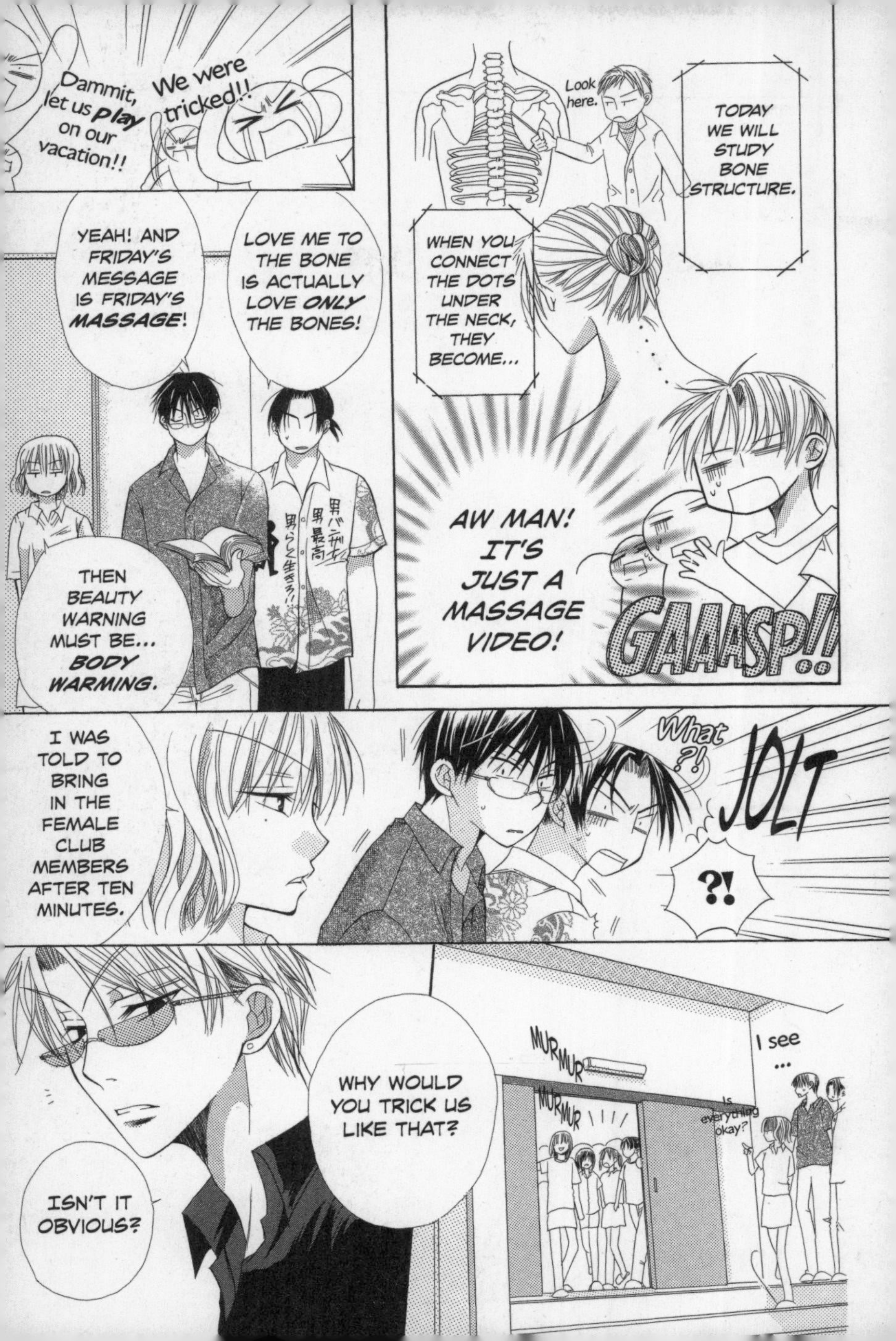
Look here.
TODAY WE WILL STUDY BONE STRUCTURE.
WHEN YOU CONNECT THE DOTS UNDER THE NECK, THEY BECOME...
AW MAN! IT'S JUST A MASSAGE VIDEO!
GAAASP!!
We were tricked!!
Dammit, let us play on our vacation!!
LOVE ME TO THE BONE IS ACTUALLY LOVE ONLY THE BONES!
YEAH! AND FRIDAY'S MESSAGE IS FRIDAY'S MASSAGE!
男バンザイ
男最高
男らしく生きろ!!
THEN BEAUTY WARNING MUST BE... BODY WARMING.
What?!
JOLT
?!
I WAS TOLD TO BRING IN THE FEMALE CLUB MEMBERS AFTER TEN MINUTES.
I see...
Is everything okay?
MURMUR
MURMUR
WHY WOULD YOU TRICK US LIKE THAT?
ISN'T IT OBVIOUS?

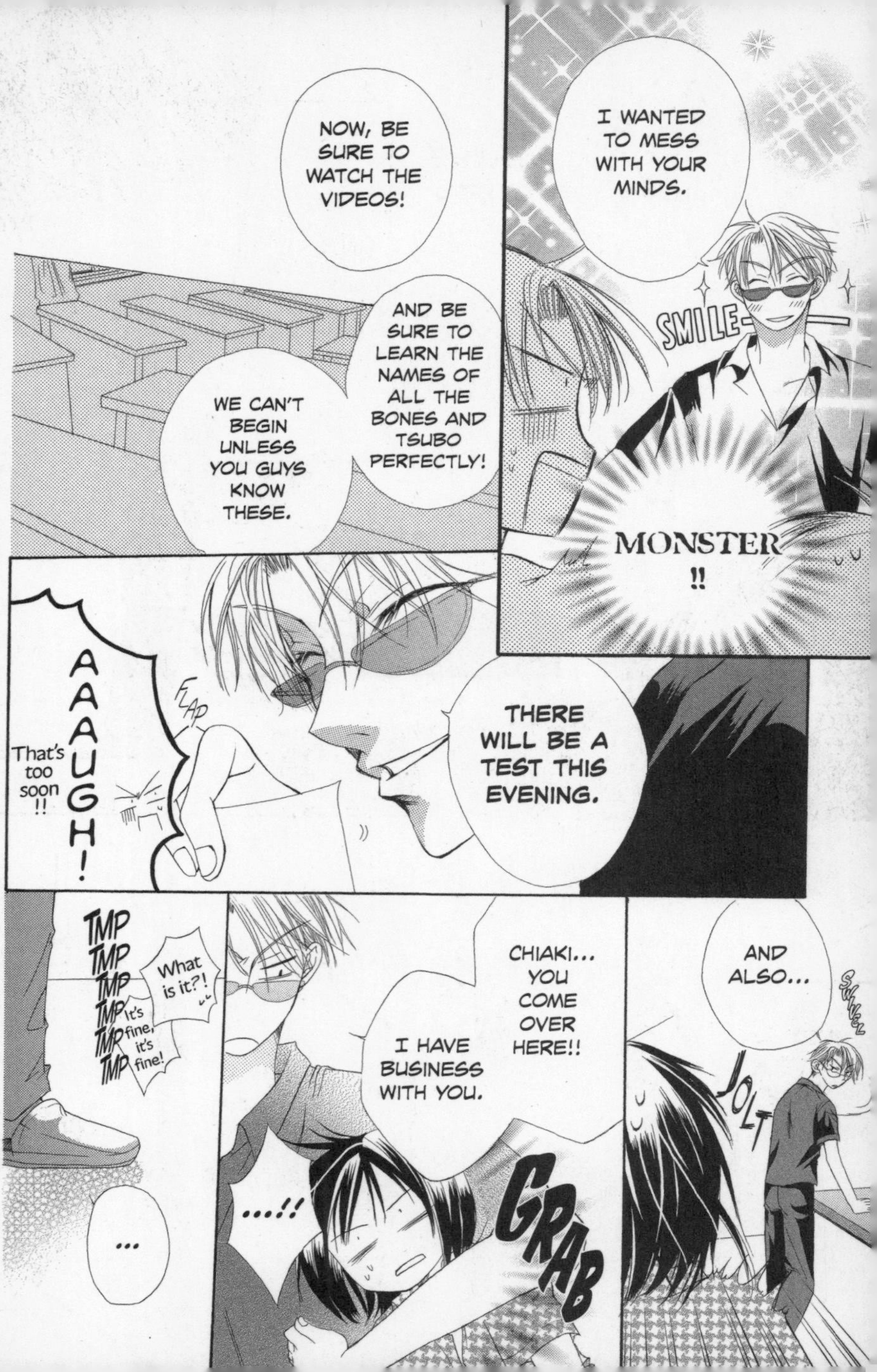
I WANTED TO MESS WITH YOUR MINDS.
SMILE-
MONSTER !!
NOW, BE SURE TO WATCH THE VIDEOS!
AND BE SURE TO LEARN THE NAMES OF ALL THE BONES AND TSUBO PERFECTLY!
WE CAN'T BEGIN UNLESS YOU GUYS KNOW THESE.
THERE WILL BE A TEST THIS EVENING.
FLAP
AAAAUGH!
That's too soon !!
AND ALSO...
JOLT
CHIAKI... YOU COME OVER HERE!!
I HAVE BUSINESS WITH YOU.
GRAB
...!!
TMP TMP TMP TMP TMP TMP
What is it?!
It's fine, it's fine!
...

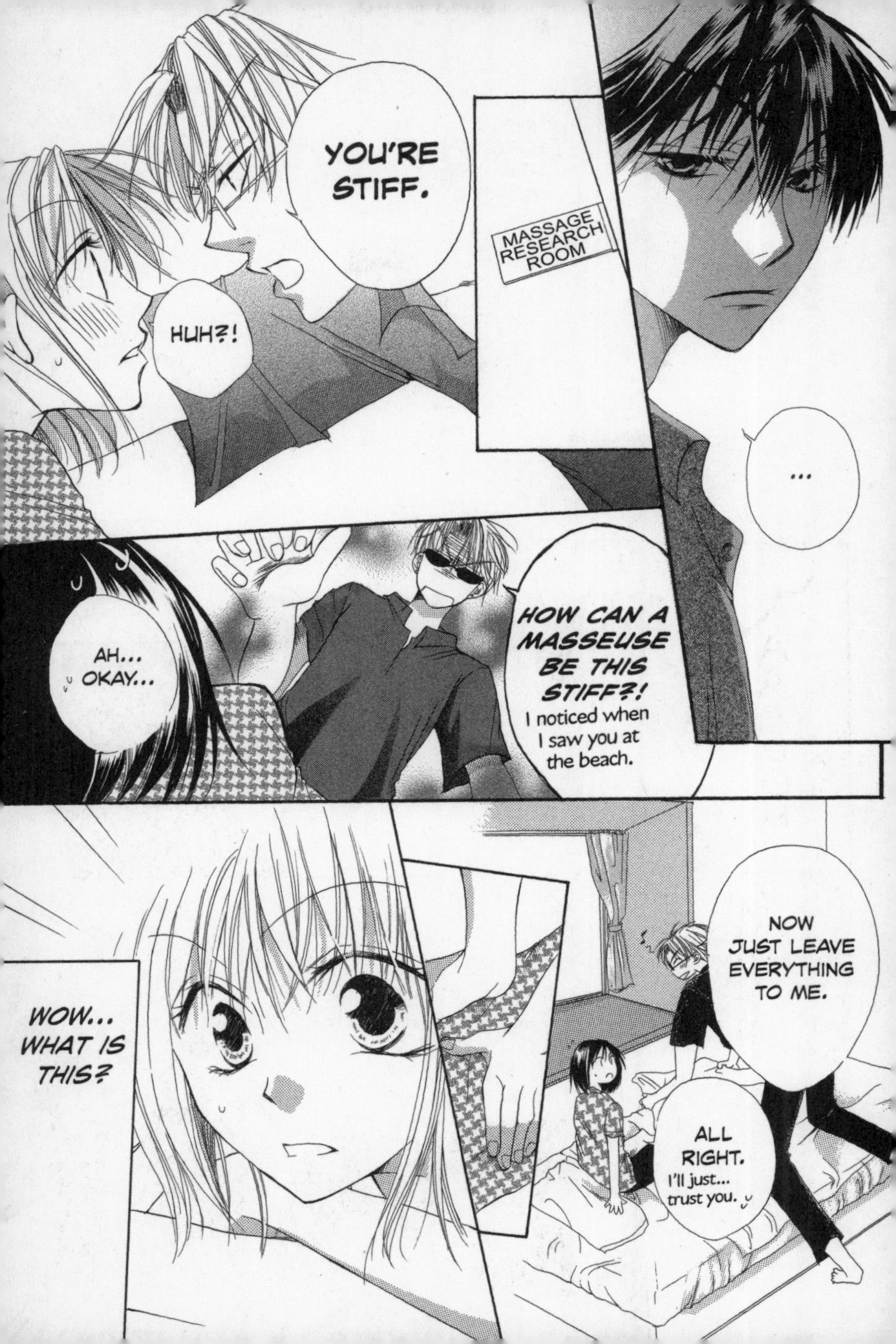
MASSAGE RESEARCH ROOM
...
YOU'RE STIFF.
HUH?!
HOW CAN A MASSEUSE BE THIS STIFF?! I noticed when I saw you at the beach.
AH... OKAY...
NOW JUST LEAVE EVERYTHING TO ME.
ALL RIGHT. I'll just... trust you.
WOW... WHAT IS THIS?

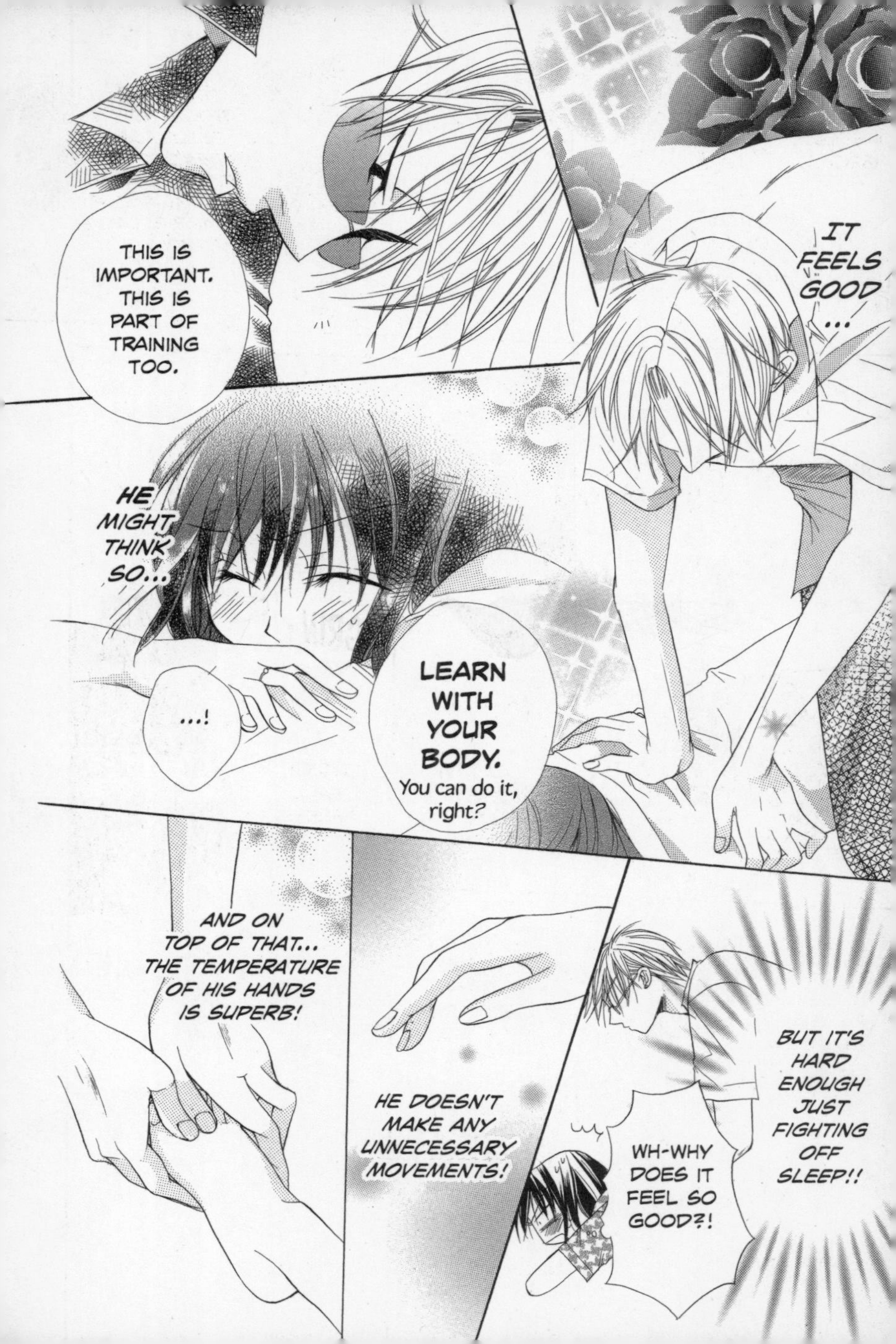
IT FEELS GOOD...
THIS IS IMPORTANT. THIS IS PART OF TRAINING TOO.
LEARN WITH YOUR BODY. You can do it, right?
...!
HE MIGHT THINK SO...
BUT IT'S HARD ENOUGH JUST FIGHTING OFF SLEEP!!
WH-WHY DOES IT FEEL SO GOOD?!
HE DOESN'T MAKE ANY UNNECESSARY MOVEMENTS!
AND ON TOP OF THAT... THE TEMPERATURE OF HIS HANDS IS SUPERB!

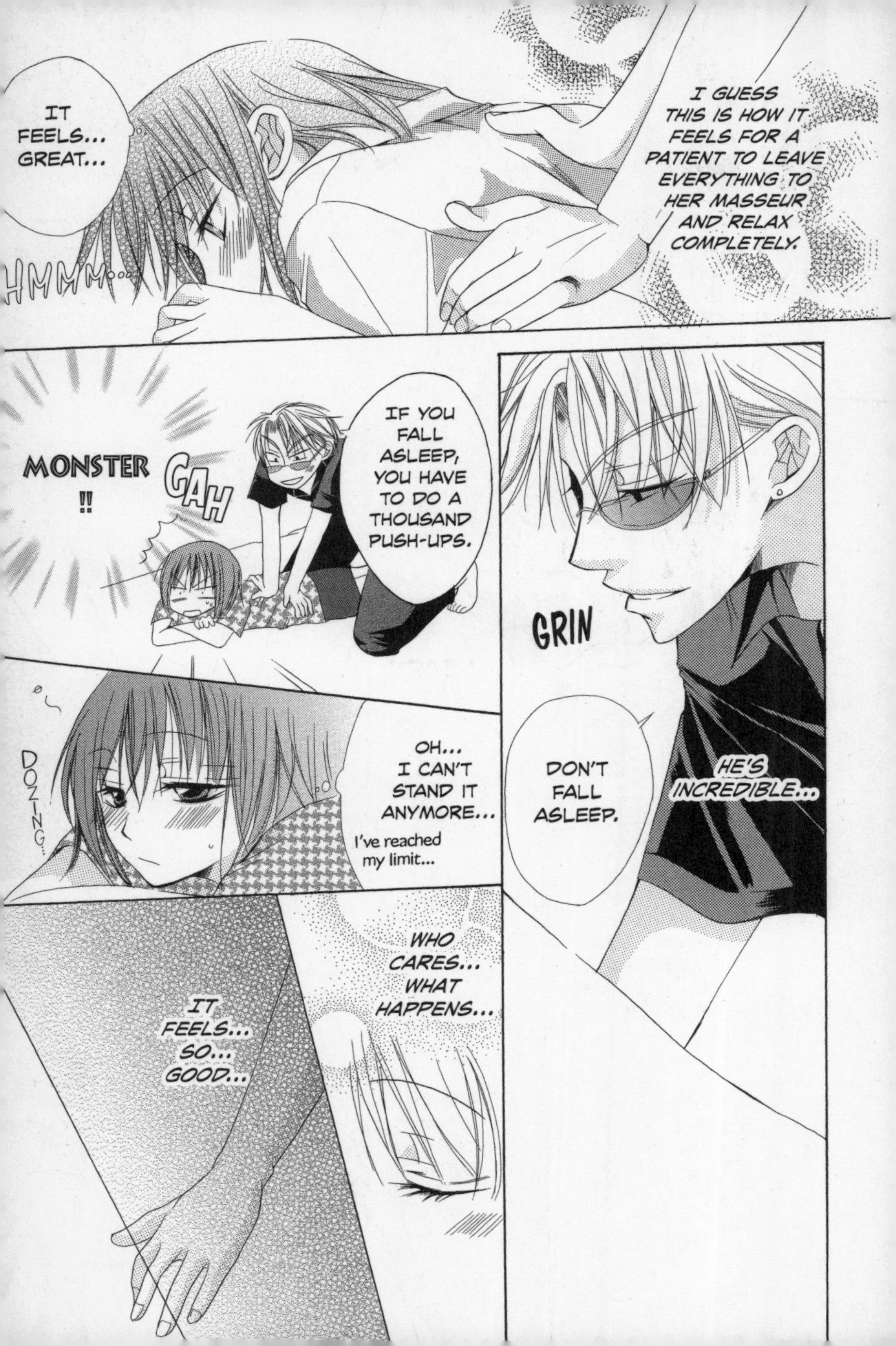
I GUESS THIS IS HOW IT FEELS FOR A PATIENT TO LEAVE EVERYTHING TO HER MASSEUR AND RELAX COMPLETELY.
IT FEELS... GREAT...
HMMMM...
GRIN
HE'S INCREDIBLE...
DON'T FALL ASLEEP.
IF YOU FALL ASLEEP, YOU HAVE TO DO A THOUSAND PUSH-UPS.
GAH
MONSTER !!
OH... I CAN'T STAND IT ANYMORE...
I've reached my limit...
DOZING...
WHO CARES... WHAT HAPPENS...
IT FEELS... SO... GOOD...

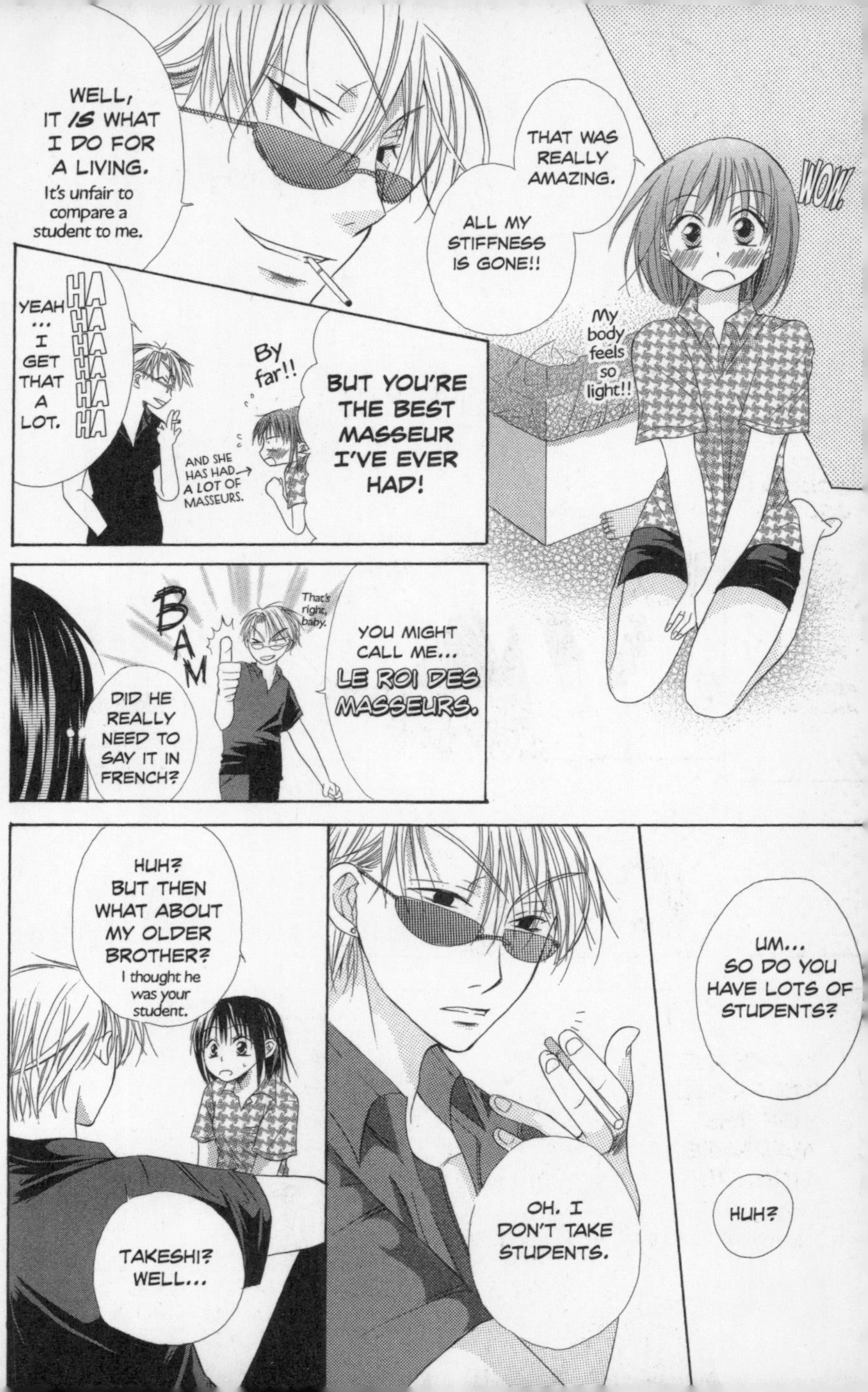
THAT WAS REALLY AMAZING.
ALL MY STIFFNESS IS GONE!!
WOW!
My body feels so light!!
WELL, IT IS WHAT I DO FOR A LIVING.
It's unfair to compare a student to me.
BUT YOU'RE THE BEST MASSEUR I'VE EVER HAD!
By far!!
AND SHE HAS HAD A LOT OF MASSEURS.
HA HA HA HA HA HA HA
YEAH... I GET THAT A LOT.
YOU MIGHT CALL ME... LE ROI DES MASSEURS.
That's right, baby.
BAM
DID HE REALLY NEED TO SAY IT IN FRENCH?
UM... SO DO YOU HAVE LOTS OF STUDENTS?
HUH?
OH. I DON'T TAKE STUDENTS.
HUH? BUT THEN WHAT ABOUT MY OLDER BROTHER?
I thought he was your student.
TAKESHI? WELL...

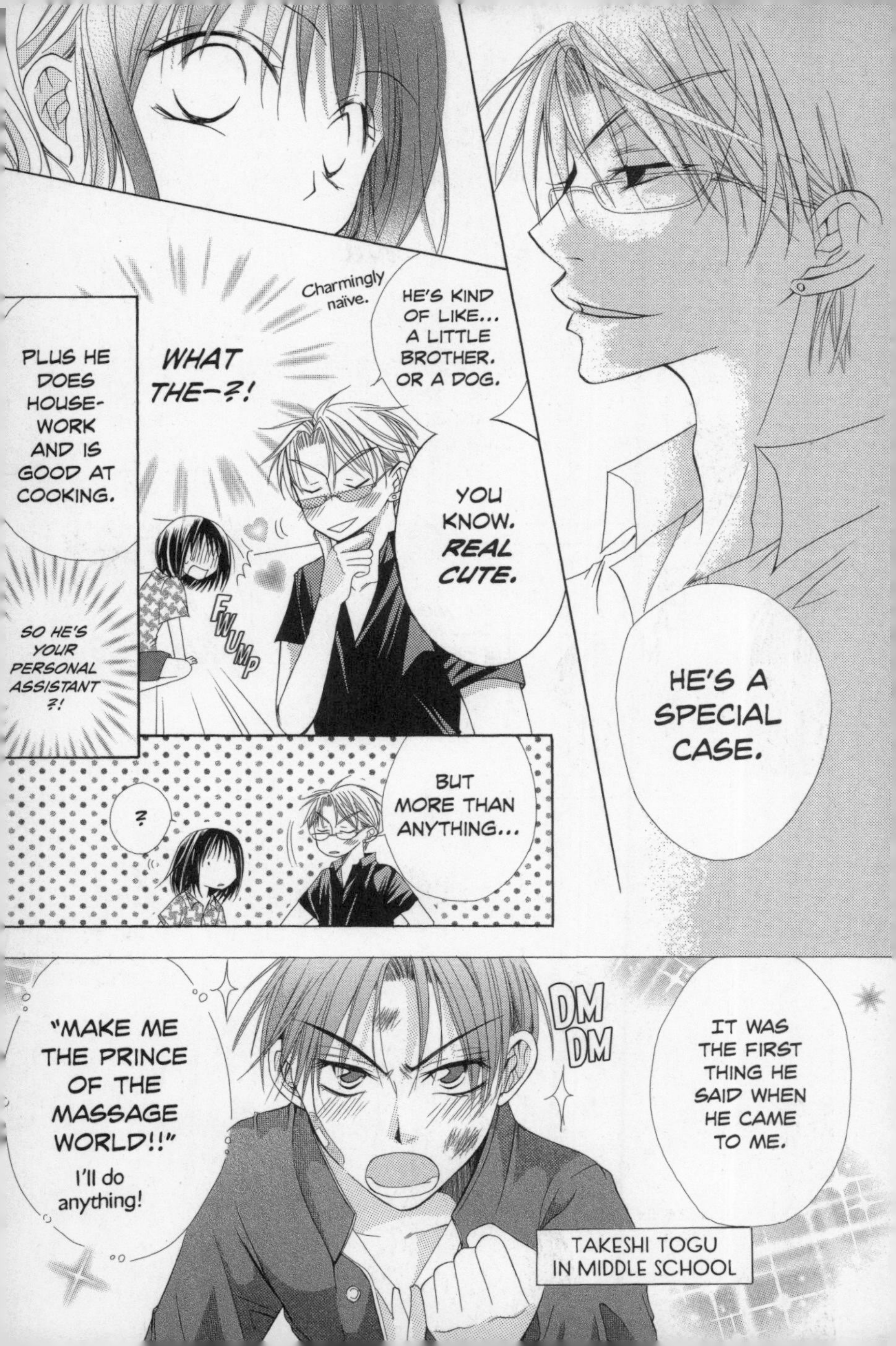
HE'S A SPECIAL CASE.
HE'S KIND OF LIKE... A LITTLE BROTHER. OR A DOG.
Charmingly naïve.
YOU KNOW. REAL CUTE.
WHAT THE-?!
FWUMP
PLUS HE DOES HOUSE-WORK AND IS GOOD AT COOKING.
SO HE'S YOUR PERSONAL ASSISTANT?!
BUT MORE THAN ANYTHING...
?
IT WAS THE FIRST THING HE SAID WHEN HE CAME TO ME.
DM DM
TAKESHI TOGU IN MIDDLE SCHOOL
"MAKE ME THE PRINCE OF THE MASSAGE WORLD!!"
I'll do anything!

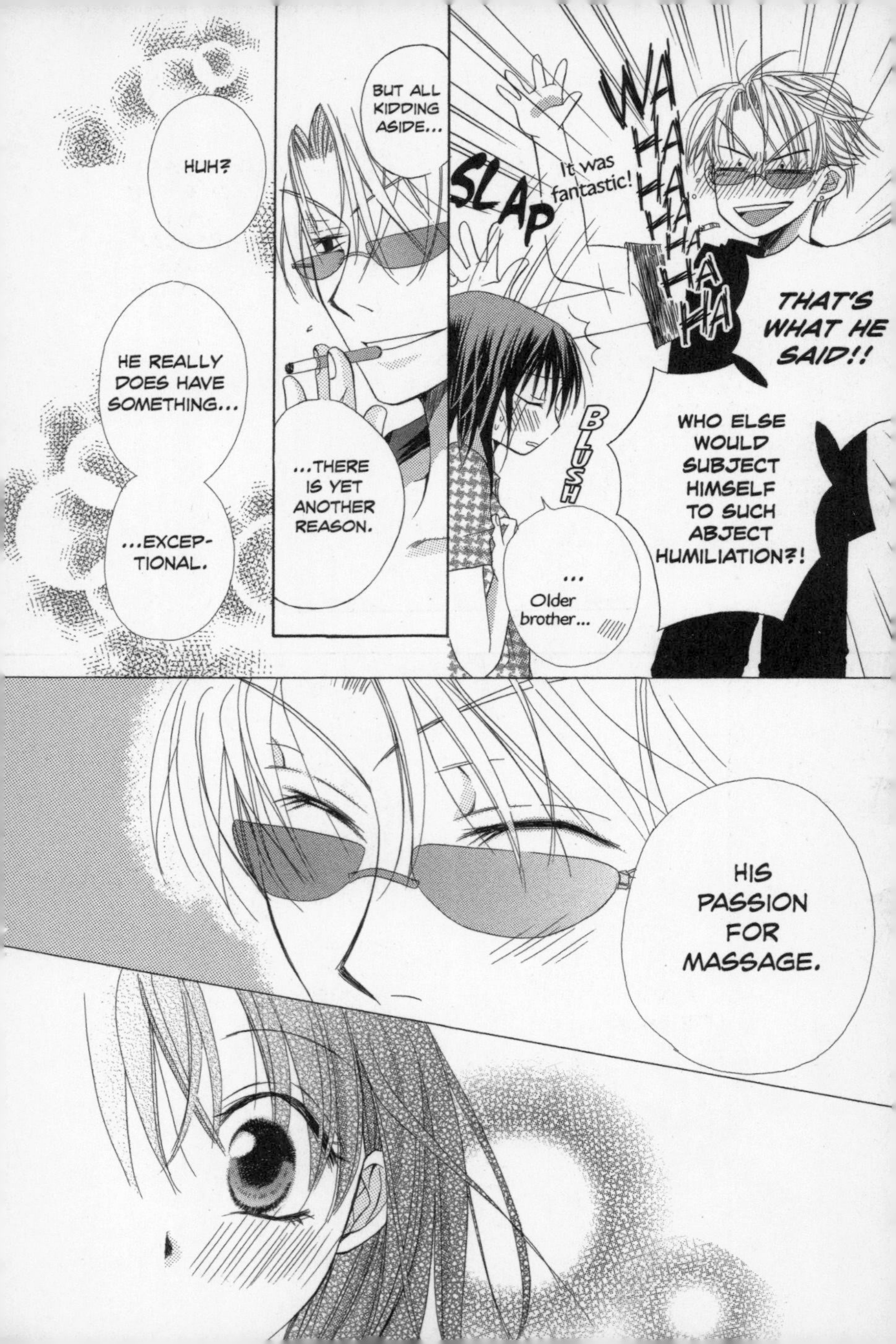
WAHAHAHAHAHAHA
It was fantastic!
SLAP
THAT'S WHAT HE SAID!!
WHO ELSE WOULD SUBJECT HIMSELF TO SUCH ABJECT HUMILIATION?!
BLUSH
... Older brother...
BUT ALL KIDDING ASIDE...
...THERE IS YET ANOTHER REASON.
HUH?
HE REALLY DOES HAVE SOMETHING...
...EXCEP-TIONAL.
HIS PASSION FOR MASSAGE.

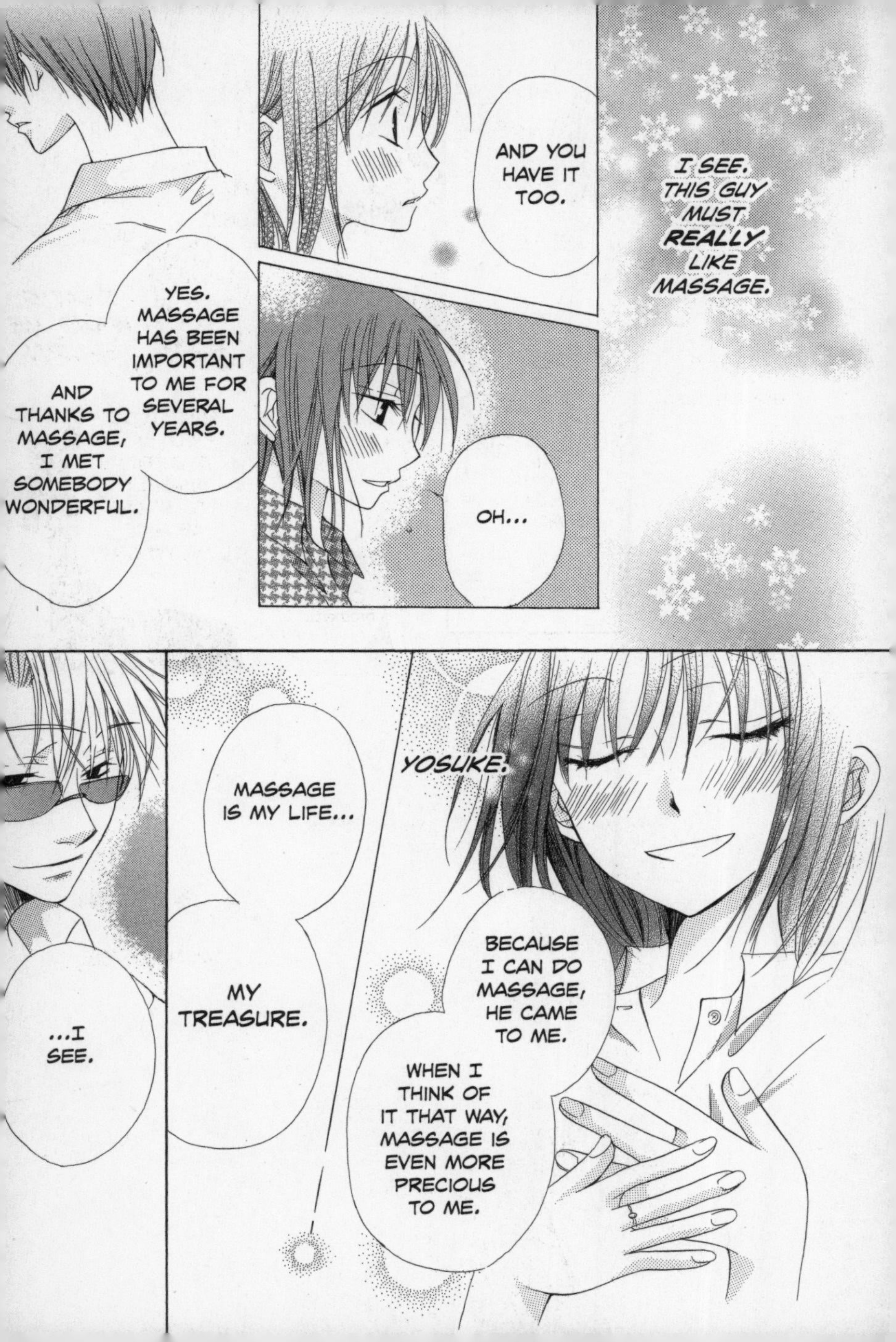
I SEE. THIS GUY MUST REALLY LIKE MASSAGE.
AND YOU HAVE IT TOO.
OH...
YES. MASSAGE HAS BEEN IMPORTANT TO ME FOR SEVERAL YEARS.
AND THANKS TO MASSAGE, I MET SOMEBODY WONDERFUL.
YOSUKE.
BECAUSE I CAN DO MASSAGE, HE CAME TO ME.
WHEN I THINK OF IT THAT WAY, MASSAGE IS EVEN MORE PRECIOUS TO ME.
MASSAGE IS MY LIFE...
MY TREASURE.
...I SEE.

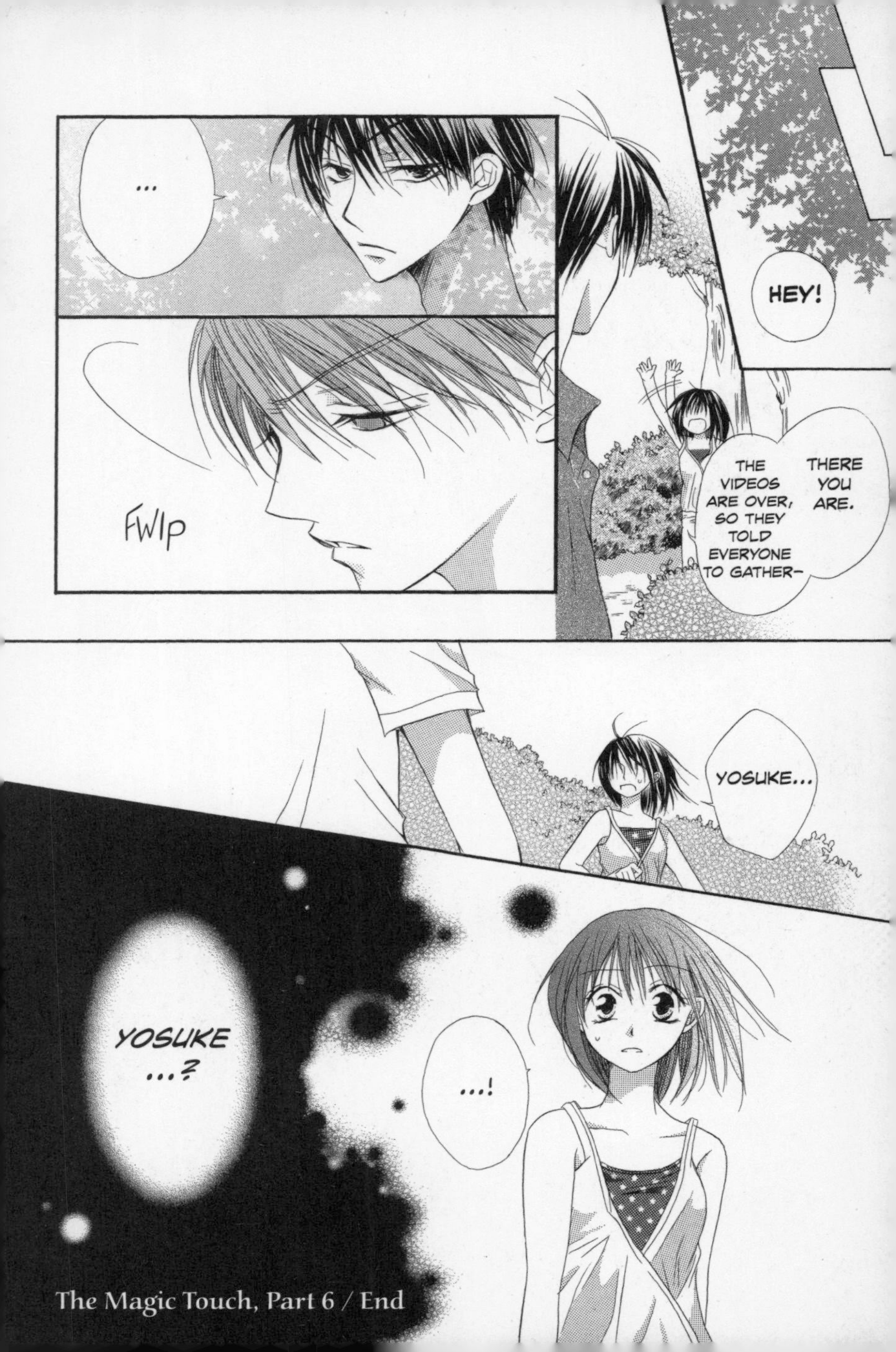
HEY!
THERE YOU ARE.
THE VIDEOS ARE OVER, SO THEY TOLD EVERYONE TO GATHER–
...
FWIP
YOSUKE...
...!
YOSUKE ...?

The Magic Touch, Part 6 / End

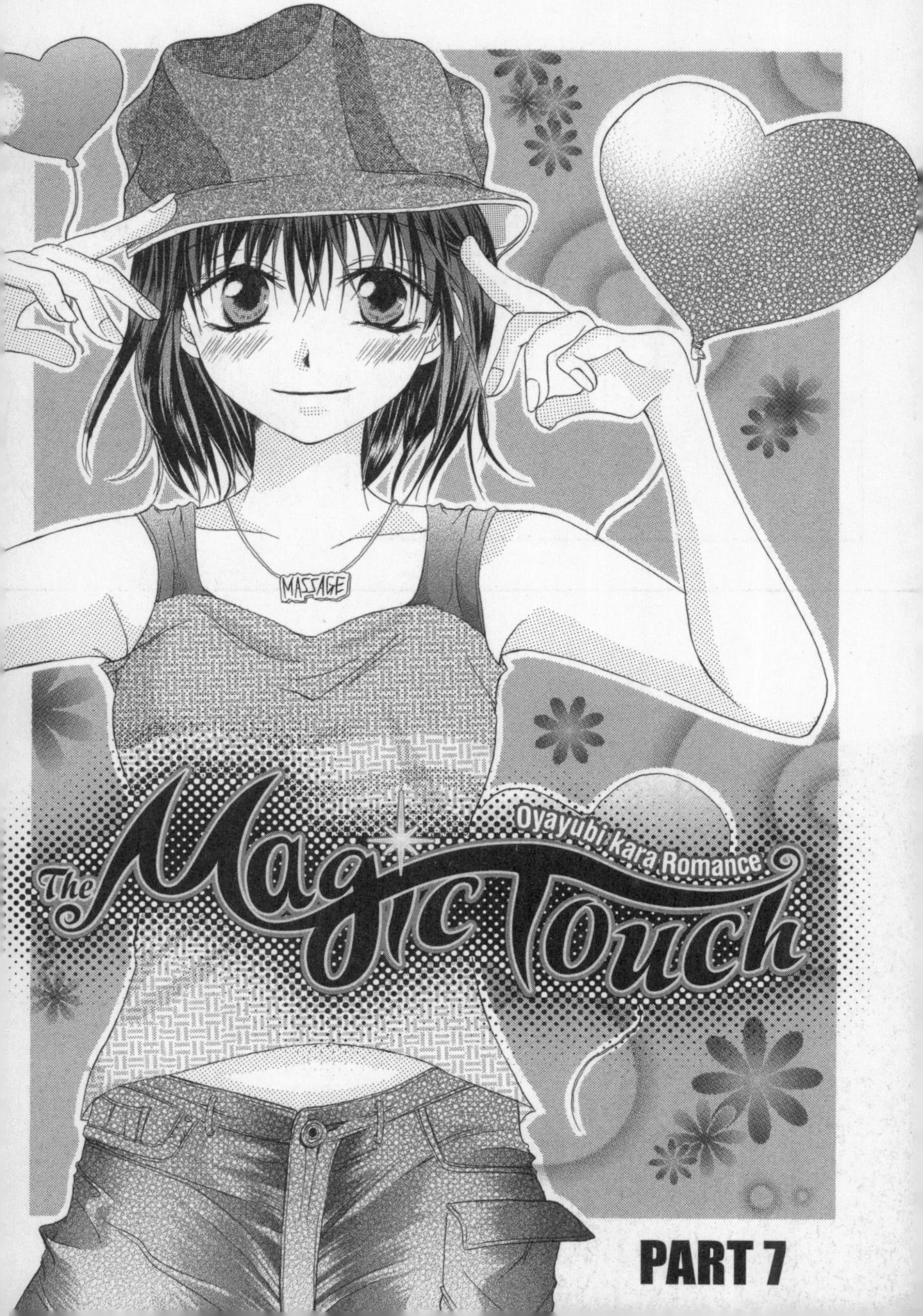
MASSAGE
The Magic Touch
Oyayubi kara Romance
PART 7

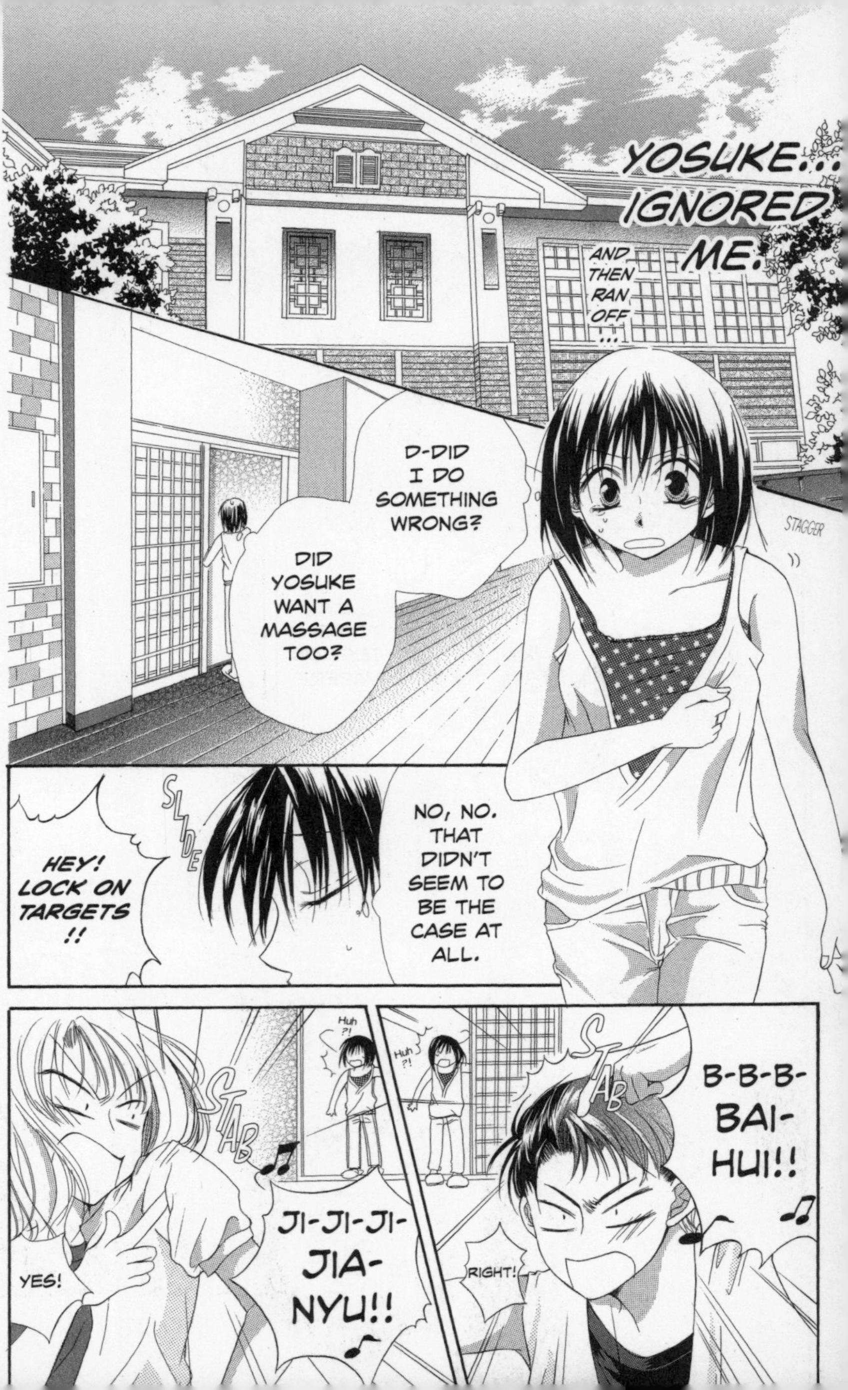
YOSUKE... IGNORED ME.
AND THEN RAN OFF...
D-DID I DO SOMETHING WRONG?
DID YOSUKE WANT A MASSAGE TOO?
STAGGER
NO, NO. THAT DIDN'T SEEM TO BE THE CASE AT ALL.
SLIDE
HEY! LOCK ON TARGETS!!
STAB
B-B-B-BAI-HUI!!
RIGHT!
Huh ?!
Huh ?!
STAB
JI-JI-JI-JIA-NYU!!
YES!

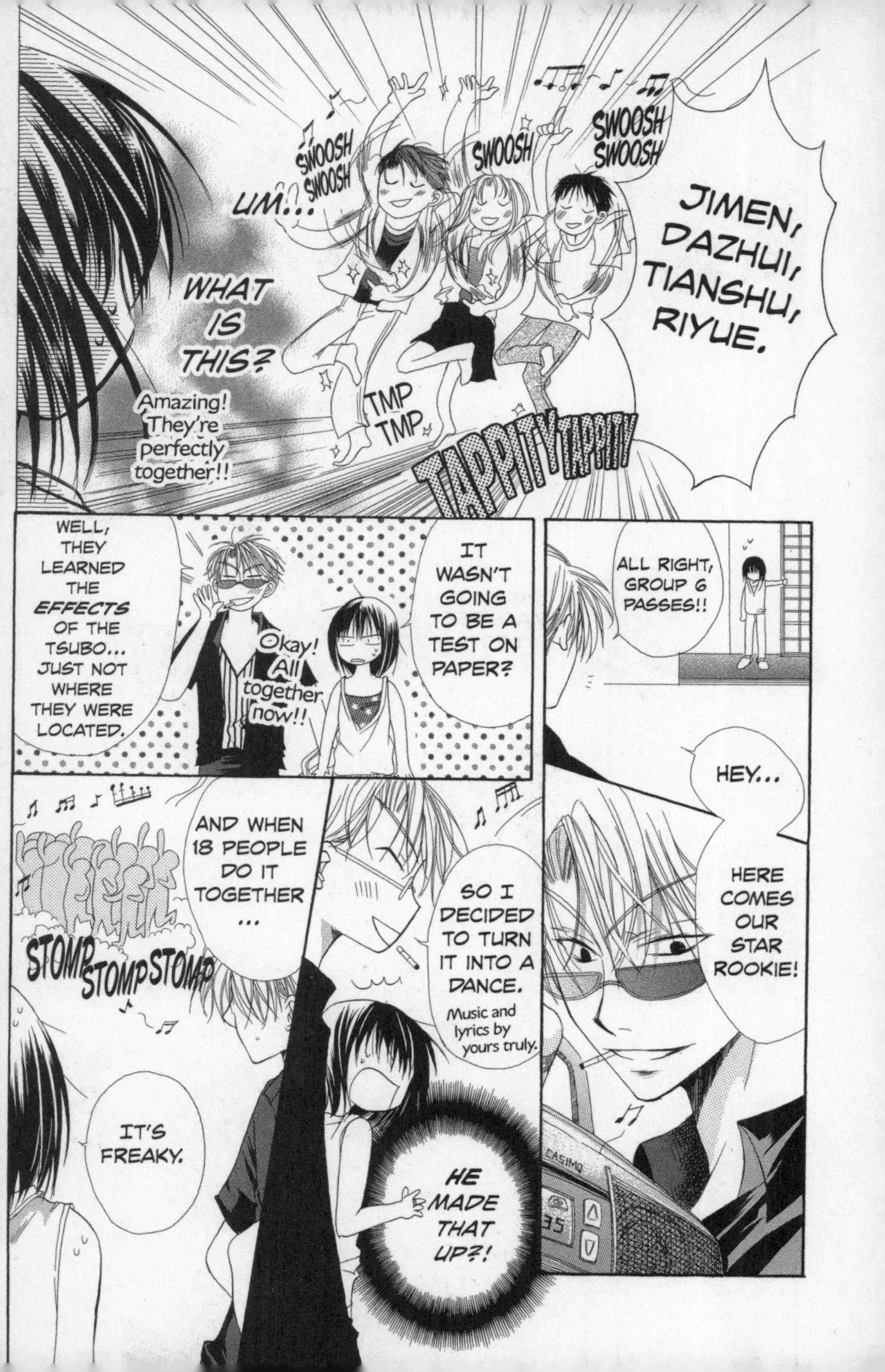
JIMEN, DAZHUI, TIANSHU, RIYUE.
SWOOSH SWOOSH
SWOOSH
SWOOSH SWOOSH
UM...
WHAT IS THIS?
Amazing! They're perfectly together!!
TMP TMP
TAPPITY TAPPITY
ALL RIGHT, GROUP 6 PASSES!!
IT WASN'T GOING TO BE A TEST ON PAPER?
Okay! All together now!!
WELL, THEY LEARNED THE *EFFECTS* OF THE TSUBO... JUST NOT WHERE THEY WERE LOCATED.
HEY...
HERE COMES OUR STAR ROOKIE!
SO I DECIDED TO TURN IT INTO A DANCE.
Music and lyrics by yours truly.
AND WHEN 18 PEOPLE DO IT TOGETHER ...
STOMP STOMP STOMP
CASIMO
HE MADE THAT UP?!
IT'S FREAKY.

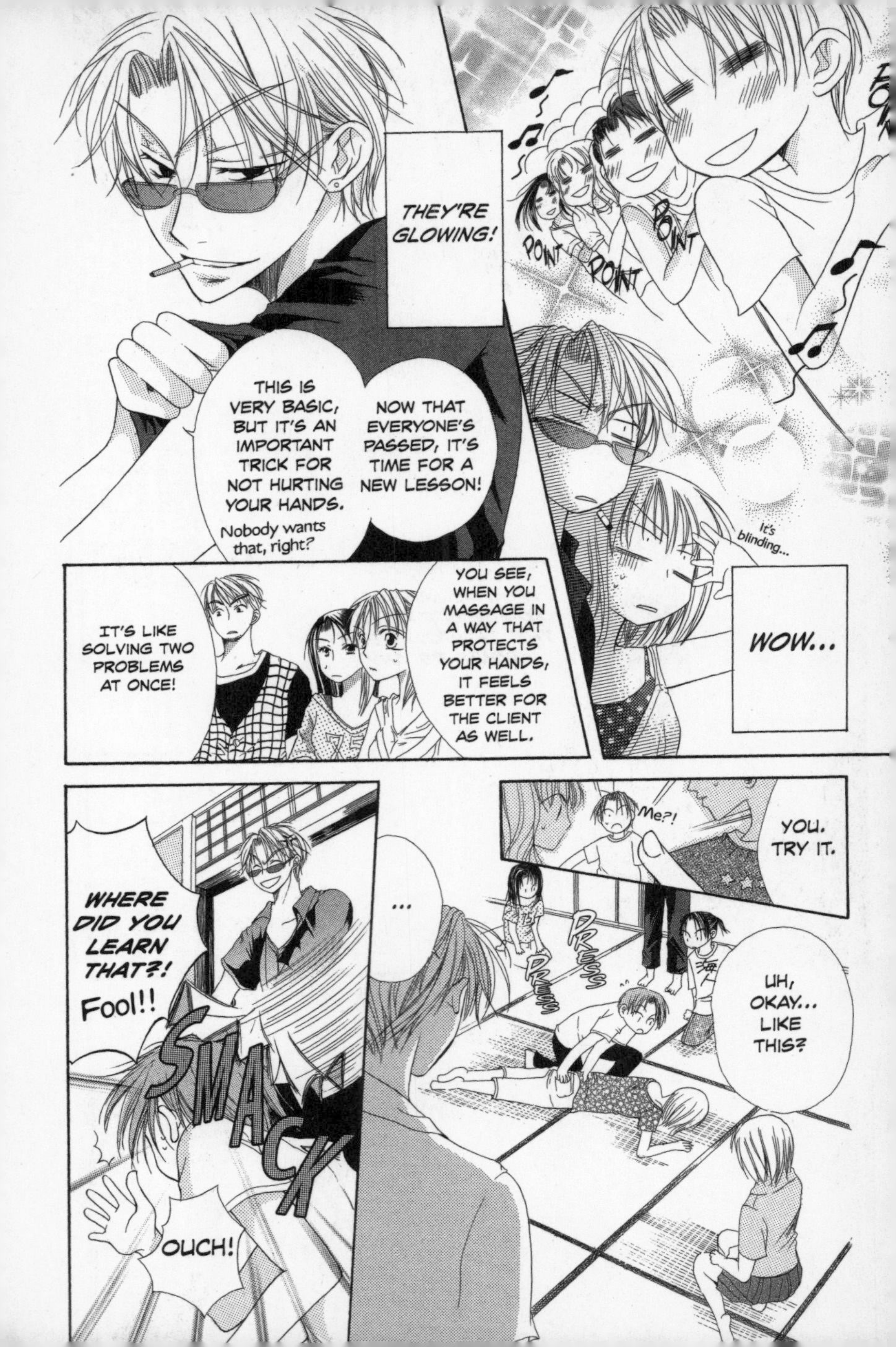
NOW THAT EVERYONE'S PASSED, IT'S TIME FOR A NEW LESSON!
THIS IS VERY BASIC, BUT IT'S AN IMPORTANT TRICK FOR NOT HURTING YOUR HANDS.
Nobody wants that, right?
YOU SEE, WHEN YOU MASSAGE IN A WAY THAT PROTECTS YOUR HANDS, IT FEELS BETTER FOR THE CLIENT AS WELL.
IT'S LIKE SOLVING TWO PROBLEMS AT ONCE!
THEY'RE GLOWING!
POINT
POINT
POINT
It's blinding...
WOW...
YOU. TRY IT.
Me?!
UH, OKAY... LIKE THIS?
PRESS
PRESS
...
WHERE DID YOU LEARN THAT?!
Fool!!
SMACK
OUCH!

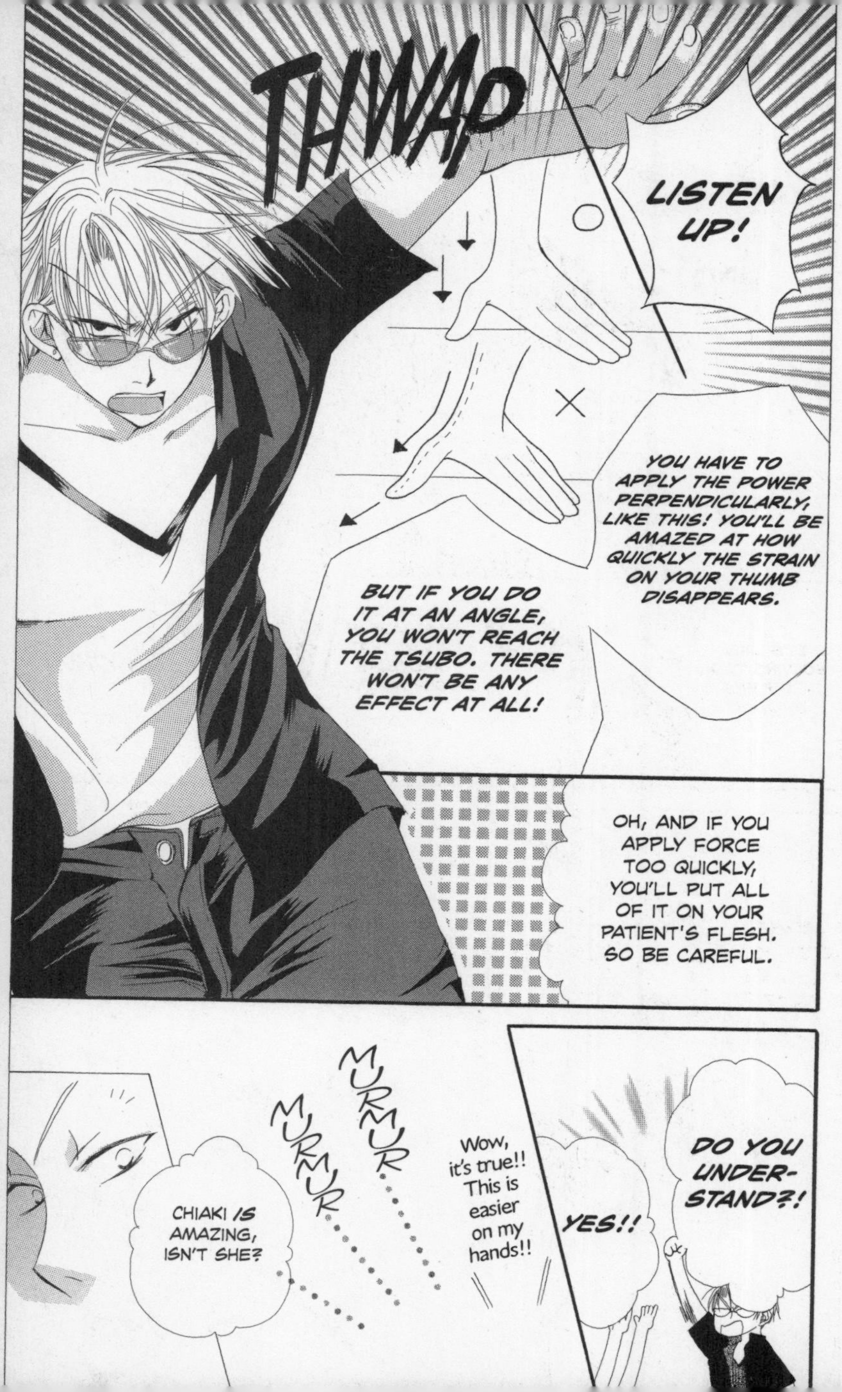
THWAP
LISTEN UP!
YOU HAVE TO APPLY THE POWER PERPENDICULARLY, LIKE THIS! YOU'LL BE AMAZED AT HOW QUICKLY THE STRAIN ON YOUR THUMB DISAPPEARS.
BUT IF YOU DO IT AT AN ANGLE, YOU WON'T REACH THE TSUBO. THERE WON'T BE ANY EFFECT AT ALL!
OH, AND IF YOU APPLY FORCE TOO QUICKLY, YOU'LL PUT ALL OF IT ON YOUR PATIENT'S FLESH. SO BE CAREFUL.
DO YOU UNDER-STAND?!
YES!!
MURMUR
MURMUR
Wow, it's true!! This is easier on my hands!!
CHIAKI IS AMAZING, ISN'T SHE?

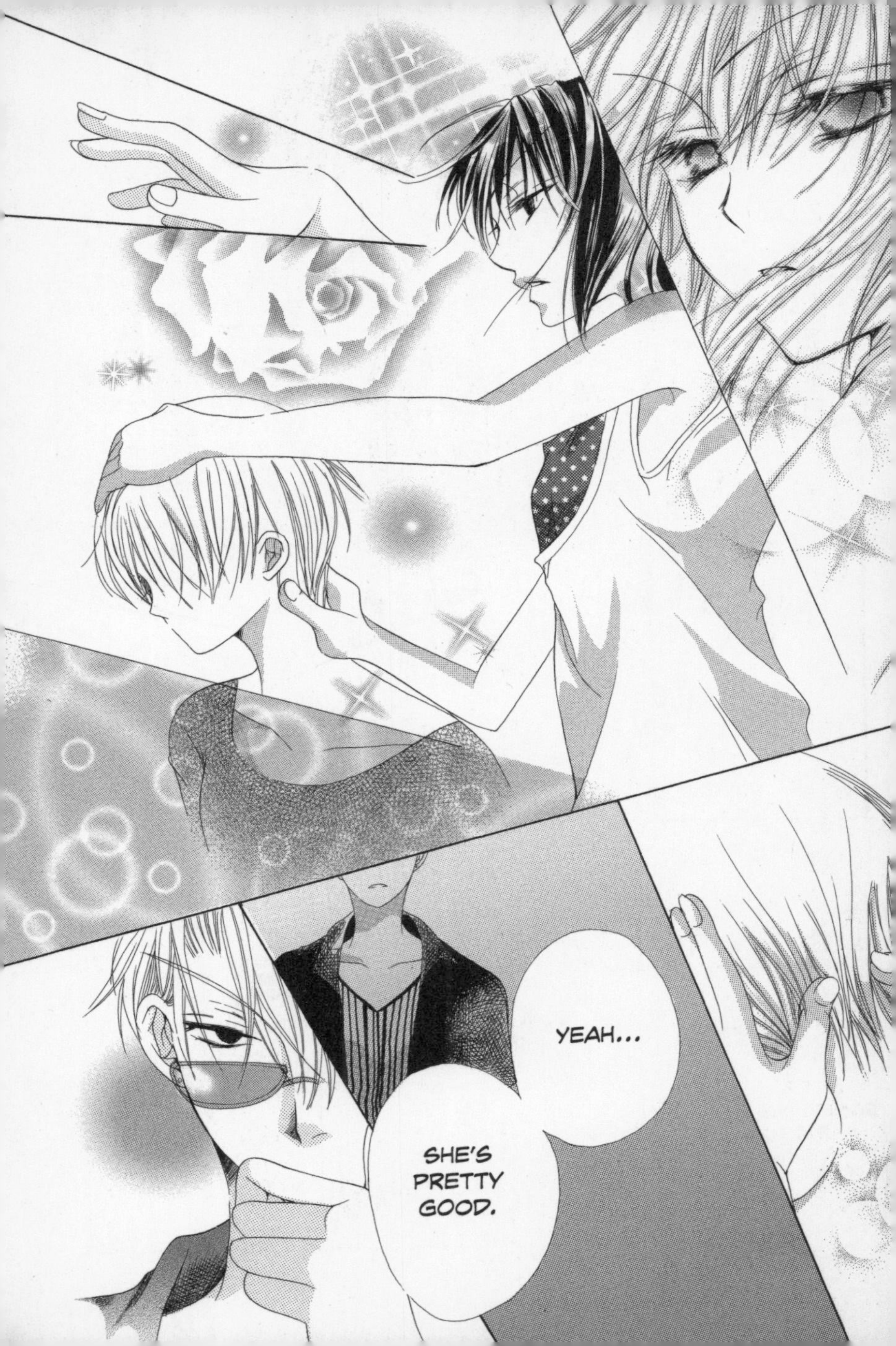
YEAH...
SHE'S PRETTY GOOD.

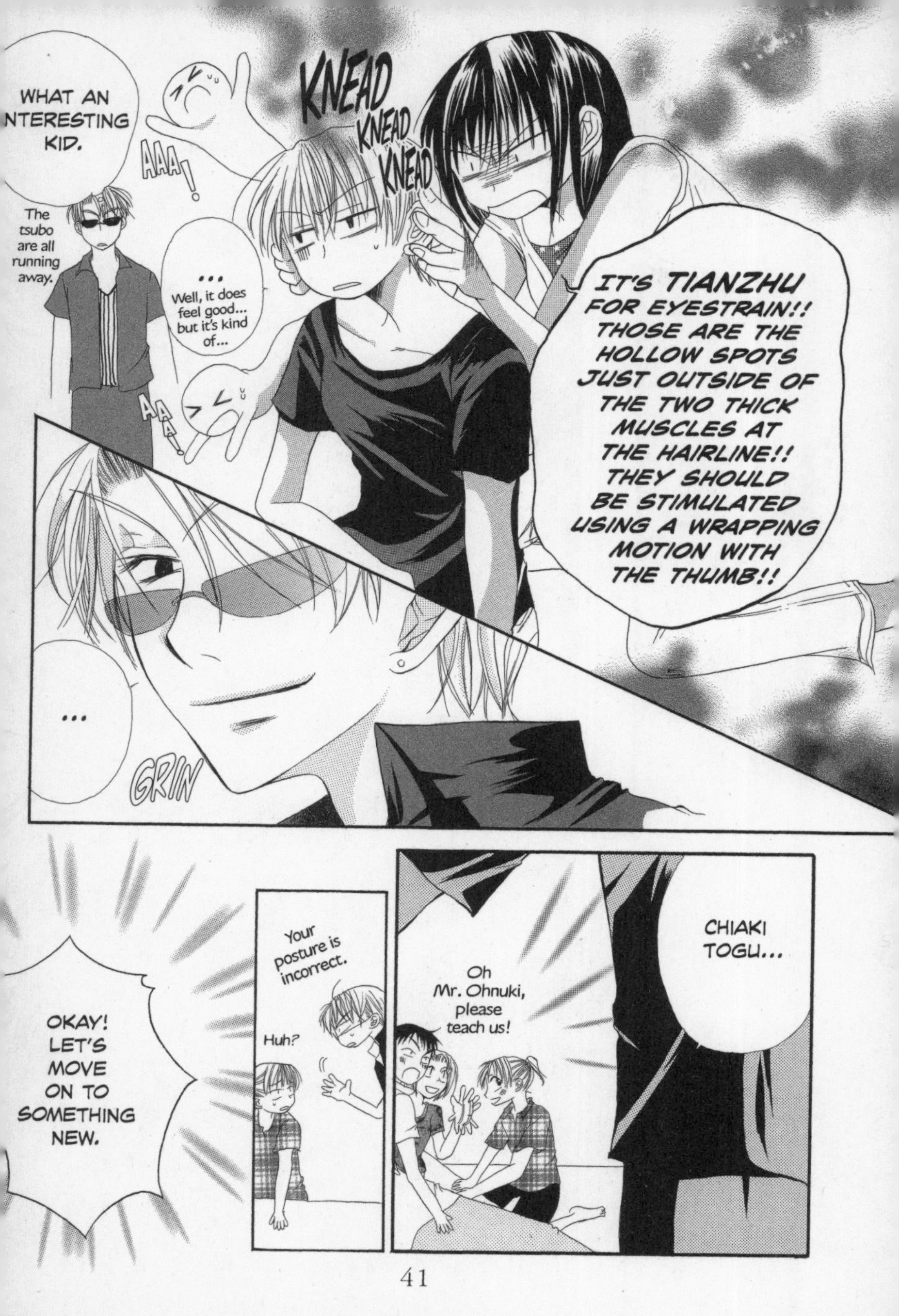

KNEAD
KNEAD
KNEAD
IT'S TIANZHU FOR EYESTRAIN!! THOSE ARE THE HOLLOW SPOTS JUST OUTSIDE OF THE TWO THICK MUSCLES AT THE HAIRLINE!! THEY SHOULD BE STIMULATED USING A WRAPPING MOTION WITH THE THUMB!!
... Well, it does feel good... but it's kind of...
AAA!
AAA!
WHAT AN NTERESTING KID.
The tsubo are all running away.
...
GRIN
CHIAKI TOGU...
Oh Mr. Ohnuki, please teach us!
Your posture is incorrect.
Huh?
OKAY! LET'S MOVE ON TO SOMETHING NEW.

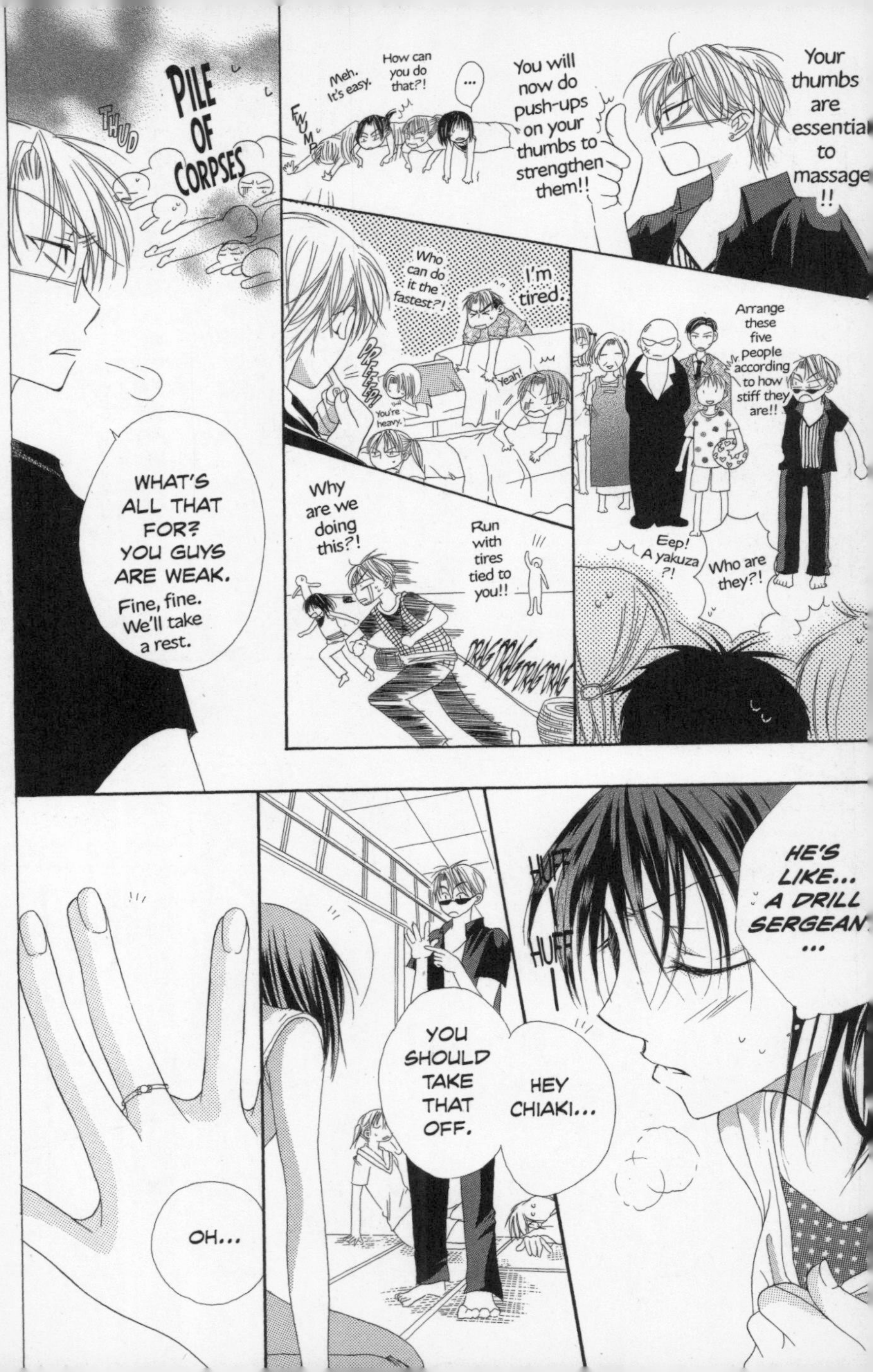
Your thumbs are essentia to massage !!
You will now do push-ups on your thumbs to strengthen them!!
...
How can you do that?!
Meh. It's easy.
FWUMP
Arrange these five people according to how stiff they are!!
Who are they?!
Eep! A yakuza?!
I'm tired.
Who can do it the fastest?!
Yeah!
PREEEEP
You're heavy.
Run with tires tied to you!!
Why are we doing this?!
DRAG DRAG DRAG DRAG
PILE OF CORPSES
THUD
WHAT'S ALL THAT FOR? YOU GUYS ARE WEAK.
Fine, fine. We'll take a rest.
HE'S LIKE... A DRILL SERGEAN...
HUFF HUFF
HEY CHIAKI...
YOU SHOULD TAKE THAT OFF.
OH...

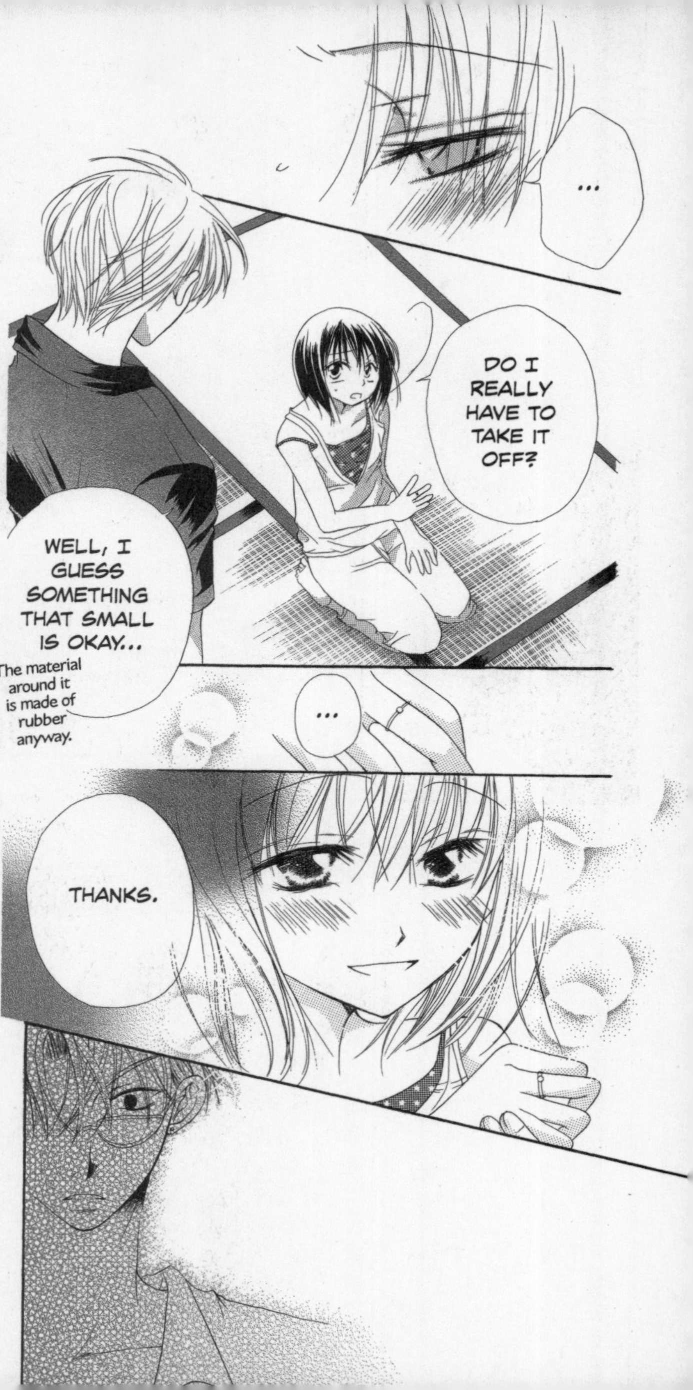
...
DO I REALLY HAVE TO TAKE IT OFF?
WELL, I GUESS SOMETHING THAT SMALL IS OKAY...
The material around it is made of rubber anyway.
...
THANKS.

Daily Life

I'm a college student—I still go to school! So when my deadlines approach, my friends help me out. I'm very grateful to them! Sometimes when I'm drawing with my ink pen back in a corner of the library, people look at me funny. But everyone in my department knows I'm drawing a manga series, so they sometimes buy the magazine to look for it.

When Volume 1 went on sale:

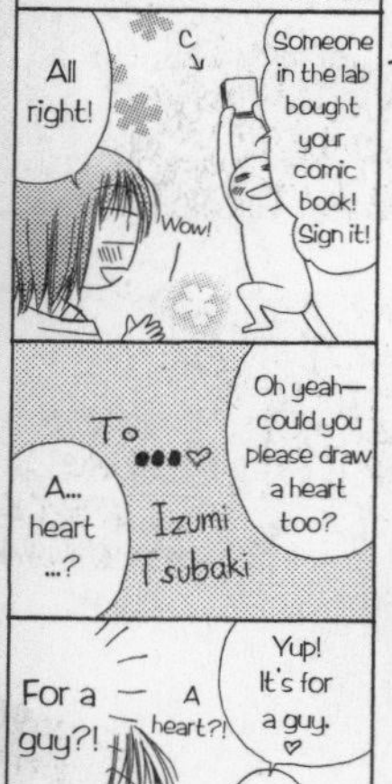
Someone in the lab bought your comic book! Sign it!
C
All right!
Wow!
Oh yeah—could you please draw a heart too?
To ●●●♡
Izumi Tsubaki
A... heart ...?
Yup! It's for a guy. ♡
A heart?!
For a guy?!
They keep a copy of your magazine at the lab.
Even though it's all guys.

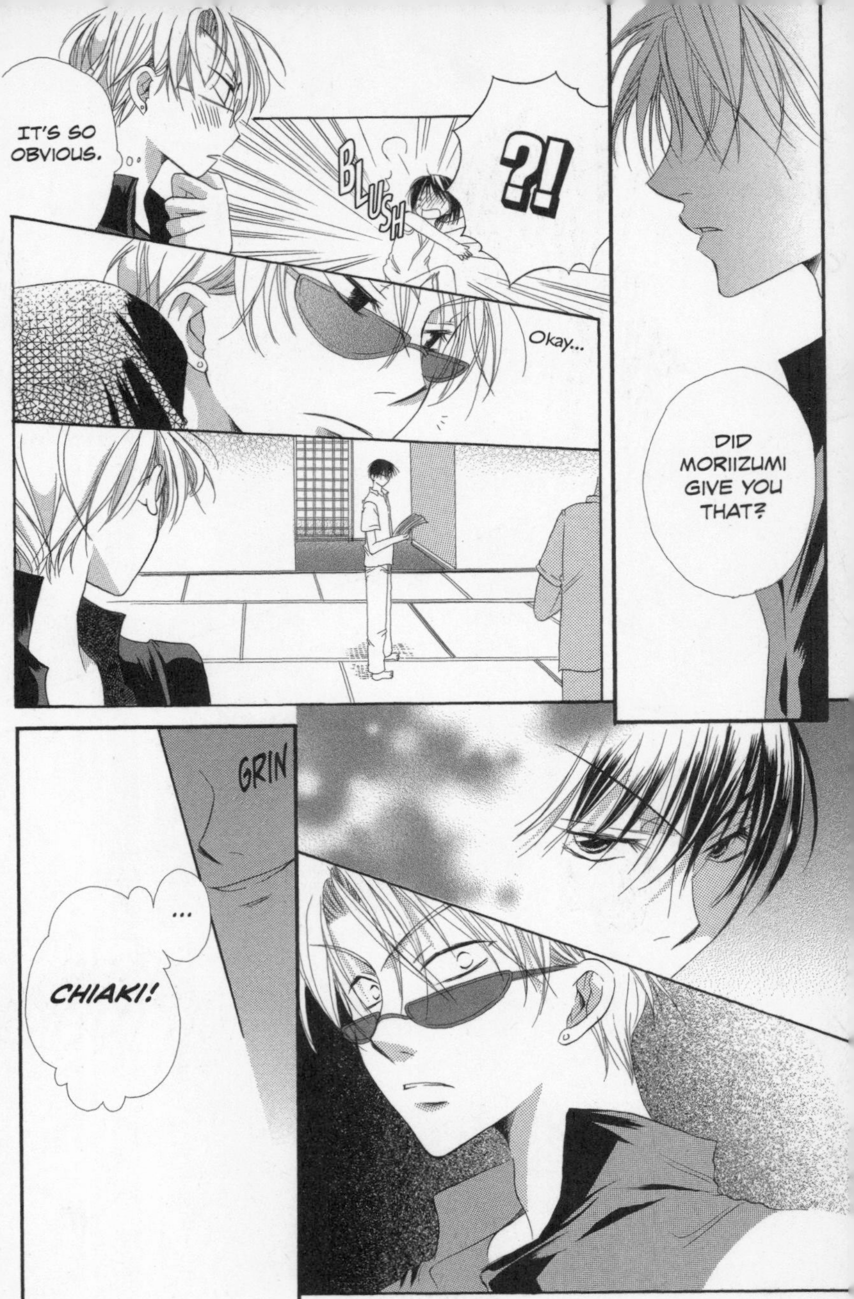
DID MORIIZUMI GIVE YOU THAT?
?!
BLUSH
IT'S SO OBVIOUS.
Okay...
GRIN
...
CHIAKI!

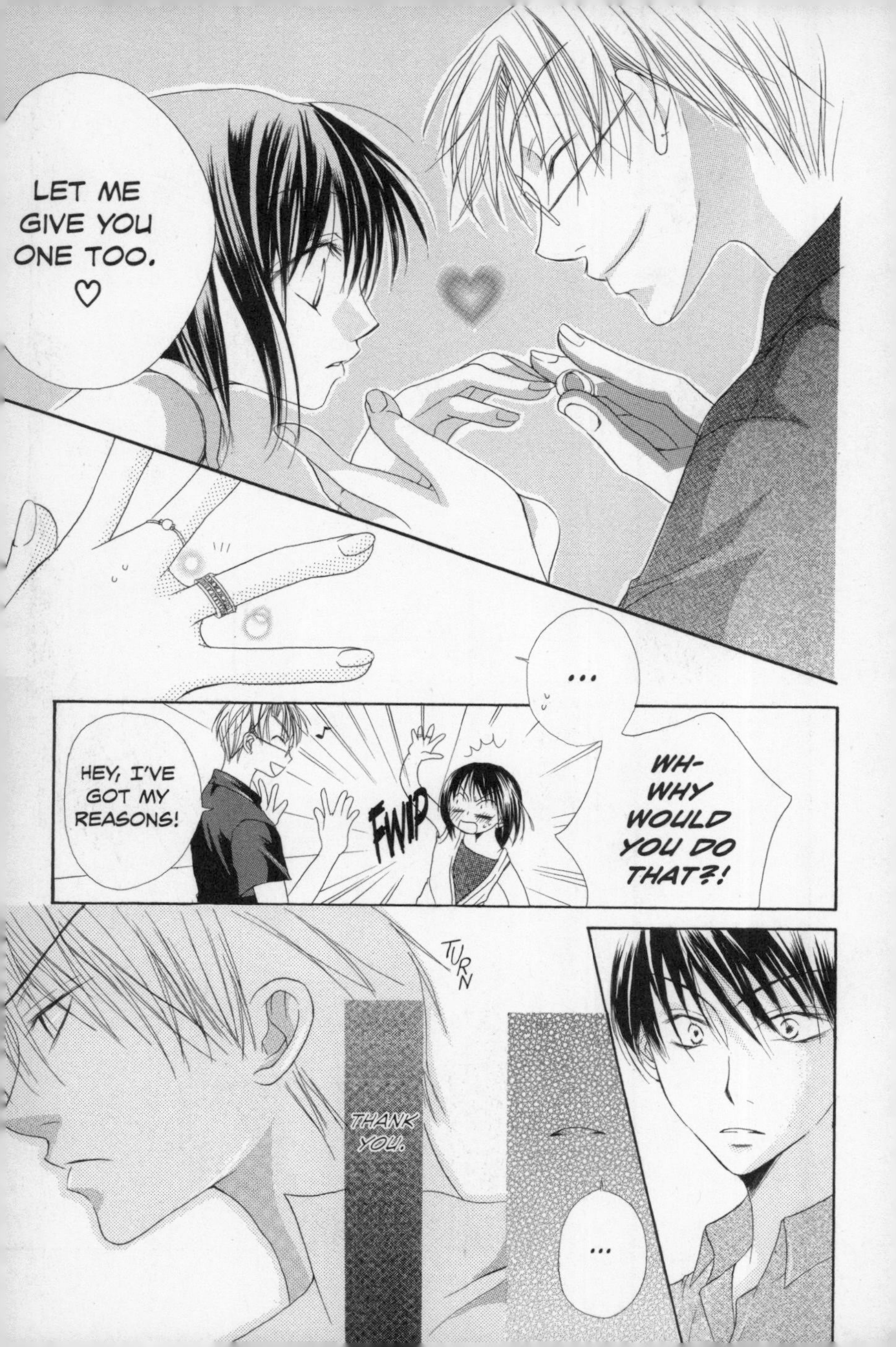
LET ME GIVE YOU ONE TOO. ♡
...
WH- WHY WOULD YOU DO THAT?!
FWIP
HEY, I'VE GOT MY REASONS!
...
TURN
THANK YOU.

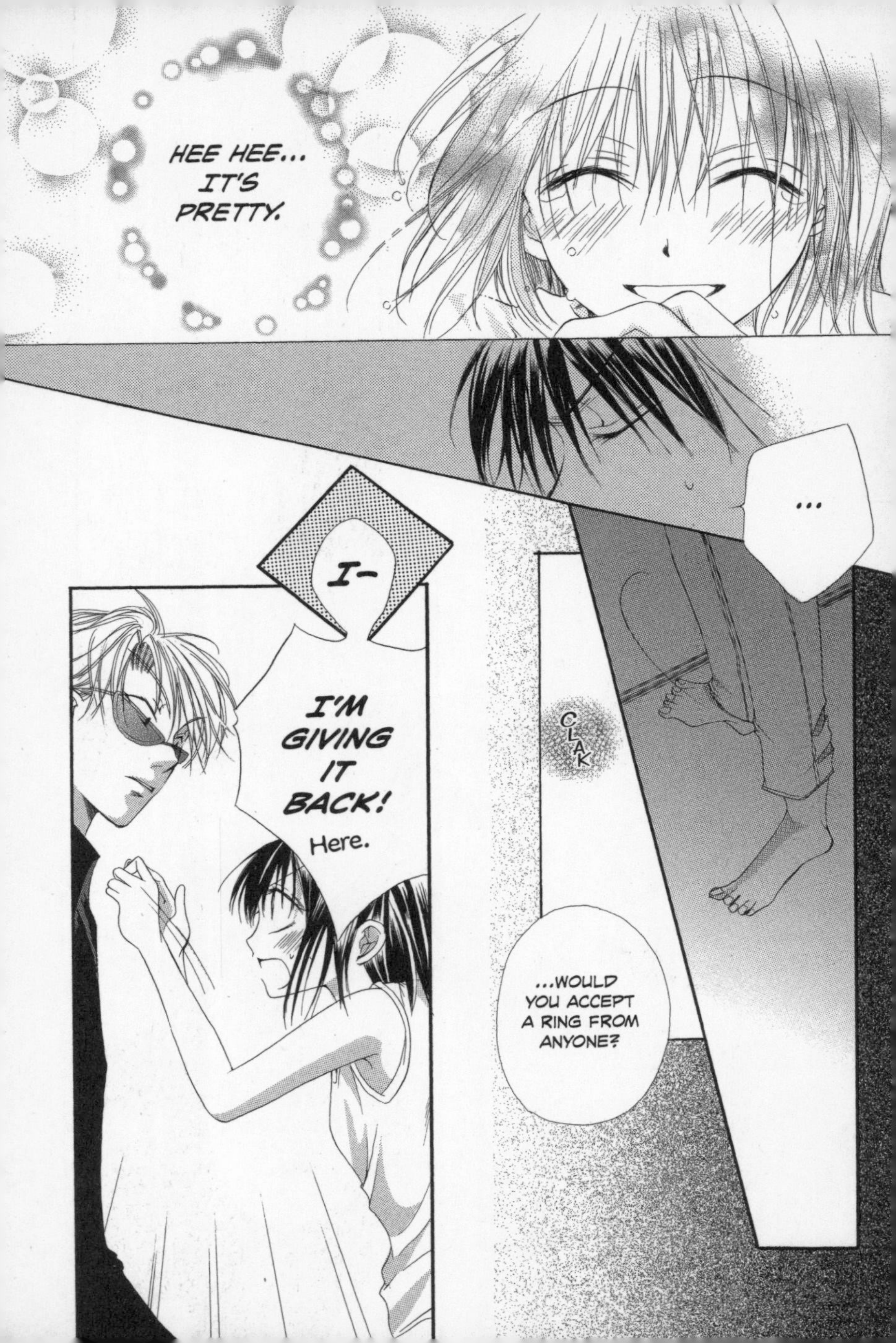
HEE HEE... IT'S PRETTY.
...
CLAK
...WOULD YOU ACCEPT A RING FROM ANYONE?
I—
I'M GIVING IT BACK!
Here.

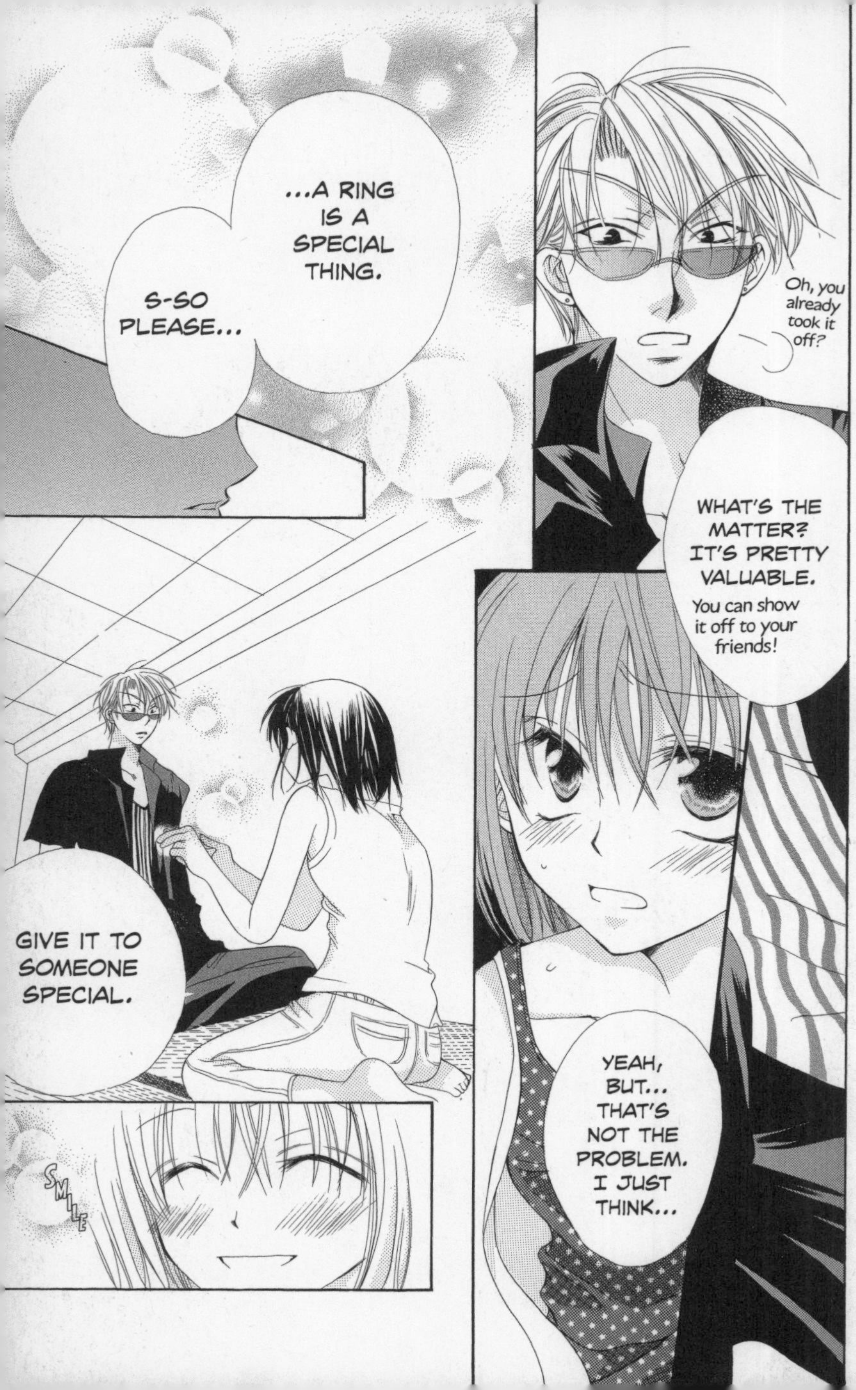
Oh, you already took it off?
WHAT'S THE MATTER? IT'S PRETTY VALUABLE.
You can show it off to your friends!
YEAH, BUT... THAT'S NOT THE PROBLEM. I JUST THINK...
...A RING IS A SPECIAL THING.
S-SO PLEASE...
GIVE IT TO SOMEONE SPECIAL.
SMILE

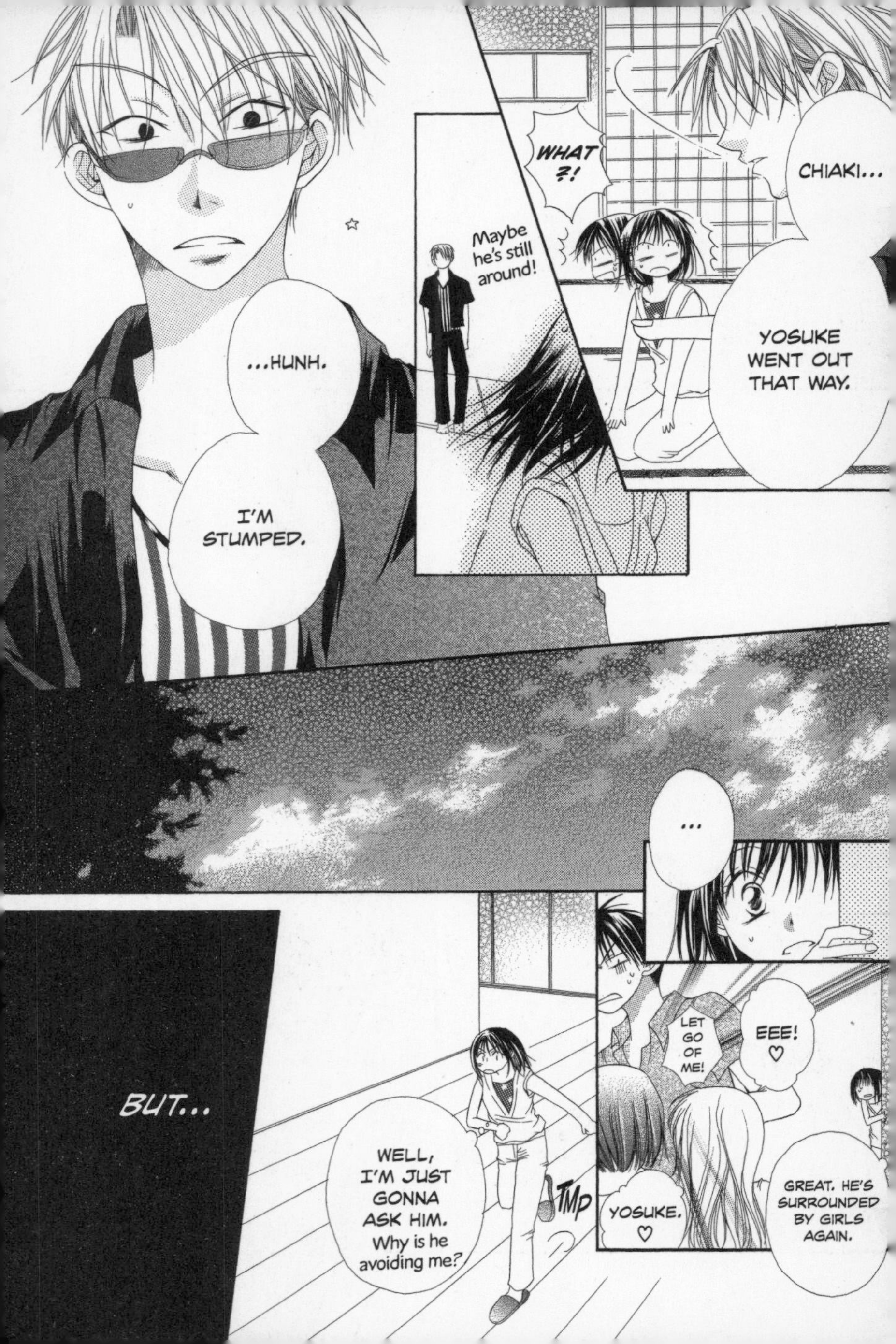
CHIAKI...
YOSUKE WENT OUT THAT WAY.
WHAT ?!
Maybe he's still around!
...HUNH.
I'M STUMPED.
...
EEE! ♡
LET GO OF ME!
GREAT. HE'S SURROUNDED BY GIRLS AGAIN.
YOSUKE. ♡
TMP
WELL, I'M JUST GONNA ASK HIM.
Why is he avoiding me?
BUT...

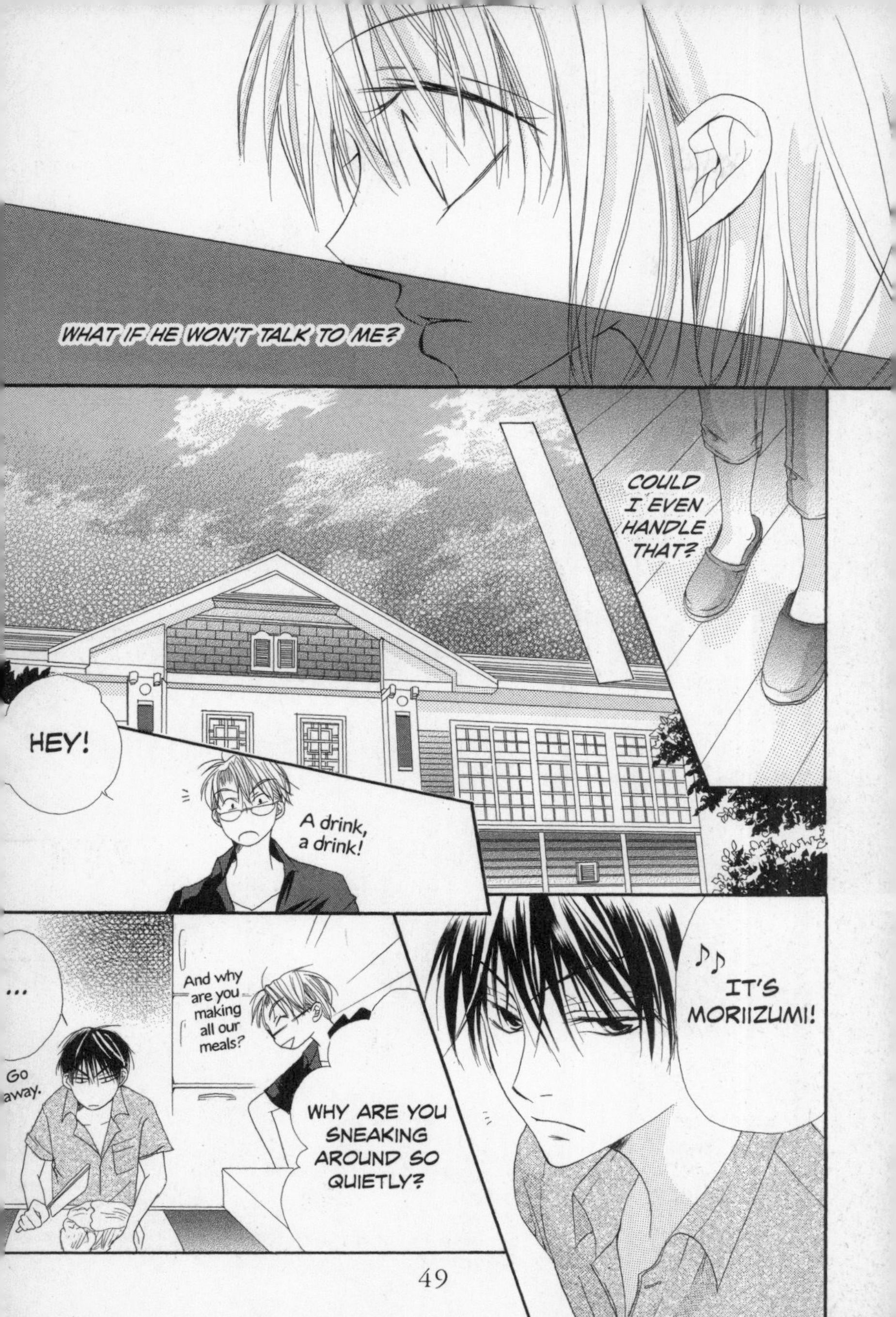
WHAT IF HE WON'T TALK TO ME?
COULD I EVEN HANDLE THAT?
HEY!
A drink, a drink!
♪♪ IT'S MORIIZUMI!
WHY ARE YOU SNEAKING AROUND SO QUIETLY?
And why are you making all our meals?
...
Go away.

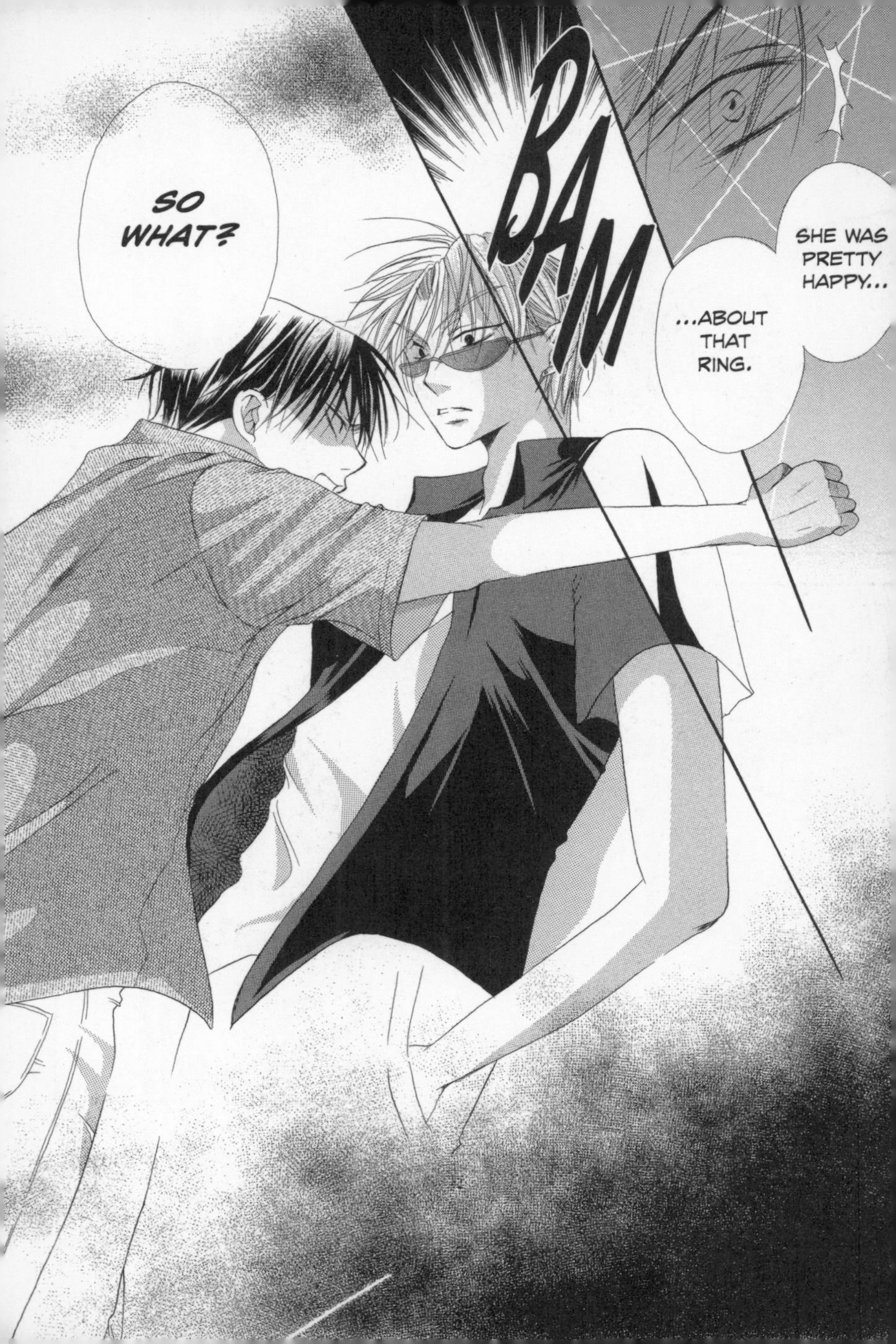
SHE WAS PRETTY HAPPY...
...ABOUT THAT RING.
BAM
SO WHAT?

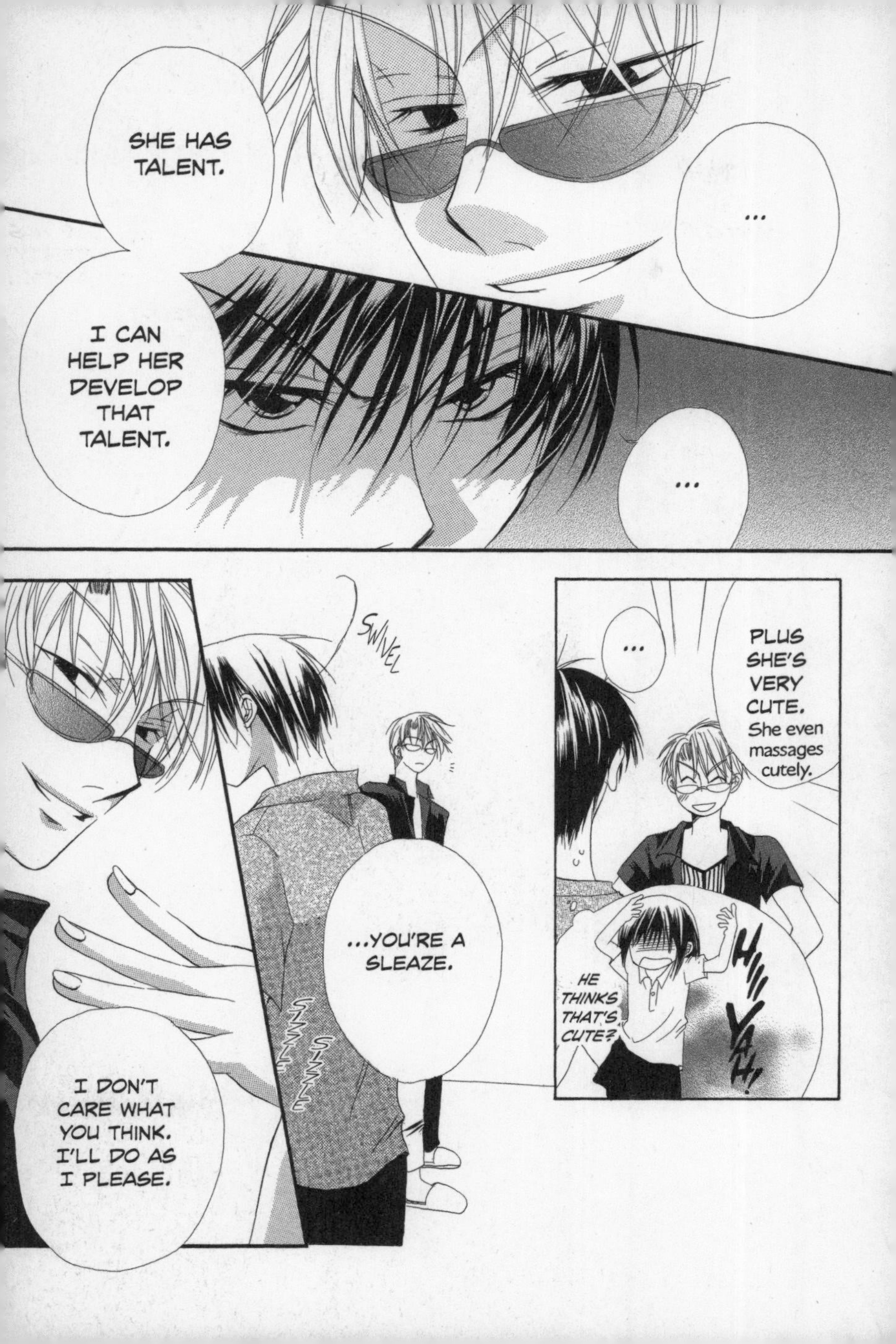
...
SHE HAS TALENT.
...
I CAN HELP HER DEVELOP THAT TALENT.
...
PLUS SHE'S VERY CUTE. She even massages cutely.
HIYAH!
HE THINKS THAT'S CUTE?
SWIVEL
...YOU'RE A SLEAZE.
SIZZLE SIZZLE
I DON'T CARE WHAT YOU THINK. I'LL DO AS I PLEASE.

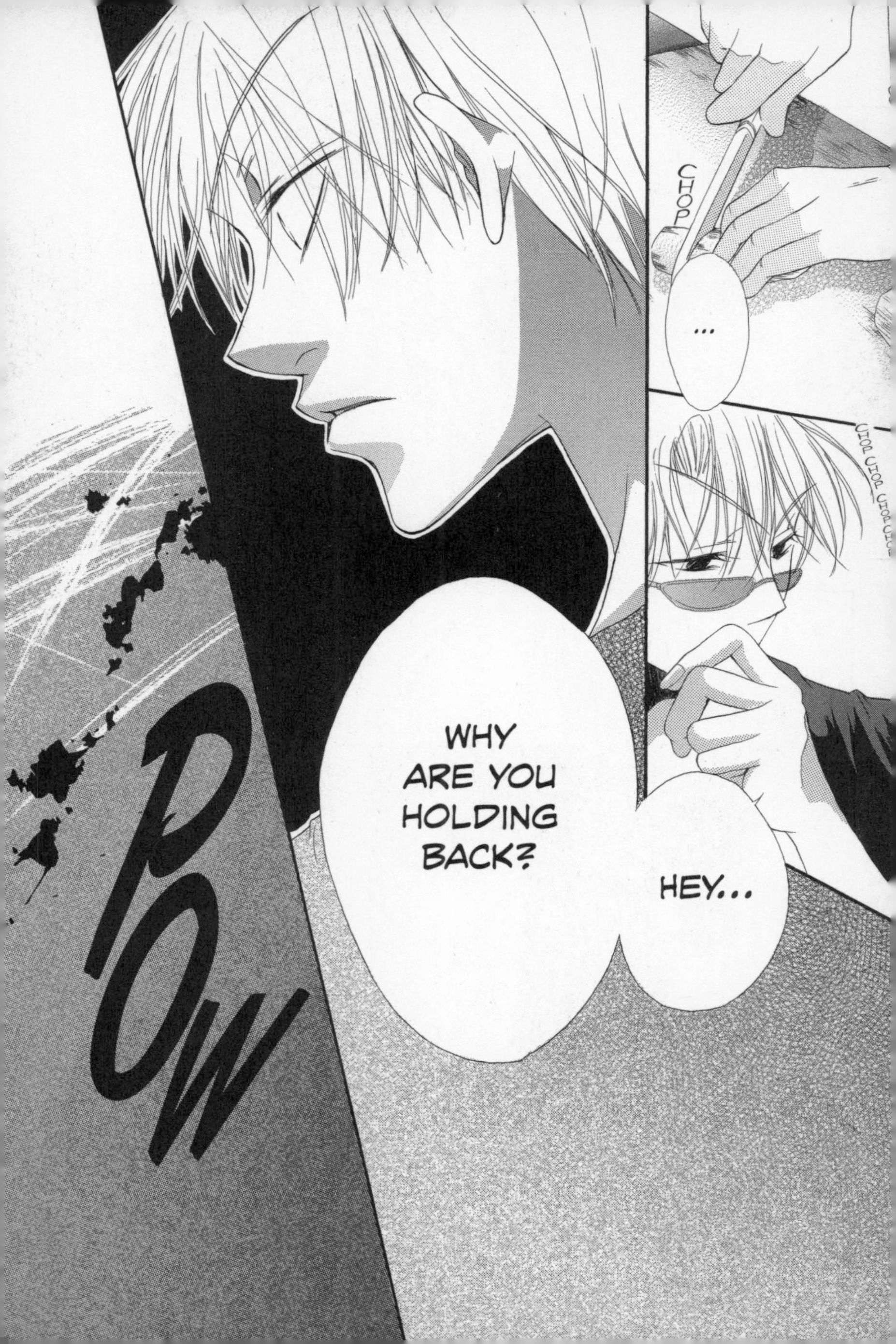
CHOP
...
CHOP CHOP CHOP
HEY...
WHY ARE YOU HOLDING BACK?
POW

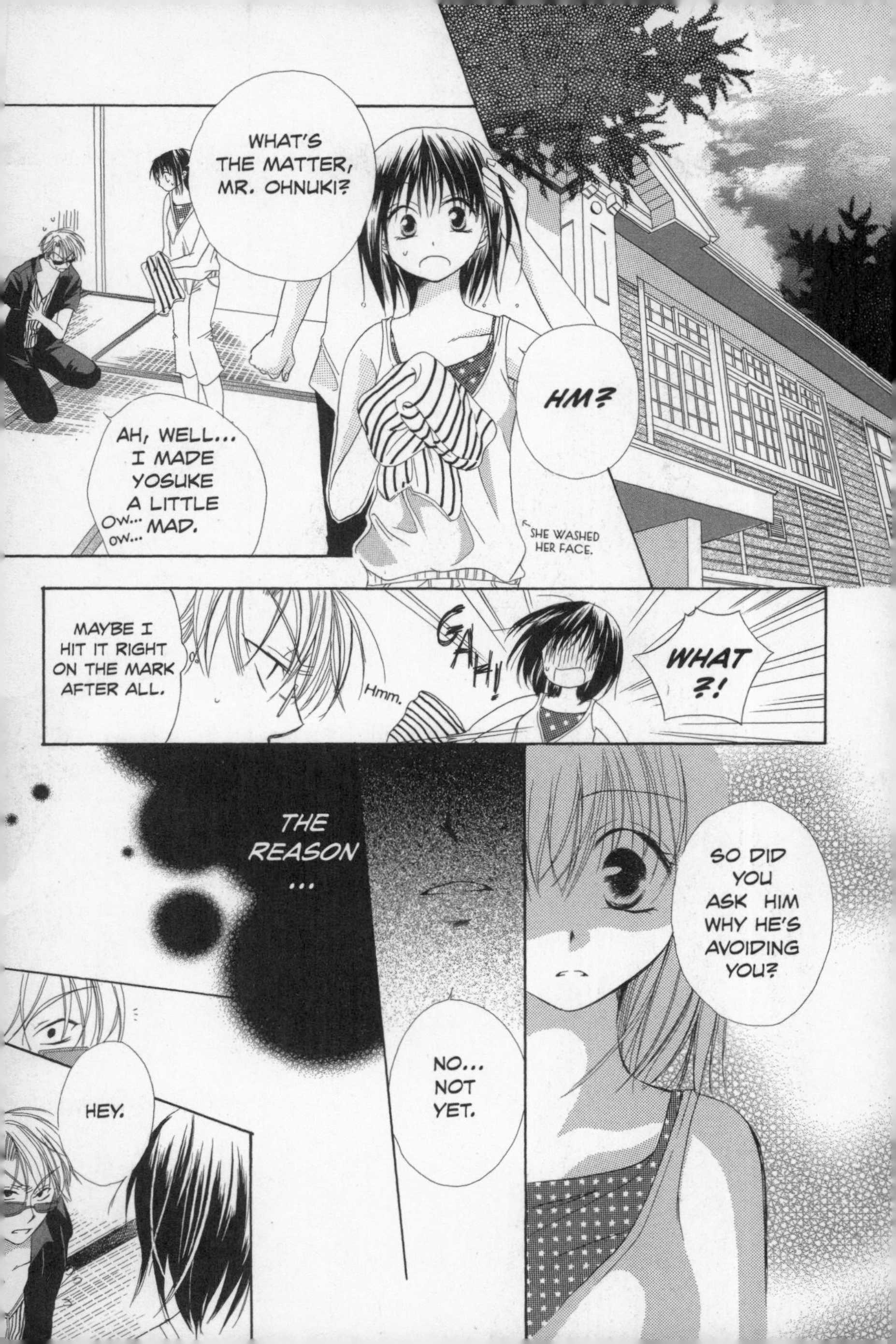
HM?
WHAT'S THE MATTER, MR. OHNUKI?
SHE WASHED HER FACE.
AH, WELL... I MADE YOSUKE A LITTLE MAD.
OW... OW...
WHAT?!
GAH!
Hmm.
MAYBE I HIT IT RIGHT ON THE MARK AFTER ALL.
SO DID YOU ASK HIM WHY HE'S AVOIDING YOU?
NO... NOT YET.
THE REASON ...
HEY.

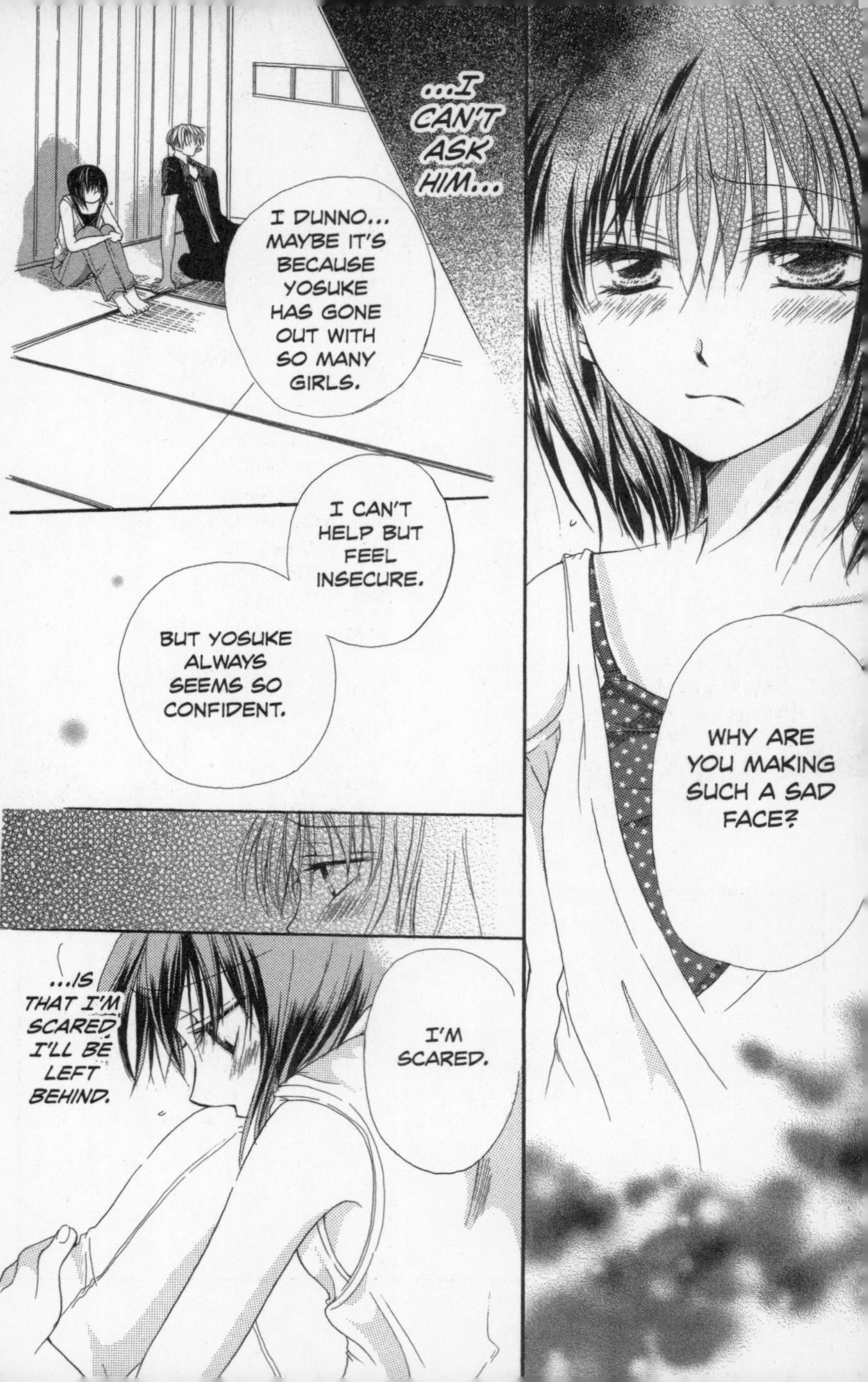
WHY ARE YOU MAKING SUCH A SAD FACE?
...I CAN'T ASK HIM...
I DUNNO... MAYBE IT'S BECAUSE YOSUKE HAS GONE OUT WITH SO MANY GIRLS.
I CAN'T HELP BUT FEEL INSECURE.
BUT YOSUKE ALWAYS SEEMS SO CONFIDENT.
I'M SCARED.
...IS THAT I'M SCARED I'LL BE LEFT BEHIND.

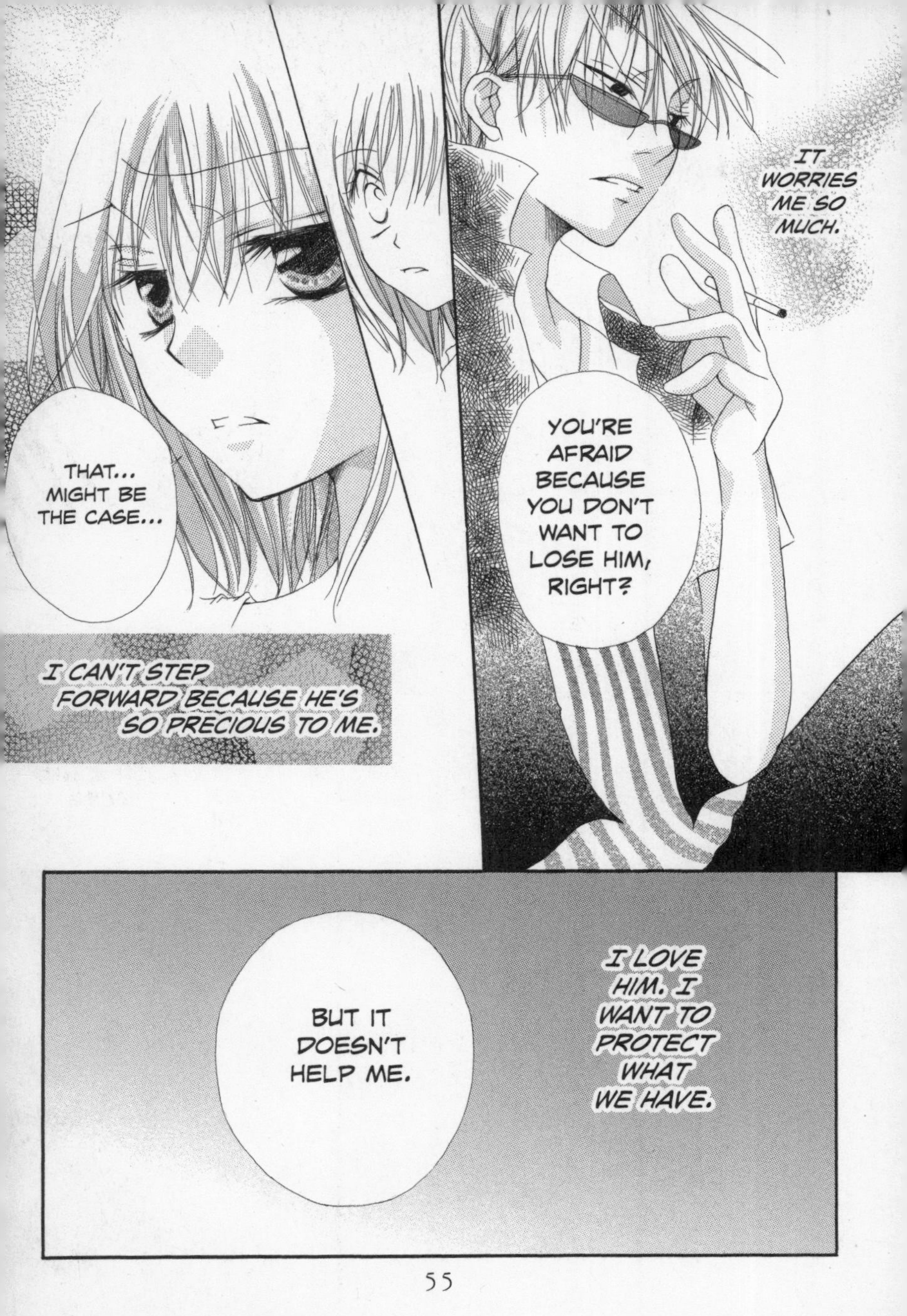
IT WORRIES ME SO MUCH.
YOU'RE AFRAID BECAUSE YOU DON'T WANT TO LOSE HIM, RIGHT?
THAT... MIGHT BE THE CASE...
I CAN'T STEP FORWARD BECAUSE HE'S SO PRECIOUS TO ME.
I LOVE HIM. I WANT TO PROTECT WHAT WE HAVE.
BUT IT DOESN'T HELP ME.

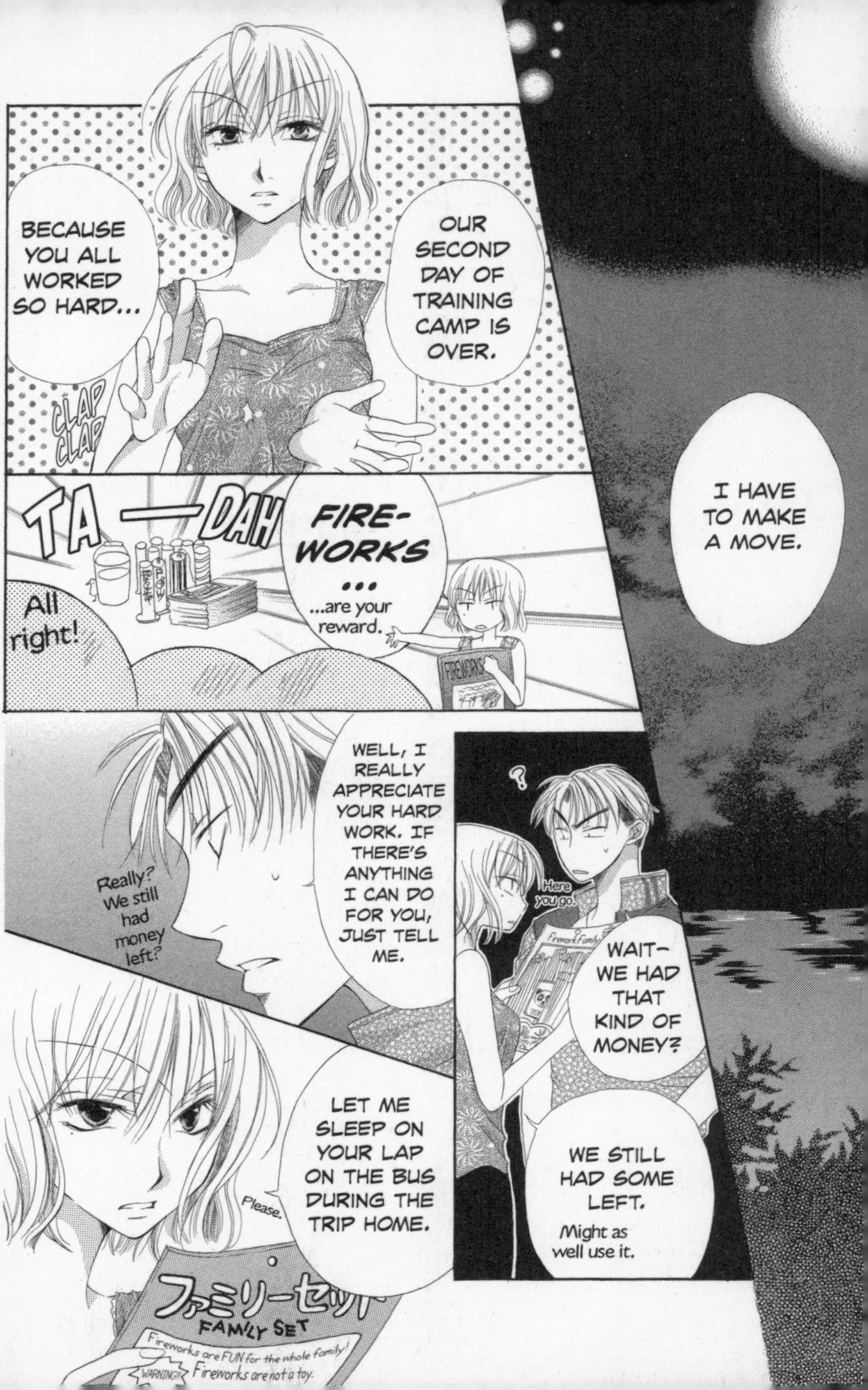
I HAVE TO MAKE A MOVE.
OUR SECOND DAY OF TRAINING CAMP IS OVER.
BECAUSE YOU ALL WORKED SO HARD...
CLAP CLAP
FIRE-WORKS...
...are your reward.
TA—DAH
All right!
FIREWORKS
Here you go.
Firework Family
WAIT- WE HAD THAT KIND OF MONEY?
WE STILL HAD SOME LEFT.
Might as well use it.
WELL, I REALLY APPRECIATE YOUR HARD WORK. IF THERE'S ANYTHING I CAN DO FOR YOU, JUST TELL ME.
Really? We still had money left?
LET ME SLEEP ON YOUR LAP ON THE BUS DURING THE TRIP HOME.
Please.
ファミリーセット
FAMILY SET
Fireworks are FUN for the whole family!
WARNING!!! Fireworks are not a toy.

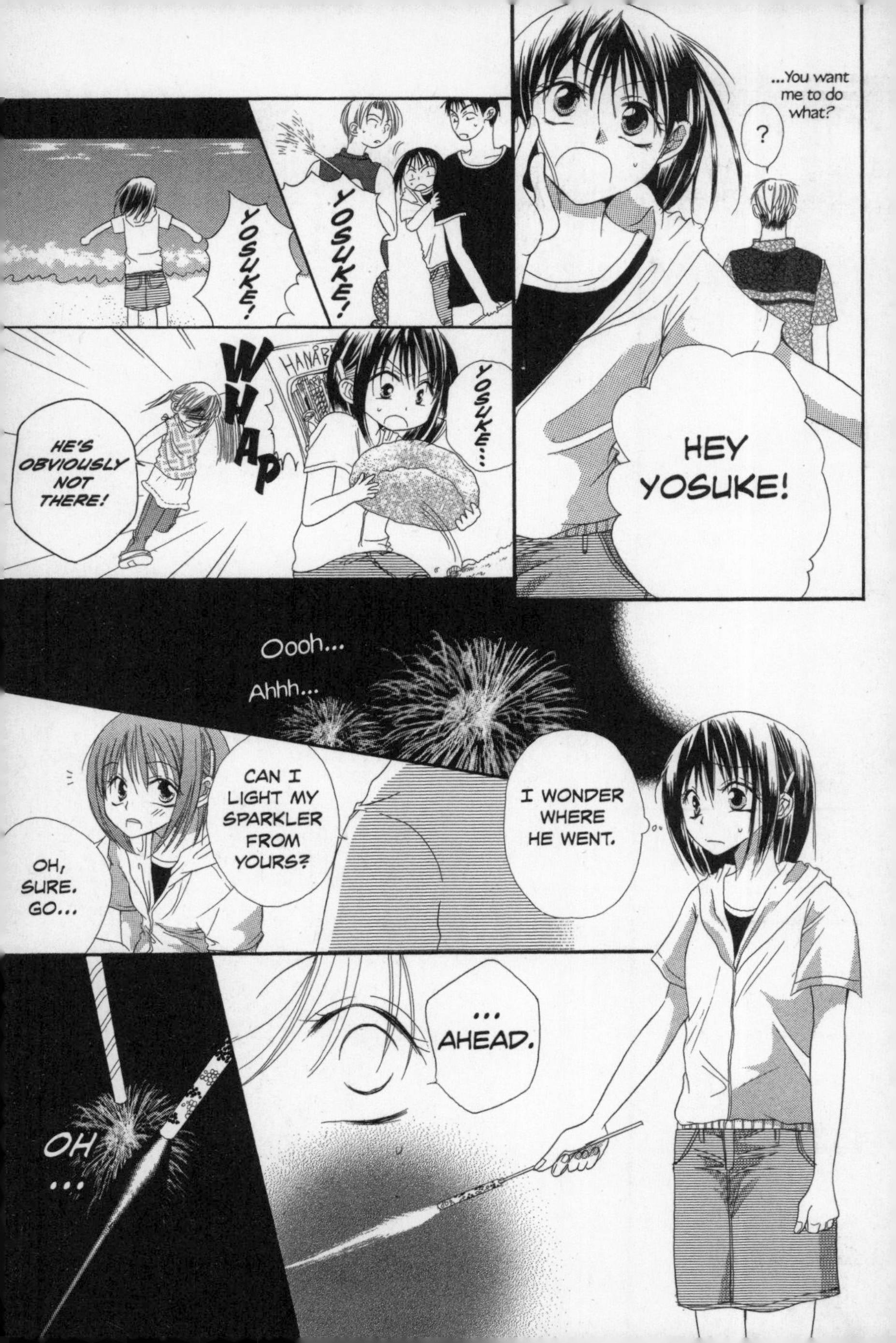
...You want me to do what?
?
HEY YOSUKE!
YOSUKE!
YOSUKE!
YOSUKE...
WHAP
HE'S OBVIOUSLY NOT THERE!
Oooh...
Ahhh...
I WONDER WHERE HE WENT.
CAN I LIGHT MY SPARKLER FROM YOURS?
OH, SURE. GO...
...AHEAD.
OH...

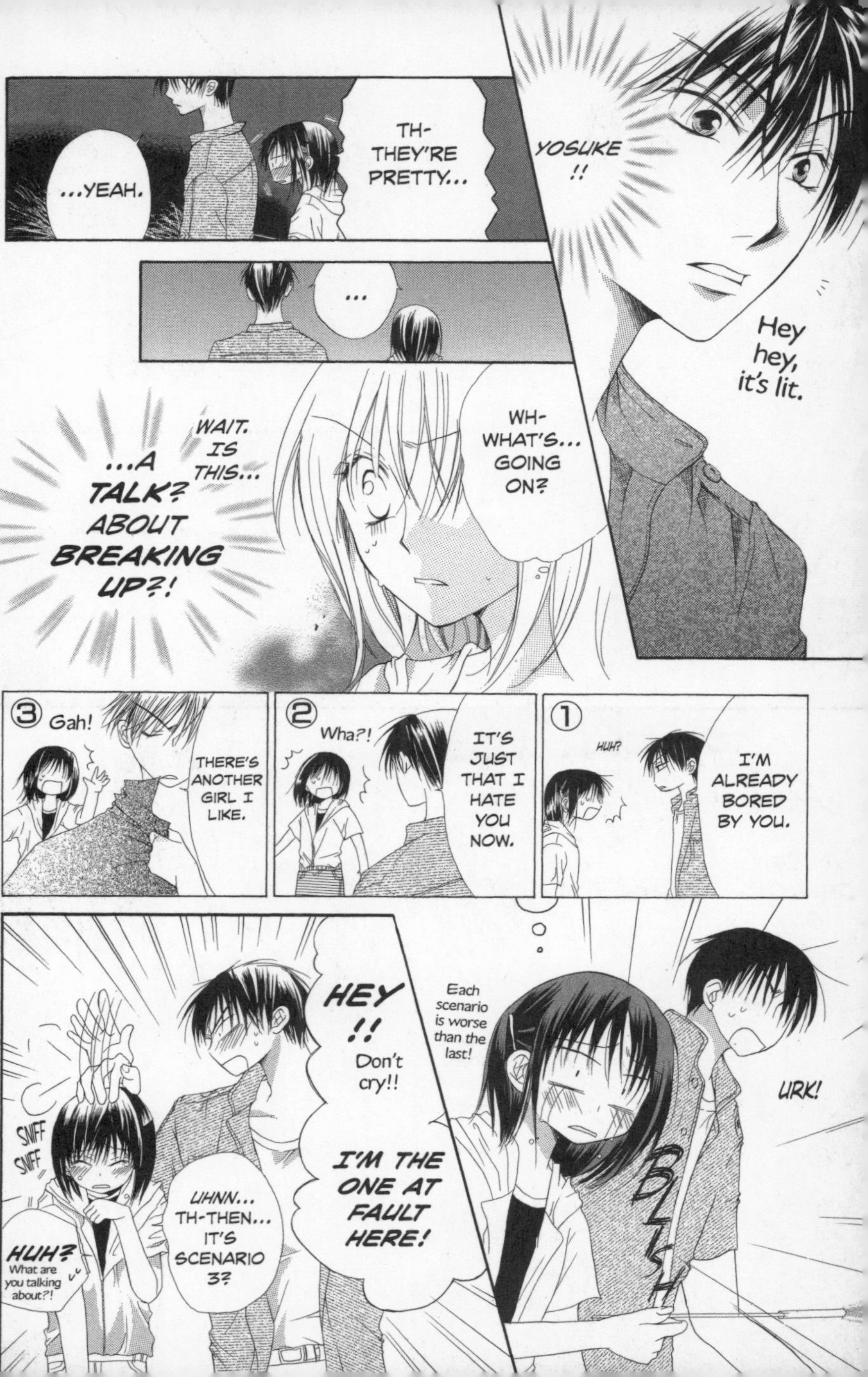
YOSUKE !!
Hey hey, it's lit.
TH- THEY'RE PRETTY...
...YEAH.
...
WH- WHAT'S... GOING ON?
WAIT. IS THIS...
...A TALK? ABOUT BREAKING UP?!
①
HUH?
I'M ALREADY BORED BY YOU.
②
Wha?!
IT'S JUST THAT I HATE YOU NOW.
③
Gah!
THERE'S ANOTHER GIRL I LIKE.
Each scenario is worse than the last!
URK!
HEY !!
Don't cry!!
I'M THE ONE AT FAULT HERE!
UHNN... TH-THEN... IT'S SCENARIO 3?
SNIFF SNIFF
HUH?
What are you talking about?!

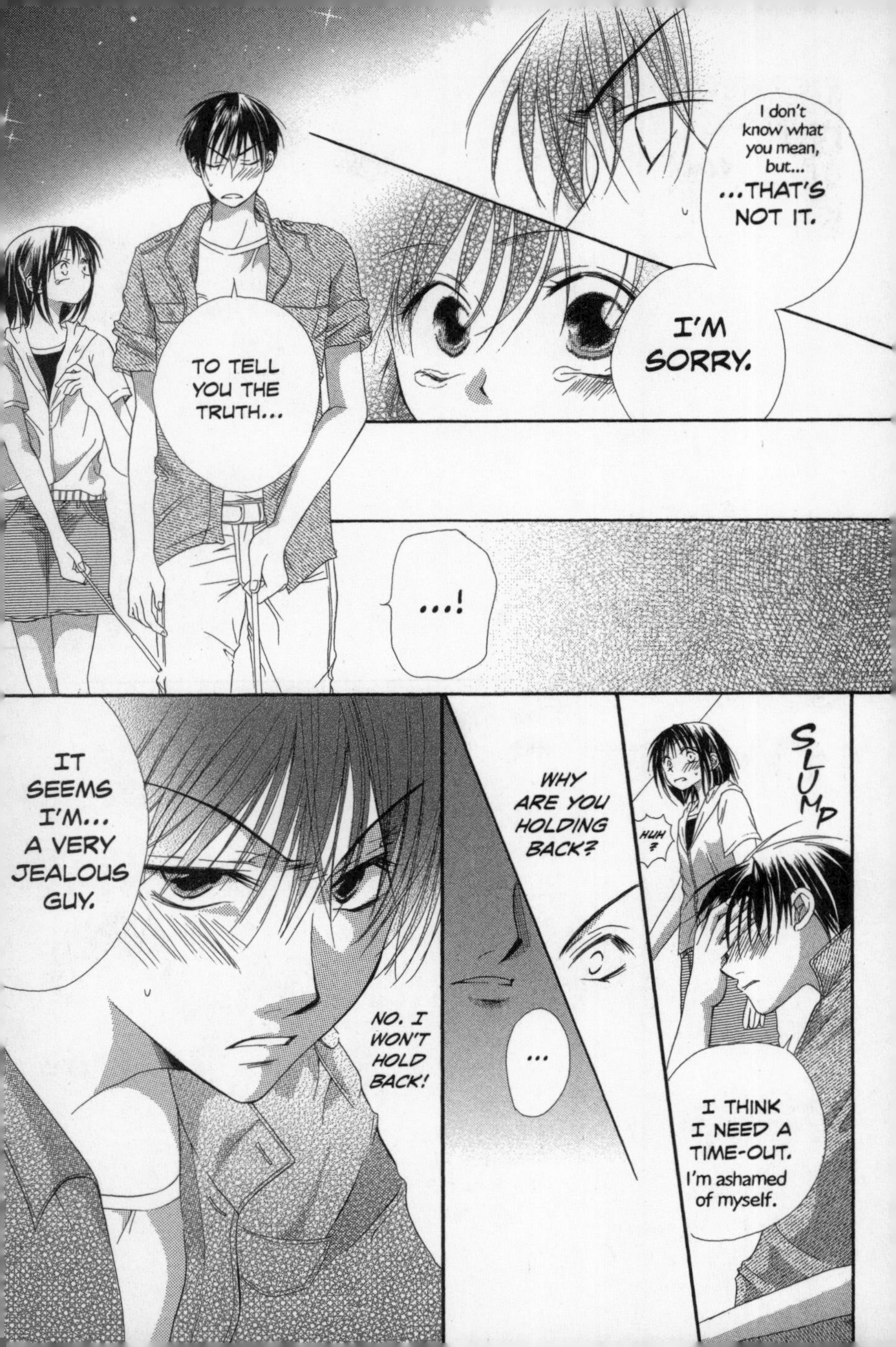
I don't know what you mean, but... ...THAT'S NOT IT.
I'M SORRY.
...!
TO TELL YOU THE TRUTH...
SLUMP
HUH?
I THINK I NEED A TIME-OUT. I'm ashamed of myself.
WHY ARE YOU HOLDING BACK?
...
IT SEEMS I'M... A VERY JEALOUS GUY.
NO. I WON'T HOLD BACK!

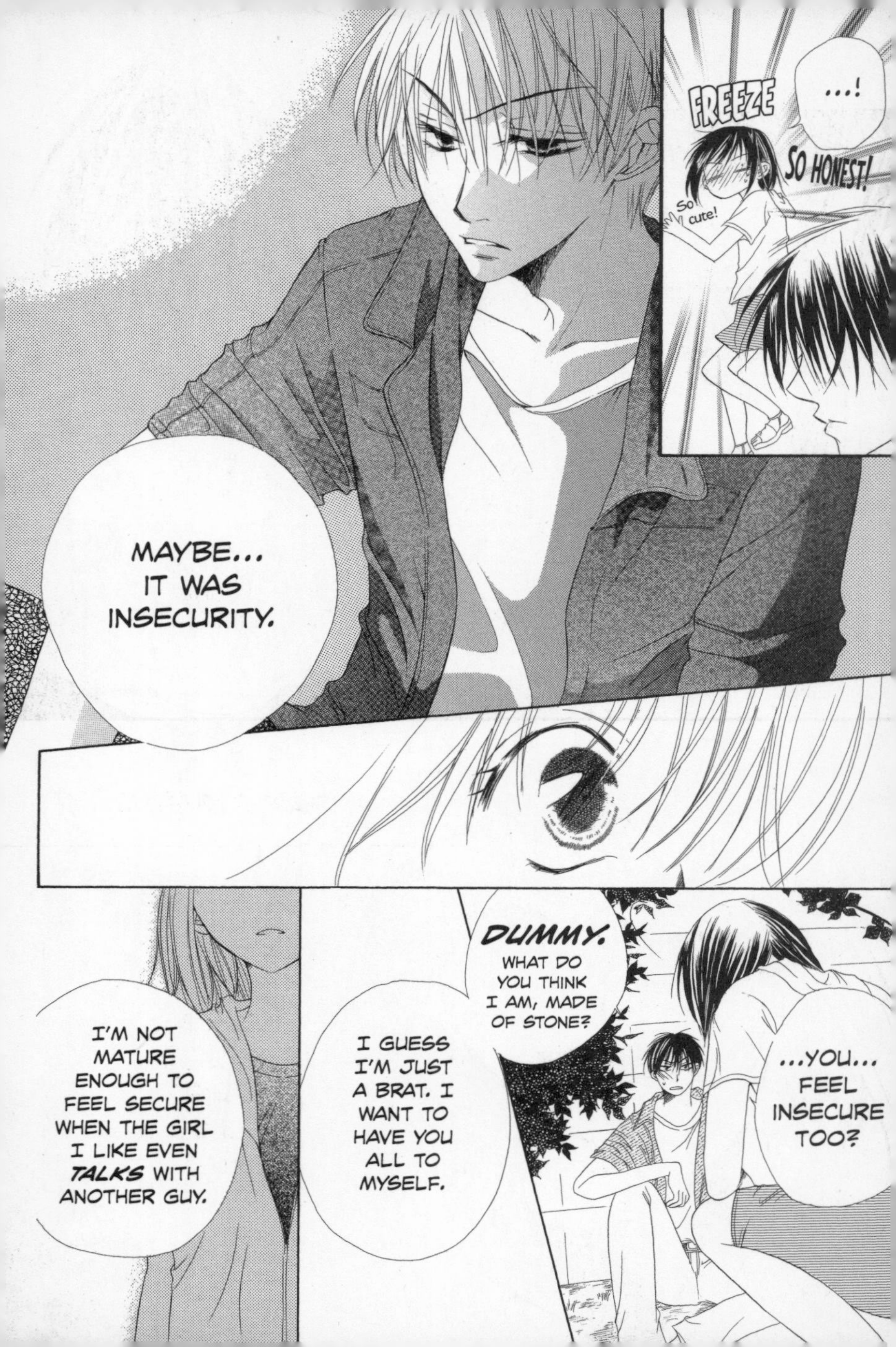
...!
FREEZE
SO HONEST!
So cute!
MAYBE... IT WAS INSECURITY.
...YOU... FEEL INSECURE TOO?
DUMMY. WHAT DO YOU THINK I AM, MADE OF STONE?
I GUESS I'M JUST A BRAT. I WANT TO HAVE YOU ALL TO MYSELF.
I'M NOT MATURE ENOUGH TO FEEL SECURE WHEN THE GIRL I LIKE EVEN TALKS WITH ANOTHER GUY.

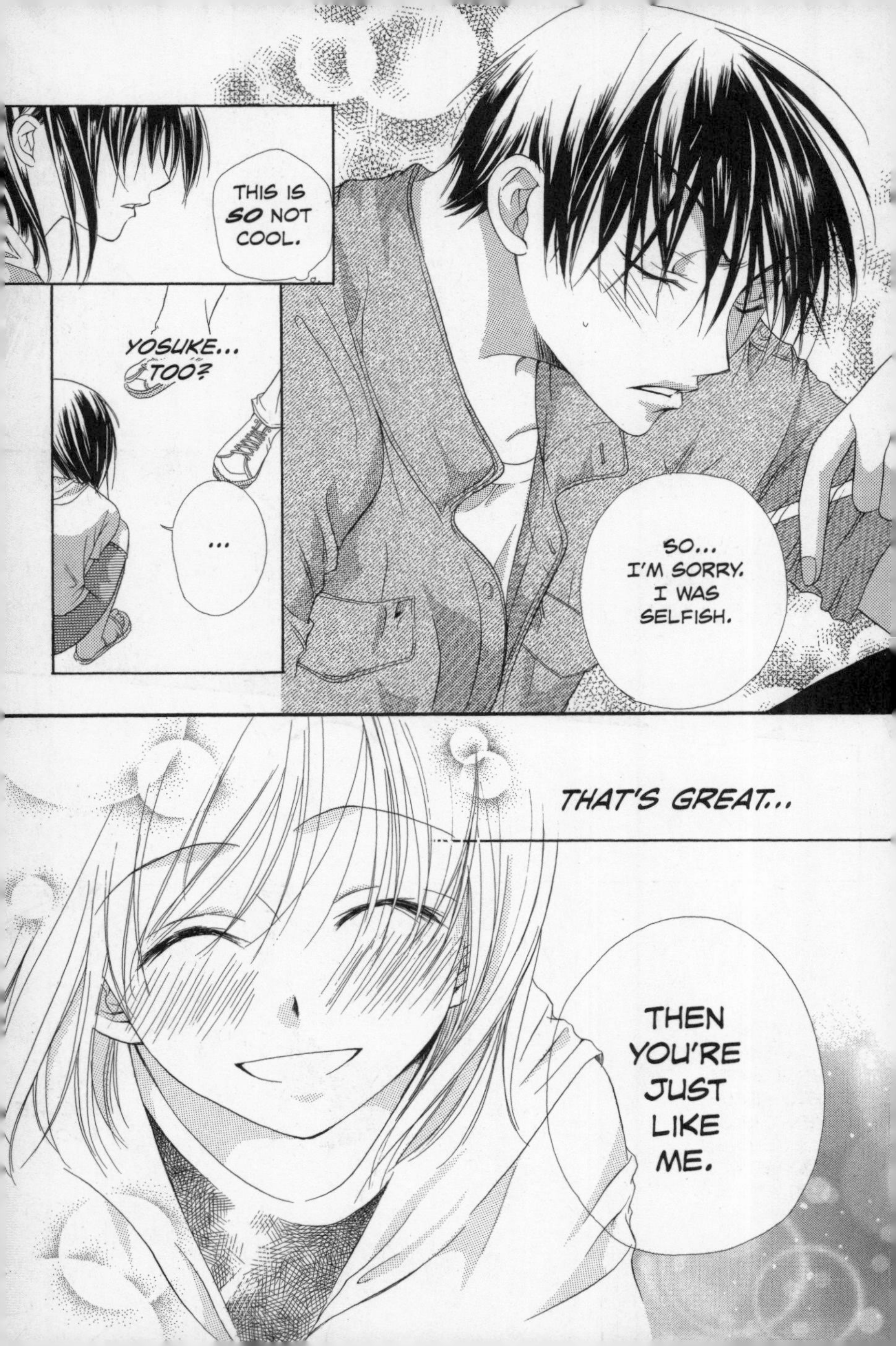
SO... I'M SORRY. I WAS SELFISH.
THIS IS SO NOT COOL.
YOSUKE... TOO?
...
THAT'S GREAT...
THEN YOU'RE JUST LIKE ME.

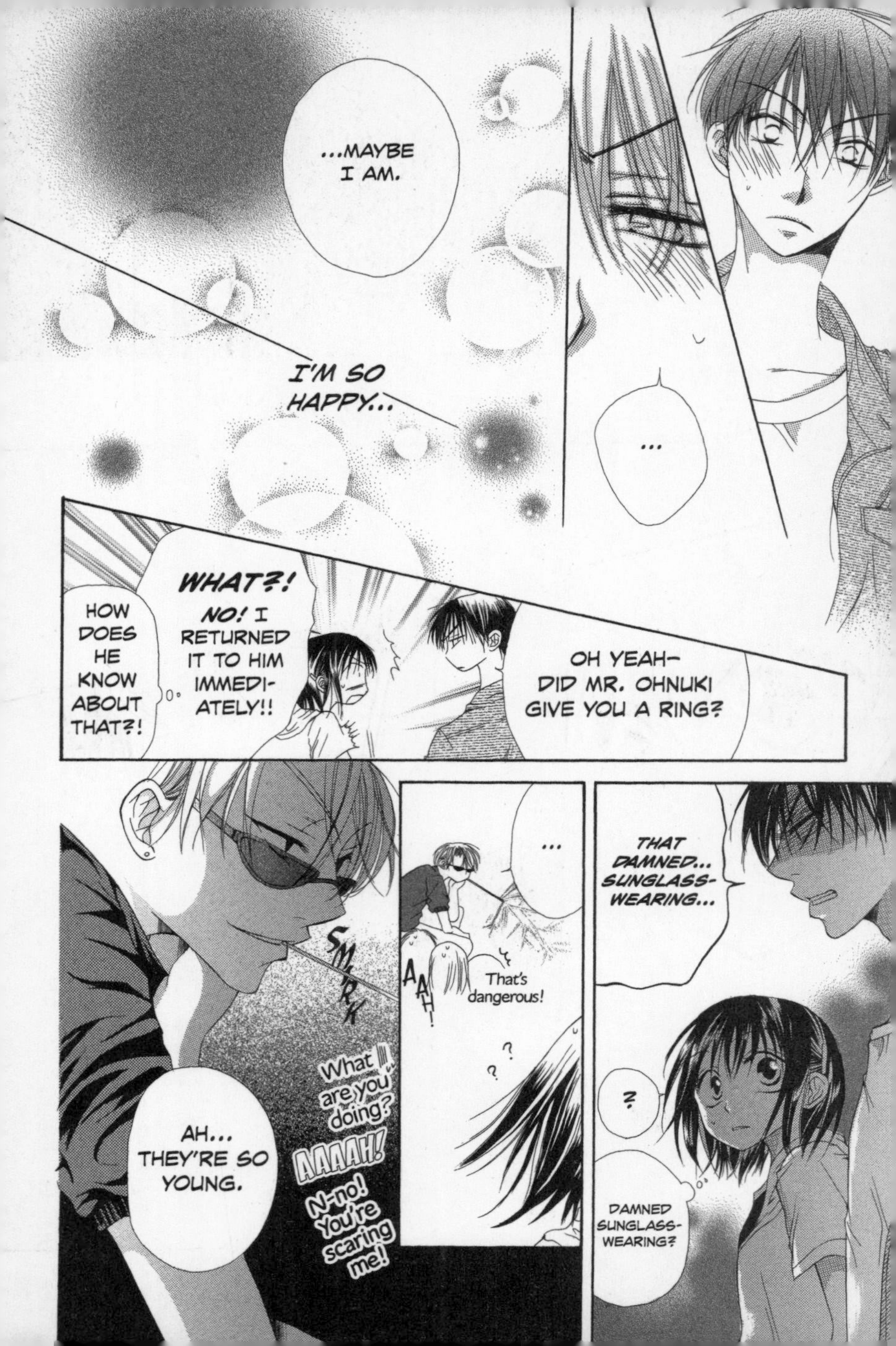
...
...MAYBE I AM.
I'M SO HAPPY...
OH YEAH- DID MR. OHNUKI GIVE YOU A RING?
WHAT?! NO! I RETURNED IT TO HIM IMMEDIATELY!!
HOW DOES HE KNOW ABOUT THAT?!
THAT DAMNED... SUNGLASS-WEARING...
?
DAMNED SUNGLASS-WEARING?
...
That's dangerous!
AAH!
?
?
SMIRK
What are you doing?
AAAAH!
N-no! You're scaring me!
AH... THEY'RE SO YOUNG.

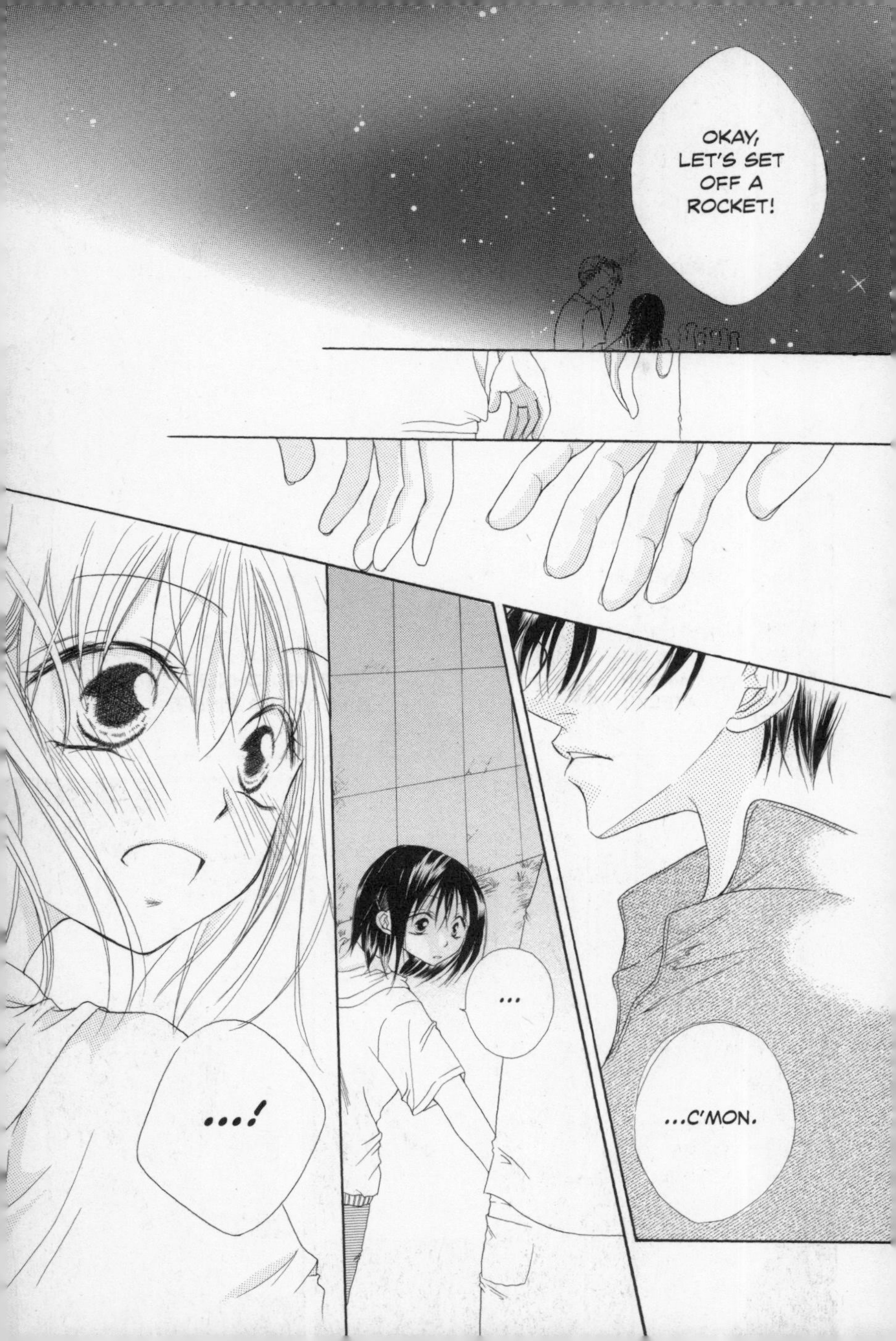
OKAY, LET'S SET OFF A ROCKET!
...C'MON.
...
...!

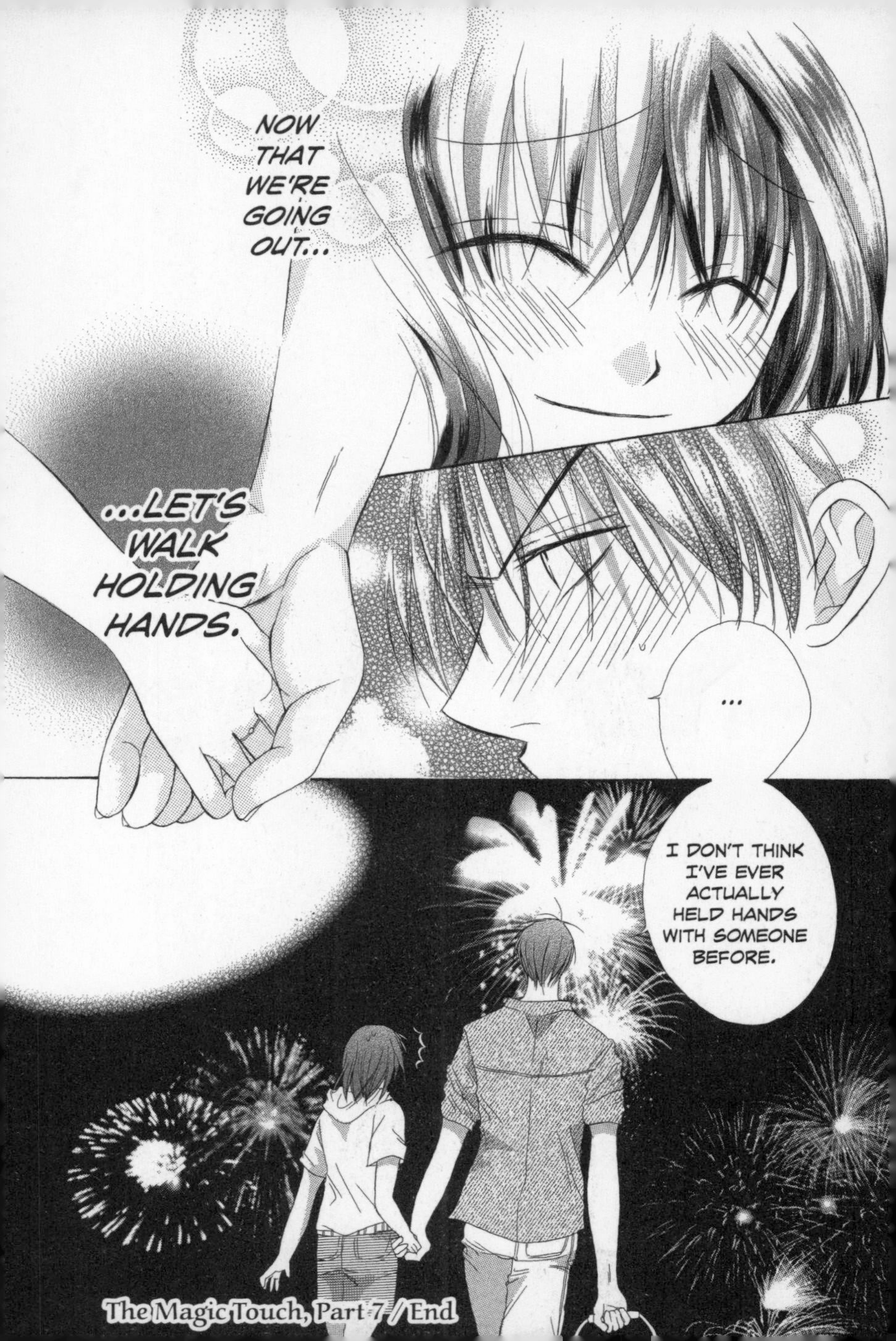
NOW THAT WE'RE GOING OUT...
...LET'S WALK HOLDING HANDS.
...
I DON'T THINK I'VE EVER ACTUALLY HELD HANDS WITH SOMEONE BEFORE.
The Magic Touch, Part 7 / End

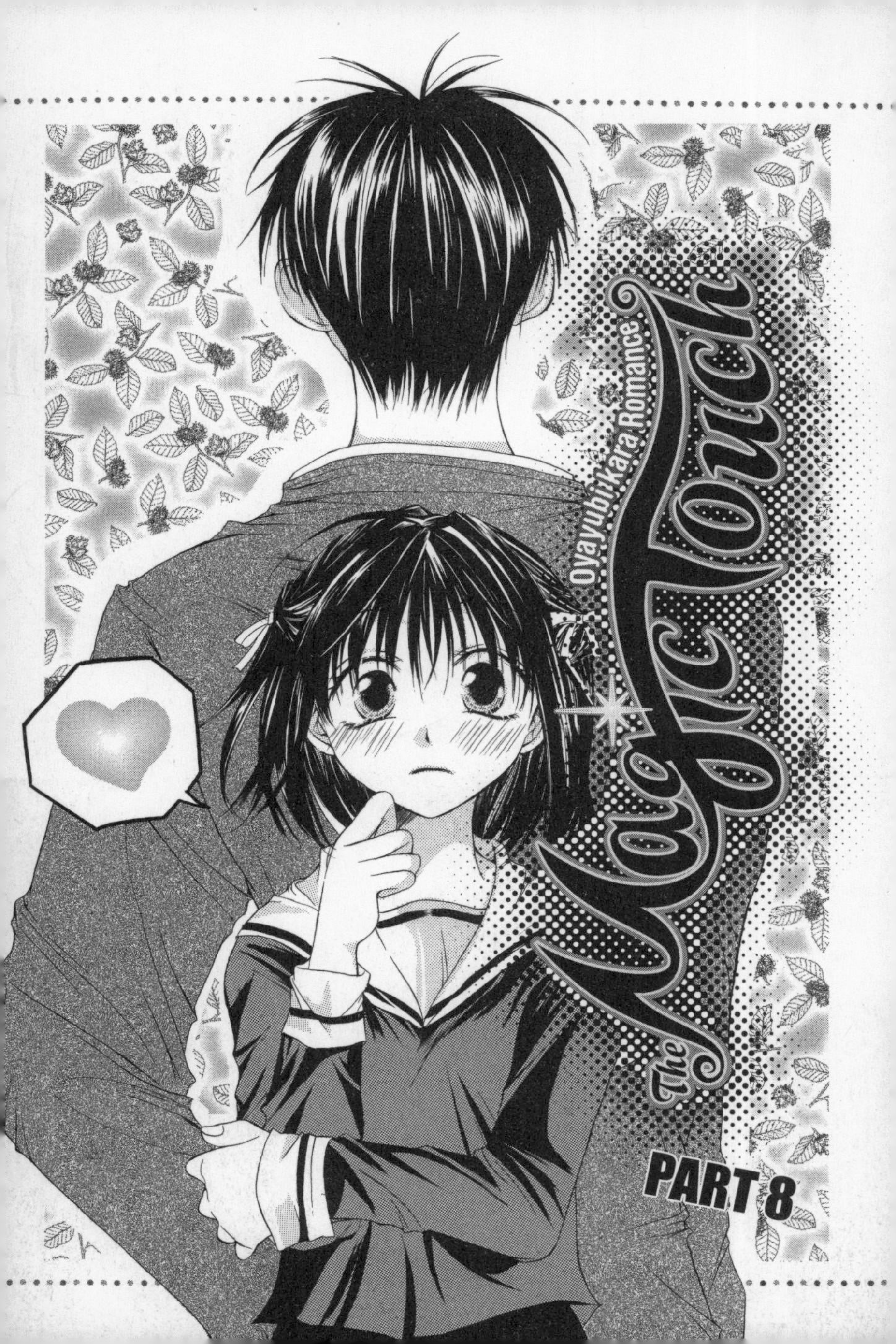
The Magic Touch
Oyayubi kara Romance
PART 8

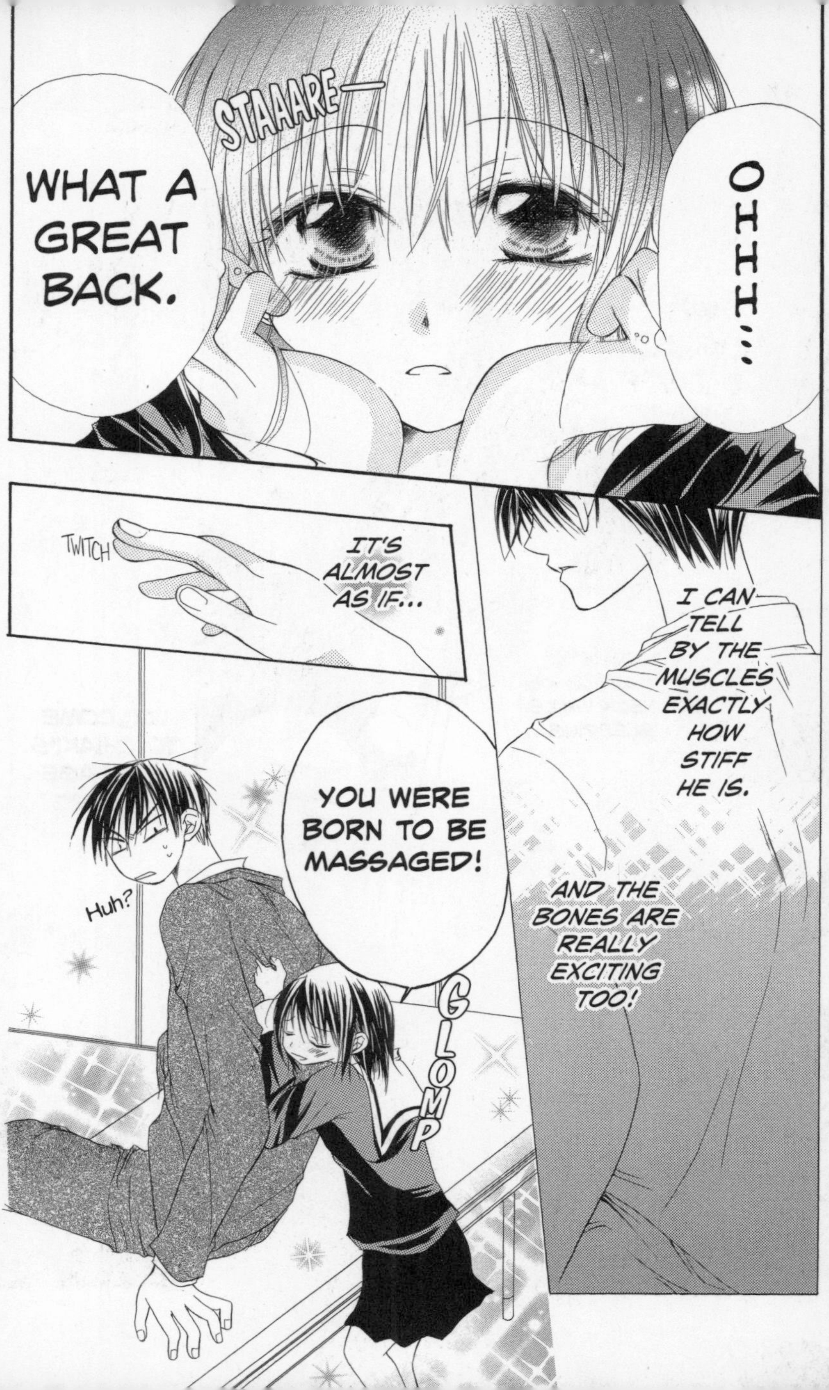
OHHH...
STAAARE—
WHAT A GREAT BACK.
I CAN TELL BY THE MUSCLES EXACTLY HOW STIFF HE IS.
AND THE BONES ARE REALLY EXCITING TOO!
TWITCH
IT'S ALMOST AS IF...
YOU WERE BORN TO BE MASSAGED!
GLOMP
Huh?

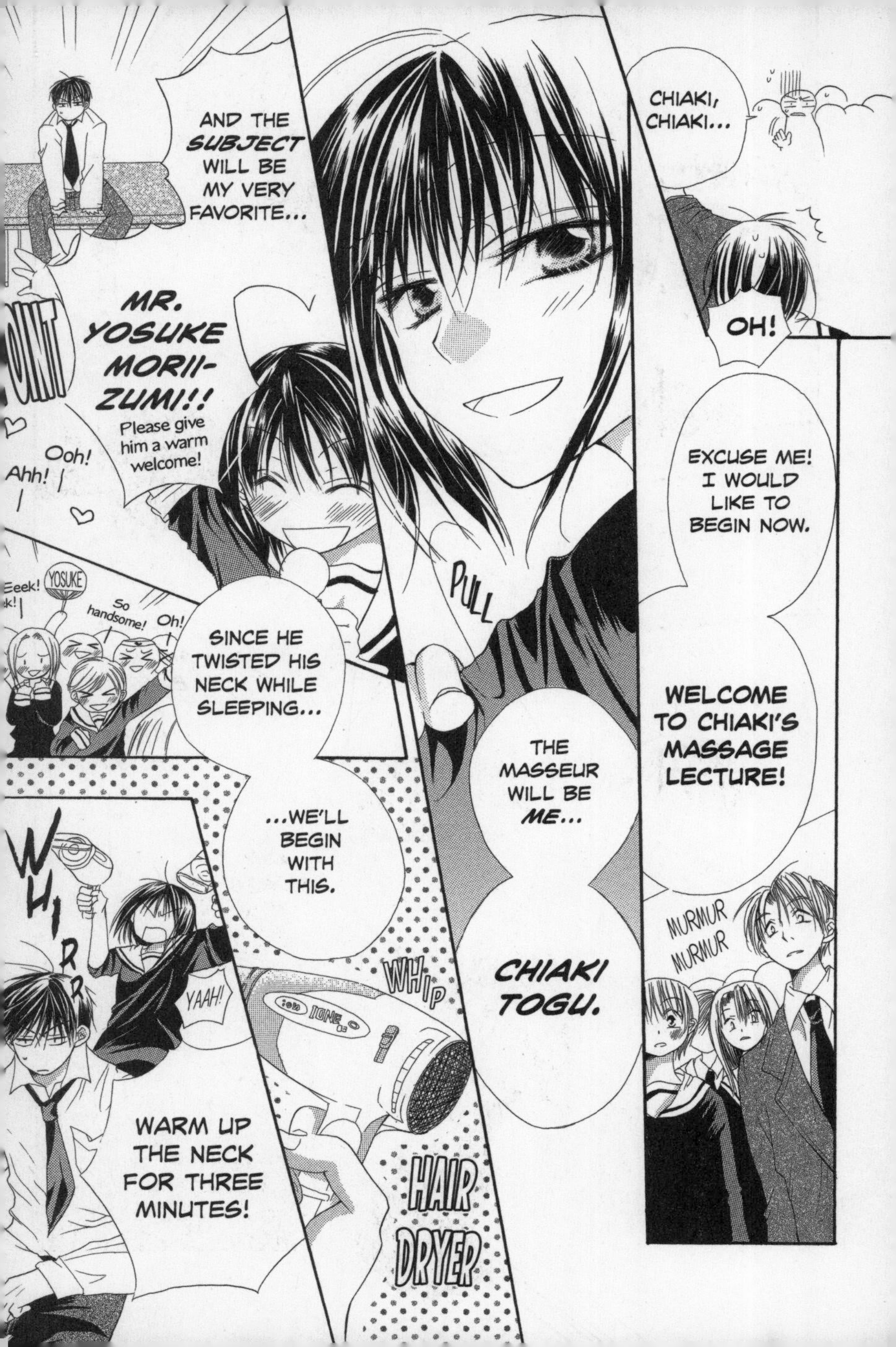
CHIAKI, CHIAKI...
OH!
EXCUSE ME! I WOULD LIKE TO BEGIN NOW.
WELCOME TO CHIAKI'S MASSAGE LECTURE!
MURMUR MURMUR
PULL
THE MASSEUR WILL BE *ME*...
CHIAKI TOGU.
AND THE *SUBJECT* WILL BE MY VERY FAVORITE...
MR. YOSUKE MORII-ZUMI!!
Please give him a warm welcome!
OINT
Ooh!
Ahh!
Eeek!
YOSUKE
So handsome!
Oh!
SINCE HE TWISTED HIS NECK WHILE SLEEPING...
...WE'LL BEGIN WITH THIS.
WHIP
HAIR DRYER
YAAH!
WHIRR
WARM UP THE NECK FOR THREE MINUTES!

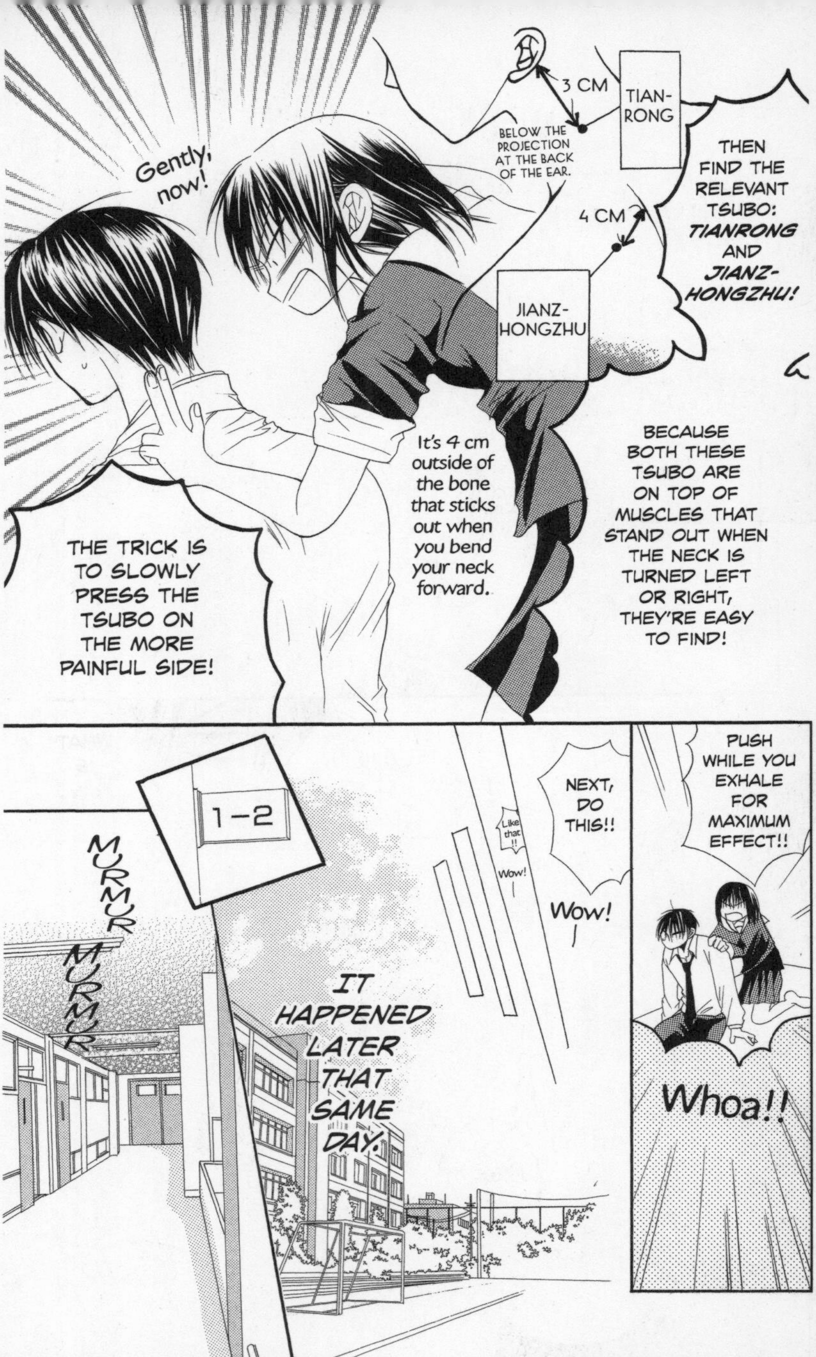

TIAN-RONG
3 CM
BELOW THE PROJECTION AT THE BACK OF THE EAR.
THEN FIND THE RELEVANT TSUBO: *TIANRONG* AND *JIANZ-HONGZHU!*
4 CM
JIANZ-HONGZHU
Gently, now!
BECAUSE BOTH THESE TSUBO ARE ON TOP OF MUSCLES THAT STAND OUT WHEN THE NECK IS TURNED LEFT OR RIGHT, THEY'RE EASY TO FIND!
It's 4 cm outside of the bone that sticks out when you bend your neck forward.
THE TRICK IS TO SLOWLY PRESS THE TSUBO ON THE MORE PAINFUL SIDE!
PUSH WHILE YOU EXHALE FOR MAXIMUM EFFECT!!
Whoa!!
NEXT, DO THIS!!
Wow!
Like that!!
Wow!
1-2
IT HAPPENED LATER THAT SAME DAY.
MURMUR MURMUR

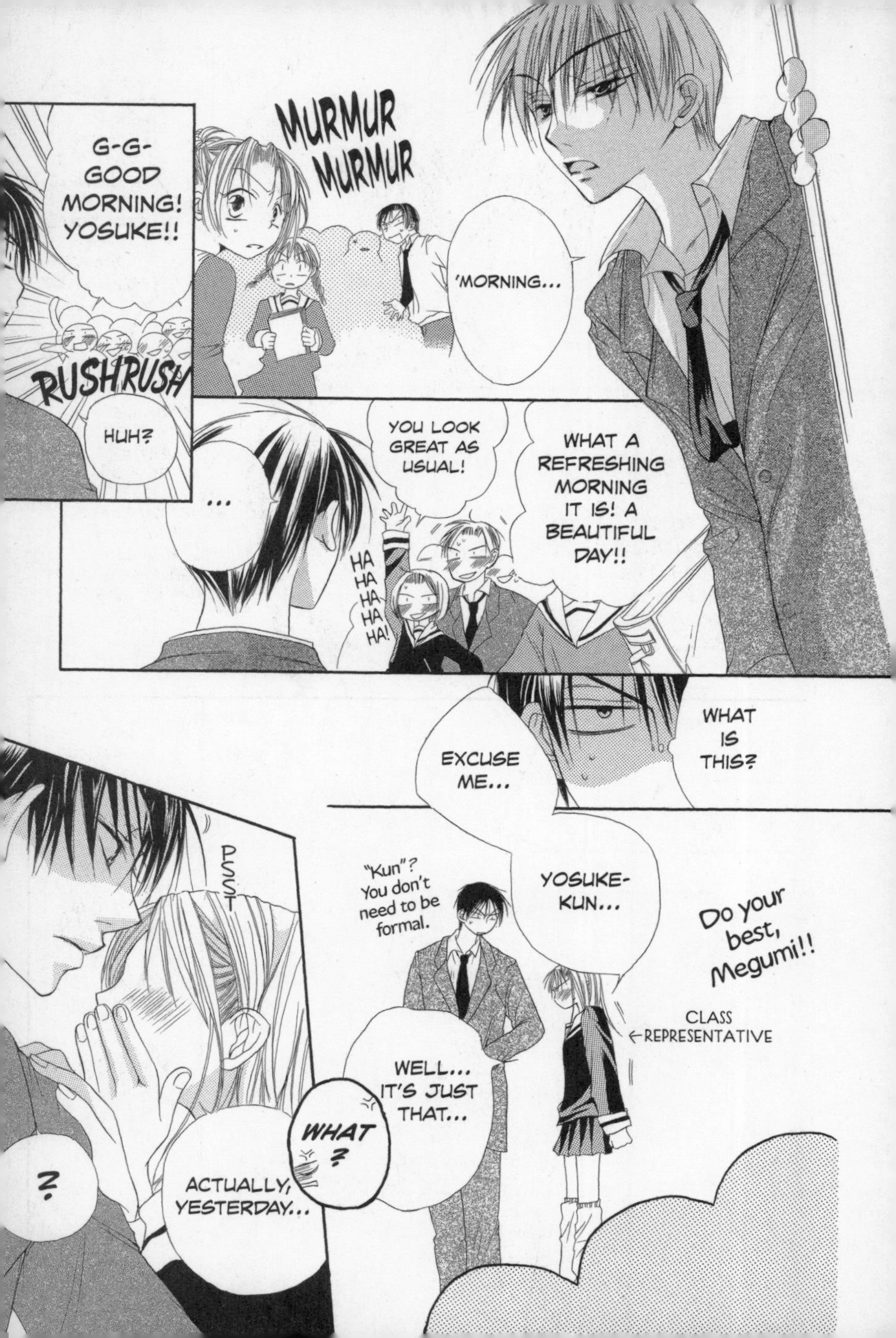
'MORNING...
MURMUR MURMUR
G-G-GOOD MORNING! YOSUKE!!
RUSHRUSH
HUH?
WHAT A REFRESHING MORNING IT IS! A BEAUTIFUL DAY!!
YOU LOOK GREAT AS USUAL!
HA HA HA HA HA!
...
WHAT IS THIS?
EXCUSE ME...
Do your best, Megumi!!
YOSUKE-KUN...
CLASS ←REPRESENTATIVE
"Kun"? You don't need to be formal.
WELL... IT'S JUST THAT...
WHAT?
PSST
ACTUALLY, YESTERDAY...
?

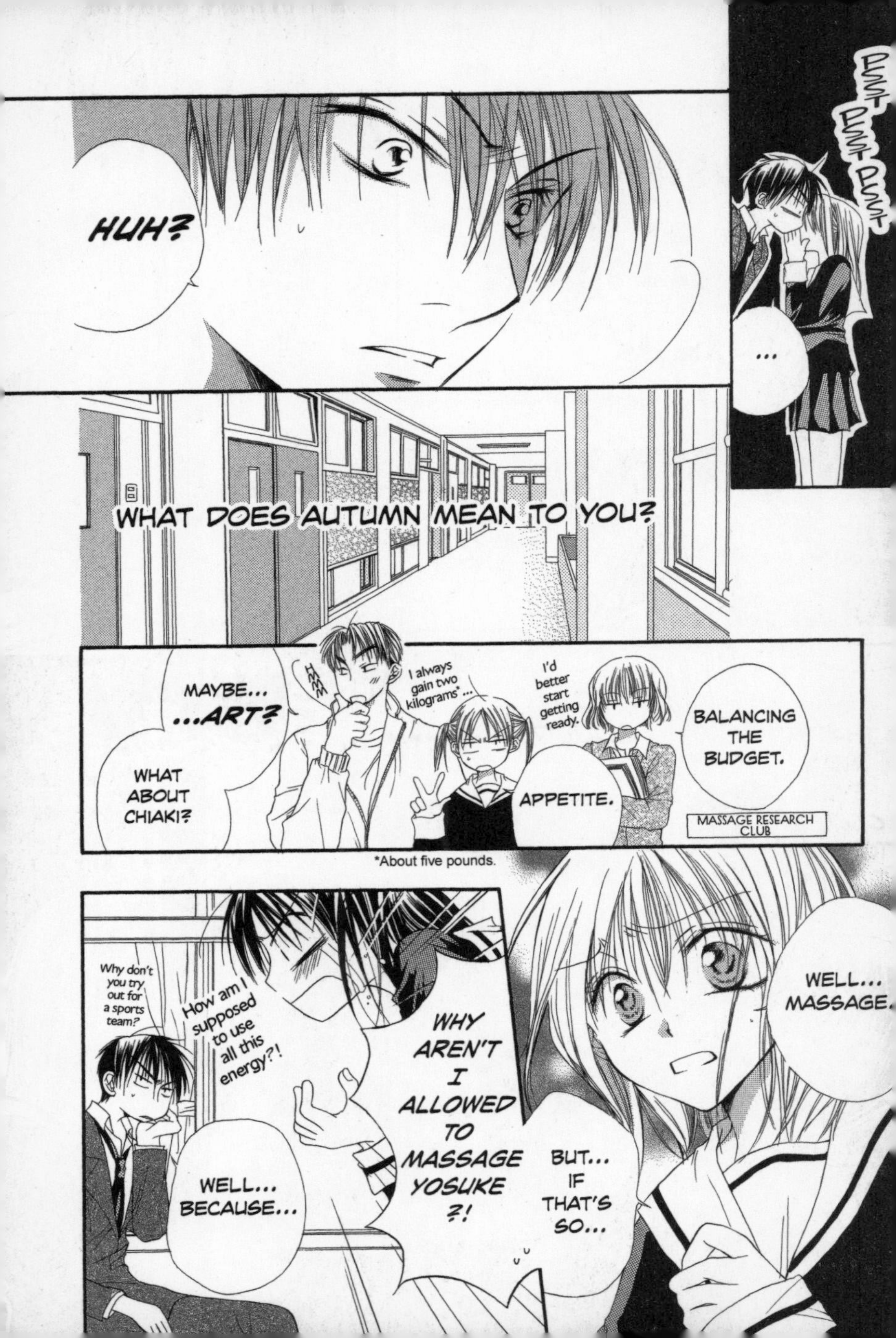
PSST PSST PSST
...
HUH?
WHAT DOES AUTUMN MEAN TO YOU?
BALANCING THE BUDGET.
MASSAGE RESEARCH CLUB
I'd better start getting ready.
APPETITE.
I always gain two kilograms*...
HMMM
MAYBE... ...ART?
WHAT ABOUT CHIAKI?
WELL... MASSAGE.
BUT... IF THAT'S SO...
WHY AREN'T I ALLOWED TO MASSAGE YOSUKE?!
How am I supposed to use all this energy?!
Why don't you try out for a sports team?
WELL... BECAUSE...

*About five pounds.

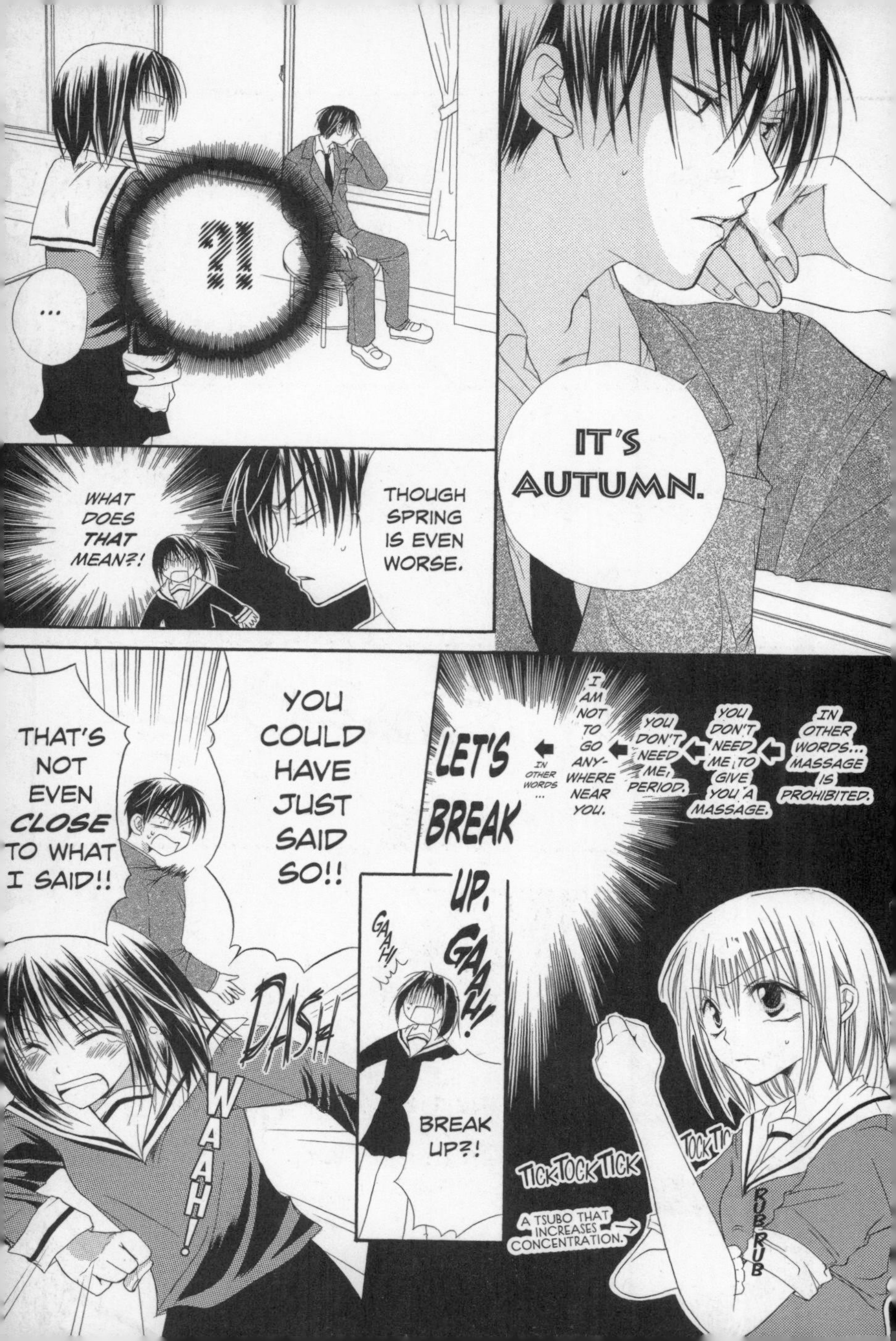
IT'S AUTUMN.
?!
...
THOUGH SPRING IS EVEN WORSE.
WHAT DOES THAT MEAN?!
TICK TOCK TICK TOCK TICK
A TSUBO THAT INCREASES CONCENTRATION.
RUB RUB
IN OTHER WORDS... MASSAGE IS PROHIBITED.
YOU DON'T NEED ME TO GIVE YOU A MASSAGE.
YOU DON'T NEED ME, PERIOD.
I AM NOT TO GO ANYWHERE NEAR YOU.
IN OTHER WORDS...
LET'S BREAK UP.
GAAH!
GAAH!
BREAK UP?!
YOU COULD HAVE JUST SAID SO!!
THAT'S NOT EVEN CLOSE TO WHAT I SAID!!
DASH
WAAAH!

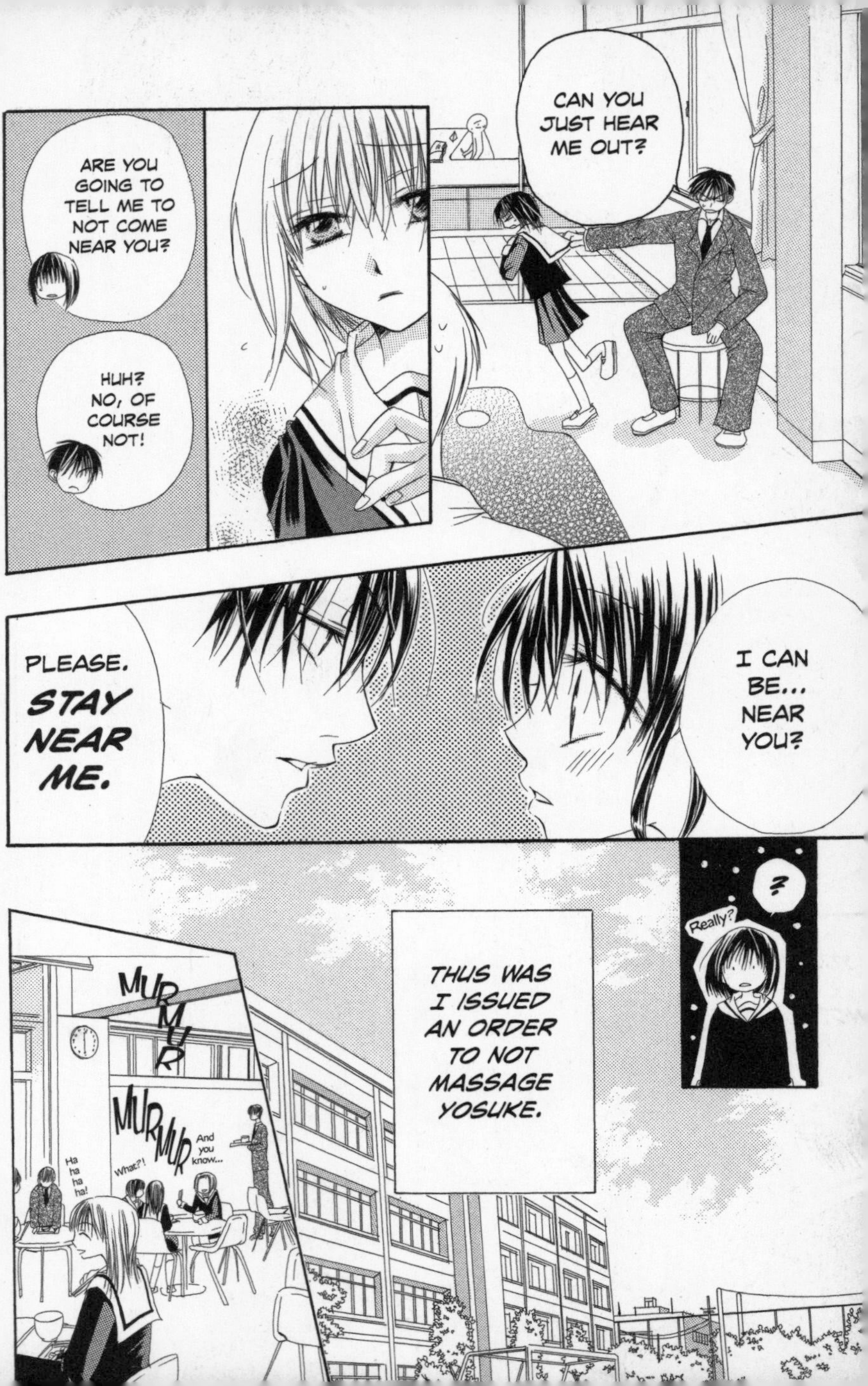
CAN YOU JUST HEAR ME OUT?
ARE YOU GOING TO TELL ME TO NOT COME NEAR YOU?
HUH? NO, OF COURSE NOT!
I CAN BE... NEAR YOU?
PLEASE. STAY NEAR ME.
?
Really?
THUS WAS I ISSUED AN ORDER TO NOT MASSAGE YOSUKE.
MURMUR
MURMUR
And you know...
What?!
Ha ha ha ha!

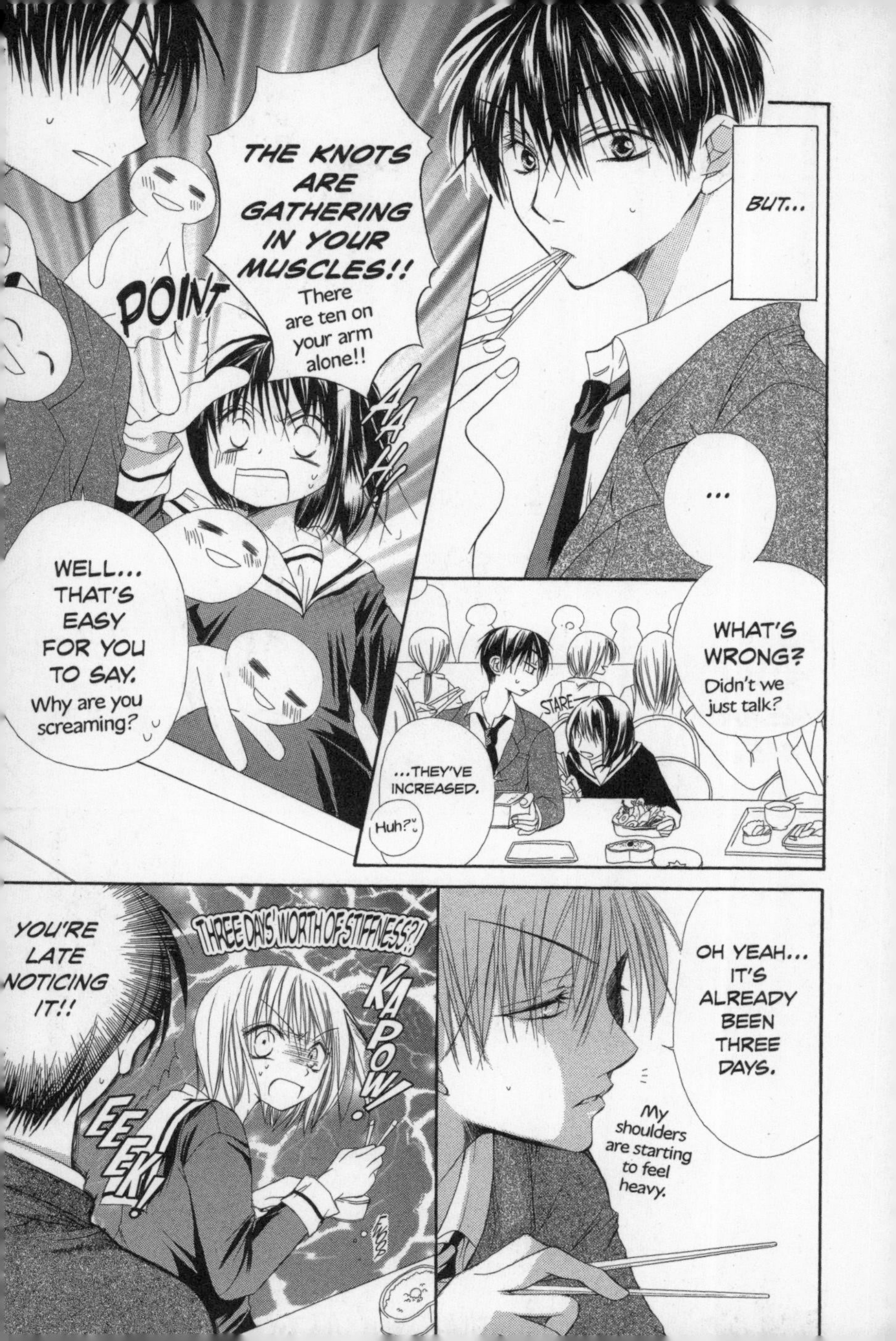
BUT...
...
WHAT'S WRONG? Didn't we just talk?
STARE
...THEY'VE INCREASED.
Huh?
THE KNOTS ARE GATHERING IN YOUR MUSCLES!! There are ten on your arm alone!!
POINT
AAAH!
WELL... THAT'S EASY FOR YOU TO SAY. Why are you screaming?
OH YEAH... IT'S ALREADY BEEN THREE DAYS.
My shoulders are starting to feel heavy.
THREE DAYS' WORTH OF STIFFNESS?!
KAPOW!
YOU'RE LATE NOTICING IT!!
EEEK!

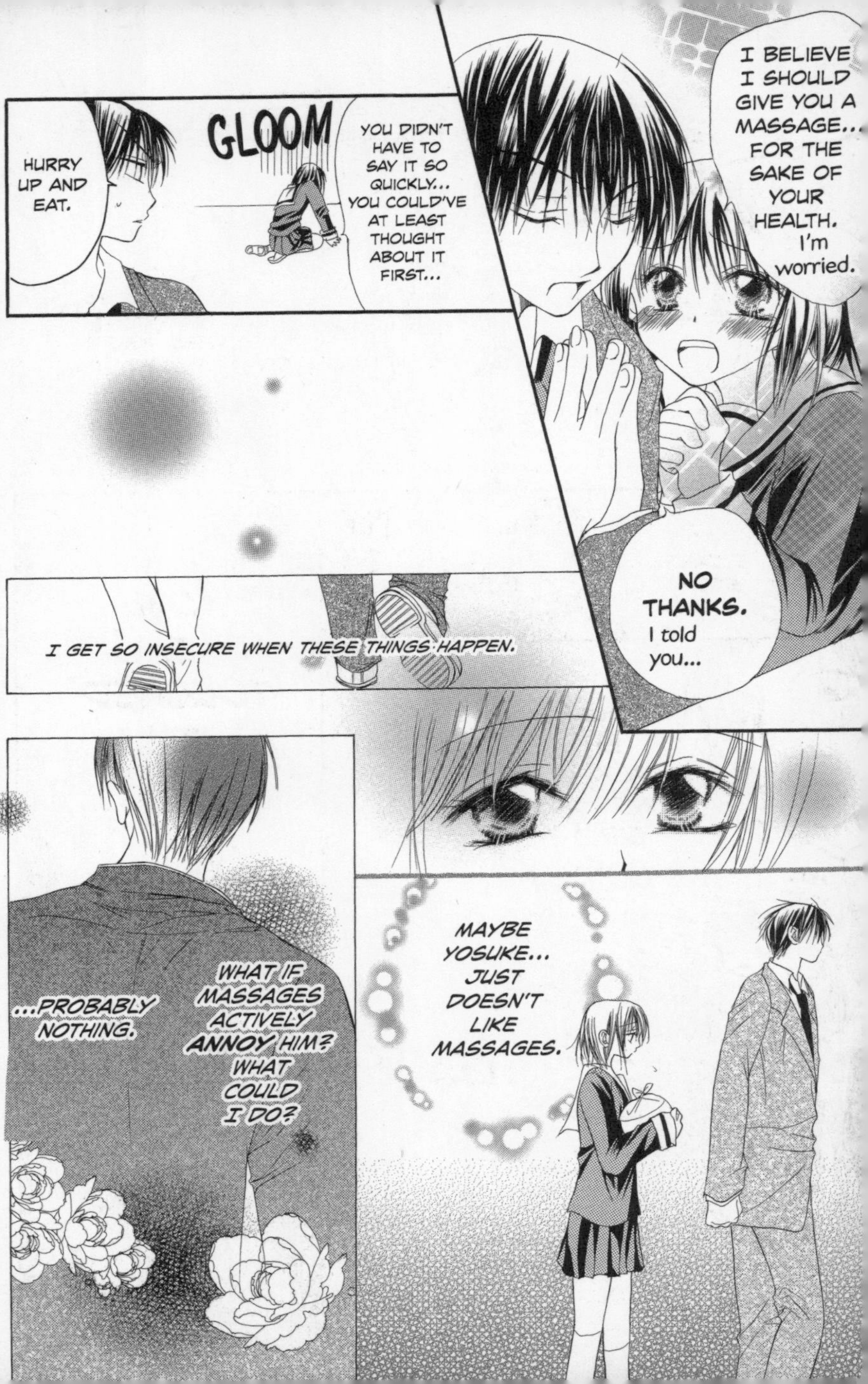
I BELIEVE I SHOULD GIVE YOU A MASSAGE... FOR THE SAKE OF YOUR HEALTH. I'm worried.
NO THANKS. I told you...
YOU DIDN'T HAVE TO SAY IT SO QUICKLY... YOU COULD'VE AT LEAST THOUGHT ABOUT IT FIRST...
GLOOM
HURRY UP AND EAT.
I GET SO INSECURE WHEN THESE THINGS HAPPEN.
MAYBE YOSUKE... JUST DOESN'T LIKE MASSAGES.
WHAT IF MASSAGES ACTIVELY ANNOY HIM? WHAT COULD I DO?
...PROBABLY NOTHING.

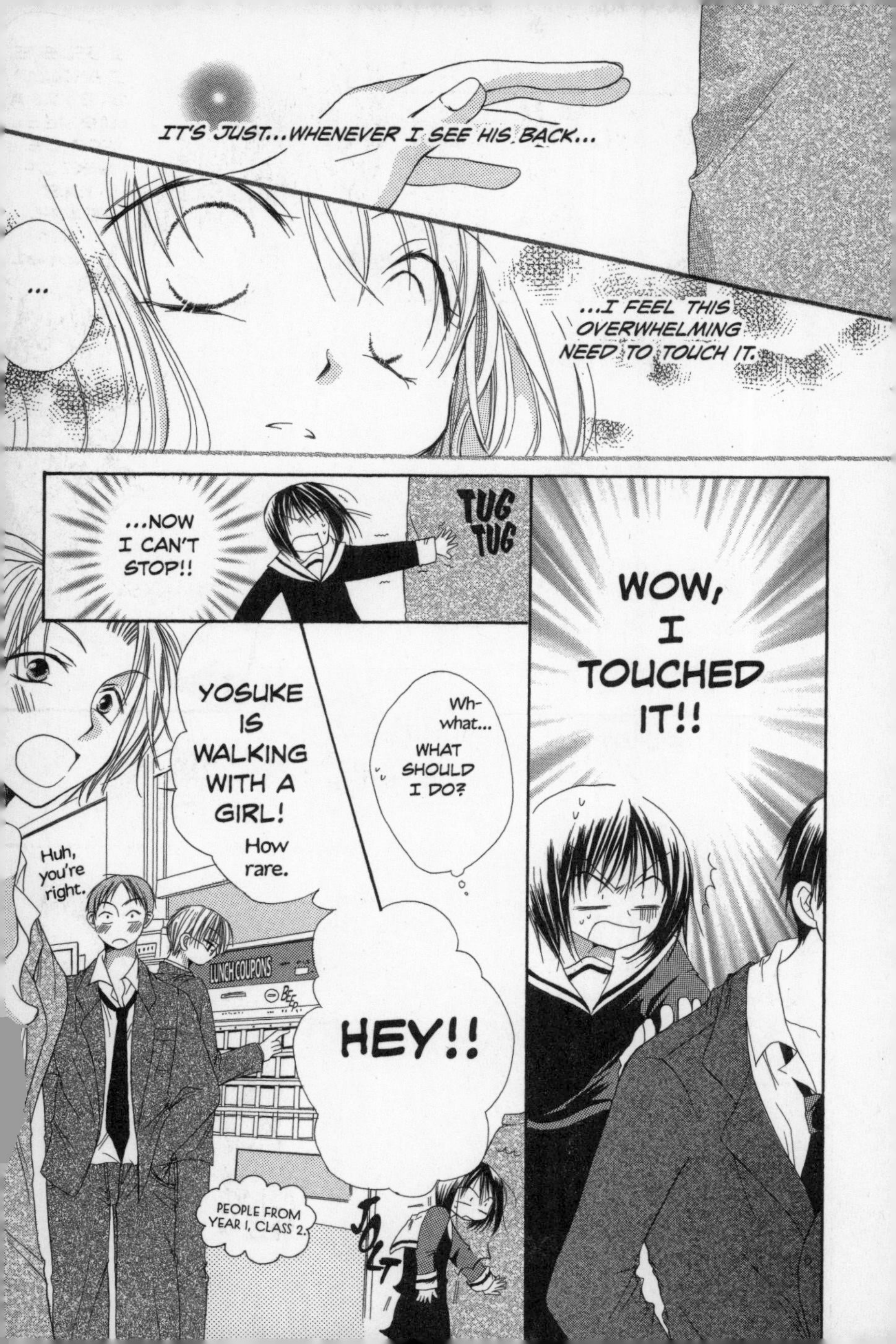
IT'S JUST...WHENEVER I SEE HIS BACK...
...I FEEL THIS OVERWHELMING NEED TO TOUCH IT.
...
WOW, I TOUCHED IT!!
TUG TUG
...NOW I CAN'T STOP!!
HEY!!
Wh-what... WHAT SHOULD I DO?
YOSUKE IS WALKING WITH A GIRL!
How rare.
Huh, you're right.
LUNCH COUPONS
BEEP
PEOPLE FROM YEAR 1, CLASS 2.
JOLT

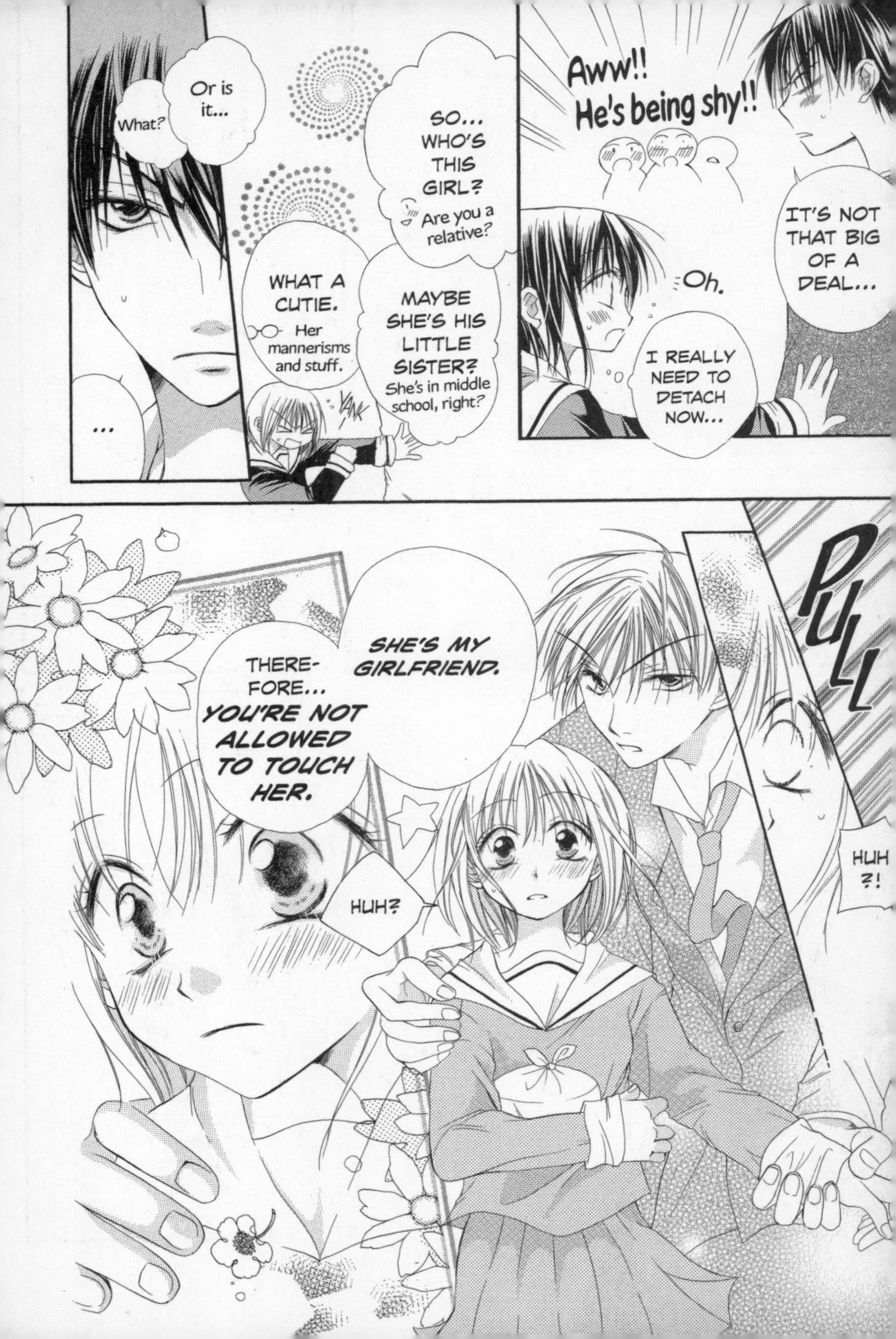
Aww!! He's being shy!!
IT'S NOT THAT BIG OF A DEAL...
Oh.
I REALLY NEED TO DETACH NOW...
SO... WHO'S THIS GIRL? Are you a relative?
Or is it...
What?
MAYBE SHE'S HIS LITTLE SISTER? She's in middle school, right?
WHAT A CUTIE. Her mannerisms and stuff.
YANK
...
PULL
HUH ?!
SHE'S MY GIRLFRIEND.
THERE-FORE... YOU'RE NOT ALLOWED TO TOUCH HER.
HUH?

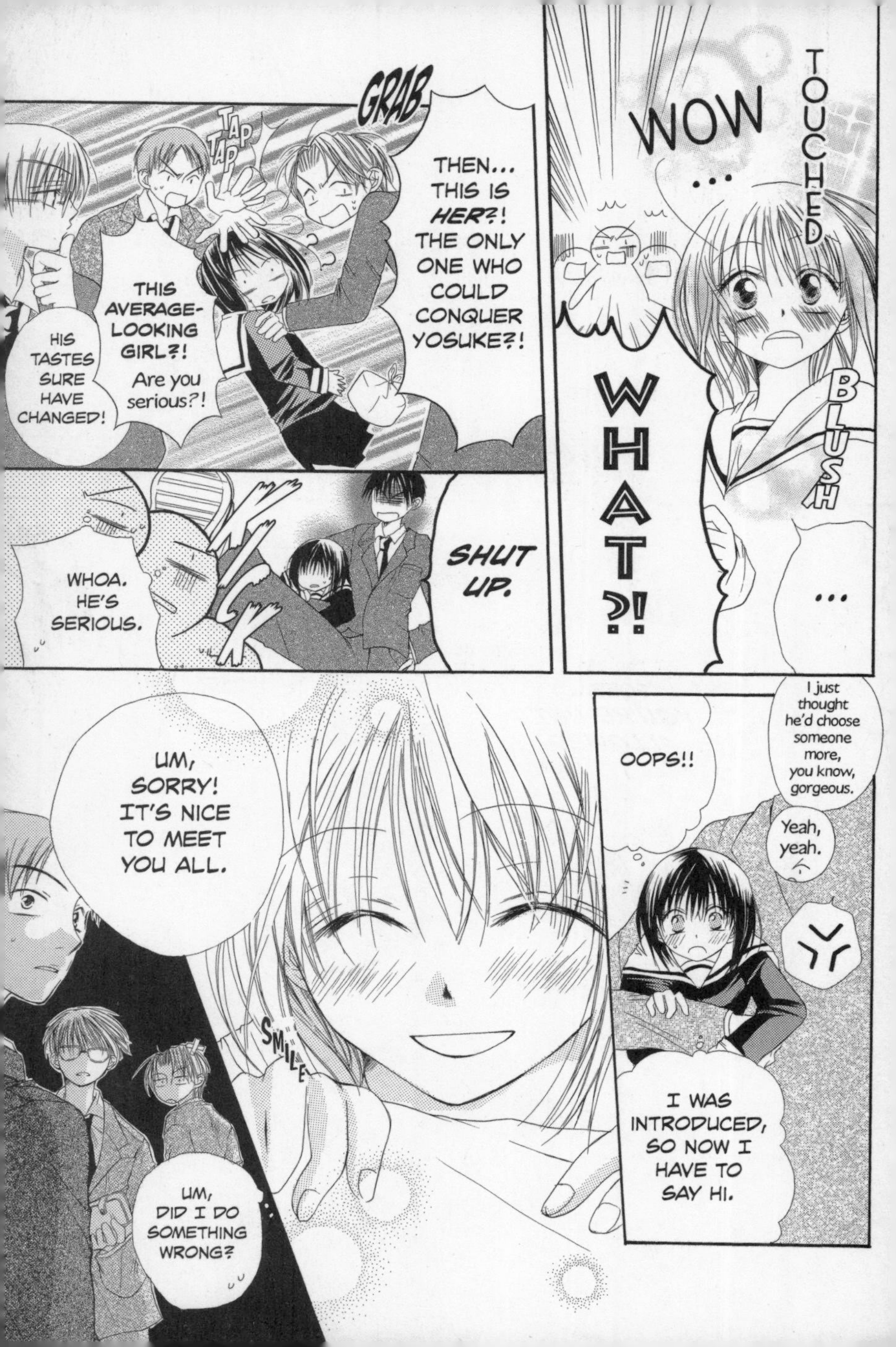
WOW...
TOUCHED
WHAT?!
BLUSH
...
GRAB
THEN... THIS IS HER?! THE ONLY ONE WHO COULD CONQUER YOSUKE?!
TAP TAP
THIS AVERAGE-LOOKING GIRL?!
Are you serious?!
HIS TASTES SURE HAVE CHANGED!
SHUT UP.
WHOA. HE'S SERIOUS.
I just thought he'd choose someone more, you know, gorgeous.
OOPS!!
Yeah, yeah.
I WAS INTRODUCED, SO NOW I HAVE TO SAY HI.
UM, SORRY! IT'S NICE TO MEET YOU ALL.
SMILE
UM, DID I DO SOMETHING WRONG?

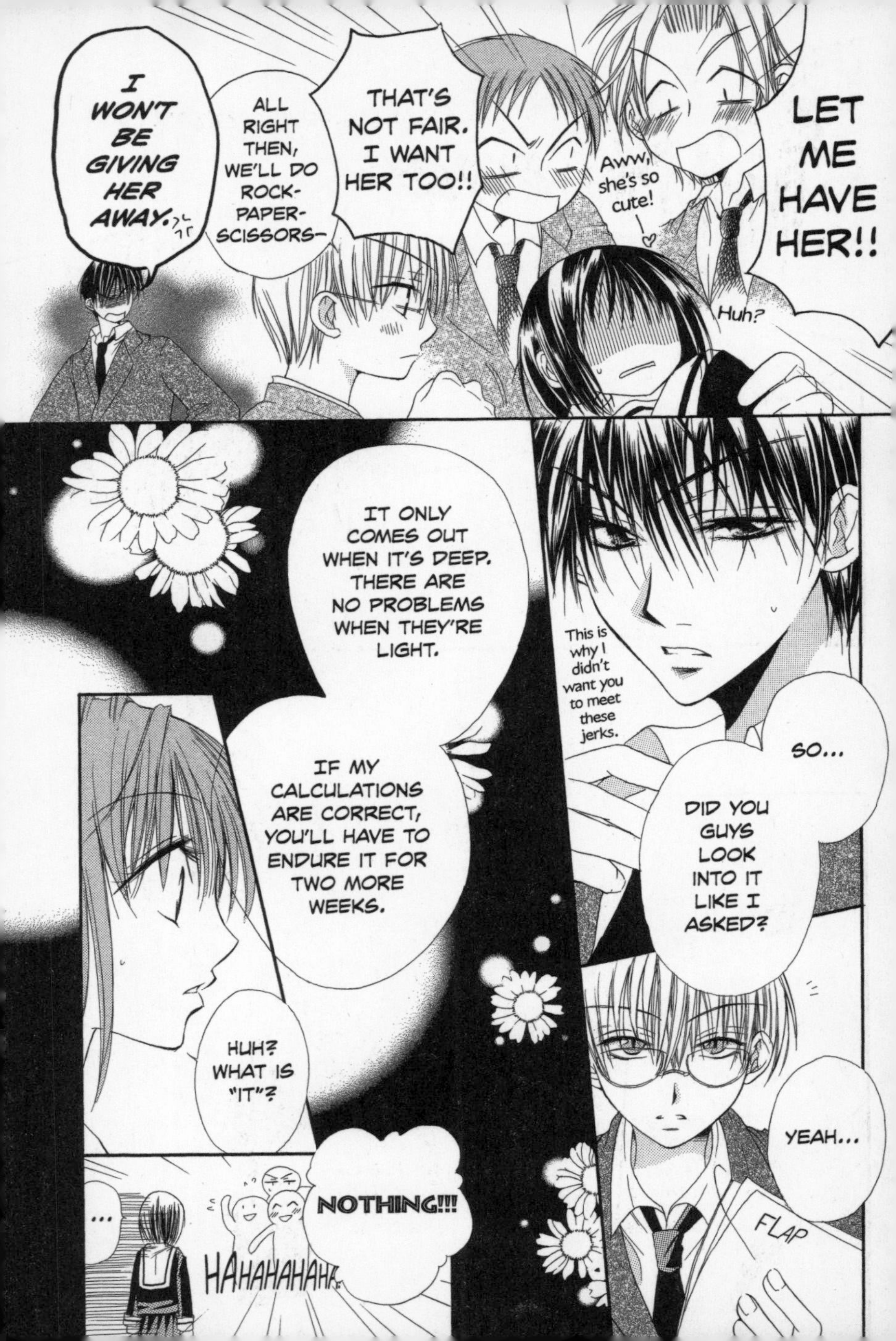
LET ME HAVE HER!!
Aww, she's so cute!
Huh?
THAT'S NOT FAIR. I WANT HER TOO!!
ALL RIGHT THEN, WE'LL DO ROCK-PAPER-SCISSORS-
I WON'T BE GIVING HER AWAY.
This is why I didn't want you to meet these jerks.
SO...
DID YOU GUYS LOOK INTO IT LIKE I ASKED?
YEAH...
FLAP
IT ONLY COMES OUT WHEN IT'S DEEP. THERE ARE NO PROBLEMS WHEN THEY'RE LIGHT.
IF MY CALCULATIONS ARE CORRECT, YOU'LL HAVE TO ENDURE IT FOR TWO MORE WEEKS.
HUH? WHAT IS "IT"?
NOTHING!!!
HAHAHAHAHAHA
...

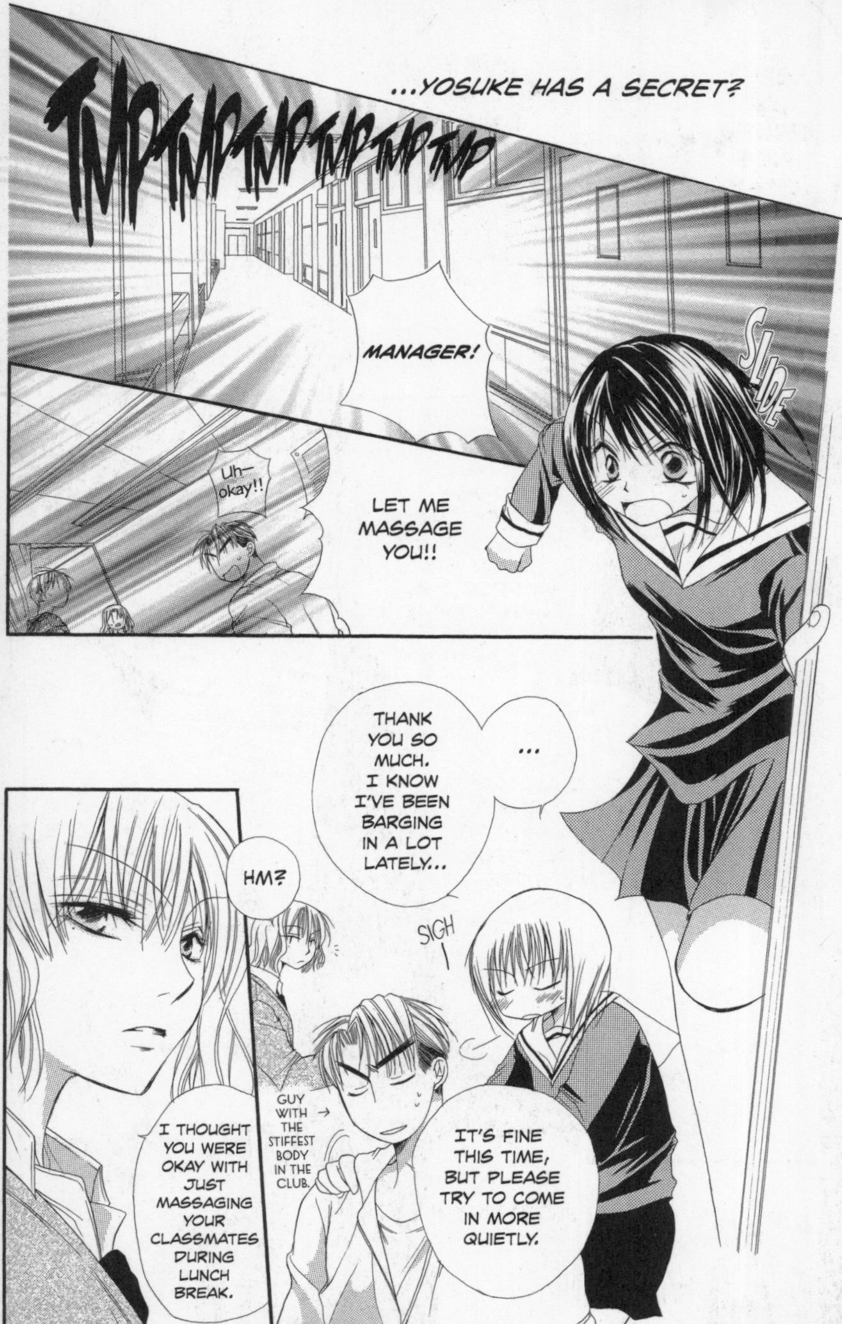
...YOSUKE HAS A SECRET?
TMP TMP TMP TMP TMP TMP
MANAGER!
SLIDE
LET ME MASSAGE YOU!!
Uh— okay!!
...
THANK YOU SO MUCH. I KNOW I'VE BEEN BARGING IN A LOT LATELY...
HM?
SIGH
IT'S FINE THIS TIME, BUT PLEASE TRY TO COME IN MORE QUIETLY.
GUY WITH THE STIFFEST BODY IN THE CLUB. →
I THOUGHT YOU WERE OKAY WITH JUST MASSAGING YOUR CLASSMATES DURING LUNCH BREAK.

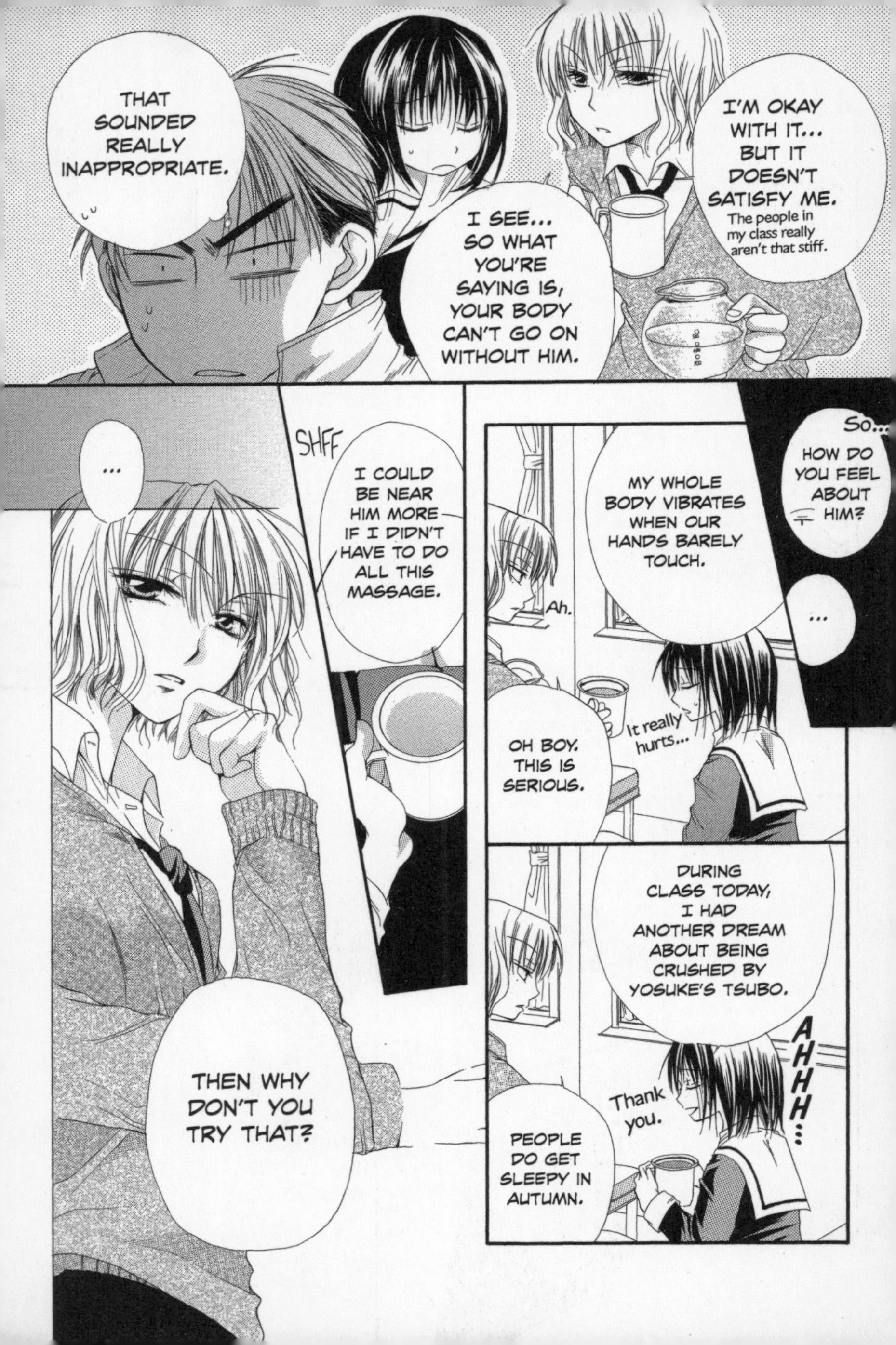
I'M OKAY WITH IT... BUT IT DOESN'T SATISFY ME.
The people in my class really aren't that stiff.
I SEE... SO WHAT YOU'RE SAYING IS, YOUR BODY CAN'T GO ON WITHOUT HIM.
THAT SOUNDED REALLY INAPPROPRIATE.
So... HOW DO YOU FEEL ABOUT HIM?
...
MY WHOLE BODY VIBRATES WHEN OUR HANDS BARELY TOUCH.
Ah.
It really hurts...
OH BOY. THIS IS SERIOUS.
DURING CLASS TODAY, I HAD ANOTHER DREAM ABOUT BEING CRUSHED BY YOSUKE'S TSUBO.
AHHH...
Thank you.
PEOPLE DO GET SLEEPY IN AUTUMN.
SHFF
I COULD BE NEAR HIM MORE IF I DIDN'T HAVE TO DO ALL THIS MASSAGE.
...
THEN WHY DON'T YOU TRY THAT?

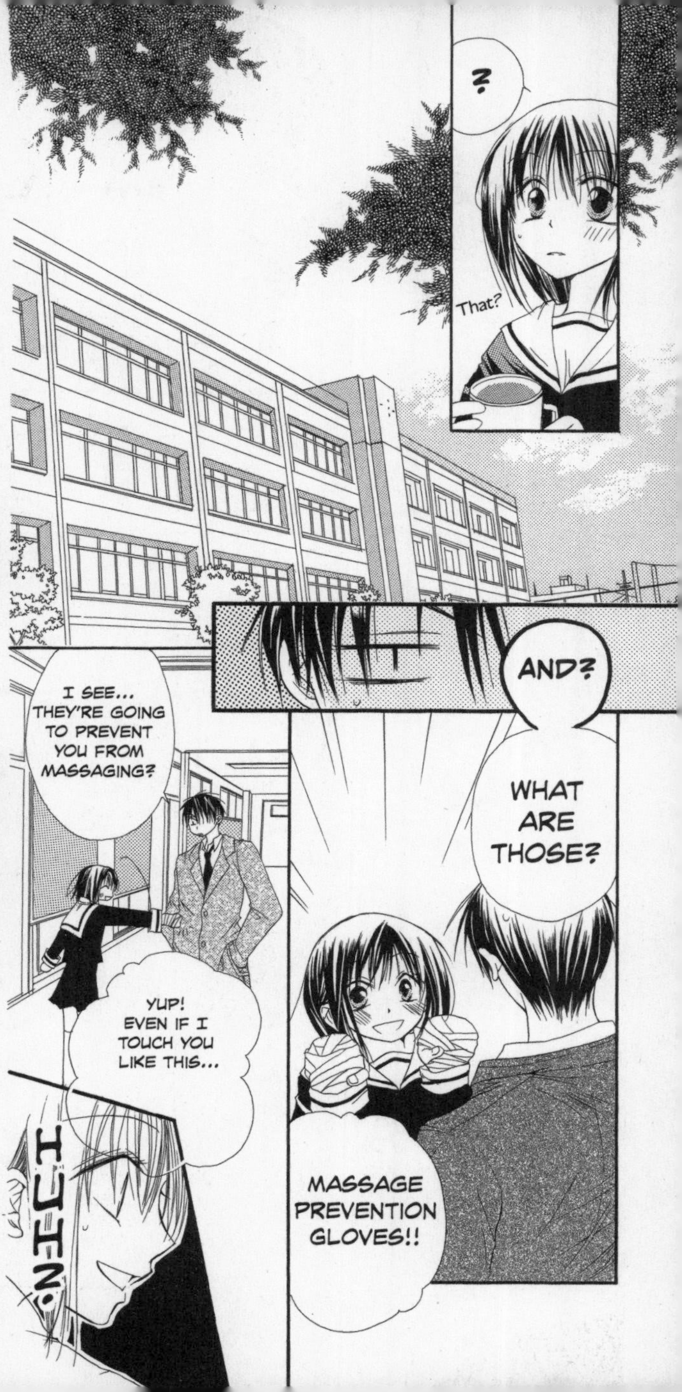
?
That?
AND?
WHAT ARE THOSE?
MASSAGE PREVENTION GLOVES!!
I SEE... THEY'RE GOING TO PREVENT YOU FROM MASSAGING?
YUP! EVEN IF I TOUCH YOU LIKE THIS...
HUH?!

This episode is a complete story in one chapter. I was asked to create a narrative that would "feel like autumn," so I wrote it with an autumn theme. (That was completely redundant, wasn't it?)

Well, since there's plenty of space left here, I'll add a "behind the scenes" story...

Mr. Ohnuki

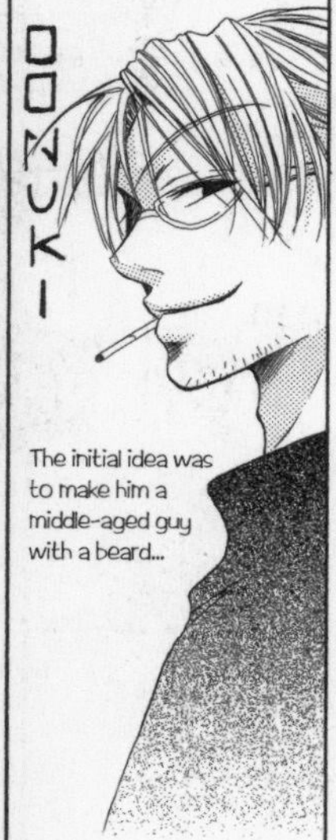
OONUKI

The initial idea was to make him a middle-aged guy with a beard...

...but he came out completely different. He's someone who's had a big influence on Takeshi Togu's personality.

He loves cigarettes.
He loves people.

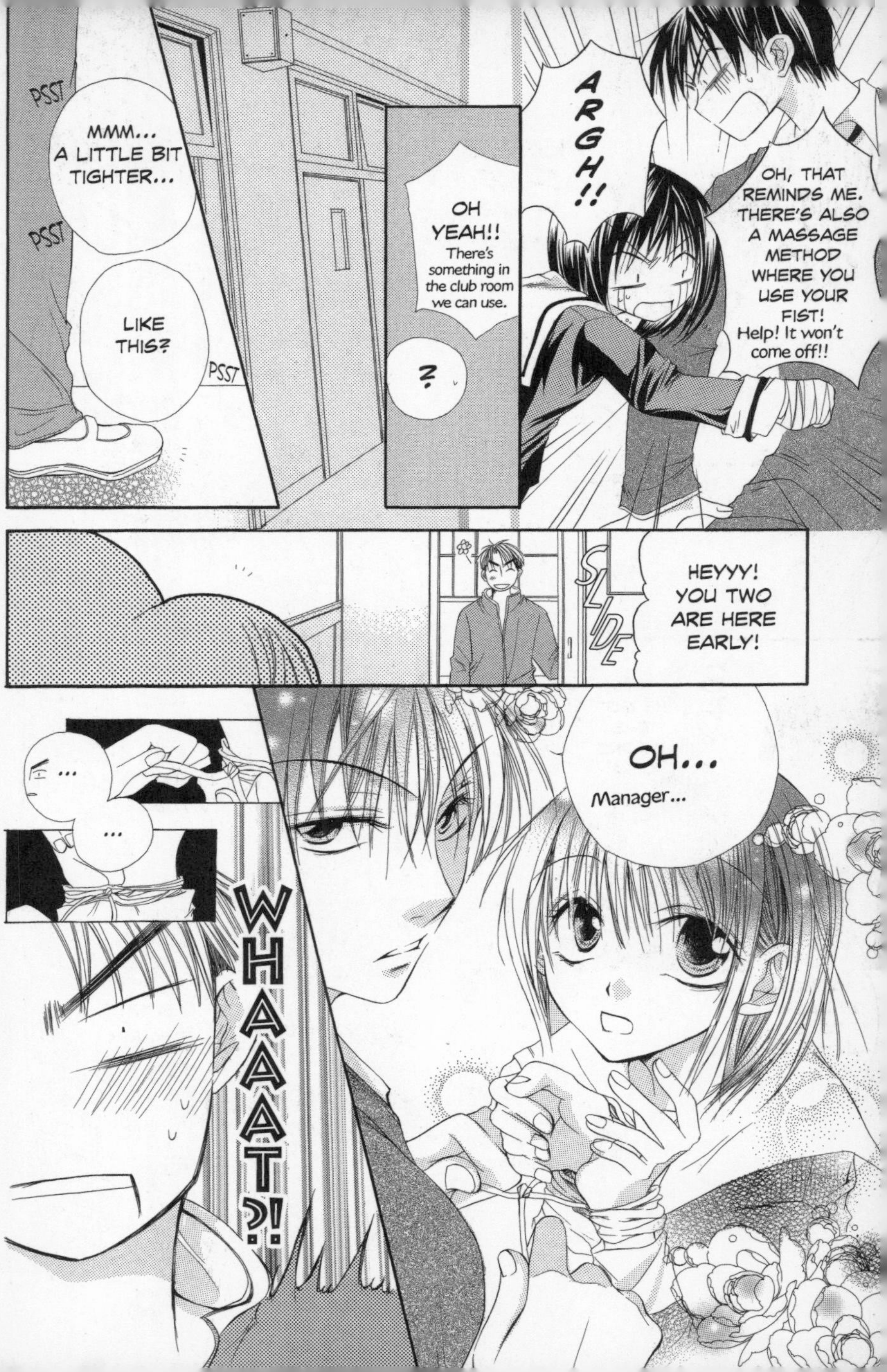
ARGH!!
OH, THAT REMINDS ME. THERE'S ALSO A MASSAGE METHOD WHERE YOU USE YOUR FIST!
Help! It won't come off!!
OH YEAH!! There's something in the club room we can use.
?
PSST
MMM... A LITTLE BIT TIGHTER...
PSST
LIKE THIS?
PSST
SLIDE
HEYYY! YOU TWO ARE HERE EARLY!
OH... Manager...
...
...
WHAAAT?!

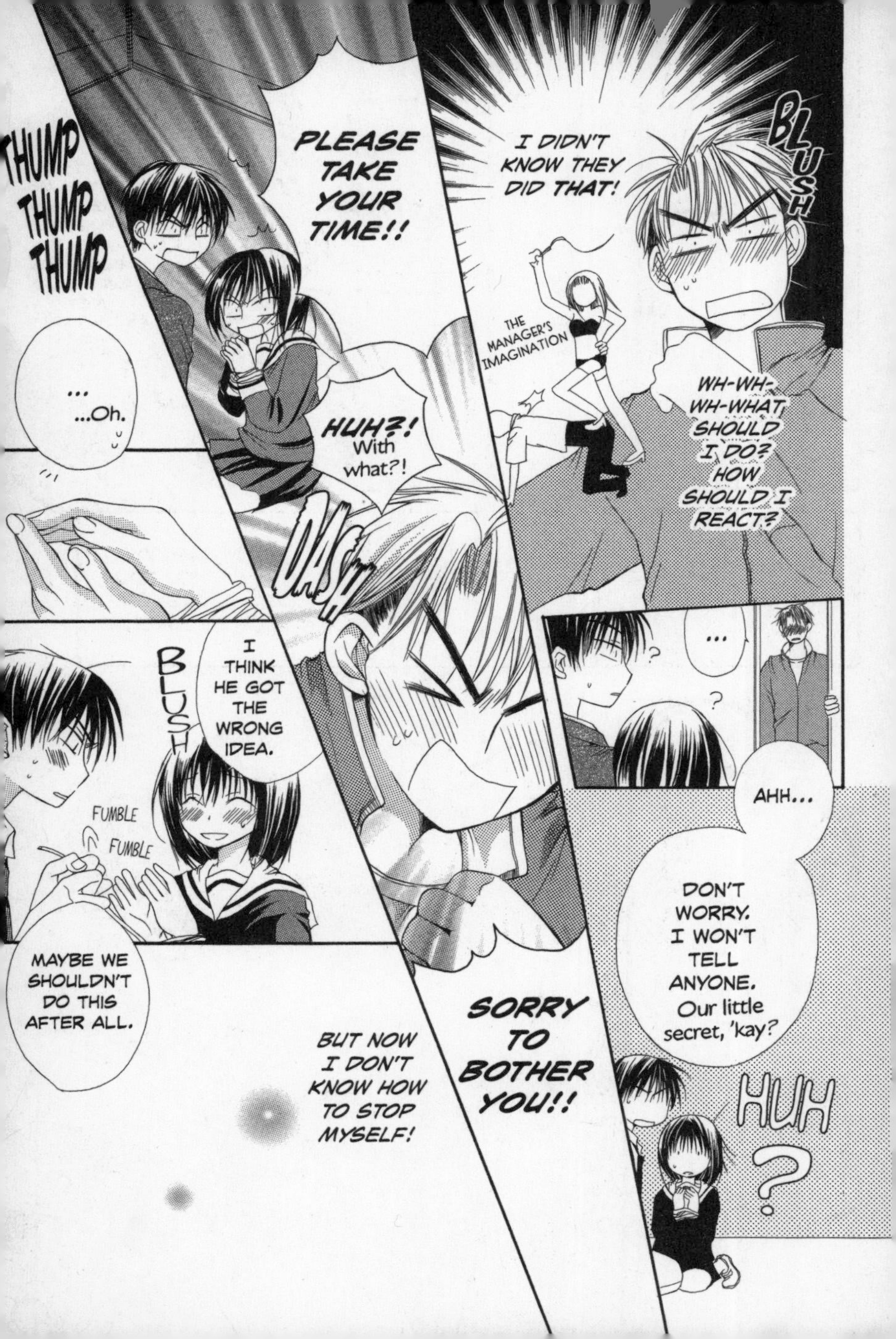
I DIDN'T KNOW THEY DID THAT!
BLUSH
THE MANAGER'S IMAGINATION
WH-WH-WH-WHAT SHOULD I DO? HOW SHOULD I REACT?
...
AHH...
DON'T WORRY. I WON'T TELL ANYONE. Our little secret, 'kay?
HUH?
PLEASE TAKE YOUR TIME!!
HUH?! With what?!
DASH
SORRY TO BOTHER YOU!!
THUMP THUMP THUMP
... ...Oh.
I THINK HE GOT THE WRONG IDEA.
BLUSH
FUMBLE FUMBLE
MAYBE WE SHOULDN'T DO THIS AFTER ALL.
BUT NOW I DON'T KNOW HOW TO STOP MYSELF!

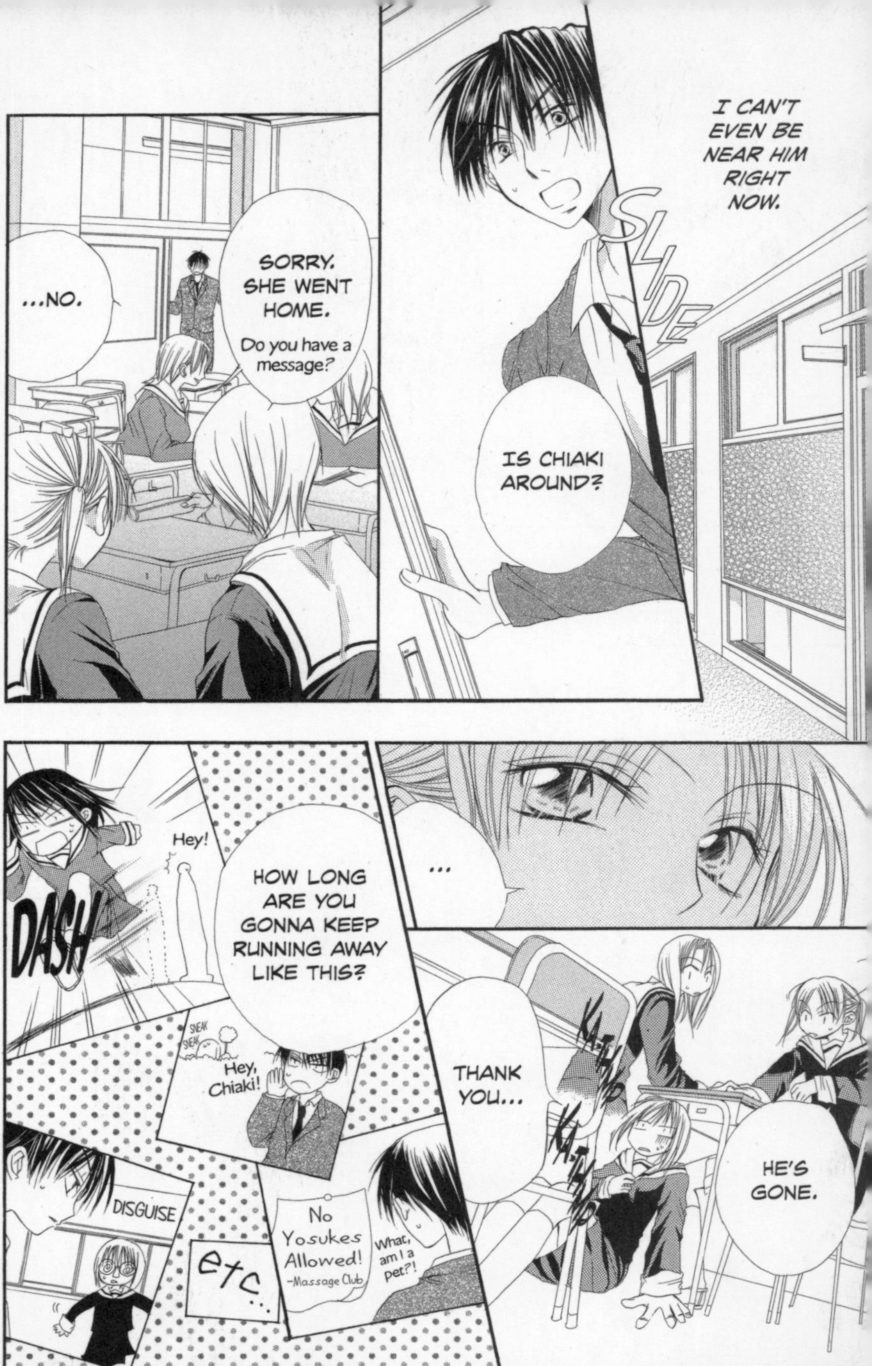
I CAN'T EVEN BE NEAR HIM RIGHT NOW.
SLIDE
IS CHIAKI AROUND?
SORRY. SHE WENT HOME.
Do you have a message?
...NO.
...
HE'S GONE.
KA-THUD
KA-THUD
THANK YOU...
HOW LONG ARE YOU GONNA KEEP RUNNING AWAY LIKE THIS?
Hey!
DASH
SNEAK SNEAK
Hey, Chiaki!
No Yosukes Allowed! –Massage Club
What, am I a pet?!
DISGUISE
etc...

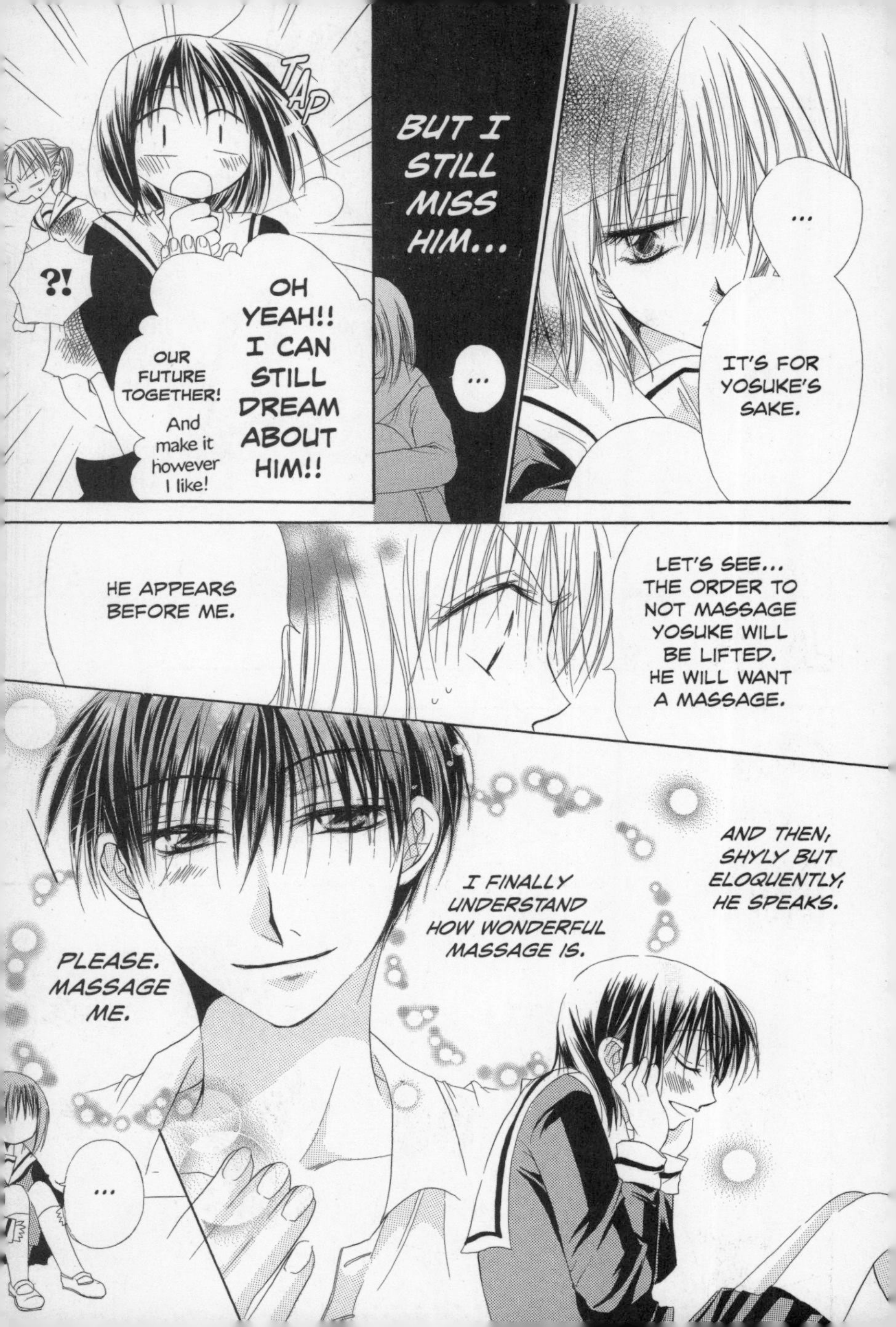
...
IT'S FOR YOSUKE'S SAKE.
BUT I STILL MISS HIM...
...
TAP
OH YEAH!! I CAN STILL DREAM ABOUT HIM!!
OUR FUTURE TOGETHER!
And make it however I like!
?!
LET'S SEE... THE ORDER TO NOT MASSAGE YOSUKE WILL BE LIFTED. HE WILL WANT A MASSAGE.
HE APPEARS BEFORE ME.
AND THEN, SHYLY BUT ELOQUENTLY, HE SPEAKS.
I FINALLY UNDERSTAND HOW WONDERFUL MASSAGE IS.
PLEASE. MASSAGE ME.
...

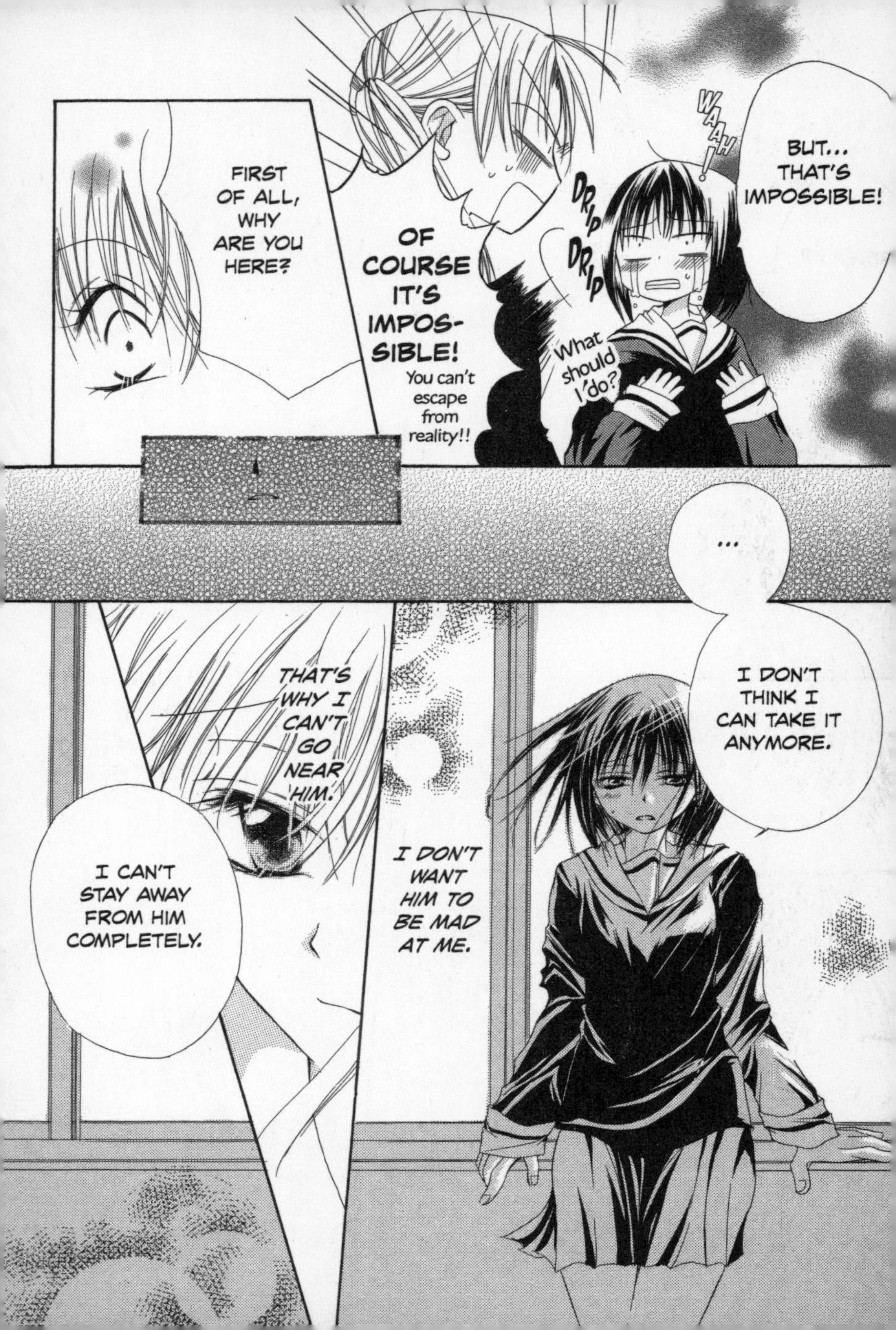
WAAH!
BUT... THAT'S IMPOSSIBLE!
DRIP DRIP
What should I do?
OF COURSE IT'S IMPOSSIBLE!
You can't escape from reality!!
FIRST OF ALL, WHY ARE YOU HERE?
...
I DON'T THINK I CAN TAKE IT ANYMORE.
I DON'T WANT HIM TO BE MAD AT ME.
THAT'S WHY I CAN'T GO NEAR HIM.
I CAN'T STAY AWAY FROM HIM COMPLETELY.

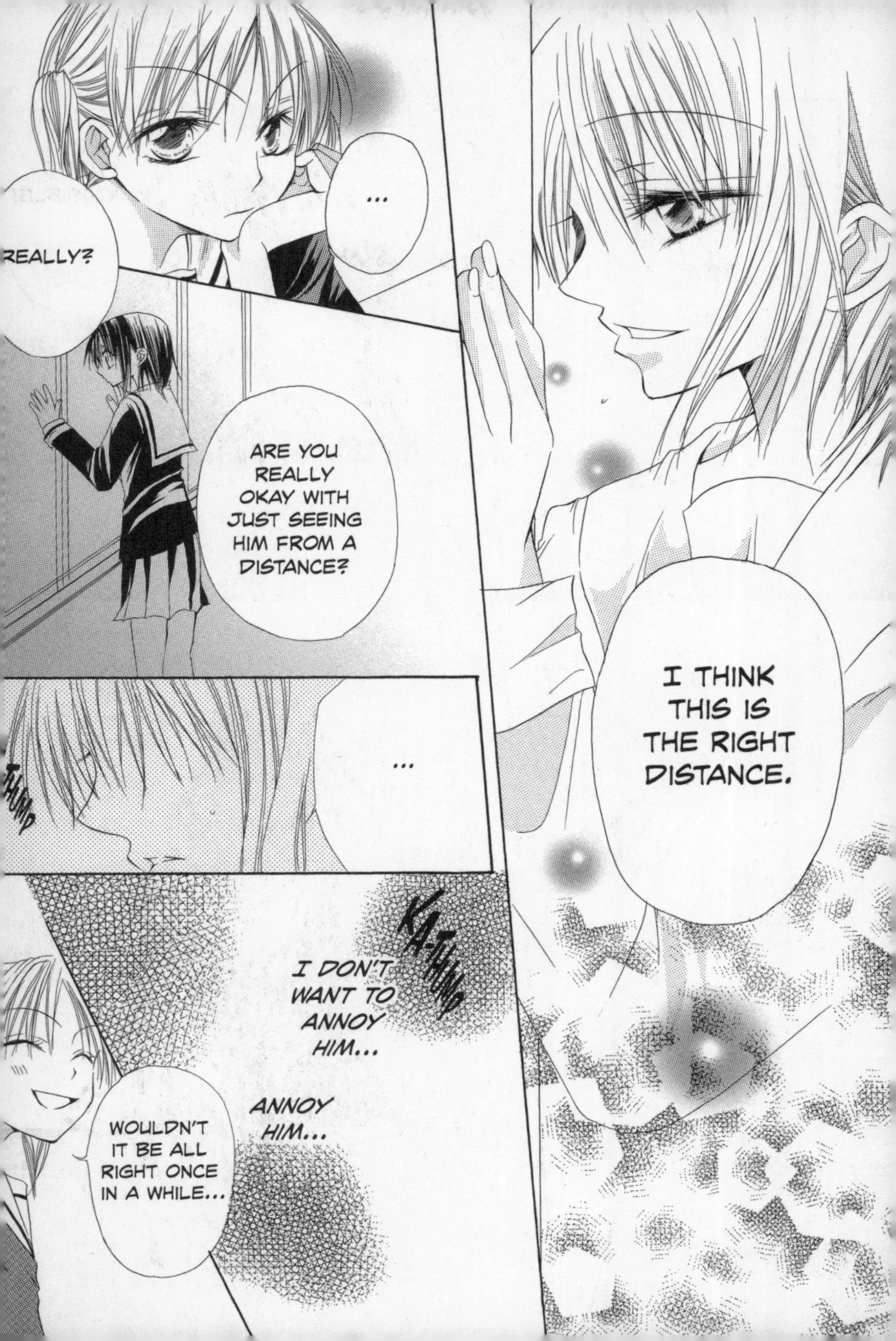
...
REALLY?
ARE YOU REALLY OKAY WITH JUST SEEING HIM FROM A DISTANCE?
...
THUMP
KA-THUMP
I DON'T WANT TO ANNOY HIM...
ANNOY HIM...
WOULDN'T IT BE ALL RIGHT ONCE IN A WHILE...
I THINK THIS IS THE RIGHT DISTANCE.

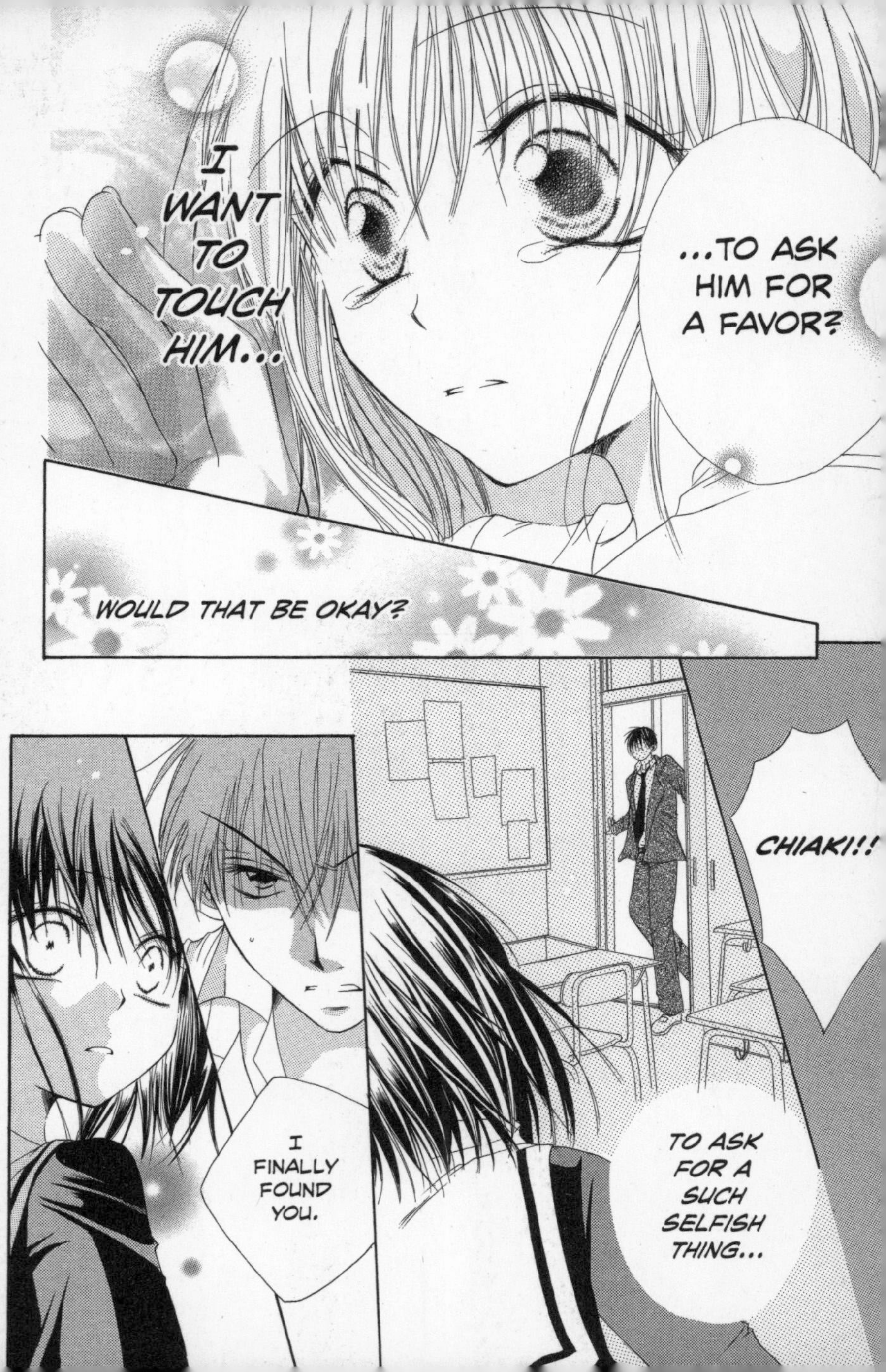
I WANT TO TOUCH HIM...
...TO ASK HIM FOR A FAVOR?
WOULD THAT BE OKAY?
CHIAKI!!
TO ASK FOR A SUCH SELFISH THING...
I FINALLY FOUND YOU.

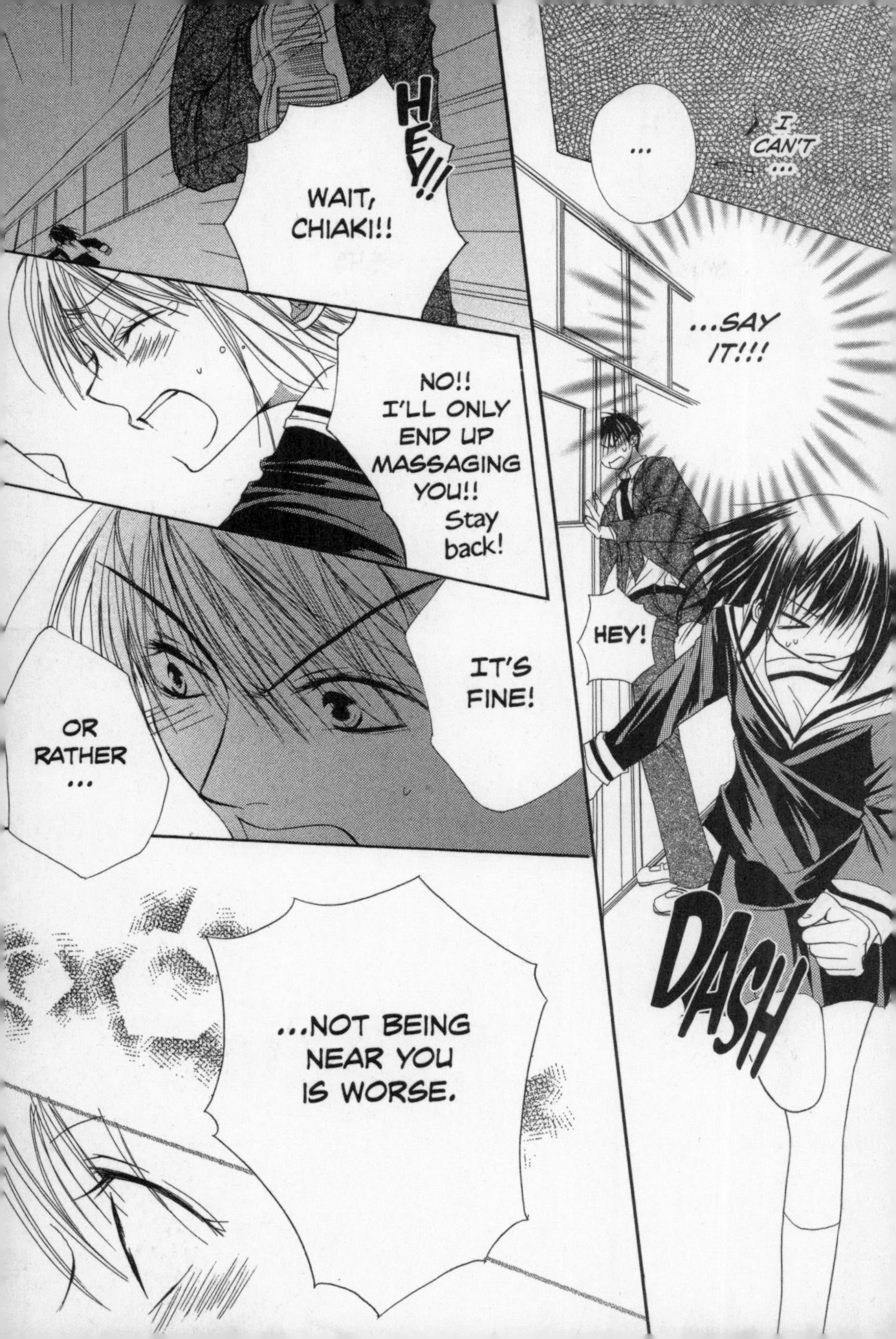
...
I CAN'T ...
...SAY IT!!!
HEY!
DASH
HEY!!
WAIT, CHIAKI!!
NO!! I'LL ONLY END UP MASSAGING YOU!!
Stay back!
IT'S FINE!
OR RATHER ...
...NOT BEING NEAR YOU IS WORSE.

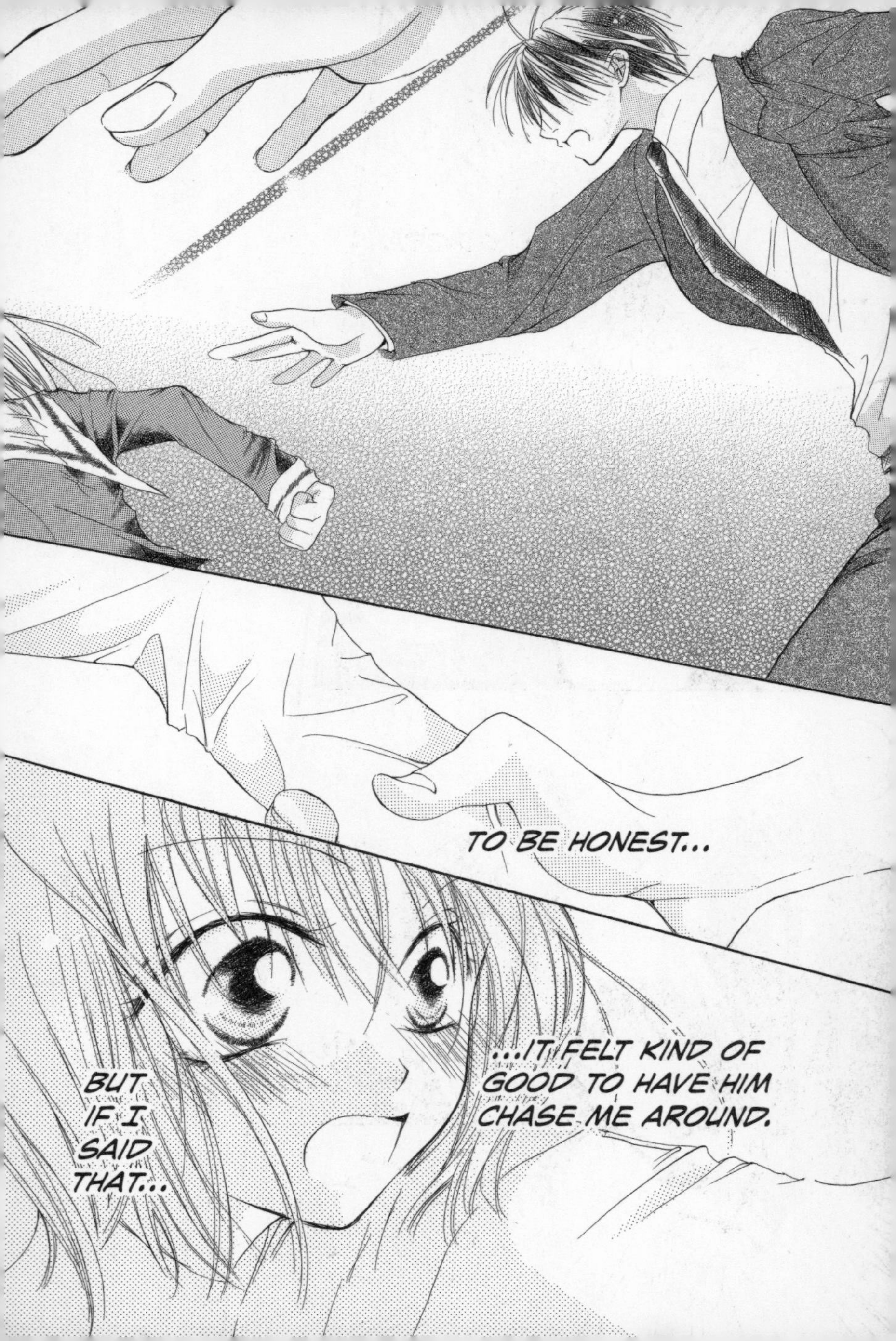
TO BE HONEST...
...IT FELT KIND OF GOOD TO HAVE HIM CHASE ME AROUND.
BUT IF I SAID THAT...

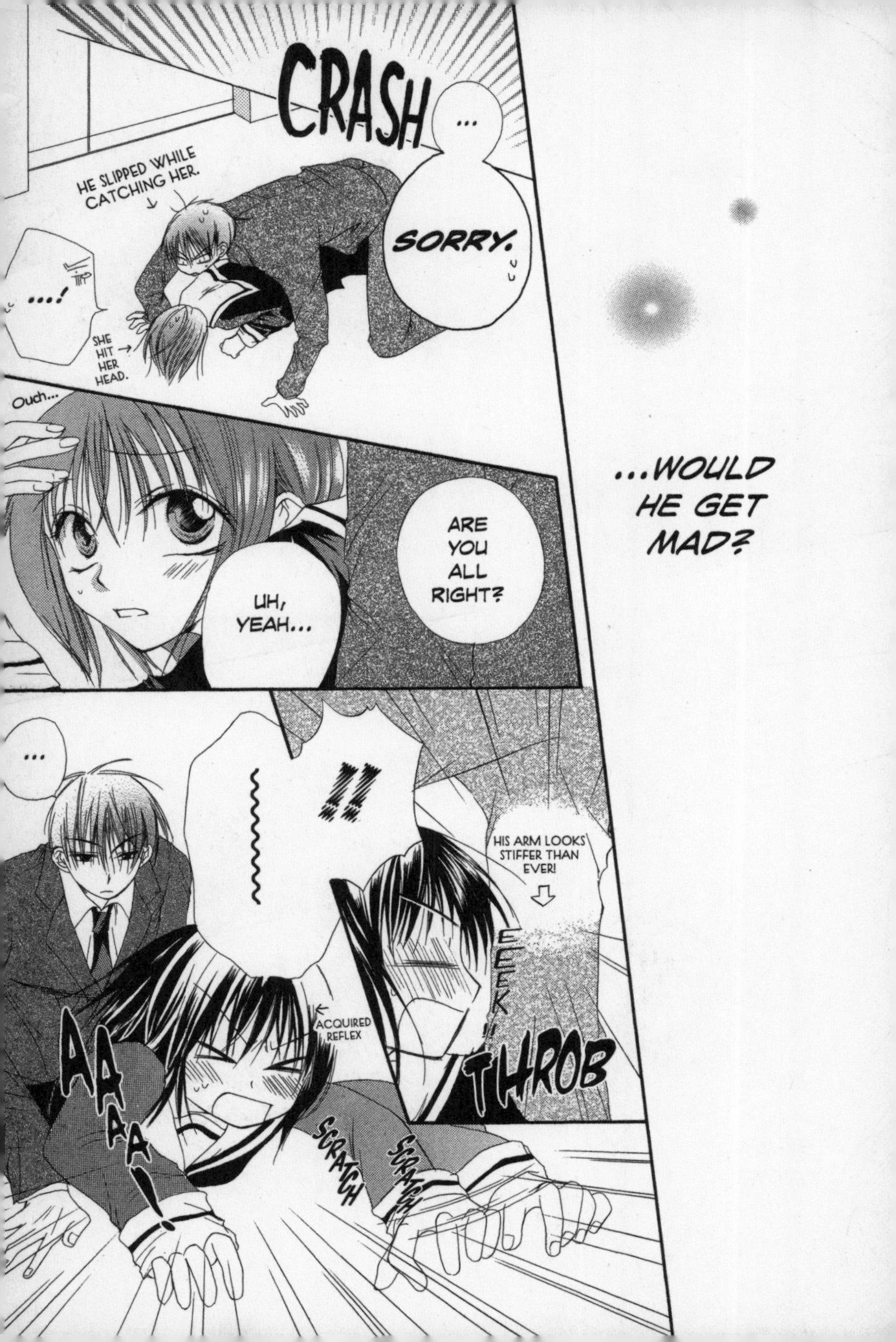

...WOULD HE GET MAD?
CRASH
...
SORRY.
HE SLIPPED WHILE CATCHING HER.
...!
SHE HIT HER HEAD.
ARE YOU ALL RIGHT?
Ouch...
UH, YEAH...
!!
HIS ARM LOOKS STIFFER THAN EVER!
EEEK!!
THROB
...
ACQUIRED REFLEX
SCRATCH
SCRATCH
AAAAA!

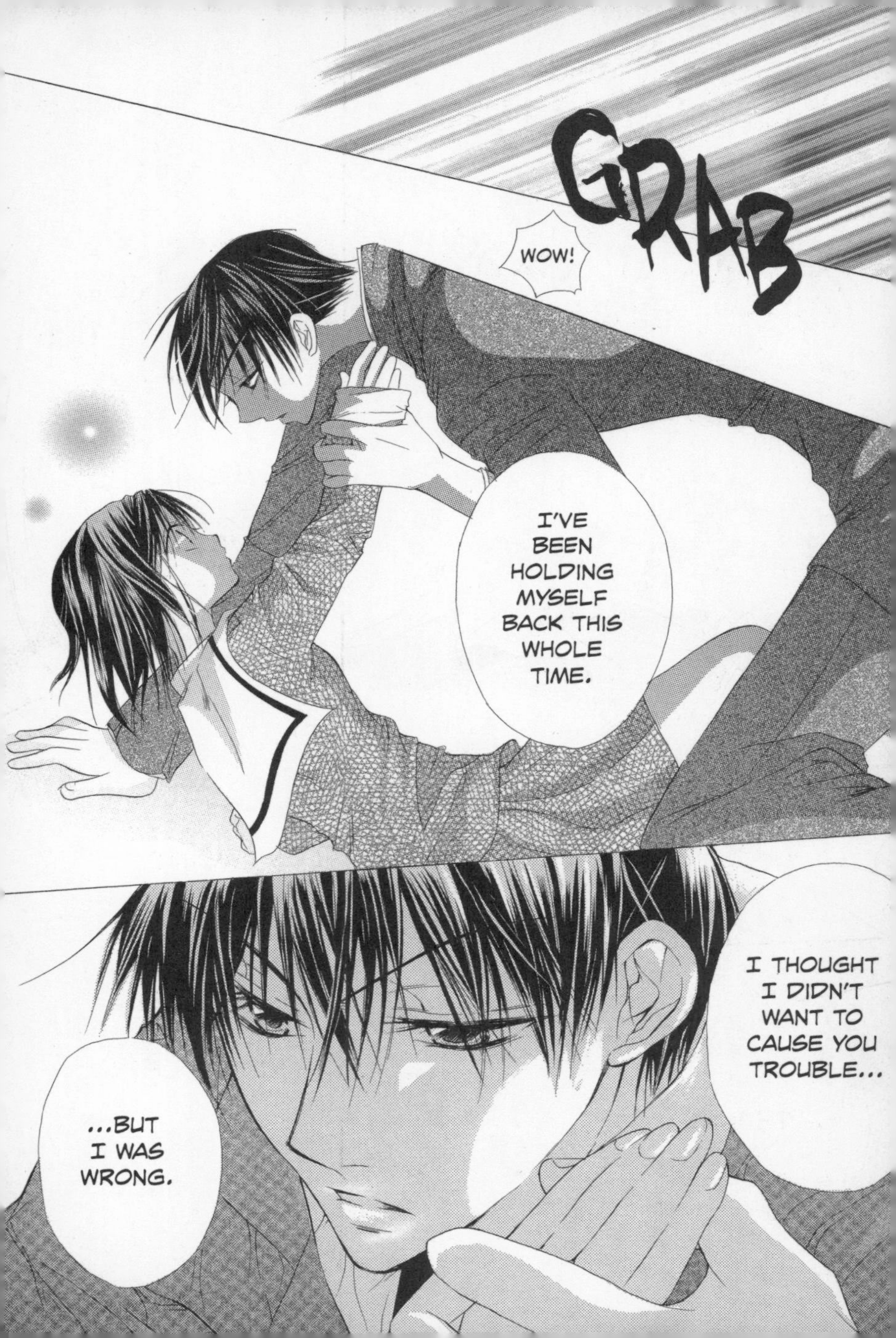
GRAB
WOW!
I'VE BEEN HOLDING MYSELF BACK THIS WHOLE TIME.
I THOUGHT I DIDN'T WANT TO CAUSE YOU TROUBLE...
...BUT I WAS WRONG.

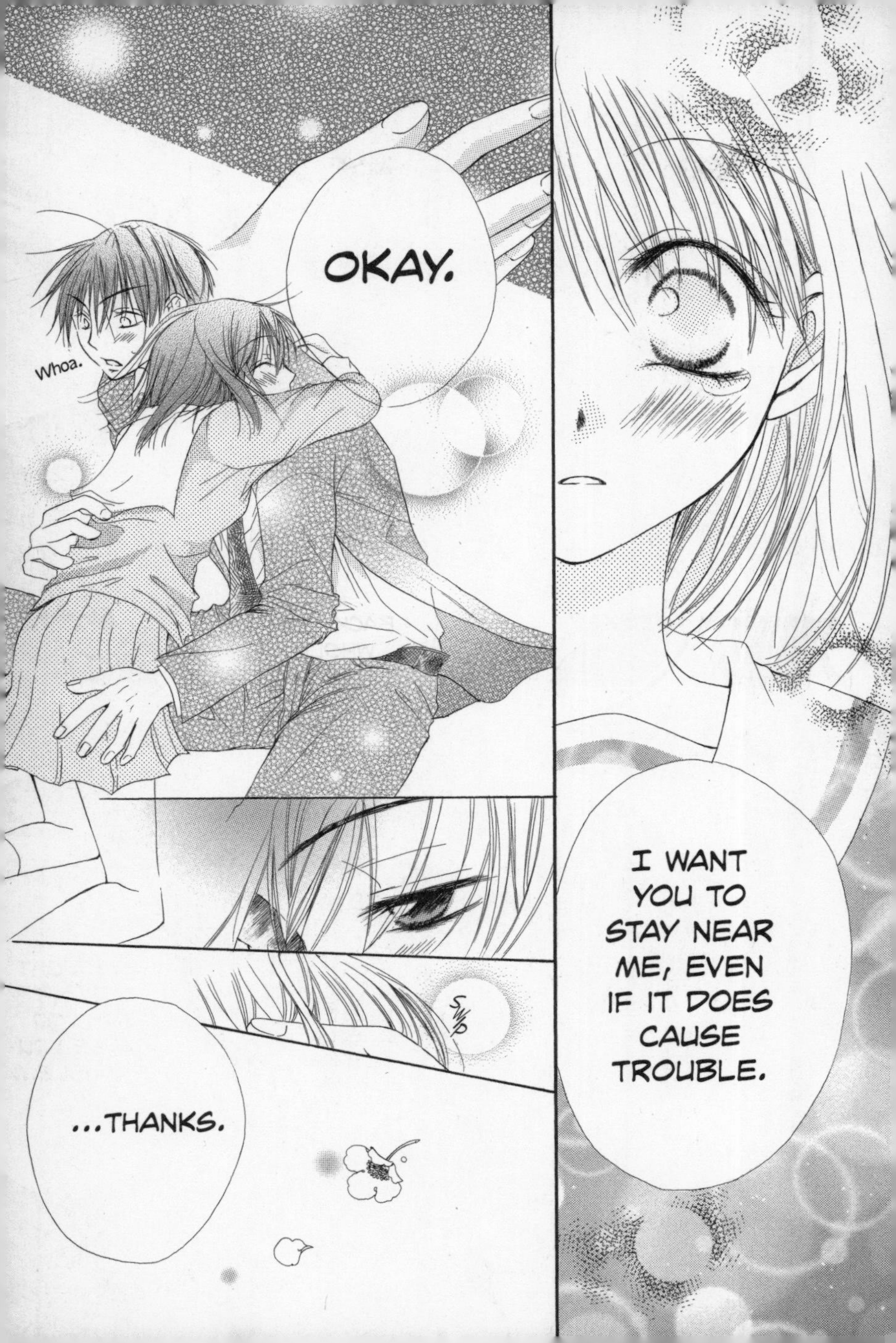
I WANT YOU TO STAY NEAR ME, EVEN IF IT DOES CAUSE TROUBLE.
OKAY.
Whoa.
SWIP
...THANKS.

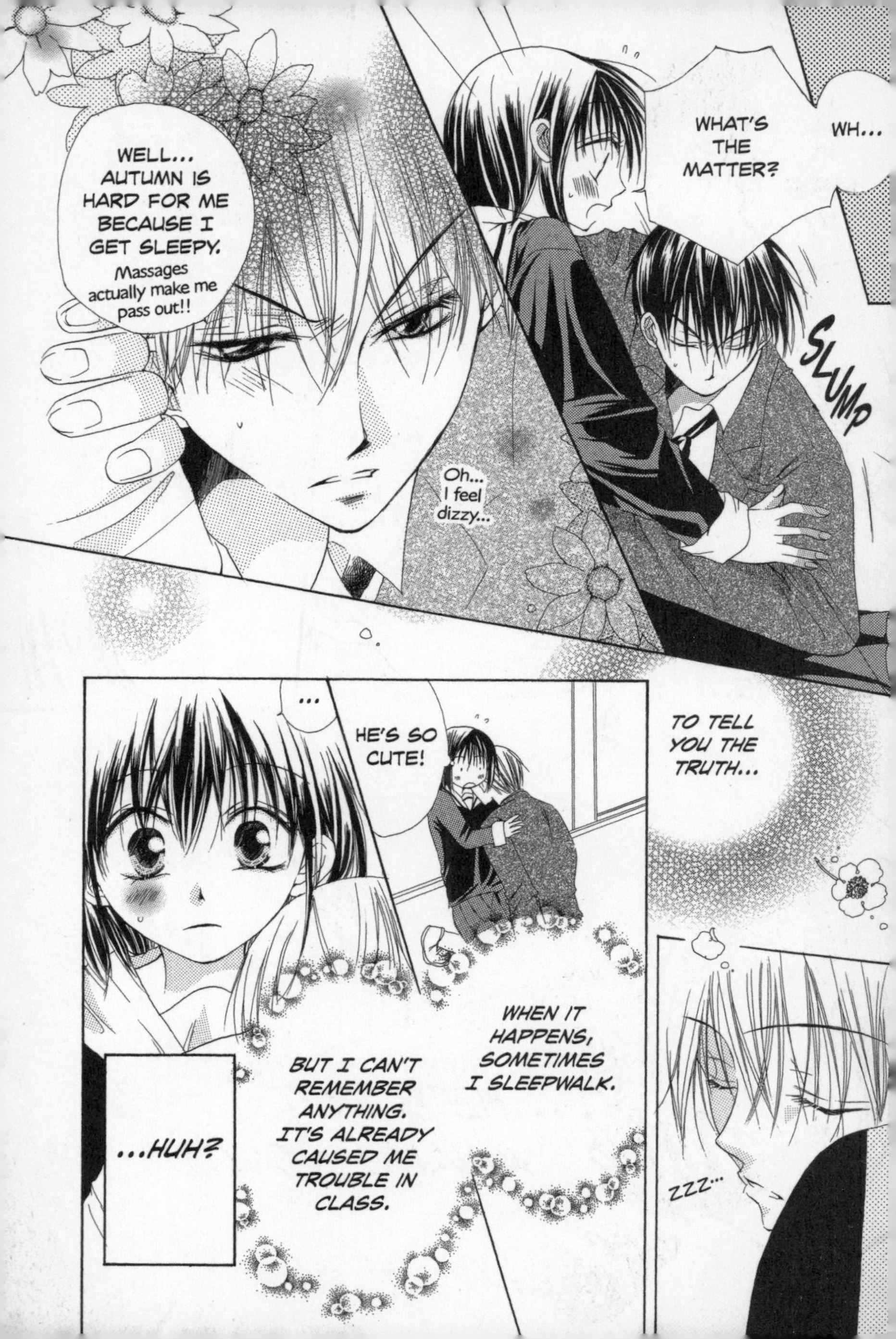
WH...
WHAT'S THE MATTER?
SLUMP
WELL... AUTUMN IS HARD FOR ME BECAUSE I GET SLEEPY.
Massages actually make me pass out!!
Oh... I feel dizzy...
TO TELL YOU THE TRUTH...
ZZZ...
WHEN IT HAPPENS, SOMETIMES I SLEEPWALK.
BUT I CAN'T REMEMBER ANYTHING. IT'S ALREADY CAUSED ME TROUBLE IN CLASS.
...
HE'S SO CUTE!
...HUH?

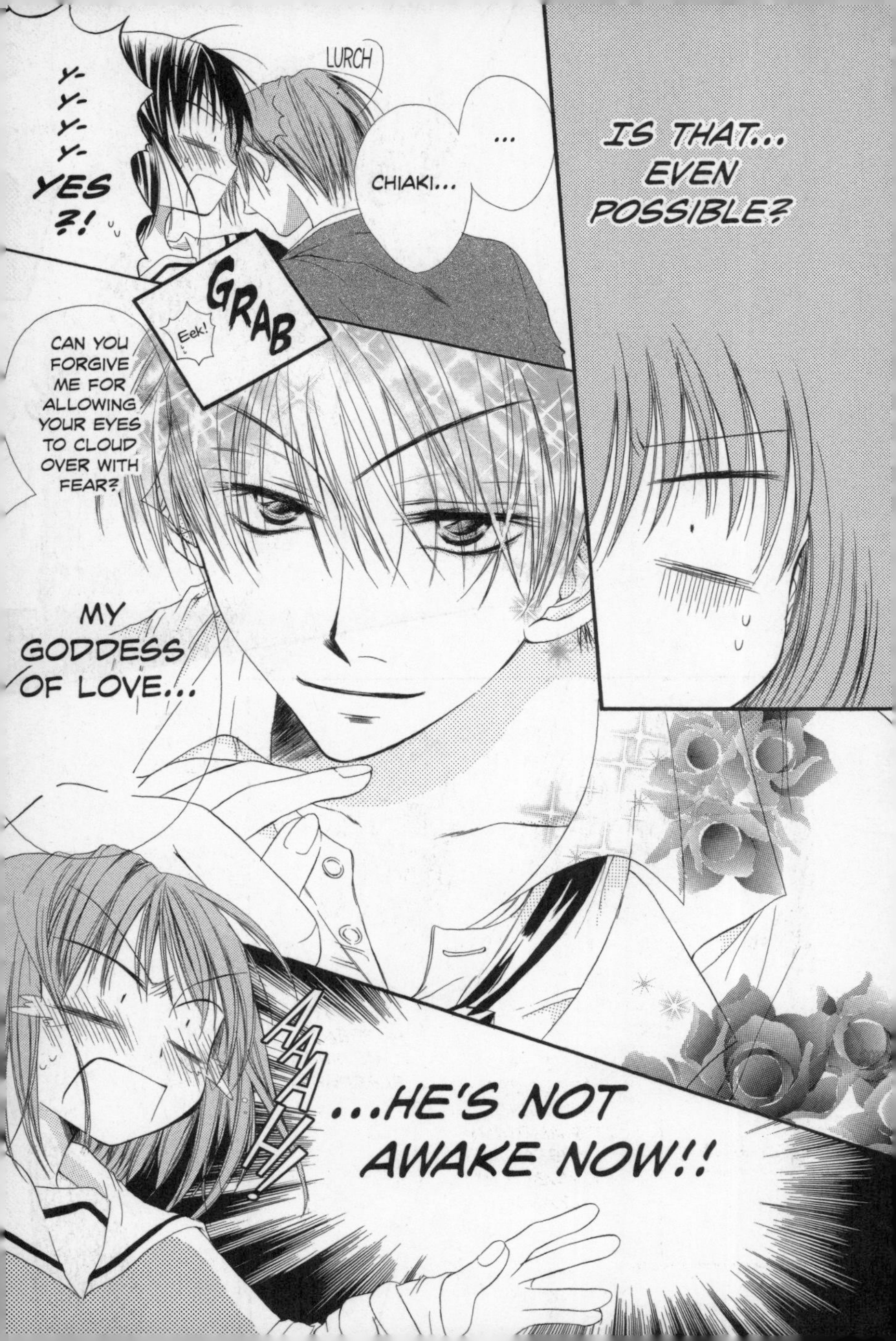

IS THAT... EVEN POSSIBLE?
LURCH
...
CHIAKI...
Y-Y-Y-Y-YES?!
GRAB
Eek!
CAN YOU FORGIVE ME FOR ALLOWING YOUR EYES TO CLOUD OVER WITH FEAR?
MY GODDESS OF LOVE...
...HE'S NOT AWAKE NOW!!
AAAAH!

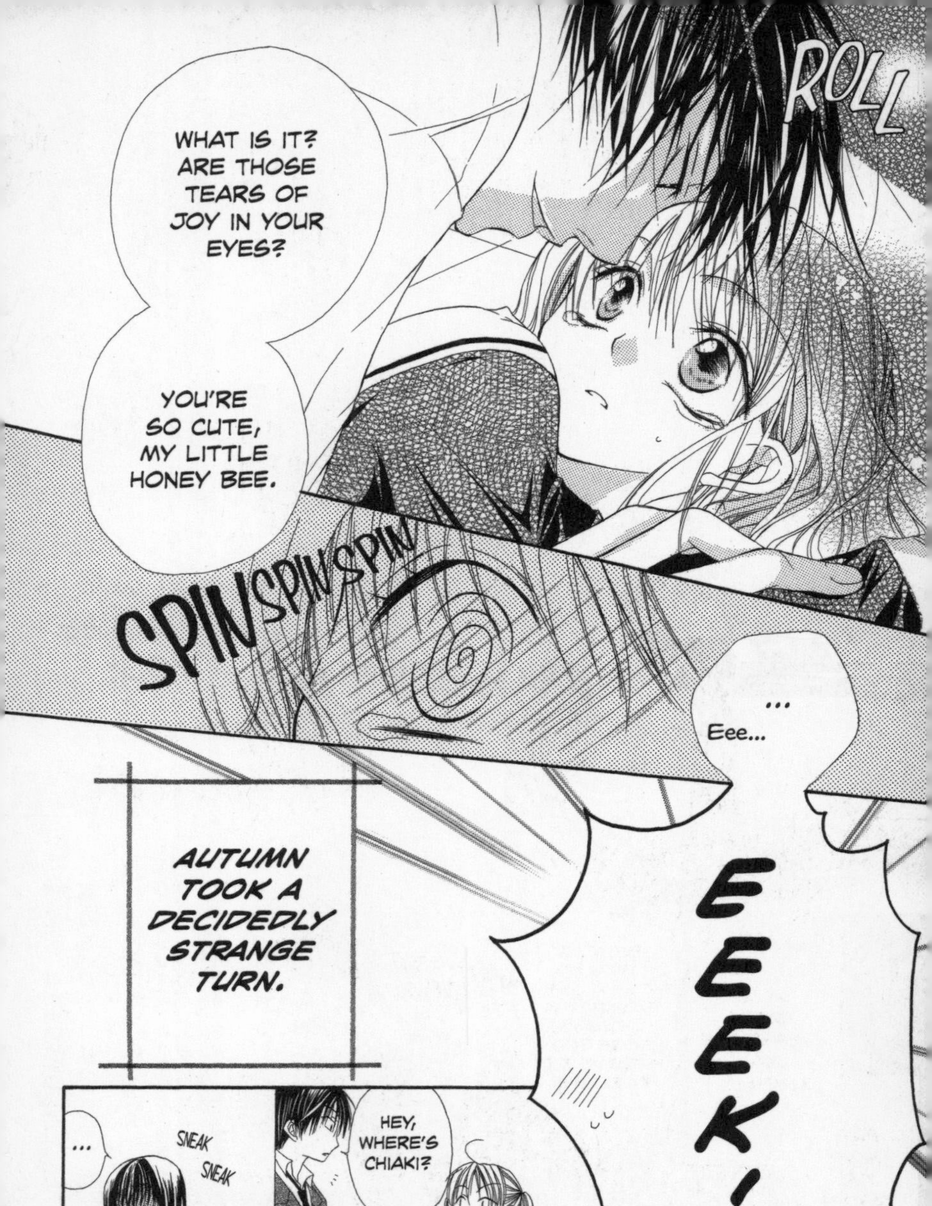
ROLL
WHAT IS IT? ARE THOSE TEARS OF JOY IN YOUR EYES?
YOU'RE SO CUTE, MY LITTLE HONEY BEE.
SPIN SPIN SPIN
...
Eee...
EEEEK!
AUTUMN TOOK A DECIDEDLY STRANGE TURN.
HEY, WHERE'S CHIAKI?
?
Dunno.
...
SNEAK
SNEAK

The Magic Touch, Part 8 / End

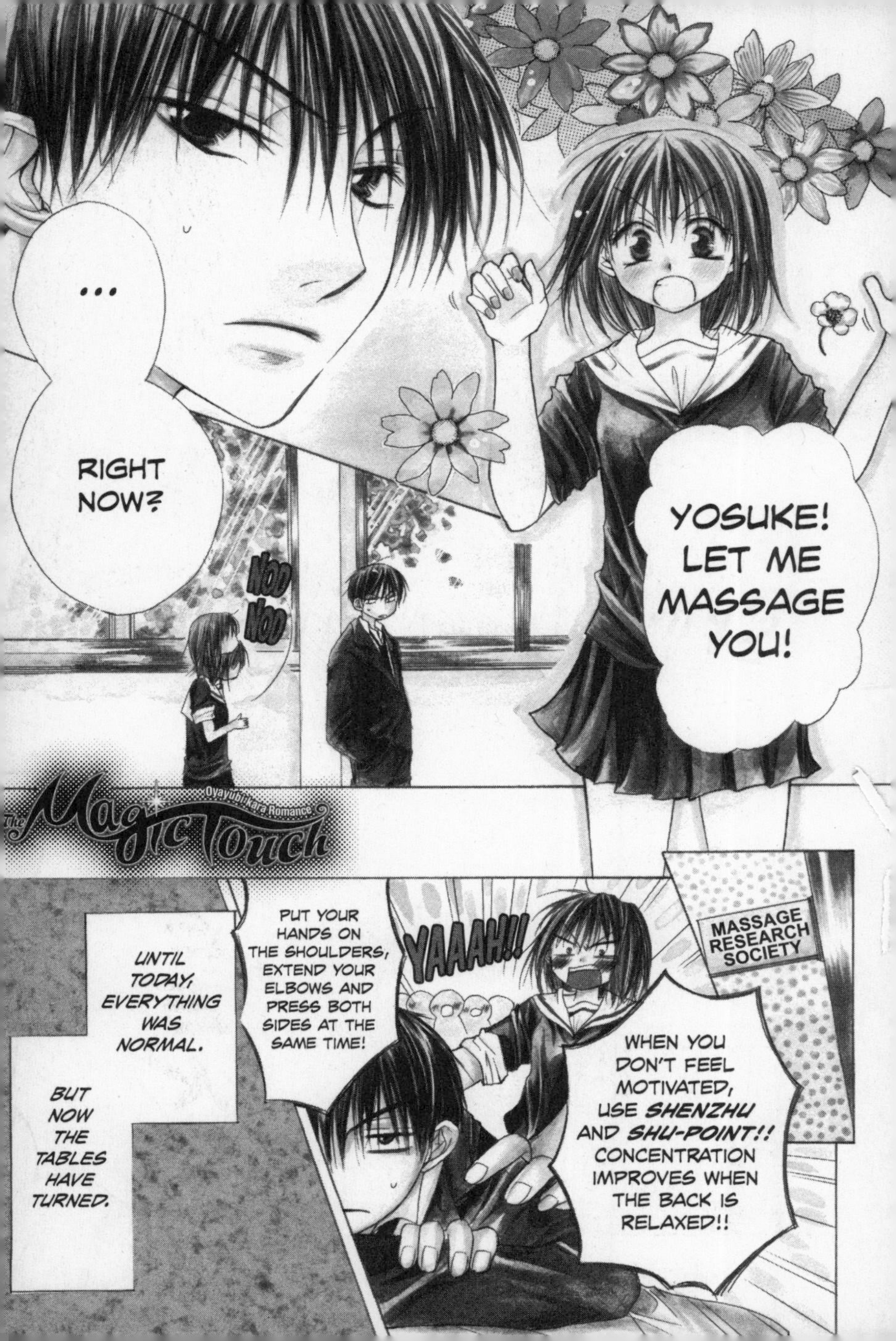
YOSUKE! LET ME MASSAGE YOU!
...
RIGHT NOW?
NOD NOD
The Magic Touch
Oyayubi kara Romance
MASSAGE RESEARCH SOCIETY
YAAAH!!
PUT YOUR HANDS ON THE SHOULDERS, EXTEND YOUR ELBOWS AND PRESS BOTH SIDES AT THE SAME TIME!
WHEN YOU DON'T FEEL MOTIVATED, USE SHENZHU AND SHU-POINT!! CONCENTRATION IMPROVES WHEN THE BACK IS RELAXED!!
UNTIL TODAY, EVERYTHING WAS NORMAL.
BUT NOW THE TABLES HAVE TURNED.

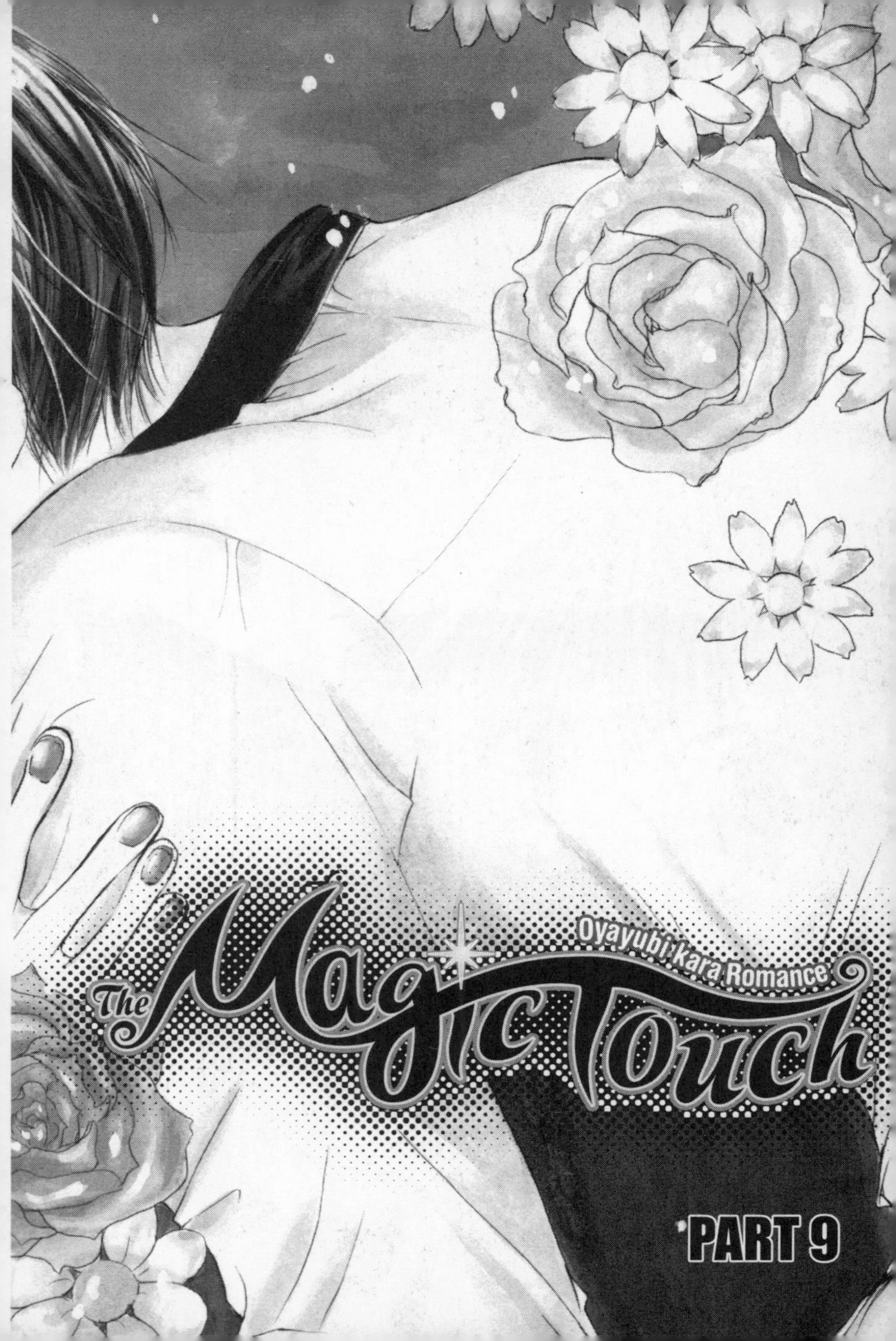
The Magic Touch
Oyayubi kara Romance
PART 9

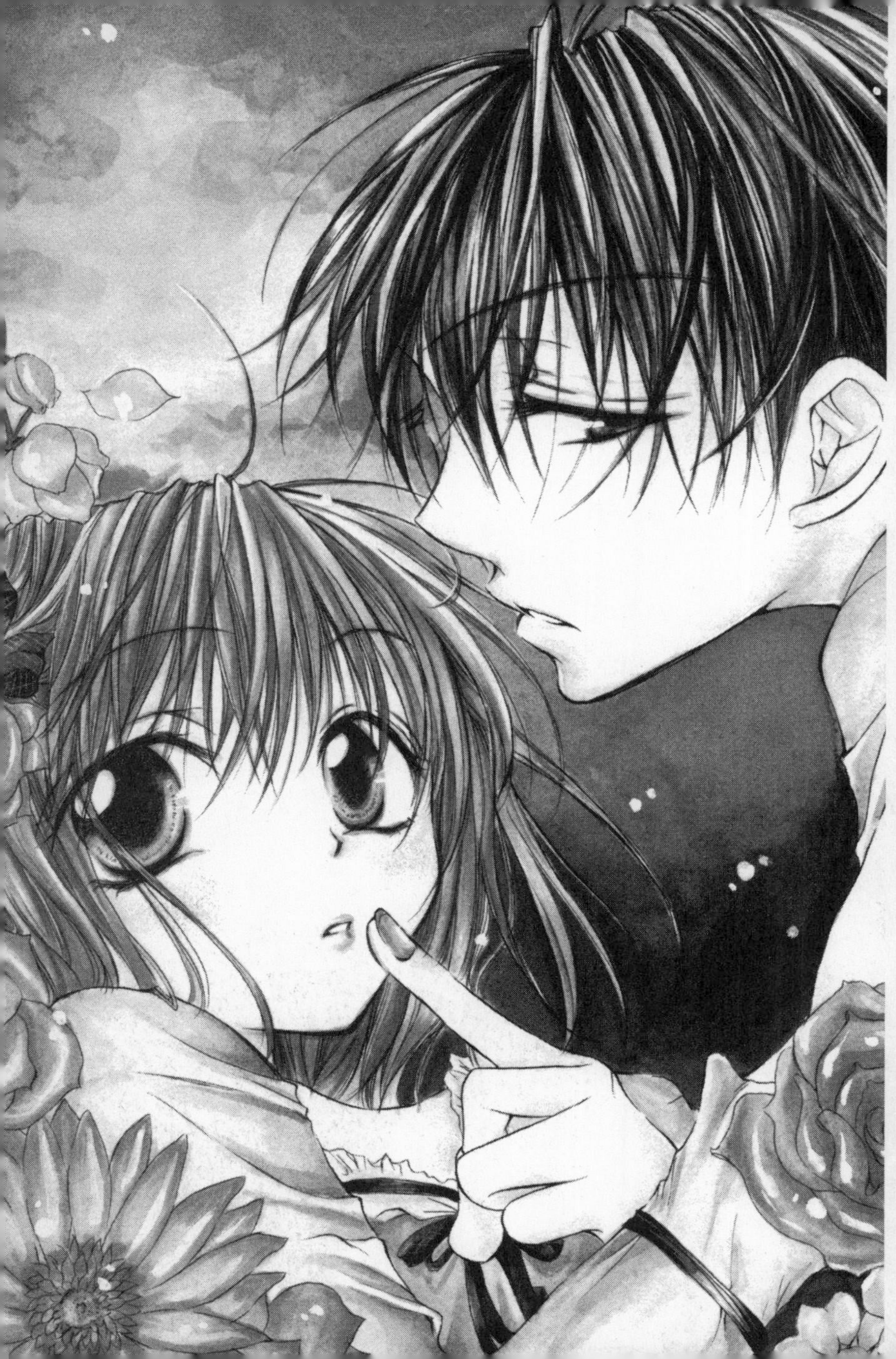

AFTER THE TRAINING CAMP

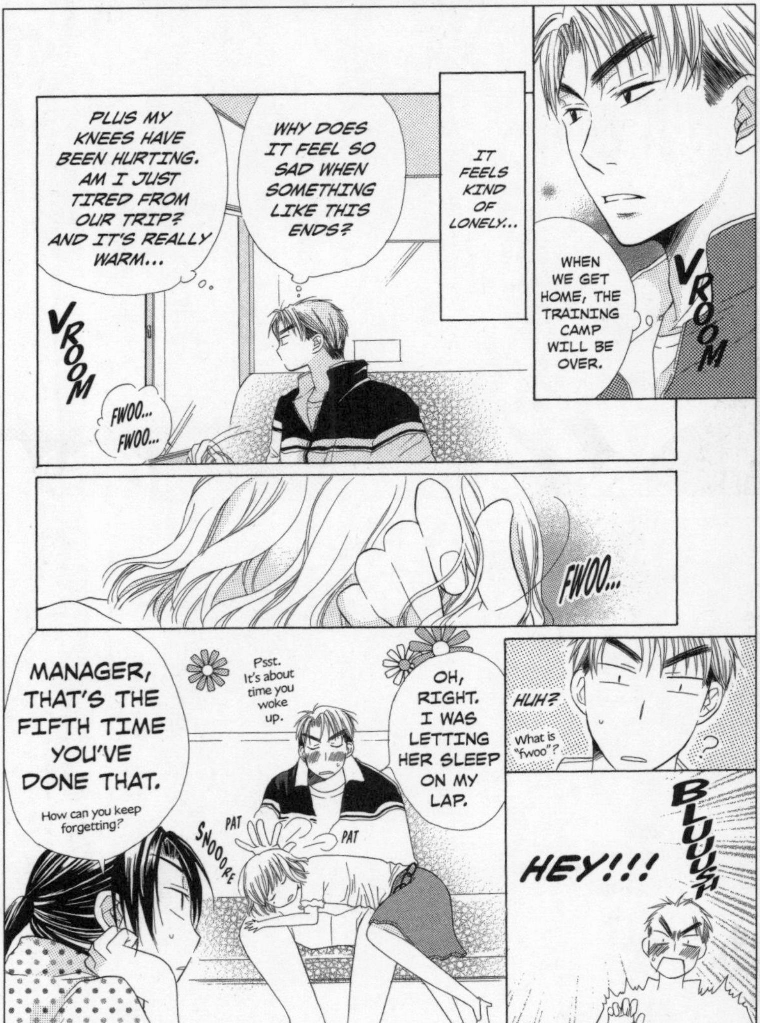

WHEN WE GET HOME, THE TRAINING CAMP WILL BE OVER.
VROOM
IT FEELS KIND OF LONELY...
WHY DOES IT FEEL SO SAD WHEN SOMETHING LIKE THIS ENDS?
PLUS MY KNEES HAVE BEEN HURTING. AM I JUST TIRED FROM OUR TRIP? AND IT'S REALLY WARM...
VROOM
FWOO... FWOO...
FWOO...
HUH?
What is "fwoo"?
HEY!!!
BLUUUSH
OH, RIGHT. I WAS LETTING HER SLEEP ON MY LAP.
Psst. It's about time you woke up.
MANAGER, THAT'S THE FIFTH TIME YOU'VE DONE THAT.
How can you keep forgetting?
PAT PAT
SNOOORE

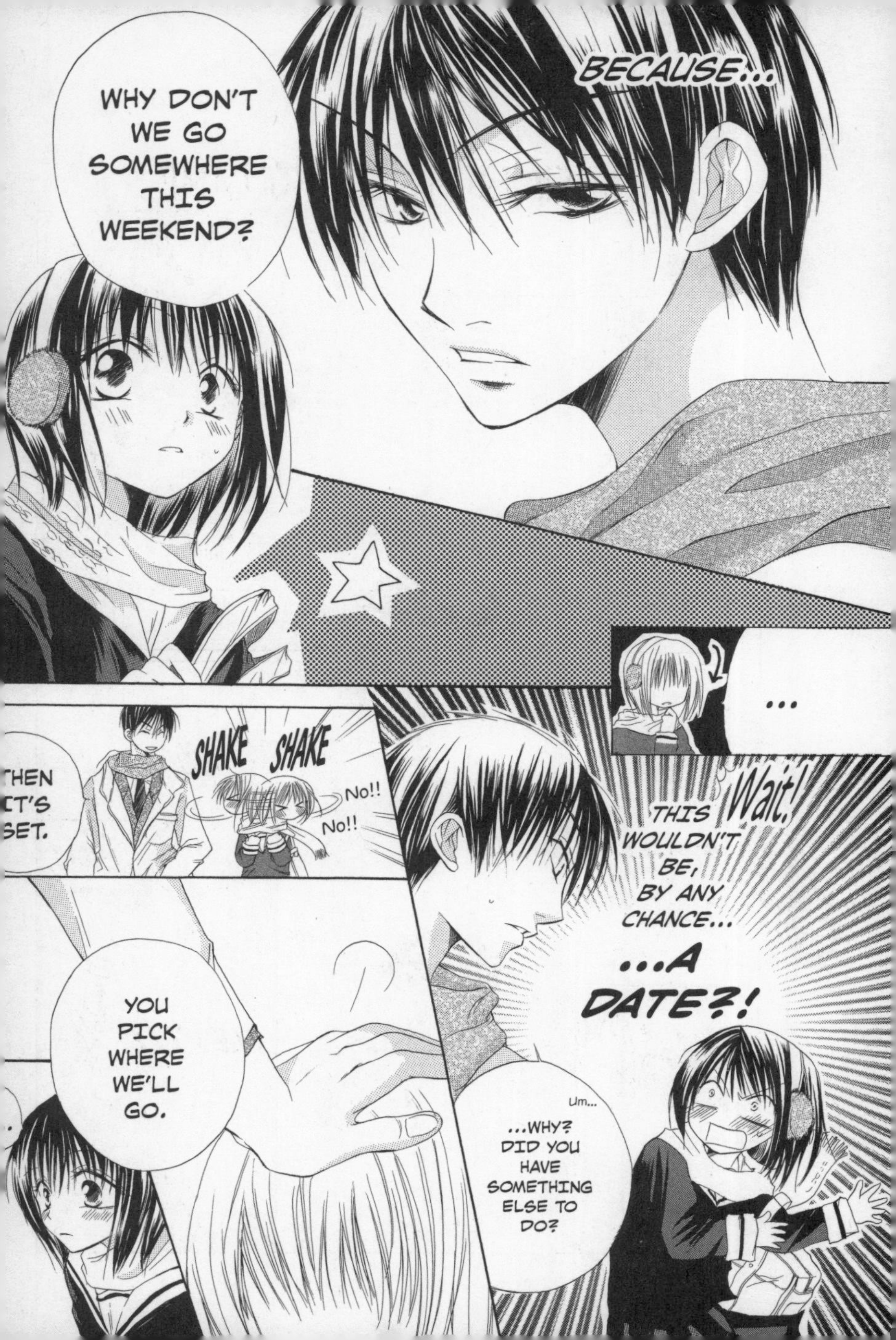
BECAUSE...
WHY DON'T WE GO SOMEWHERE THIS WEEKEND?
...
Wait!
THIS WOULDN'T BE, BY ANY CHANCE...
...A DATE?!
Um...
...WHY? DID YOU HAVE SOMETHING ELSE TO DO?
SHAKE SHAKE
No!! No!!
THEN T'S SET.
YOU PICK WHERE WE'LL GO.

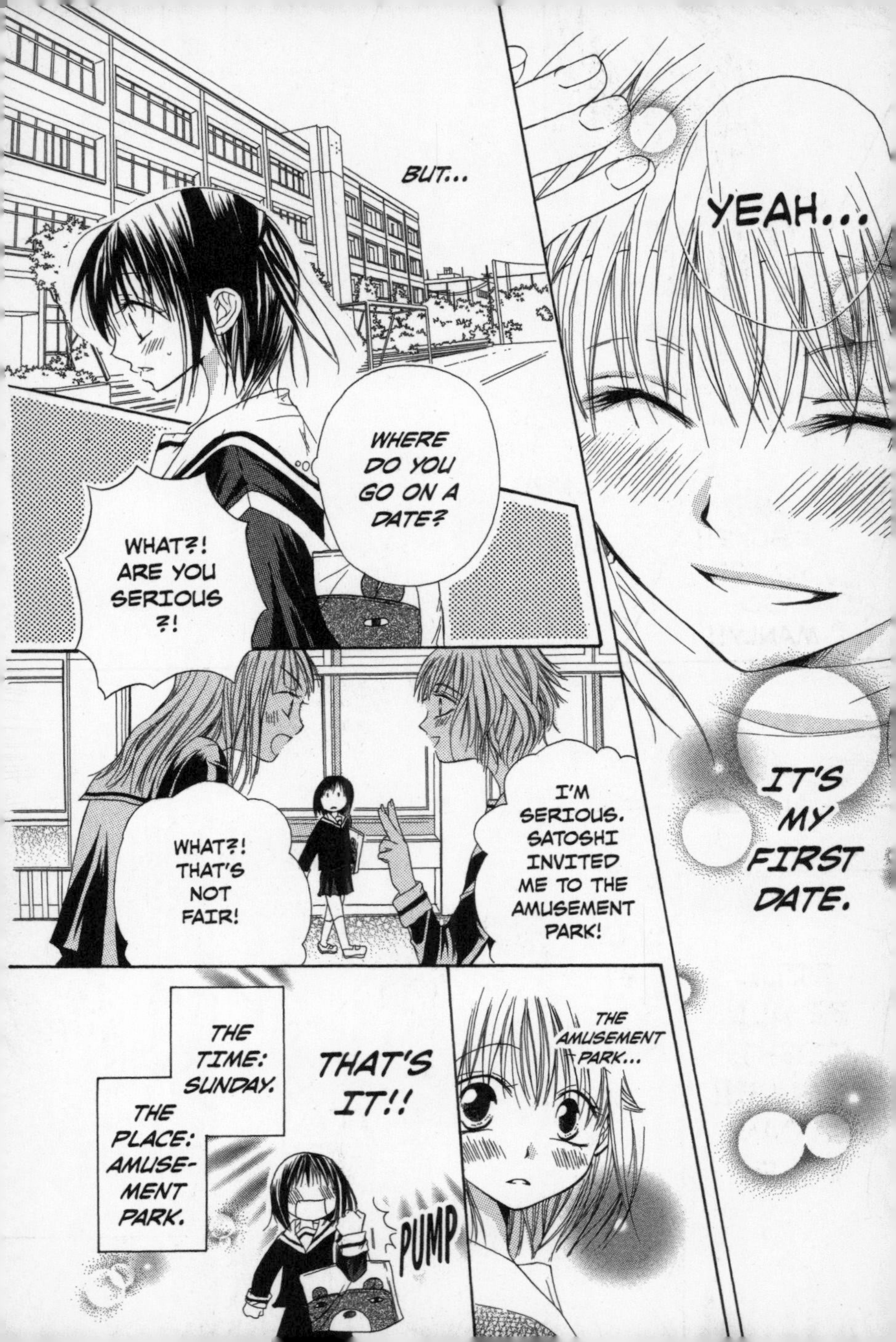
YEAH...
IT'S MY FIRST DATE.
BUT...
WHERE DO YOU GO ON A DATE?
WHAT?! ARE YOU SERIOUS?!
I'M SERIOUS. SATOSHI INVITED ME TO THE AMUSEMENT PARK!
WHAT?! THAT'S NOT FAIR!
THE AMUSEMENT PARK...
THAT'S IT!!
THE TIME: SUNDAY.
THE PLACE: AMUSEMENT PARK.
PUMP

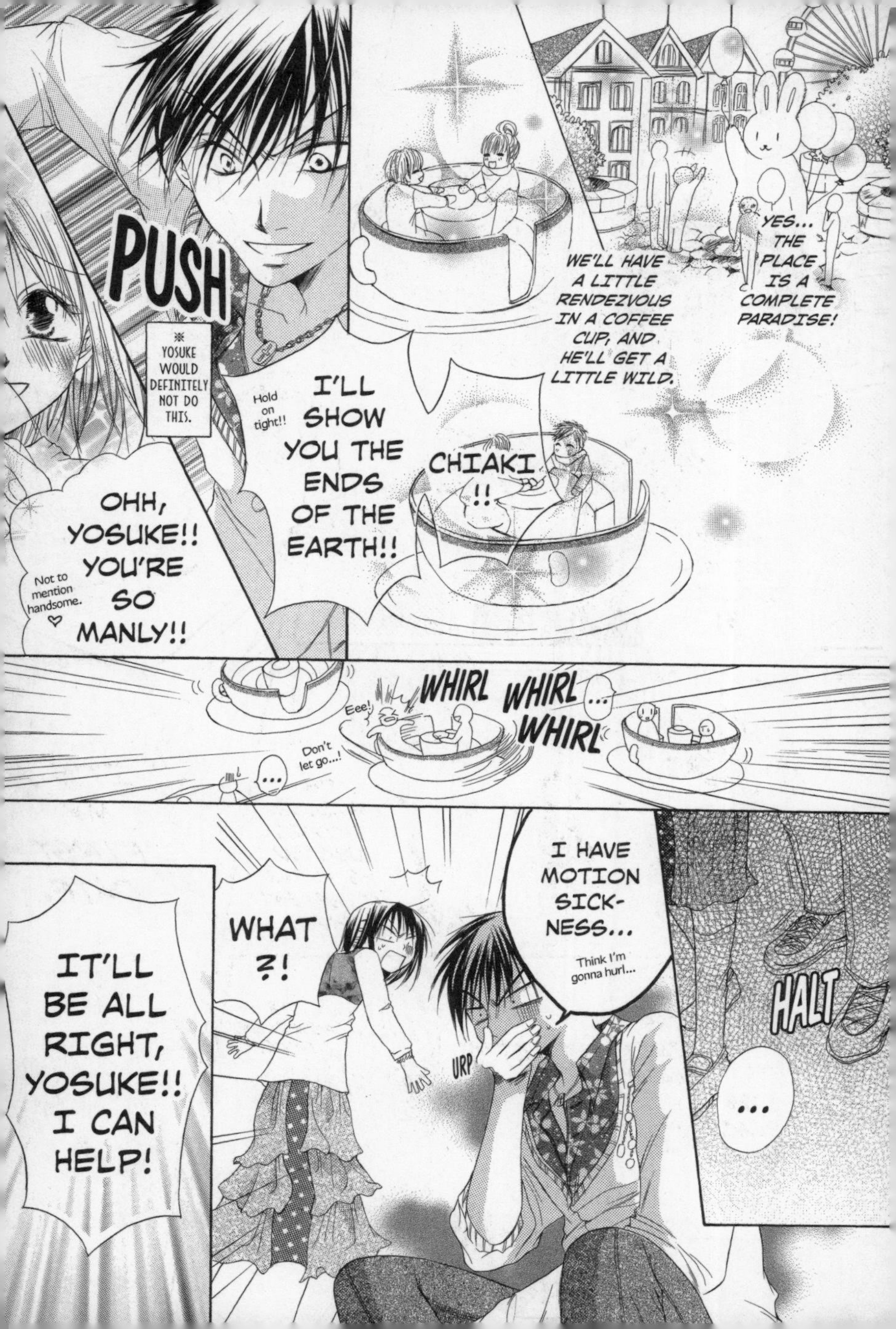
YES... THE PLACE IS A COMPLETE PARADISE!
WE'LL HAVE A LITTLE RENDEZVOUS IN A COFFEE CUP, AND HE'LL GET A LITTLE WILD.
CHIAKI !!
I'LL SHOW YOU THE ENDS OF THE EARTH!!
Hold on tight!!
PUSH
※ YOSUKE WOULD DEFINITELY NOT DO THIS.
OHH, YOSUKE!! YOU'RE SO MANLY!!
Not to mention handsome. ♡
...
WHIRL WHIRL WHIRL
Eee!
Don't let go...!
...
HALT
...
I HAVE MOTION SICK-NESS...
Think I'm gonna hurl...
URP
WHAT ?!
IT'LL BE ALL RIGHT, YOSUKE!! I CAN HELP!

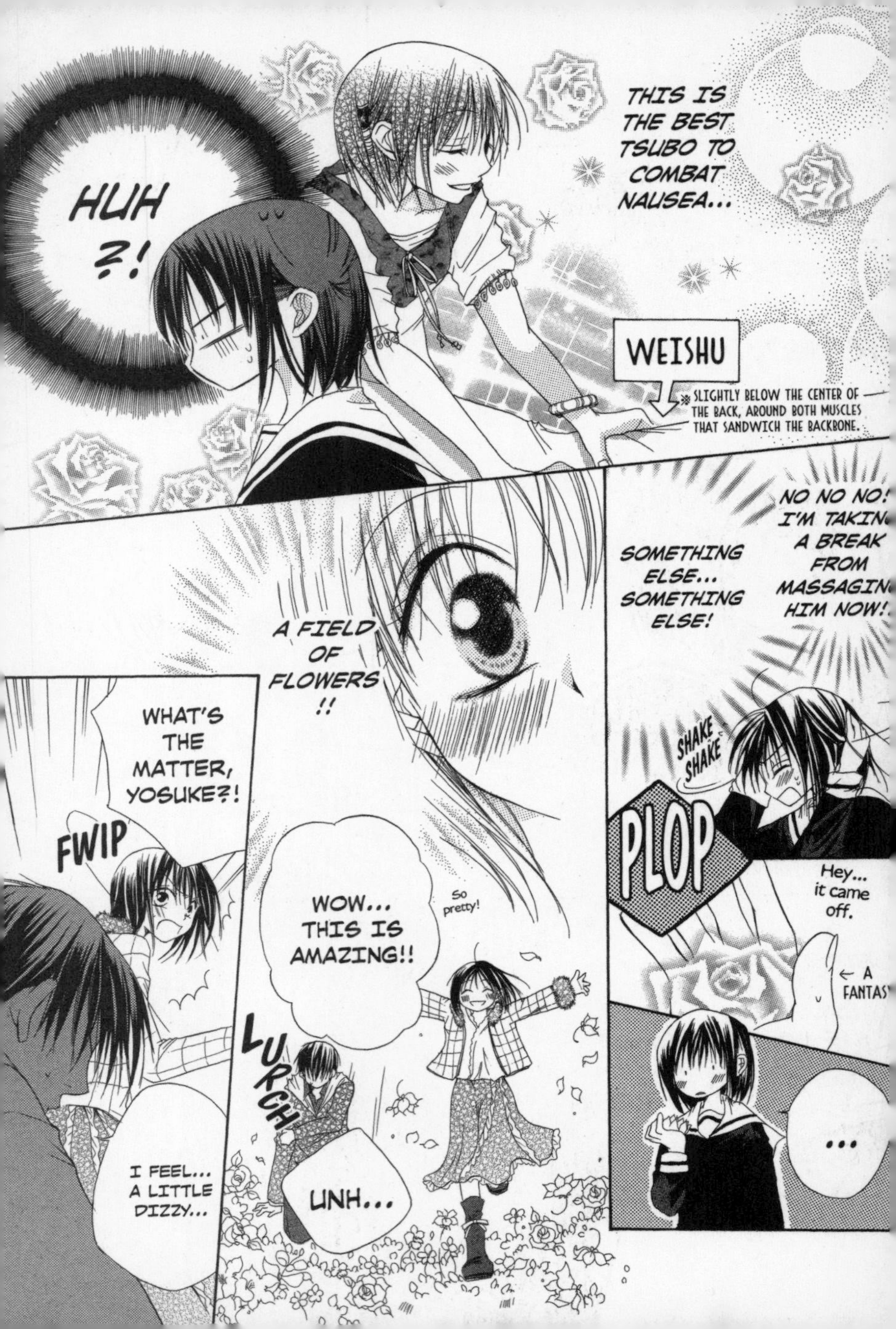
THIS IS THE BEST TSUBO TO COMBAT NAUSEA...
WEISHU
※ SLIGHTLY BELOW THE CENTER OF THE BACK, AROUND BOTH MUSCLES THAT SANDWICH THE BACKBONE.
HUH ?!
NO NO NO! I'M TAKIN A BREAK FROM MASSAGIN HIM NOW!
SOMETHING ELSE... SOMETHING ELSE!
SHAKE SHAKE
PLOP
Hey... it came off.
← A FANTAS
...
A FIELD OF FLOWERS !!
So pretty!
WOW... THIS IS AMAZING!!
LURCH
UNH...
WHAT'S THE MATTER, YOSUKE?!
FWIP
I FEEL... A LITTLE DIZZY...

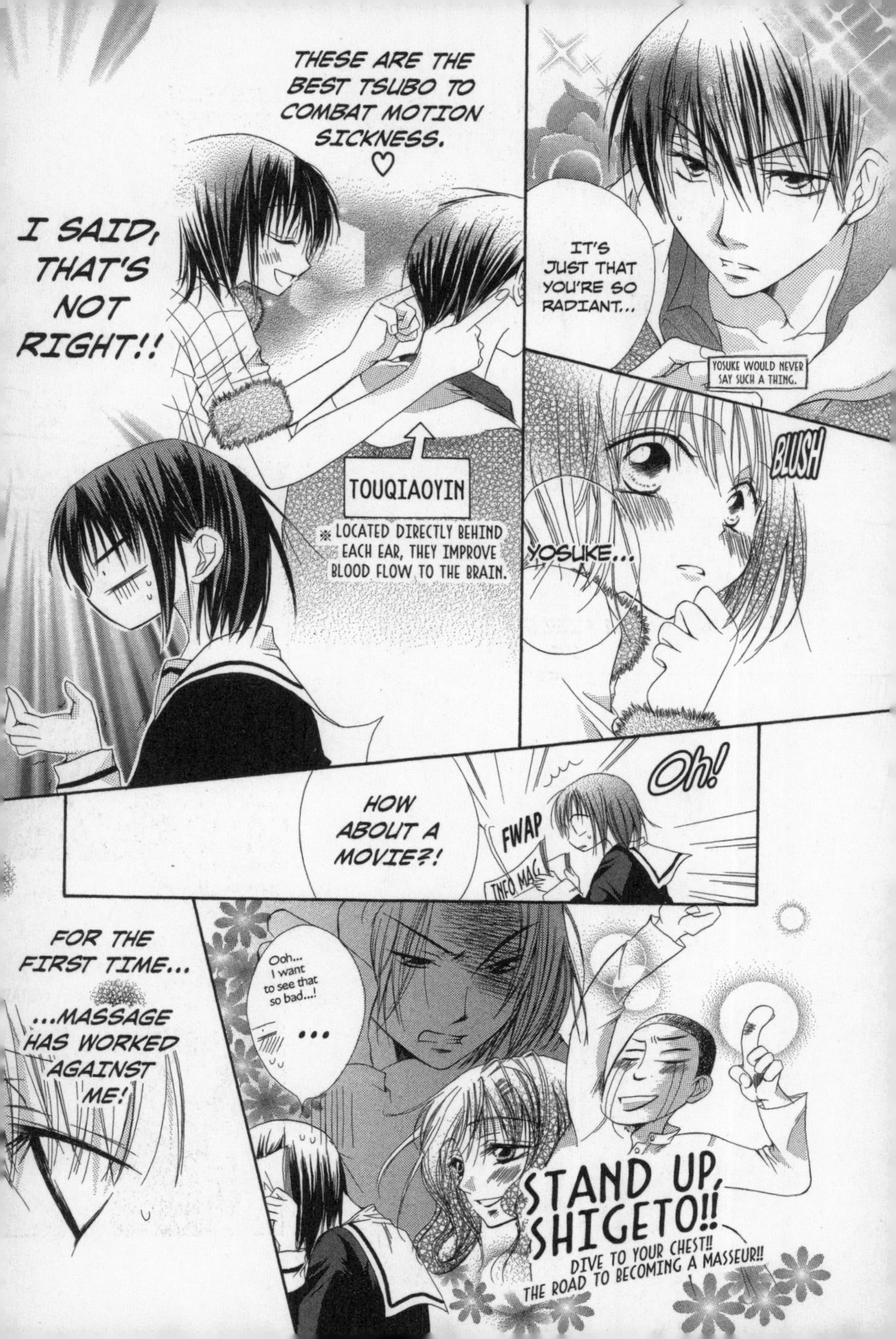
IT'S JUST THAT YOU'RE SO RADIANT...
YOSUKE WOULD NEVER SAY SUCH A THING.
BLUSH
YOSUKE...
THESE ARE THE BEST TSUBO TO COMBAT MOTION SICKNESS. ♡
I SAID, THAT'S NOT RIGHT!!
TOUQIAOYIN
※ LOCATED DIRECTLY BEHIND EACH EAR, THEY IMPROVE BLOOD FLOW TO THE BRAIN.
Oh!
FWAP
INFO MAG
HOW ABOUT A MOVIE?!
Ooh... I want to see that so bad...!
...
FOR THE FIRST TIME...
...MASSAGE HAS WORKED AGAINST ME!
STAND UP, SHIGETO!!
DIVE TO YOUR CHEST!! THE ROAD TO BECOMING A MASSEUR!!

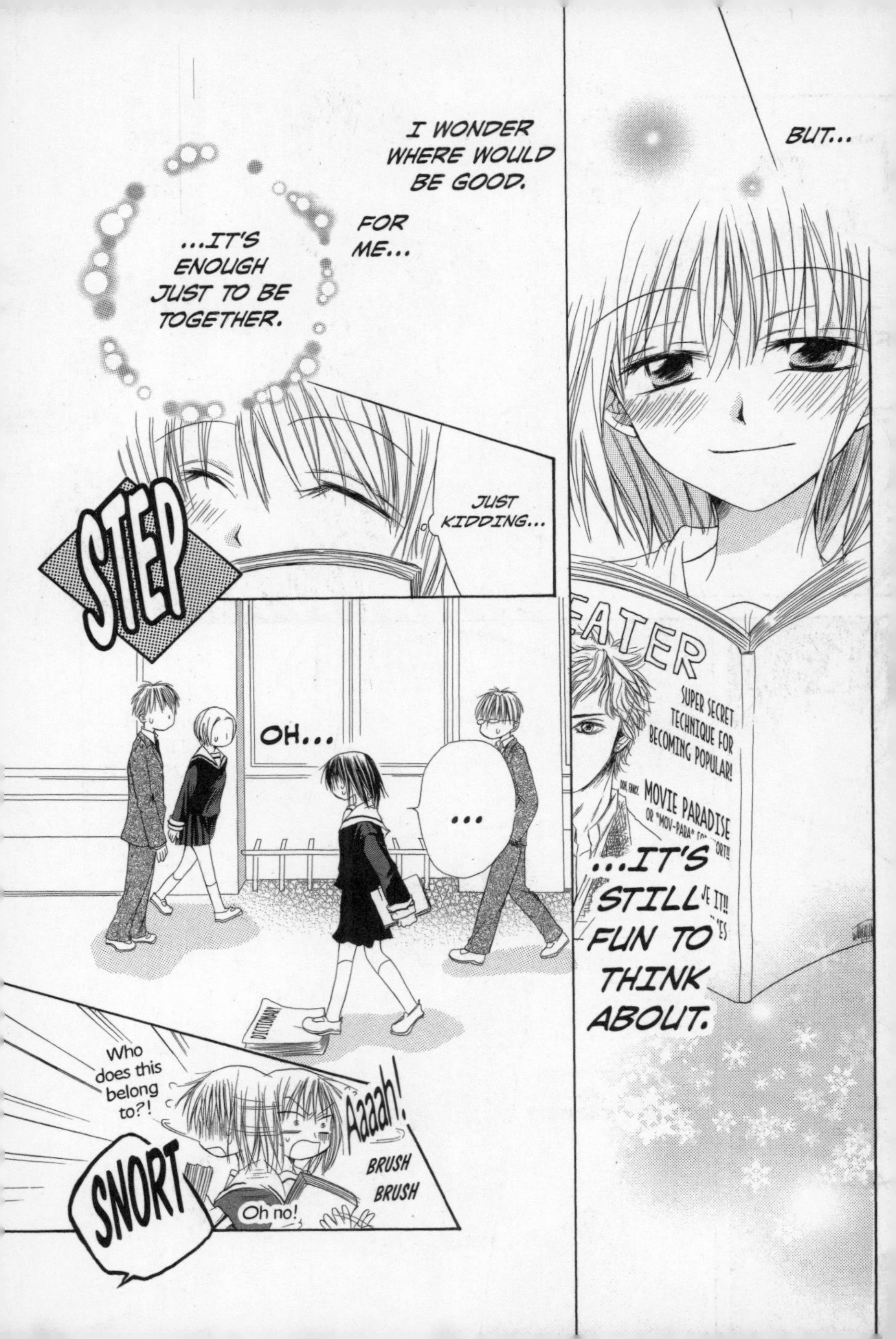
BUT...
EATER
SUPER SECRET TECHNIQUE FOR BECOMING POPULAR!
MOVIE PARADISE
...IT'S STILL FUN TO THINK ABOUT.
I WONDER WHERE WOULD BE GOOD.
FOR ME...
...IT'S ENOUGH JUST TO BE TOGETHER.
JUST KIDDING...
STEP
OH...
...
DICTIONARY
Aaaah!
Who does this belong to?!
SNORT
BRUSH BRUSH
Oh no!

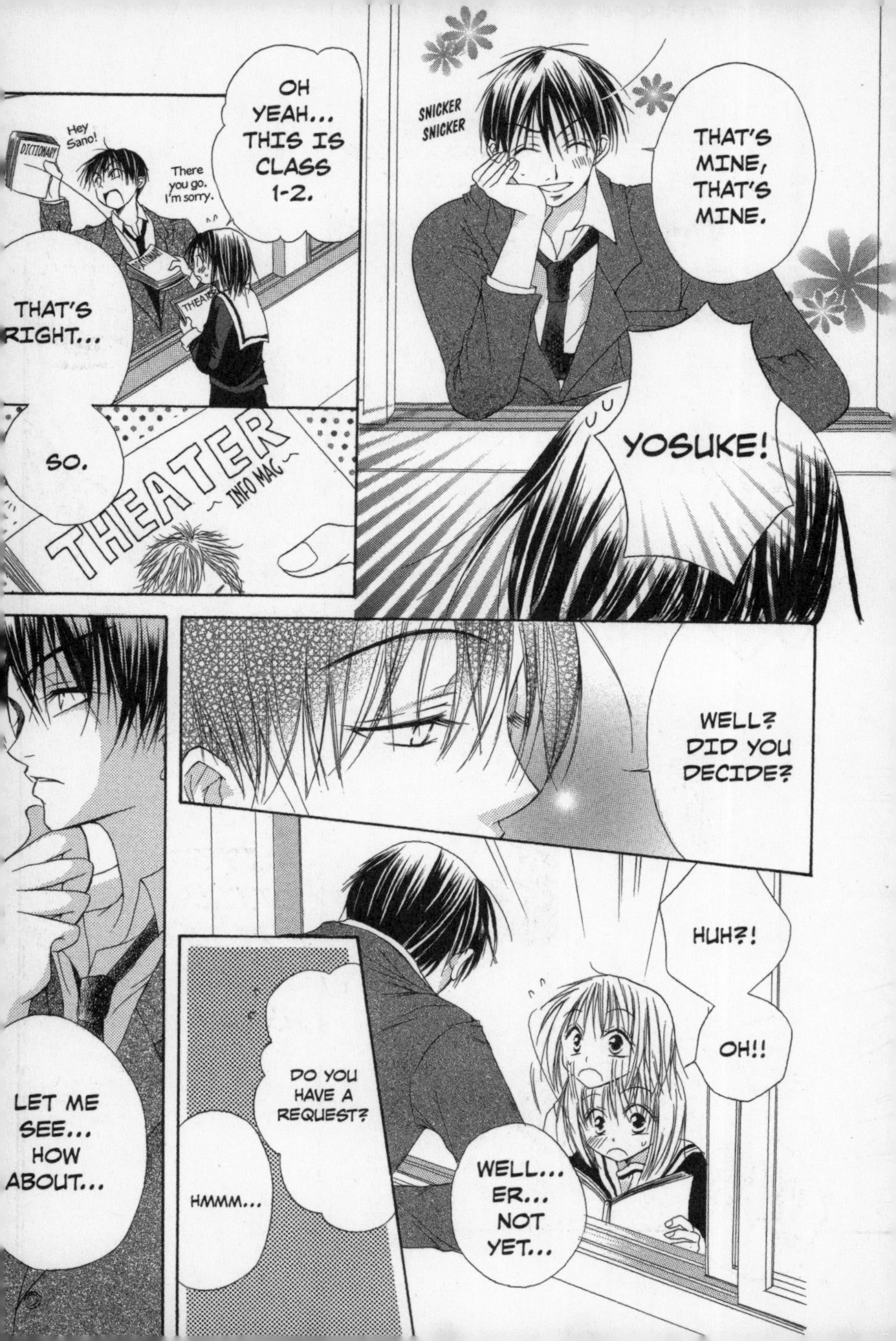
THAT'S MINE, THAT'S MINE.
SNICKER SNICKER
YOSUKE!
OH YEAH... THIS IS CLASS 1-2.
Hey Sano!
DICTIONARY
There you go. I'm sorry.
THAT'S RIGHT...
SO.
THEATER ~INFO MAG~
WELL? DID YOU DECIDE?
HUH?!
OH!!
WELL... ER... NOT YET...
DO YOU HAVE A REQUEST?
HMMM...
LET ME SEE... HOW ABOUT...

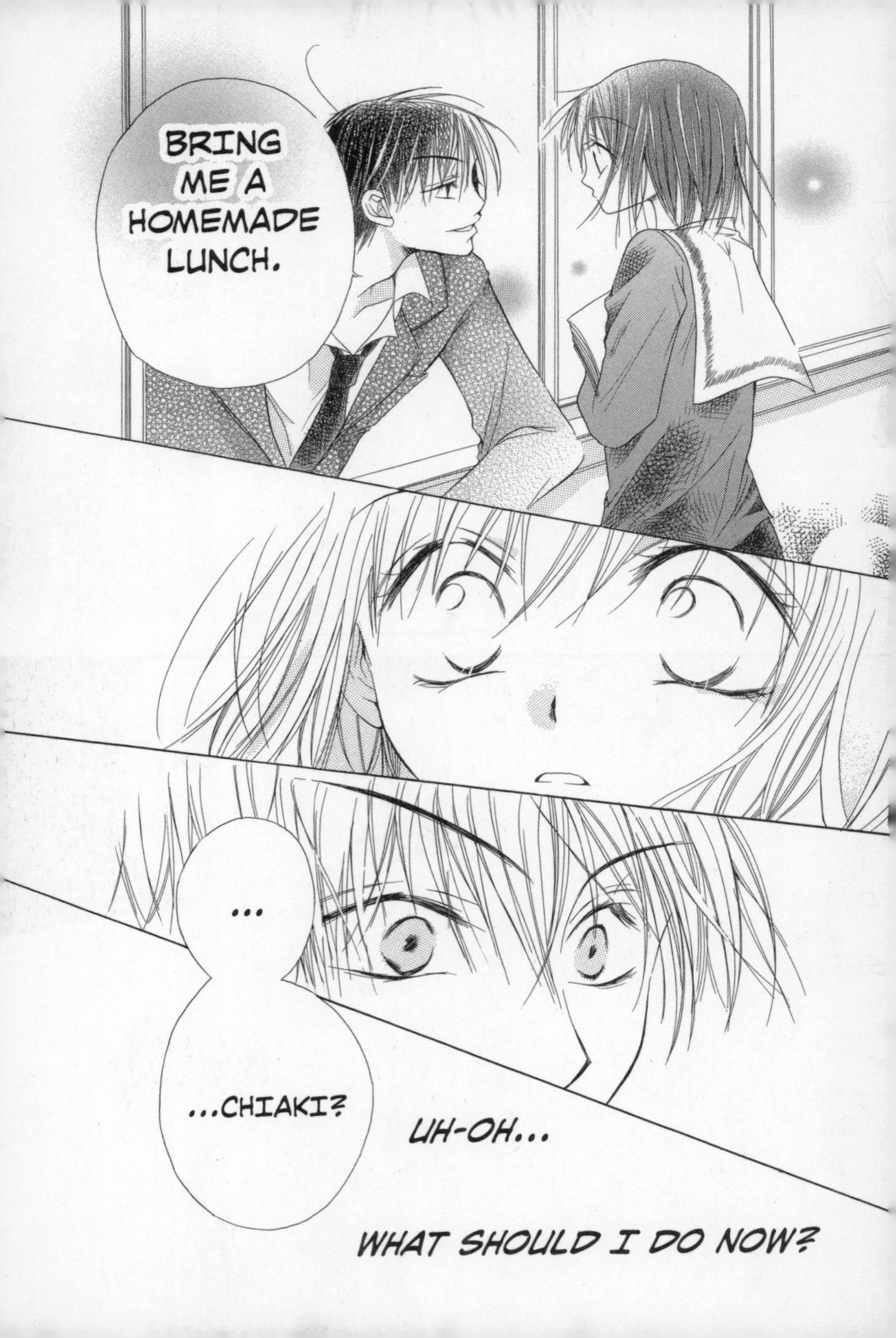
BRING ME A HOMEMADE LUNCH.
...
...CHIAKI?
UH-OH...
WHAT SHOULD I DO NOW?

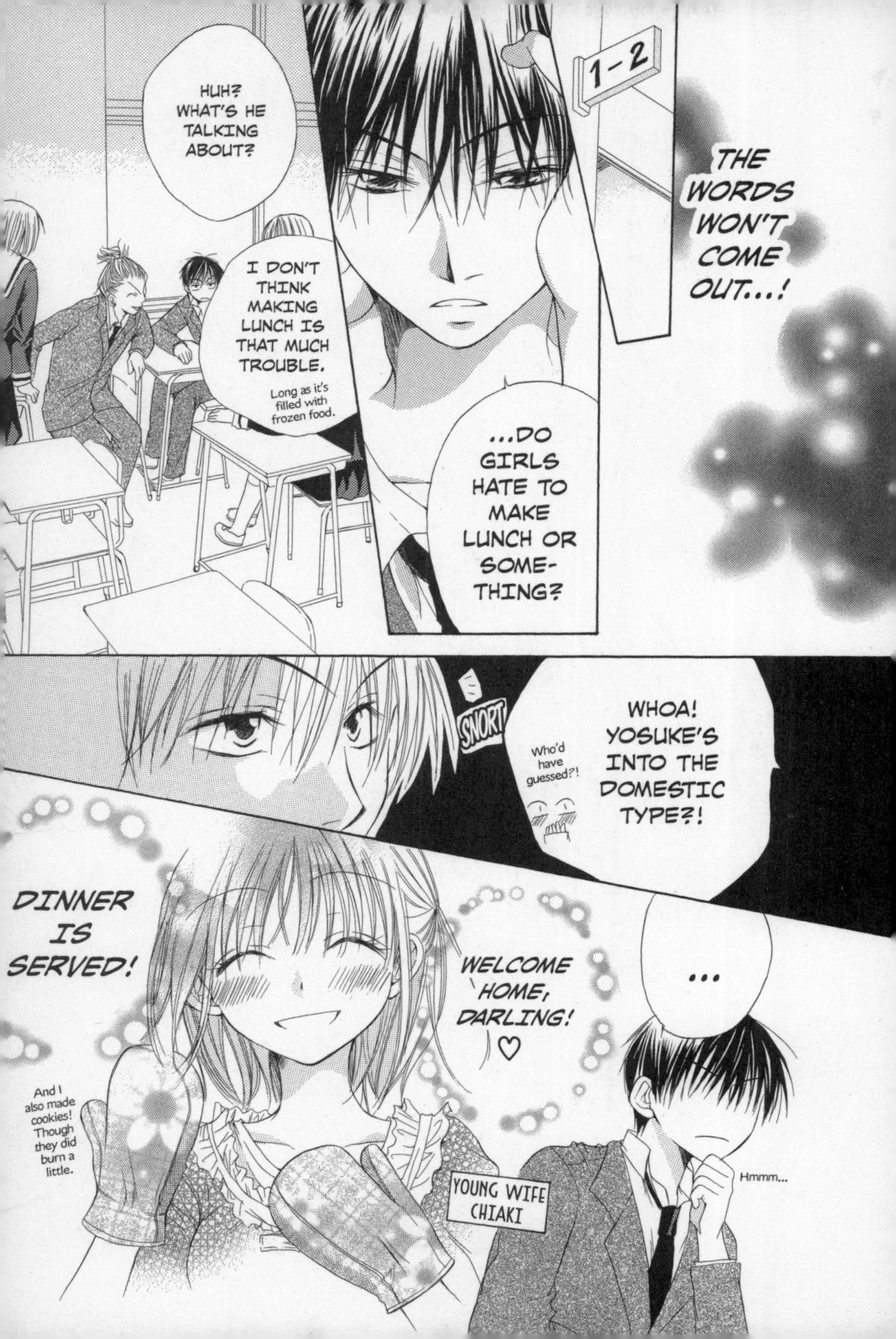
1-2
THE WORDS WON'T COME OUT...!
...DO GIRLS HATE TO MAKE LUNCH OR SOMETHING?
HUH? WHAT'S HE TALKING ABOUT?
I DON'T THINK MAKING LUNCH IS THAT MUCH TROUBLE.
Long as it's filled with frozen food.
WHOA! YOSUKE'S INTO THE DOMESTIC TYPE?!
Who'd have guessed?!
SNORT
...
Hmmm...
WELCOME HOME, DARLING! ♡
YOUNG WIFE CHIAKI
DINNER IS SERVED!
And I also made cookies! Though they did burn a little.

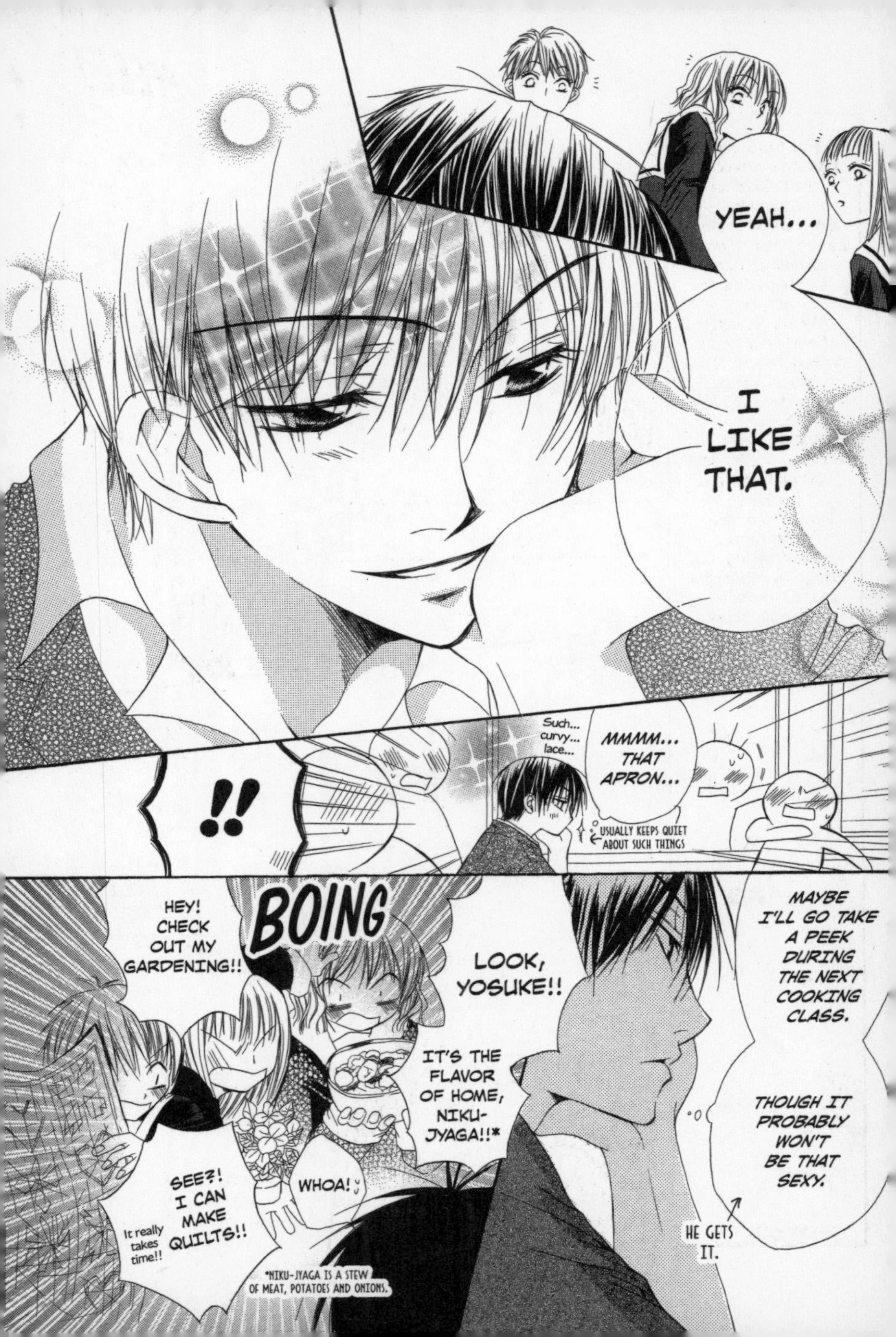
YEAH...
I LIKE THAT.
MMMM... THAT APRON...
Such... curvy... lace...
USUALLY KEEPS QUIET ABOUT SUCH THINGS
!!
MAYBE I'LL GO TAKE A PEEK DURING THE NEXT COOKING CLASS.
THOUGH IT PROBABLY WON'T BE THAT SEXY.
HE GETS IT.
LOOK, YOSUKE!!
IT'S THE FLAVOR OF HOME, NIKU-JYAGA!!*
BOING
HEY! CHECK OUT MY GARDENING!!
WHOA!
SEE?! I CAN MAKE QUILTS!!
It really takes time!!
*NIKU-JYAGA IS A STEW OF MEAT, POTATOES AND ONIONS.

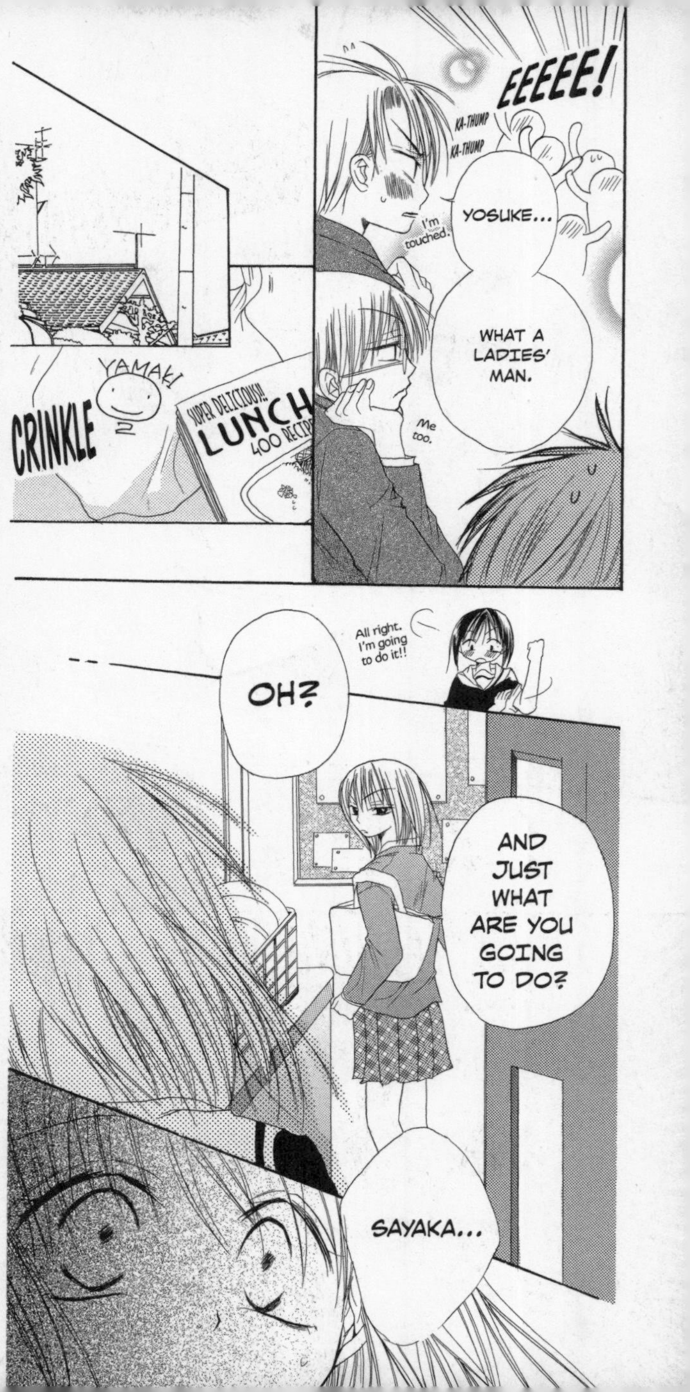
EEEEE!
KA-THUMP
KA-THUMP
YOSUKE...
I'm touched.
WHAT A LADIES' MAN.
Me too.
YAMAKI
CRINKLE
SUPER DELICIOUS!!
LUNCH
All right. I'm going to do it!!
OH?
AND JUST WHAT ARE YOU GOING TO DO?
SAYAKA...

For this story, I ended up needing the help of an assistant. So I rented a room by the week in order to decrease my commute time to school. My impressions: It was very clean. Weekly rentals today are amazing. When I first entered the room, I immediately checked underneath the bed and the locker. I watch too many horror films... I was drawing the manga by myself for a while, but it was especially scary at night.

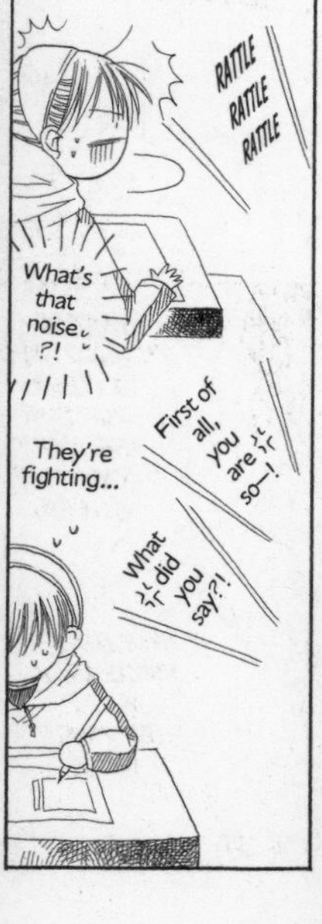
RATTLE RATTLE RATTLE
What's that noise...?!
First of all, you are so—!
They're fighting...
What did you say?!

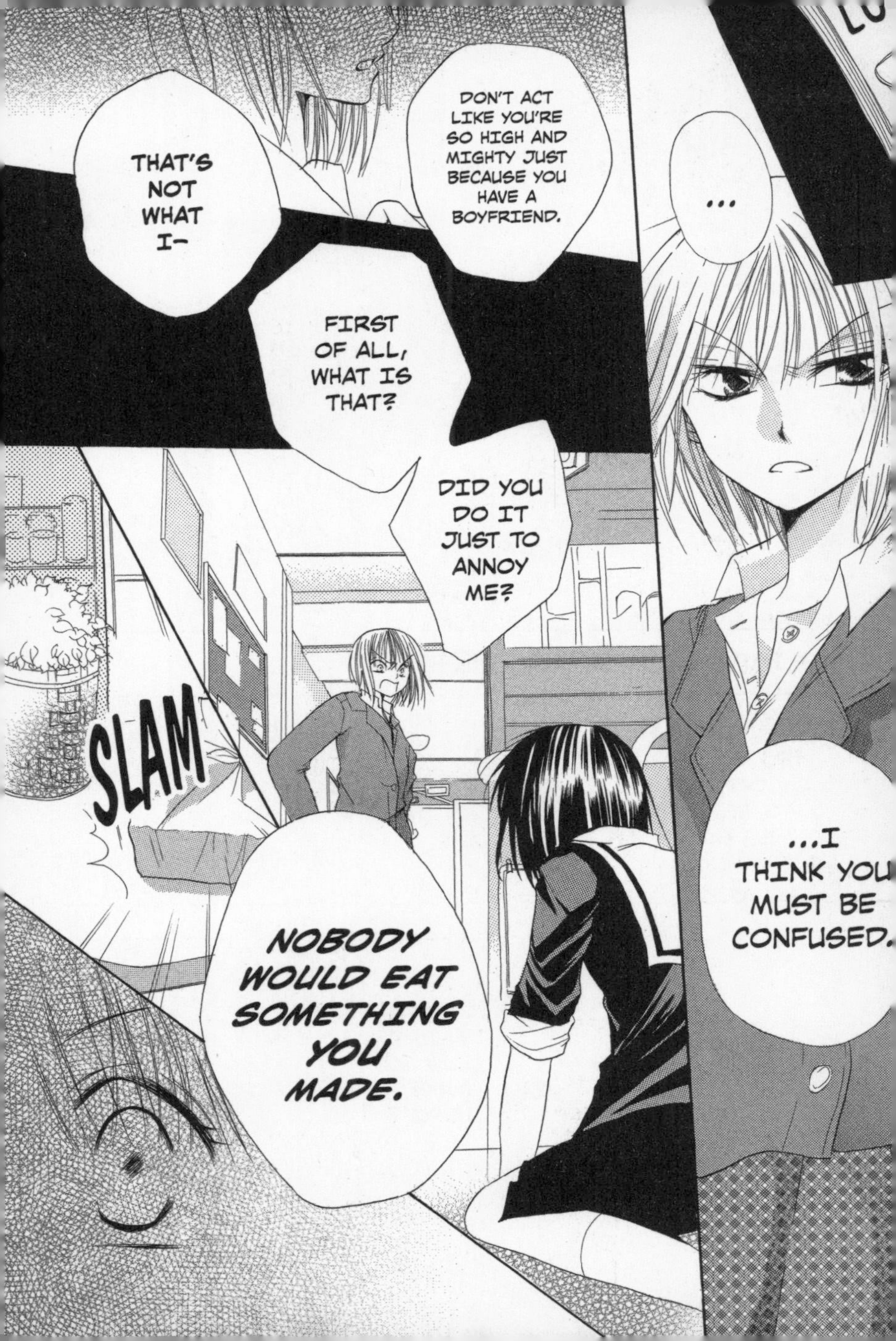
...
...I THINK YOU MUST BE CONFUSED.
DON'T ACT LIKE YOU'RE SO HIGH AND MIGHTY JUST BECAUSE YOU HAVE A BOYFRIEND.
THAT'S NOT WHAT I-
FIRST OF ALL, WHAT IS THAT?
DID YOU DO IT JUST TO ANNOY ME?
SLAM
NOBODY WOULD EAT SOMETHING YOU MADE.

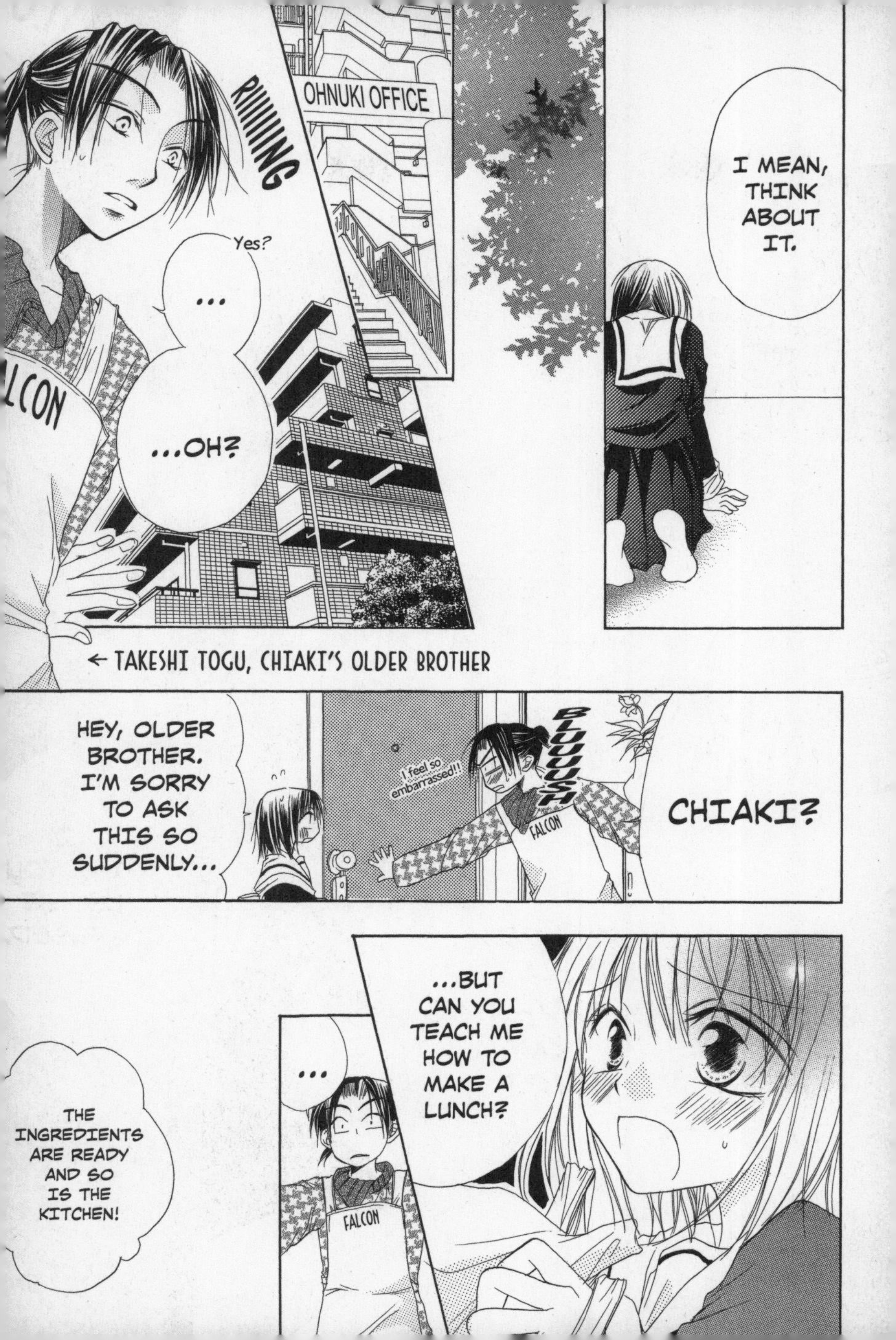
I MEAN, THINK ABOUT IT.
OHNUKI OFFICE
RIIIING
Yes?
...
...OH?
← TAKESHI TOGU, CHIAKI'S OLDER BROTHER
CHIAKI?
BLUUUUSH
I feel so embarrassed!!
HEY, OLDER BROTHER. I'M SORRY TO ASK THIS SO SUDDENLY...
...BUT CAN YOU TEACH ME HOW TO MAKE A LUNCH?
...
THE INGREDIENTS ARE READY AND SO IS THE KITCHEN!

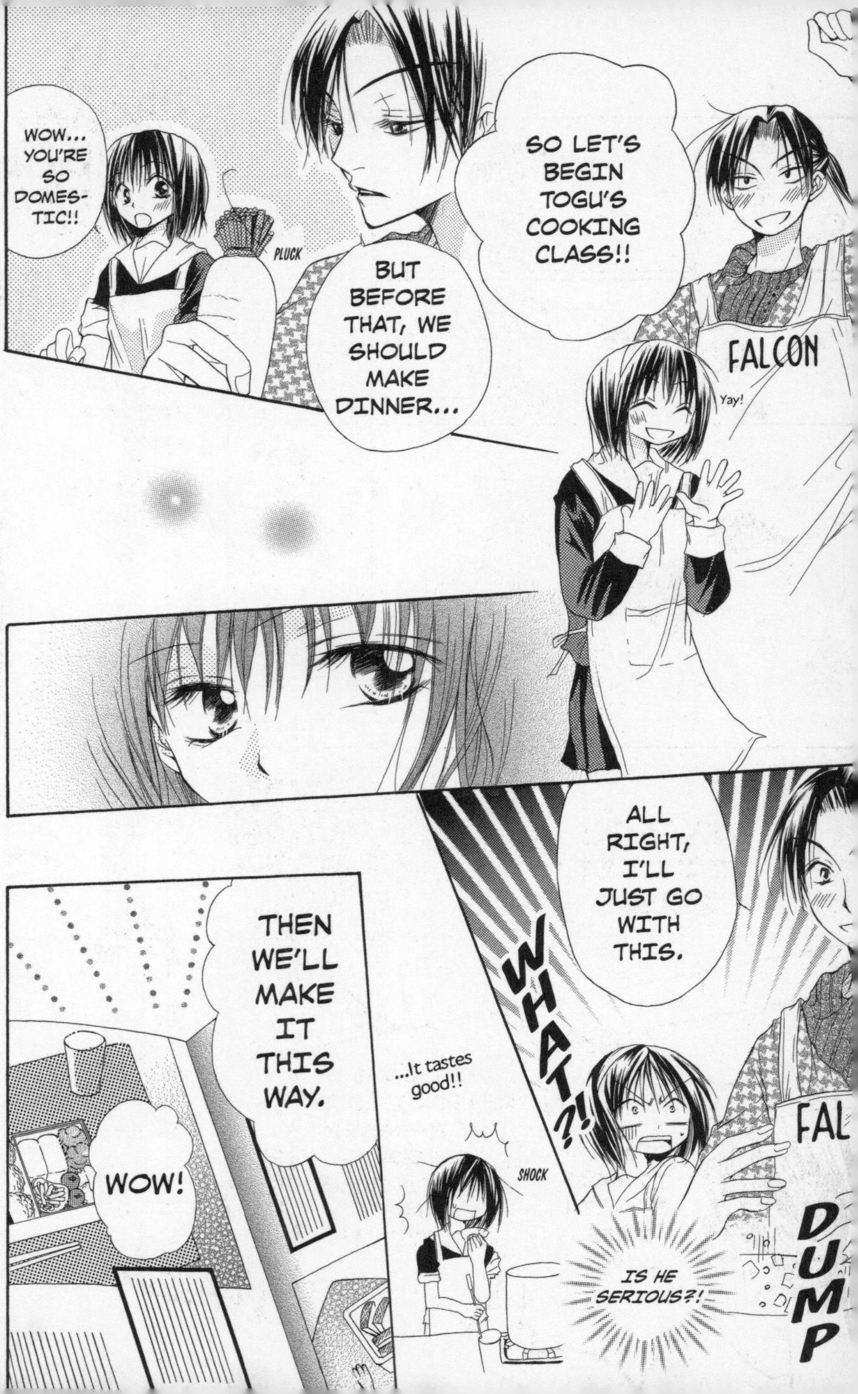
SO LET'S BEGIN TOGU'S COOKING CLASS!!
FALCON
Yay!
BUT BEFORE THAT, WE SHOULD MAKE DINNER...
PLUCK
WOW... YOU'RE SO DOMES-TIC!!
ALL RIGHT, I'LL JUST GO WITH THIS.
WHAT?!
FAL
DUMP
IS HE SERIOUS?!
SHOCK
...It tastes good!!
THEN WE'LL MAKE IT THIS WAY.
WOW!

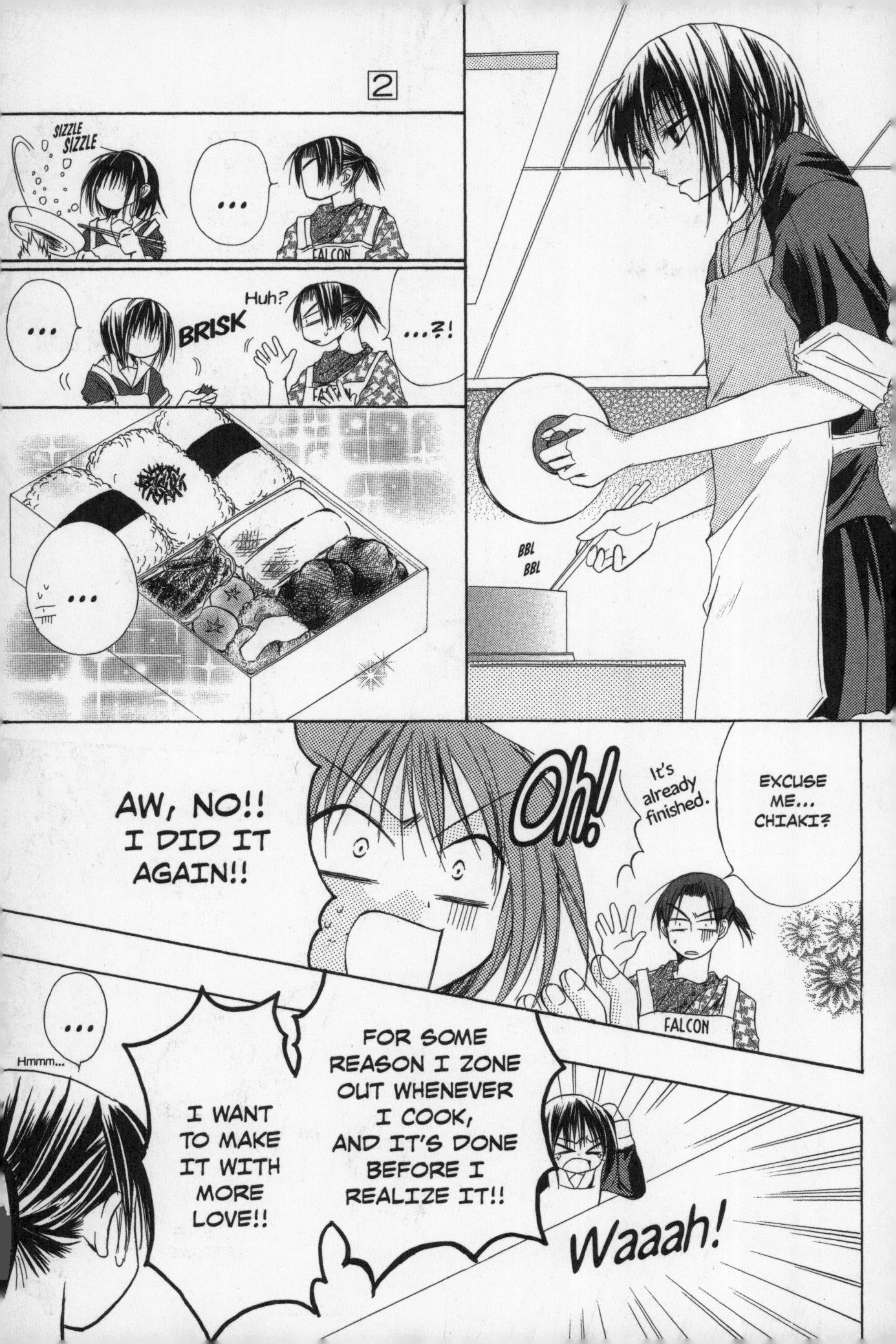
BBL
BBL
2
SIZZLE
SIZZLE
...
...?!
Huh?
BRISK
...
FALCON
...
EXCUSE ME... CHIAKI?
It's already finished.
Oh!
AW, NO!! I DID IT AGAIN!!
FALCON
Waaah!
FOR SOME REASON I ZONE OUT WHENEVER I COOK, AND IT'S DONE BEFORE I REALIZE IT!!
I WANT TO MAKE IT WITH MORE LOVE!!
...
Hmmm...

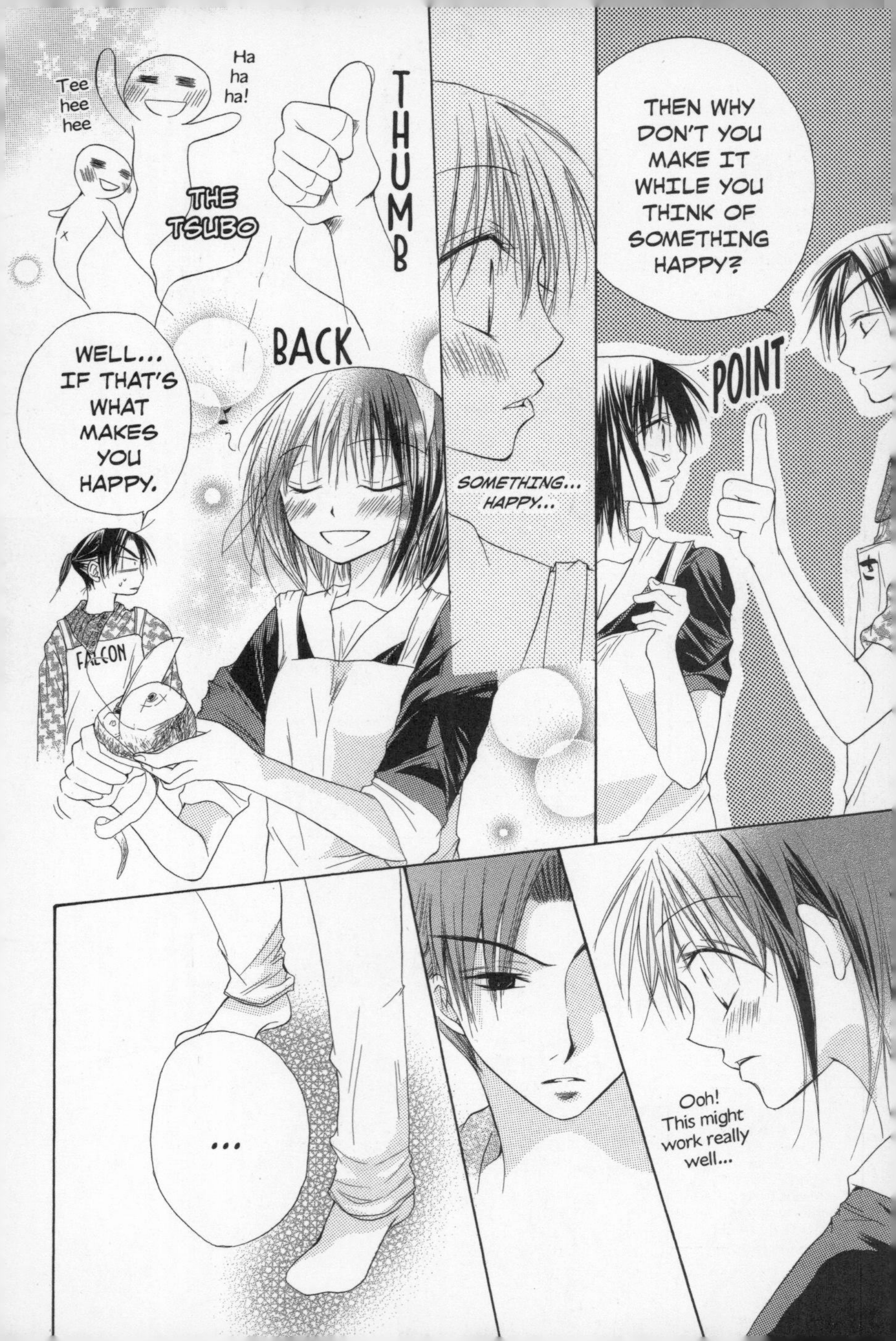

THEN WHY DON'T YOU MAKE IT WHILE YOU THINK OF SOMETHING HAPPY?
POINT
SOMETHING... HAPPY...
THUMB
Ha ha ha!
Tee hee hee
THE TSUBO
BACK
WELL... IF THAT'S WHAT MAKES YOU HAPPY.
FALCON
Ooh! This might work really well...
...

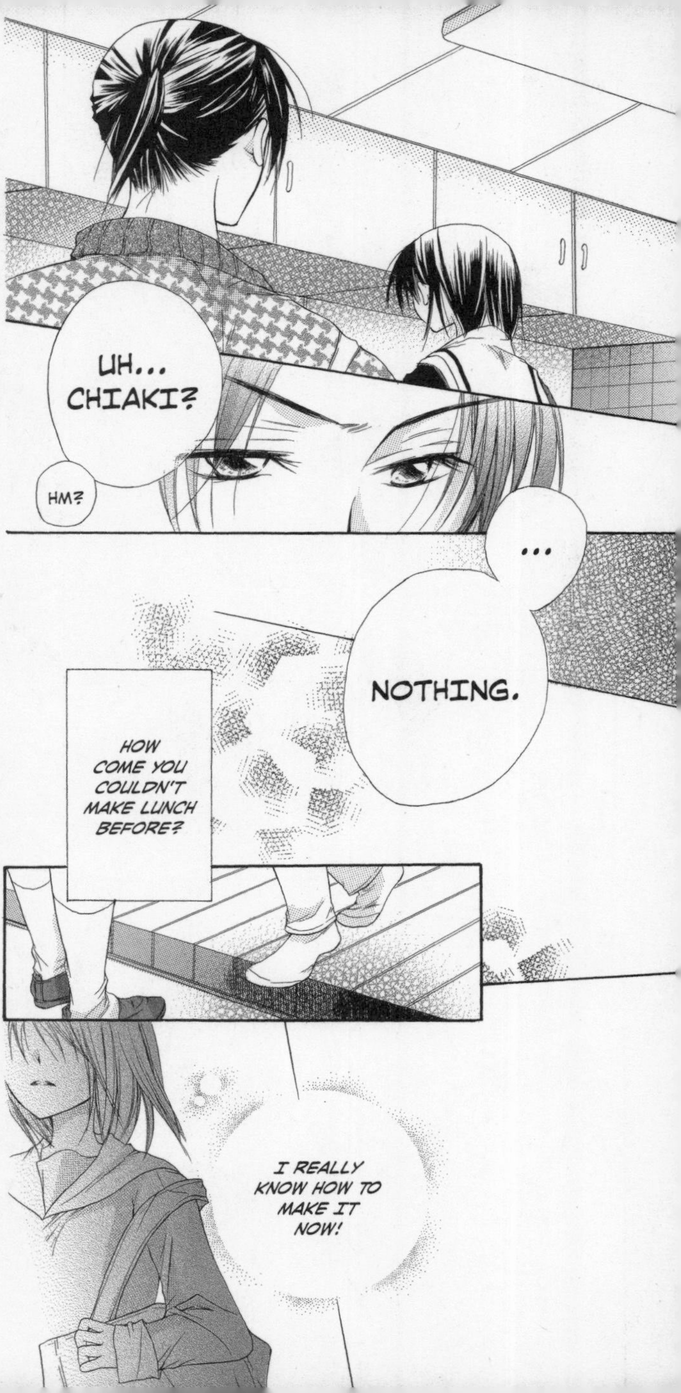
UH... CHIAKI?
HM?
...
NOTHING.
HOW COME YOU COULDN'T MAKE LUNCH BEFORE?
I REALLY KNOW HOW TO MAKE IT NOW!

An Assistant Arrived!

Actually, she was a friend. It was really fun, because we did things like go to a beef-bowl restaurant in the morning and a bento-box place and a donut store at night.

I will never forget her words: "After finishing this assistant job, I'll first go home and then go to my part-time job."
SUCH A HARD WORKER...
The Intense Pre-Deadline Crunch

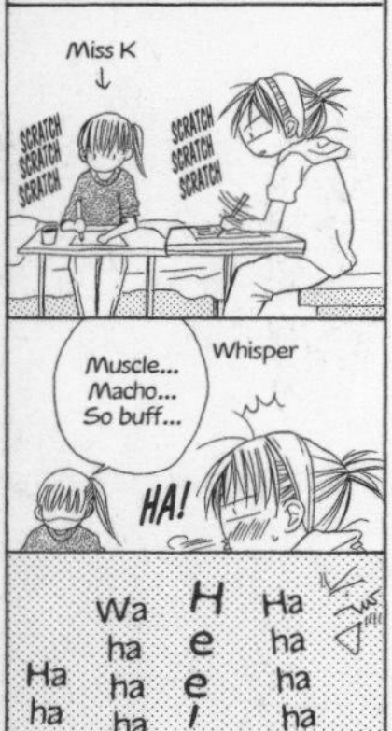
Miss K
SCRATCH SCRATCH SCRATCH
SCRATCH SCRATCH SCRATCH
Whisper
Muscle... Macho... So buff...
HA!
Ha ha ha ha ha!
Hee!
Wa ha ha ha ha ha ha!
Wa ha ha!
Ha ha ha ha ha ha ha!
...
What was so funny about that anyway?
Who knows?

REPEAT AD NAUSEUM.

I really do wonder what was funny about it... Anyway, several days later, Miss K bought a muscle manga... That's great! ☆

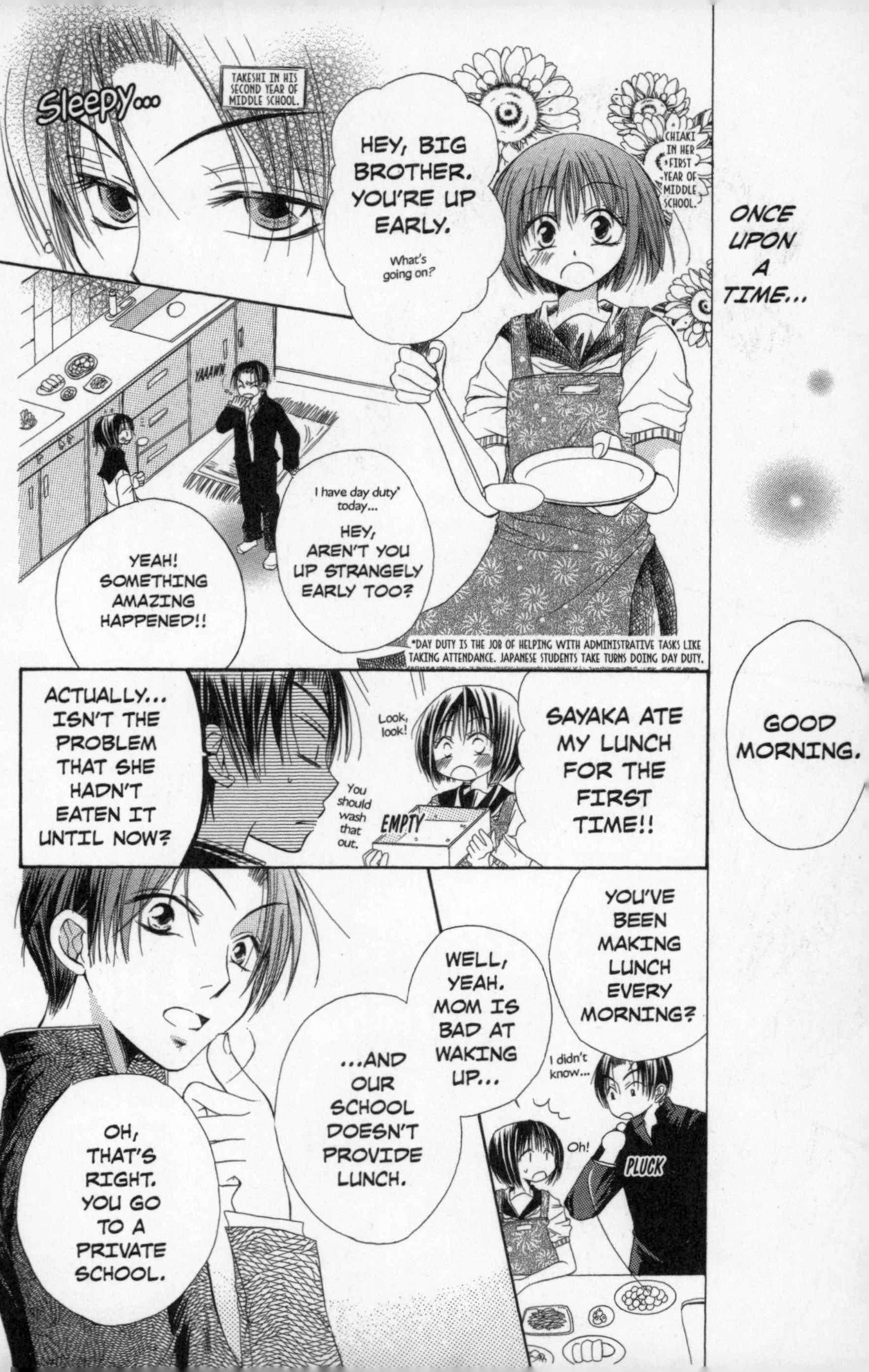
ONCE UPON A TIME...
GOOD MORNING.
CHIAKI IN HER FIRST YEAR OF MIDDLE SCHOOL.
HEY, BIG BROTHER. YOU'RE UP EARLY.
What's going on?
TAKESHI IN HIS SECOND YEAR OF MIDDLE SCHOOL.
Sleepy...
YAAAWN
I have day duty* today...
HEY, AREN'T YOU UP STRANGELY EARLY TOO?
YEAH! SOMETHING AMAZING HAPPENED!!
*DAY DUTY IS THE JOB OF HELPING WITH ADMINISTRATIVE TASKS LIKE TAKING ATTENDANCE. JAPANESE STUDENTS TAKE TURNS DOING DAY DUTY.
SAYAKA ATE MY LUNCH FOR THE FIRST TIME!!
Look, look!
EMPTY
You should wash that out.
ACTUALLY... ISN'T THE PROBLEM THAT SHE HADN'T EATEN IT UNTIL NOW?
YOU'VE BEEN MAKING LUNCH EVERY MORNING?
I didn't know...
PLUCK
Oh!
WELL, YEAH. MOM IS BAD AT WAKING UP...
...AND OUR SCHOOL DOESN'T PROVIDE LUNCH.
OH, THAT'S RIGHT. YOU GO TO A PRIVATE SCHOOL.

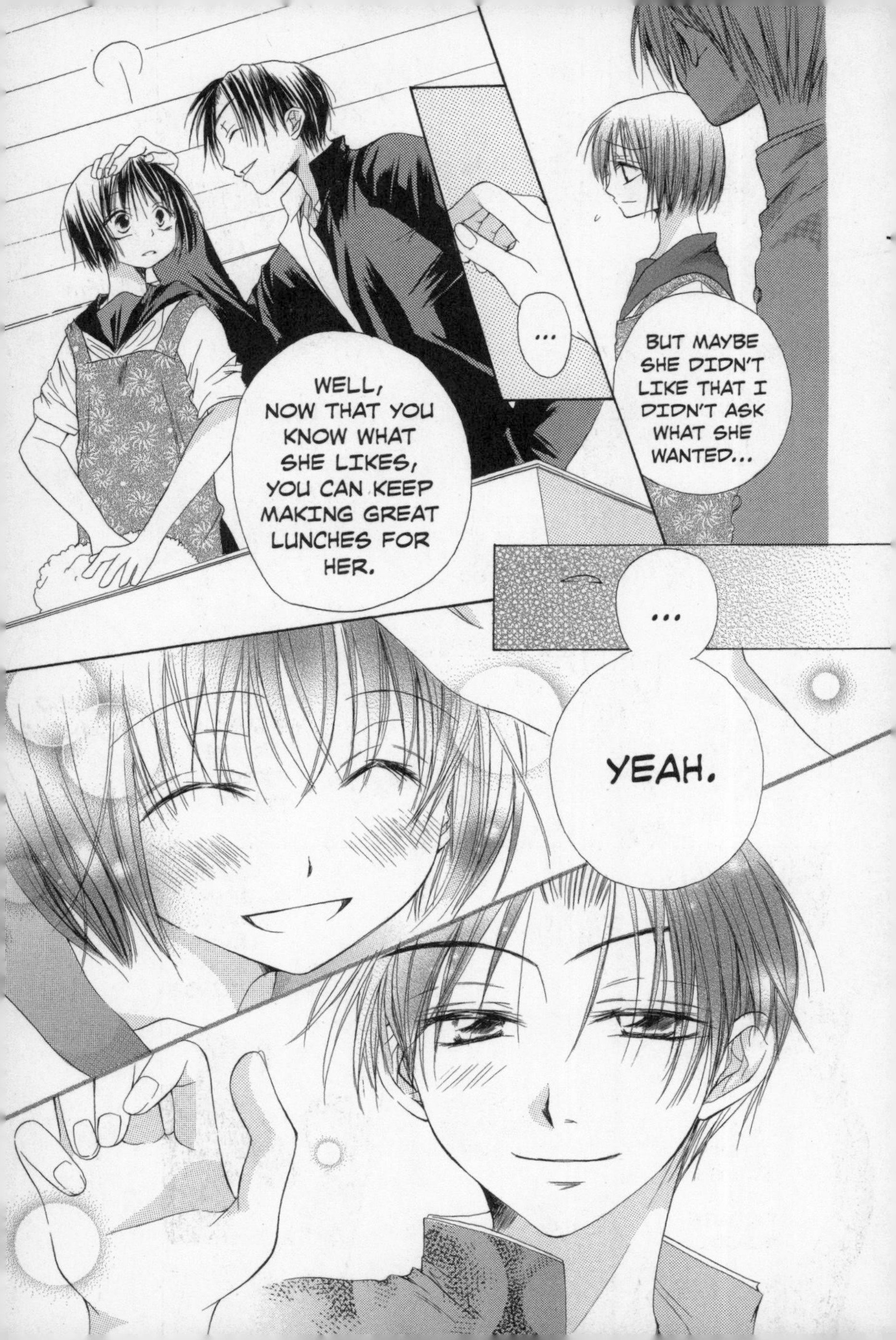
BUT MAYBE SHE DIDN'T LIKE THAT I DIDN'T ASK WHAT SHE WANTED...
...
WELL, NOW THAT YOU KNOW WHAT SHE LIKES, YOU CAN KEEP MAKING GREAT LUNCHES FOR HER.
...
YEAH.

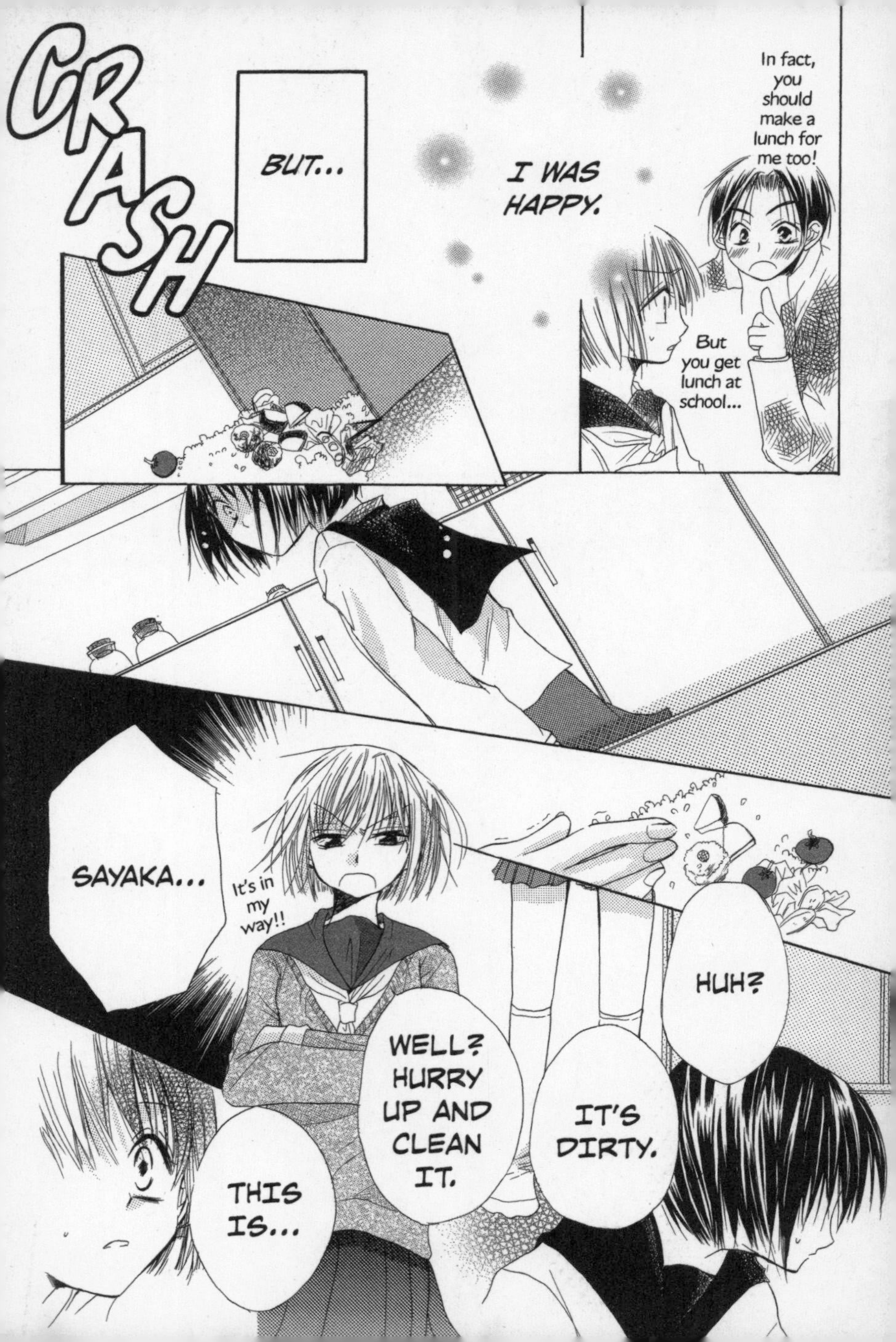
In fact, you should make a lunch for me too!
But you get lunch at school...
I WAS HAPPY.
BUT...
CRASH
HUH?
It's in my way!!
IT'S DIRTY.
WELL? HURRY UP AND CLEAN IT.
THIS IS...
SAYAKA...

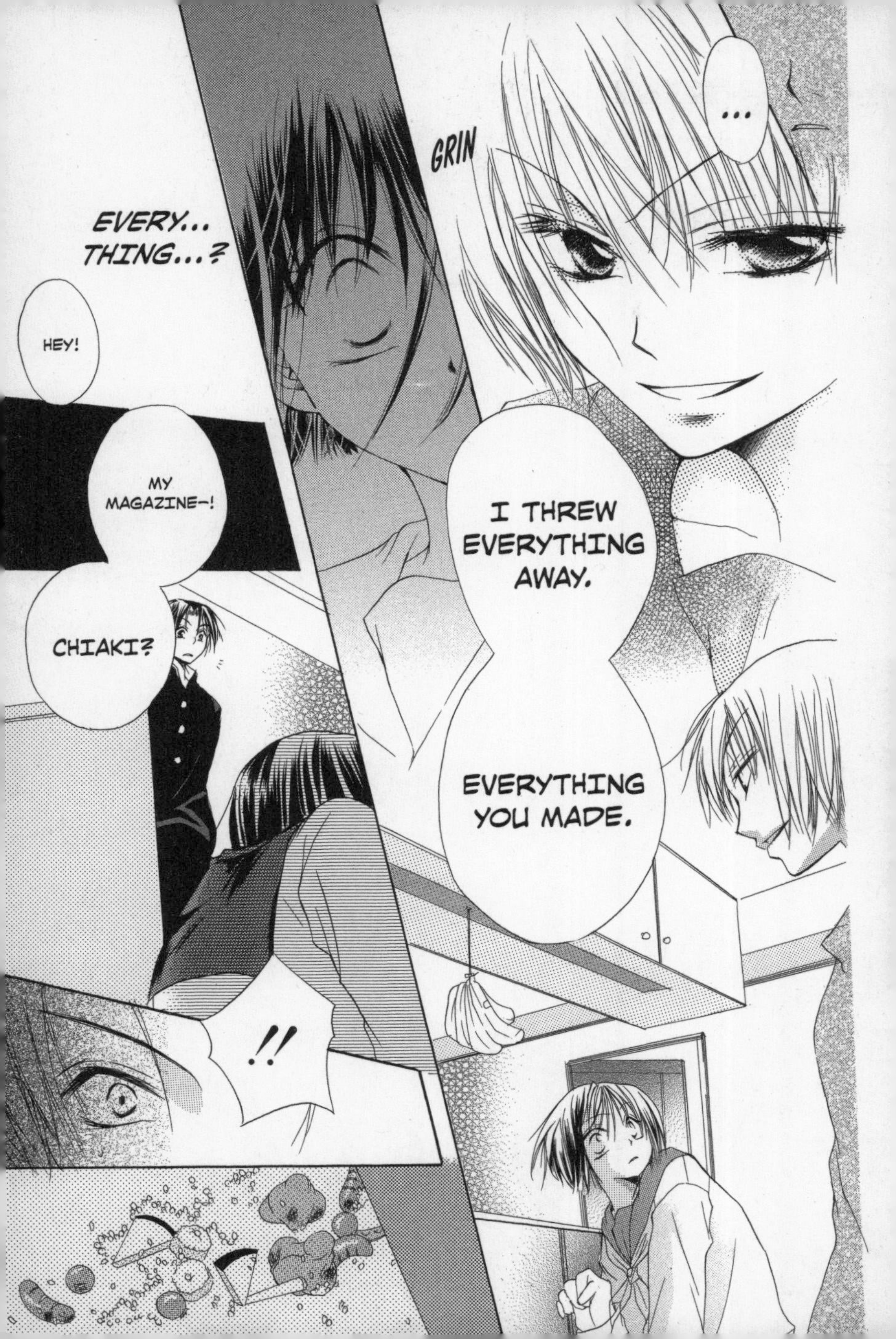
...
GRIN
I THREW EVERYTHING AWAY.
EVERYTHING YOU MADE.
EVERY... THING...?
HEY!
MY MAGAZINE--!
CHIAKI?
!!

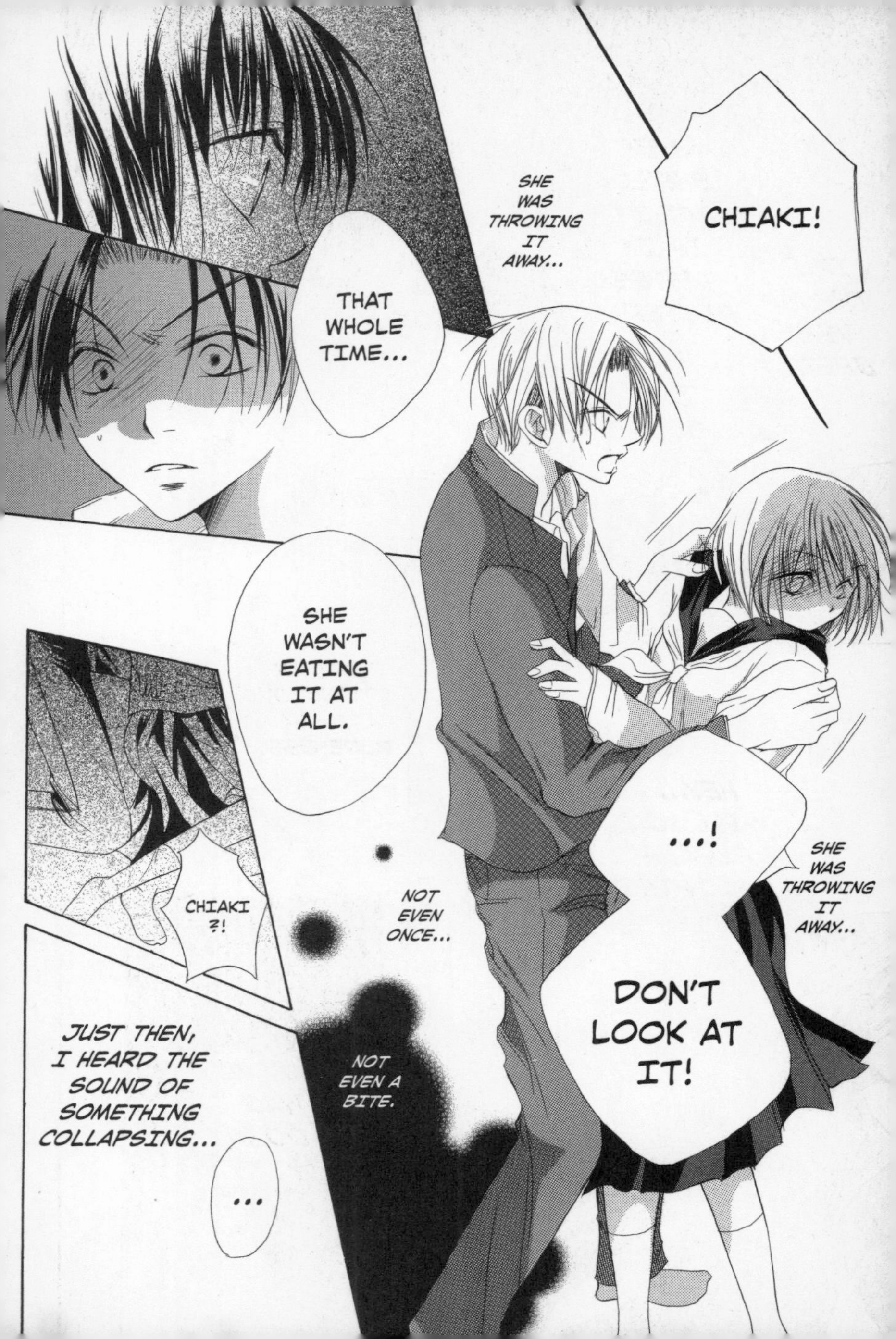
CHIAKI!
SHE WAS THROWING IT AWAY...
...!
SHE WAS THROWING IT AWAY...
DON'T LOOK AT IT!
NOT EVEN ONCE...
NOT EVEN A BITE.
THAT WHOLE TIME...
SHE WASN'T EATING IT AT ALL.
CHIAKI ?!
JUST THEN, I HEARD THE SOUND OF SOMETHING COLLAPSING...
...

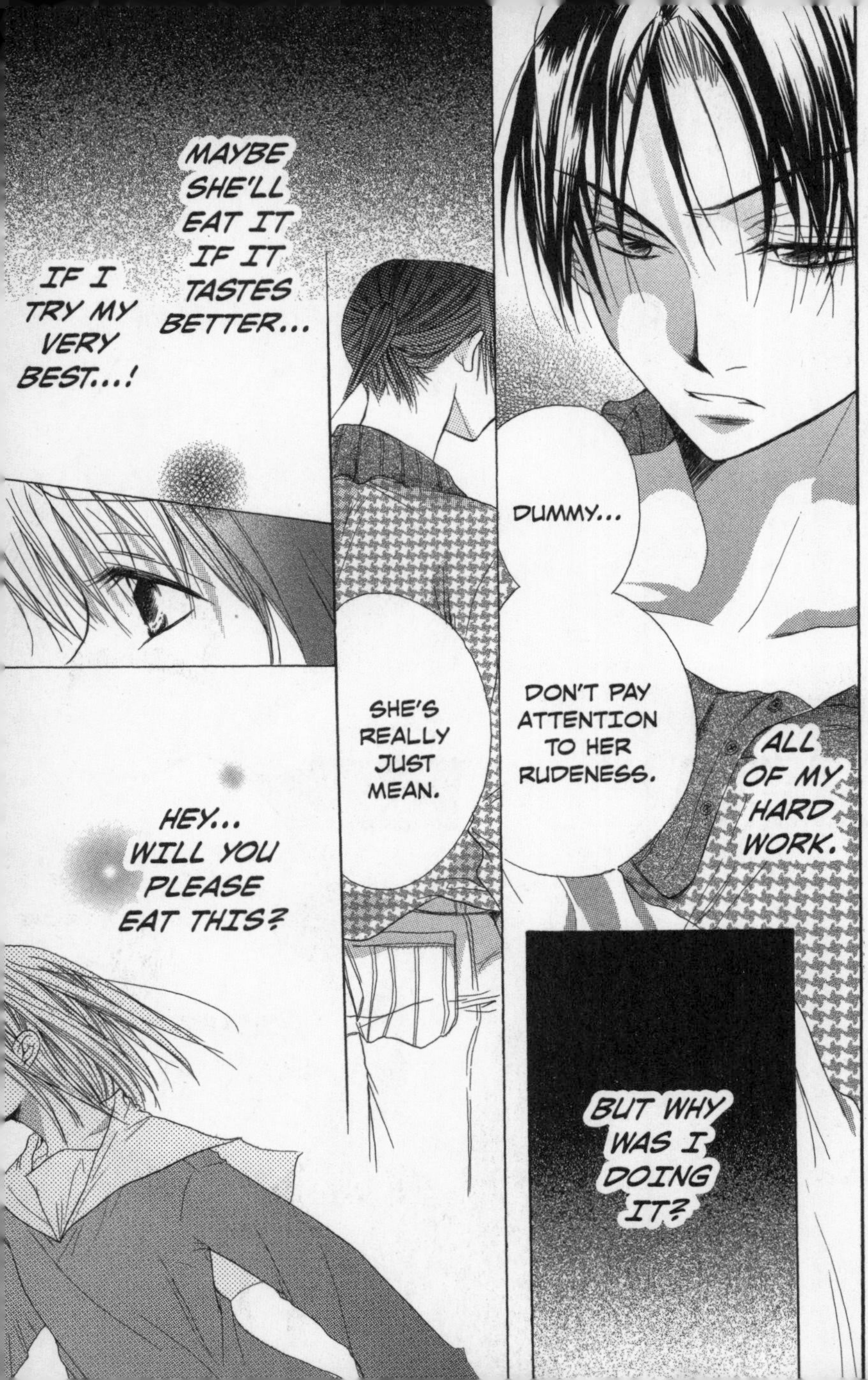
DUMMY...
DON'T PAY ATTENTION TO HER RUDENESS.
ALL OF MY HARD WORK.
BUT WHY WAS I DOING IT?
SHE'S REALLY JUST MEAN.
MAYBE SHE'LL EAT IT IF IT TASTES BETTER...
IF I TRY MY VERY BEST...!
HEY... WILL YOU PLEASE EAT THIS?

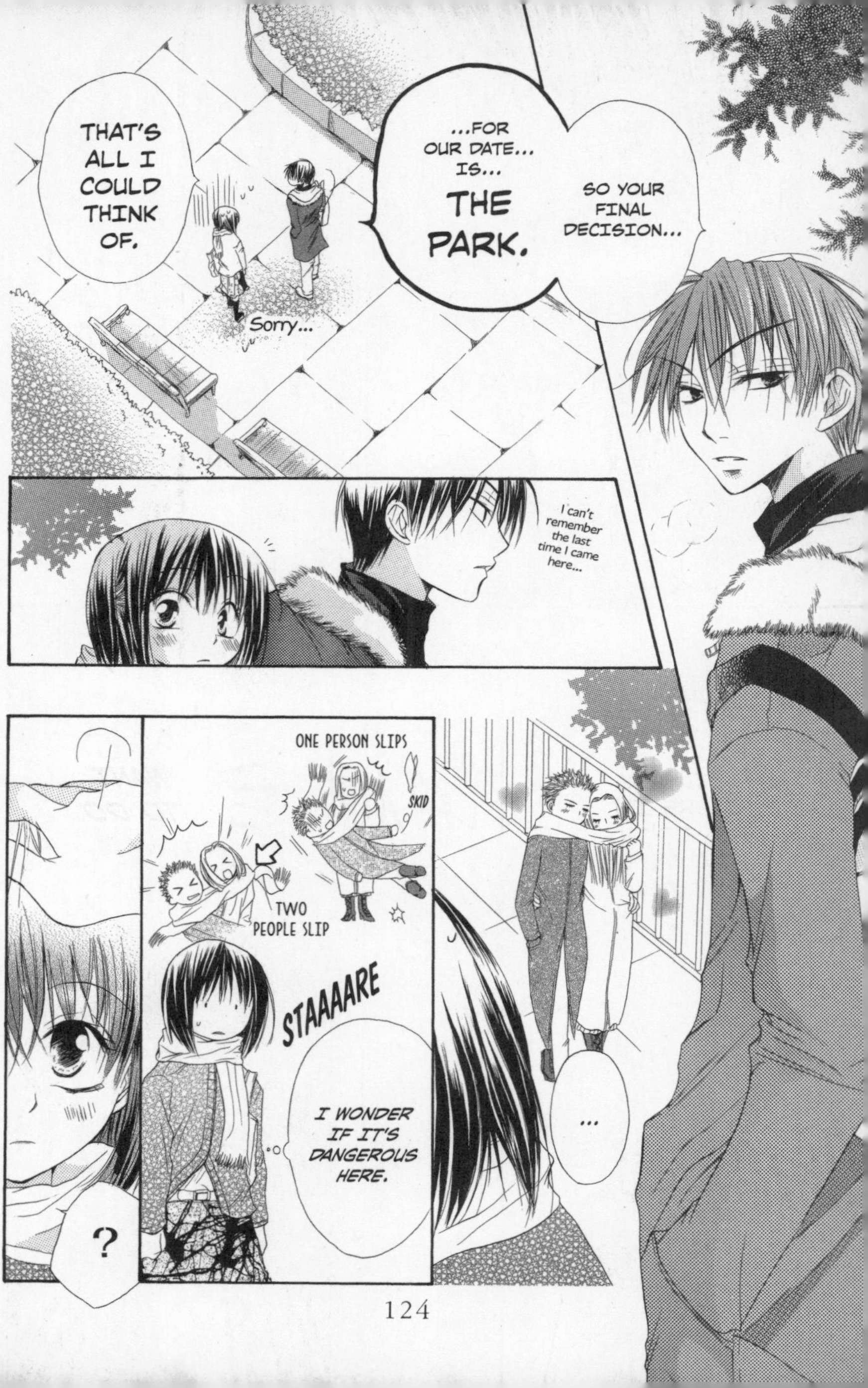
SO YOUR FINAL DECISION...
...FOR OUR DATE... IS... THE PARK.
THAT'S ALL I COULD THINK OF.
Sorry...
I can't remember the last time I came here...
...
ONE PERSON SLIPS
SKID
TWO PEOPLE SLIP
STAAAARE
I WONDER IF IT'S DANGEROUS HERE.
?

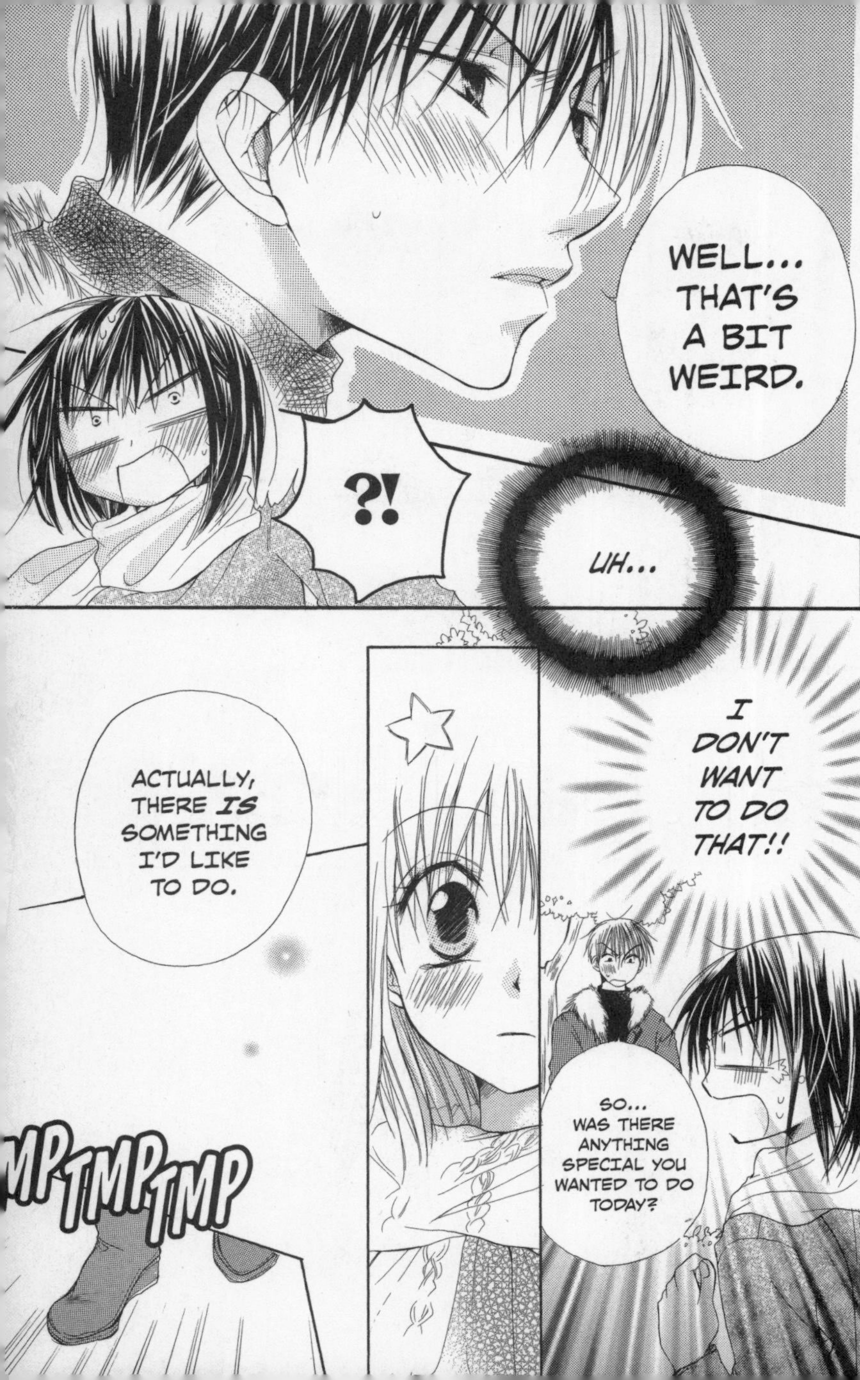
WELL... THAT'S A BIT WEIRD.
?!
UH...
I DON'T WANT TO DO THAT!!
SO... WAS THERE ANYTHING SPECIAL YOU WANTED TO DO TODAY?
ACTUALLY, THERE IS SOMETHING I'D LIKE TO DO.
MP TMP TMP

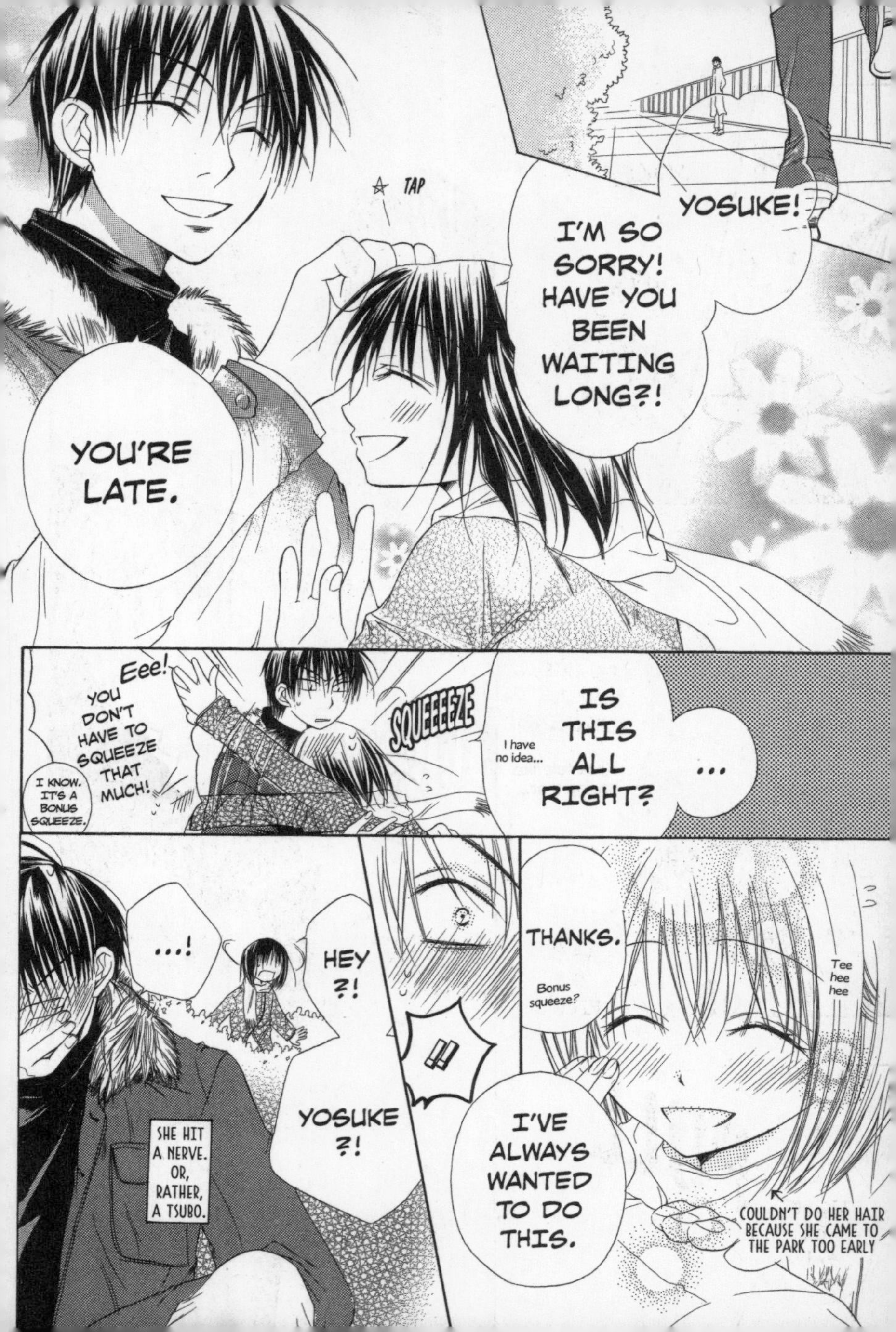
YOSUKE!
I'M SO SORRY! HAVE YOU BEEN WAITING LONG?!
TAP
YOU'RE LATE.
...
IS THIS ALL RIGHT?
I have no idea...
SQUEEEEZE
Eee! YOU DON'T HAVE TO SQUEEZE THAT MUCH!
I KNOW. IT'S A BONUS SQUEEZE.
THANKS.
Bonus squeeze?
Tee hee hee
I'VE ALWAYS WANTED TO DO THIS.
COULDN'T DO HER HAIR BECAUSE SHE CAME TO THE PARK TOO EARLY
!!
HEY?!
YOSUKE?!
...!
SHE HIT A NERVE. OR, RATHER, A TSUBO.

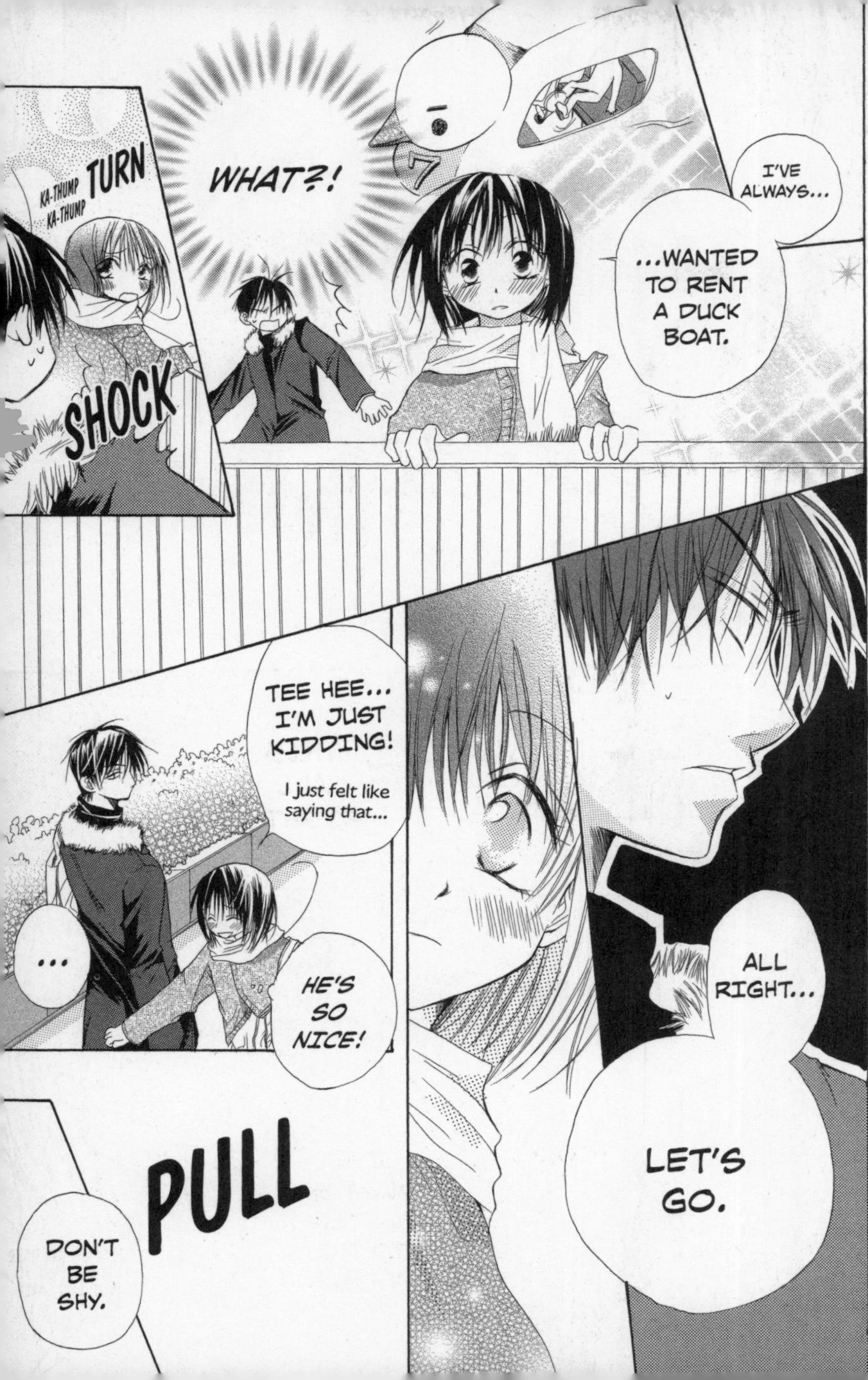
I'VE ALWAYS...
...WANTED TO RENT A DUCK BOAT.
WHAT?!
KA-THUMP KA-THUMP
TURN
SHOCK
ALL RIGHT...
LET'S GO.
TEE HEE... I'M JUST KIDDING!
I just felt like saying that...
HE'S SO NICE!
...
PULL
DON'T BE SHY.

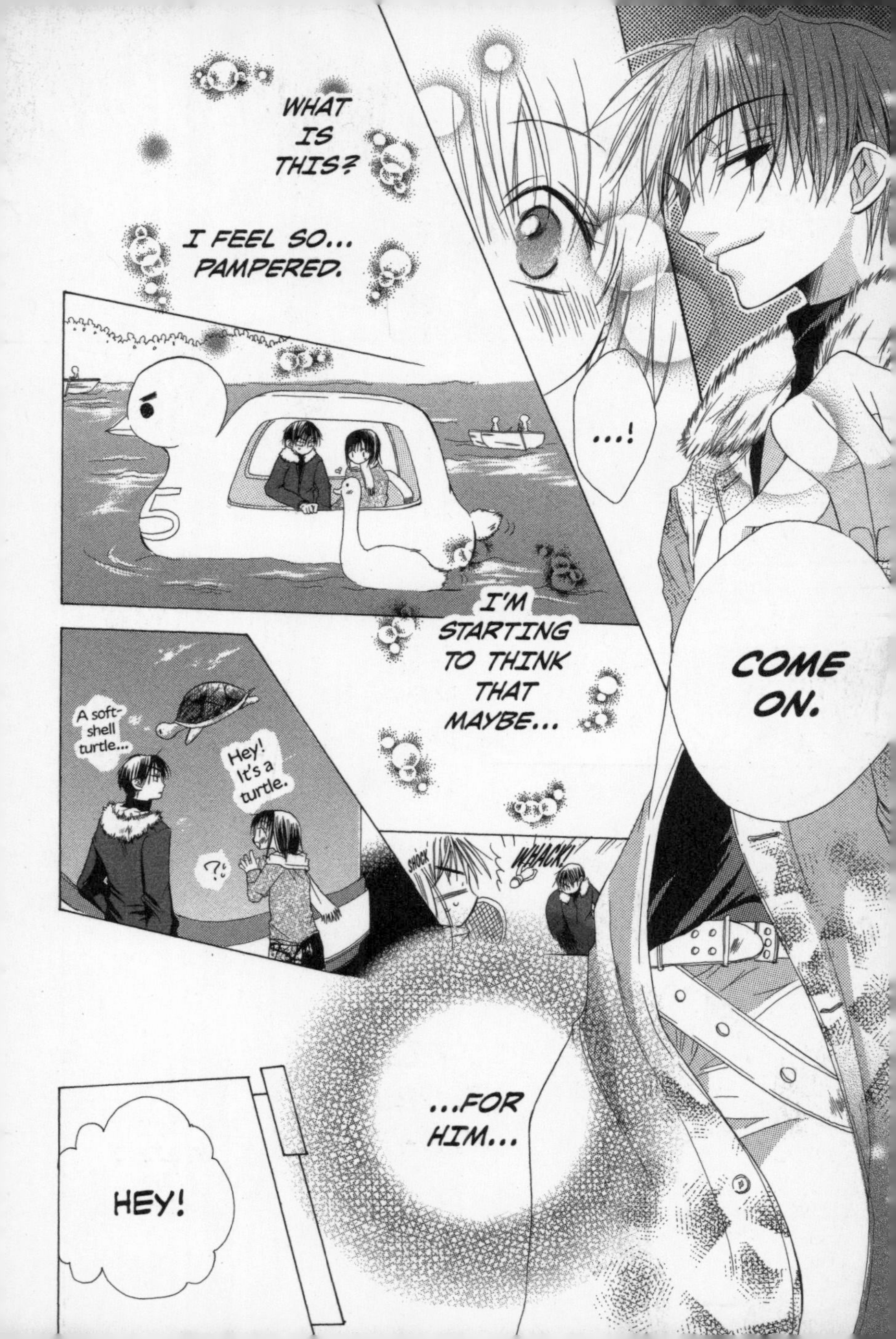
WHAT IS THIS?
I FEEL SO... PAMPERED.
Hey! It's a turtle.
A soft-shell turtle...
?!
SHOCK
WHACK!
I'M STARTING TO THINK THAT MAYBE...
...FOR HIM...
HEY!
...!
COME ON.

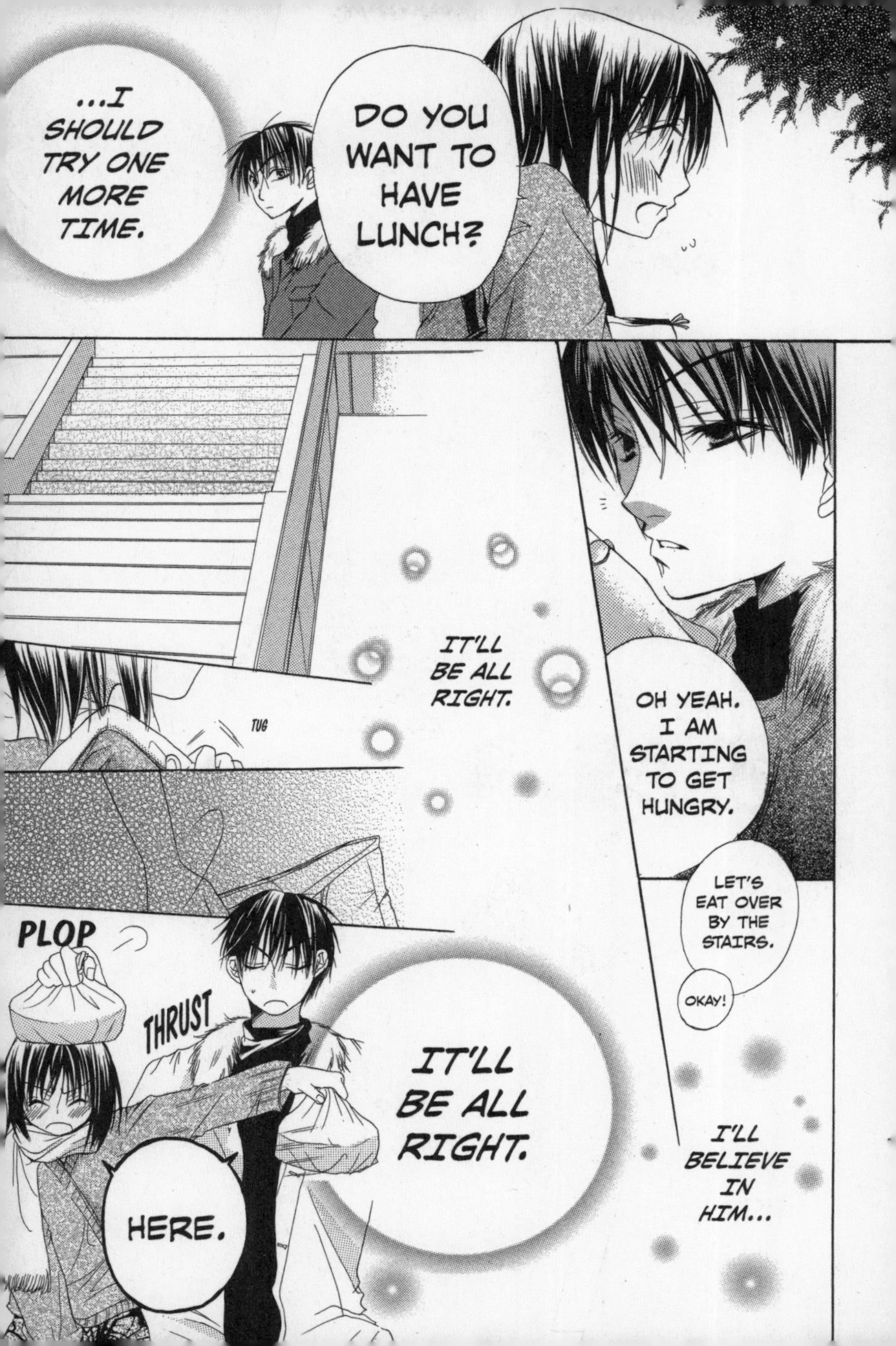
...I SHOULD TRY ONE MORE TIME.
DO YOU WANT TO HAVE LUNCH?
OH YEAH. I AM STARTING TO GET HUNGRY.
LET'S EAT OVER BY THE STAIRS.
OKAY!
I'LL BELIEVE IN HIM...
IT'LL BE ALL RIGHT.
TUG
IT'LL BE ALL RIGHT.
HERE.
THRUST
PLOP

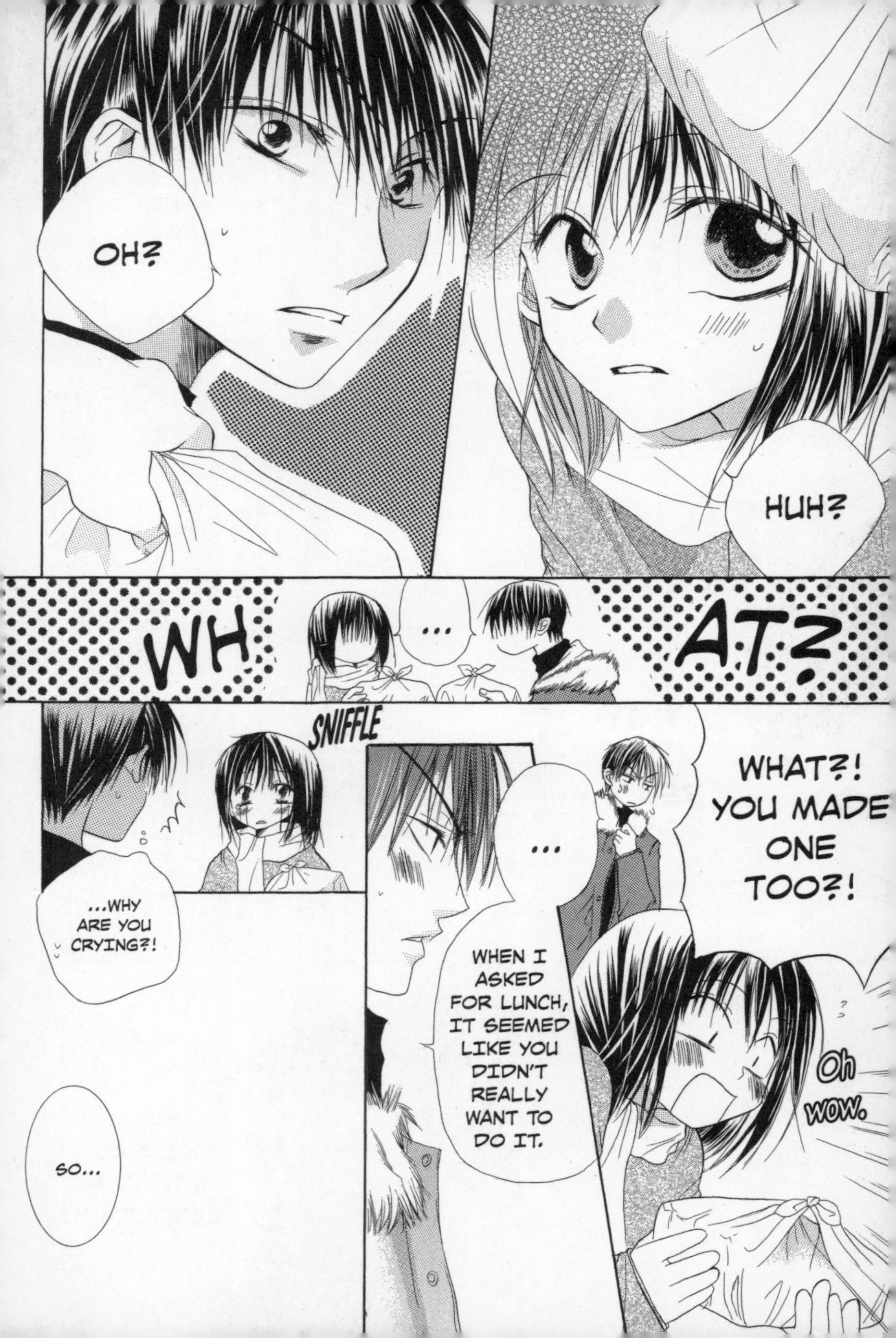
HUH?
OH?
WH
...
AT?
WHAT?! YOU MADE ONE TOO?!
Oh wow.
...
WHEN I ASKED FOR LUNCH, IT SEEMED LIKE YOU DIDN'T REALLY WANT TO DO IT.
SNIFFLE
...WHY ARE YOU CRYING?!
SO...

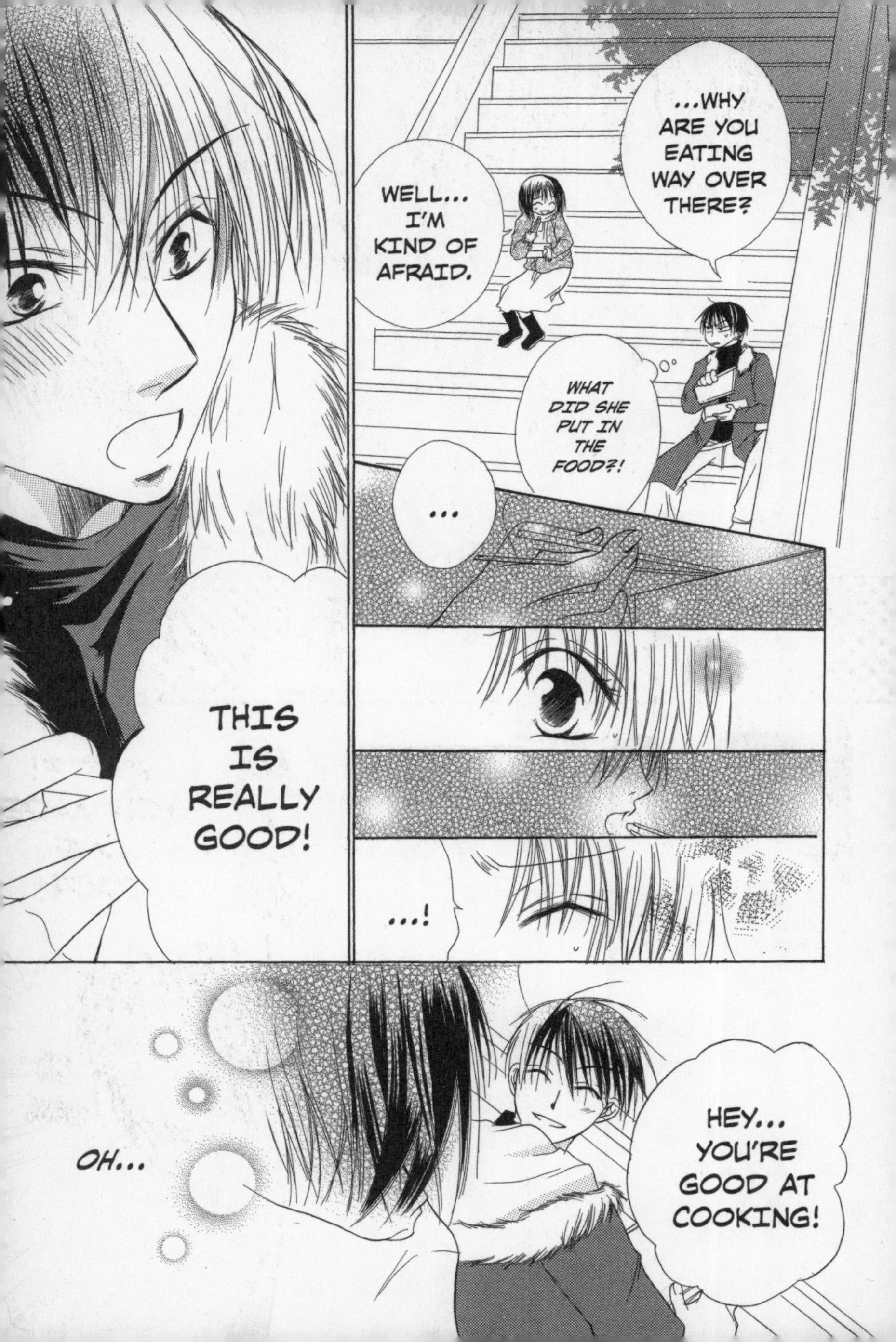
...WHY ARE YOU EATING WAY OVER THERE?
WELL... I'M KIND OF AFRAID.
WHAT DID SHE PUT IN THE FOOD?!
...
...!
THIS IS REALLY GOOD!
HEY... YOU'RE GOOD AT COOKING!
OH...

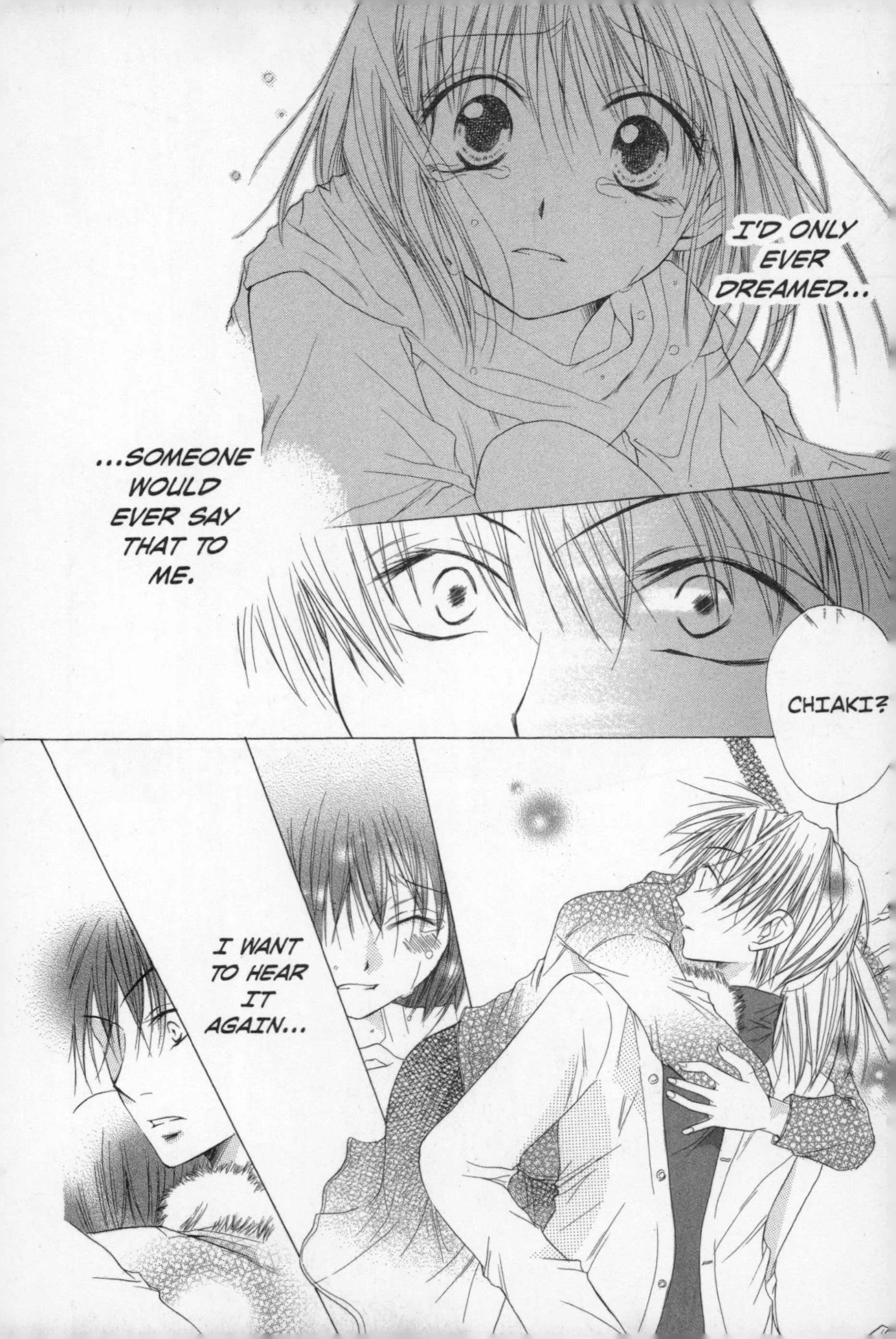
I'D ONLY EVER DREAMED...
...SOMEONE WOULD EVER SAY THAT TO ME.
CHIAKI?
I WANT TO HEAR IT AGAIN...

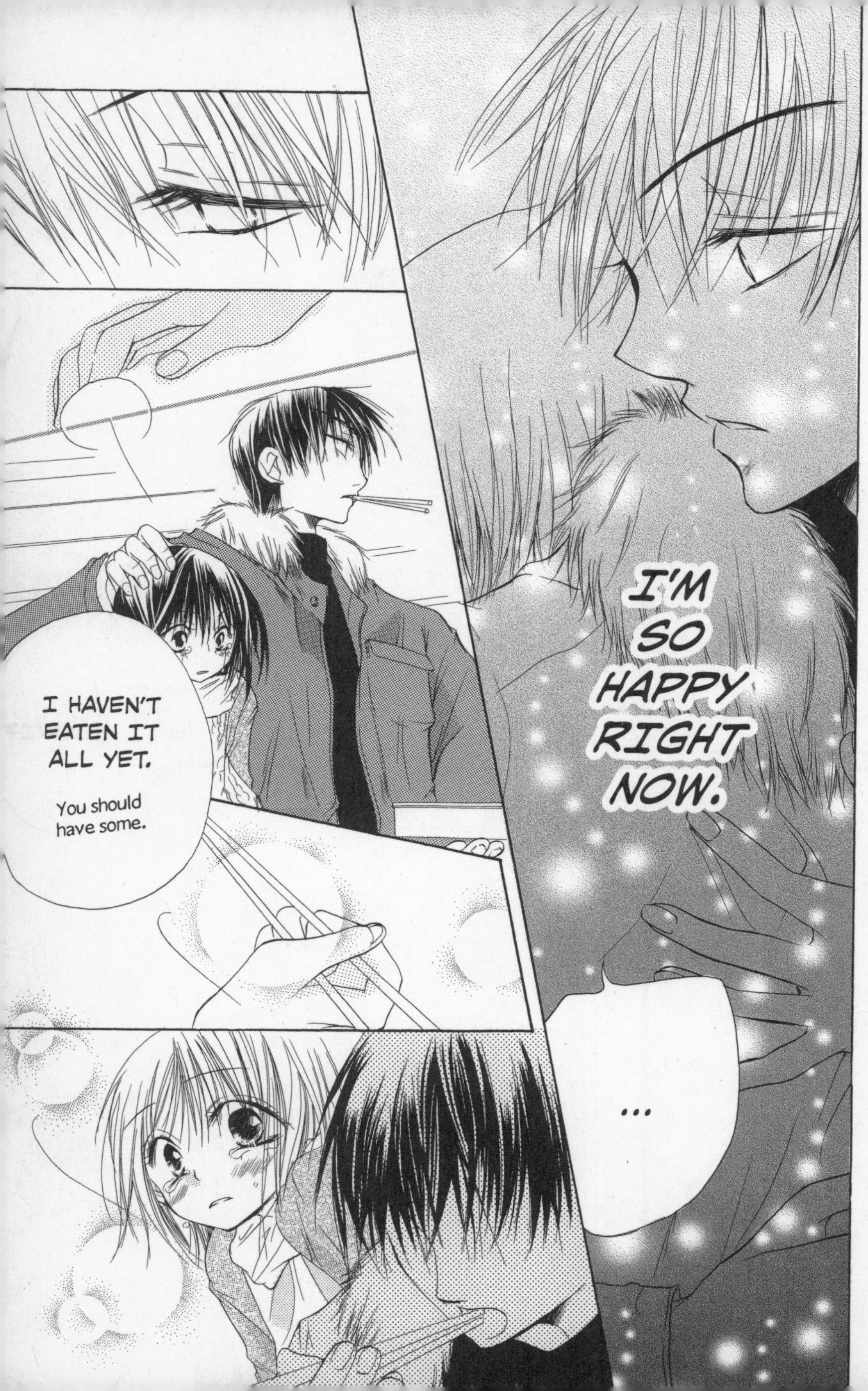

I'M SO HAPPY RIGHT NOW.
...
I HAVEN'T EATEN IT ALL YET.
You should have some.

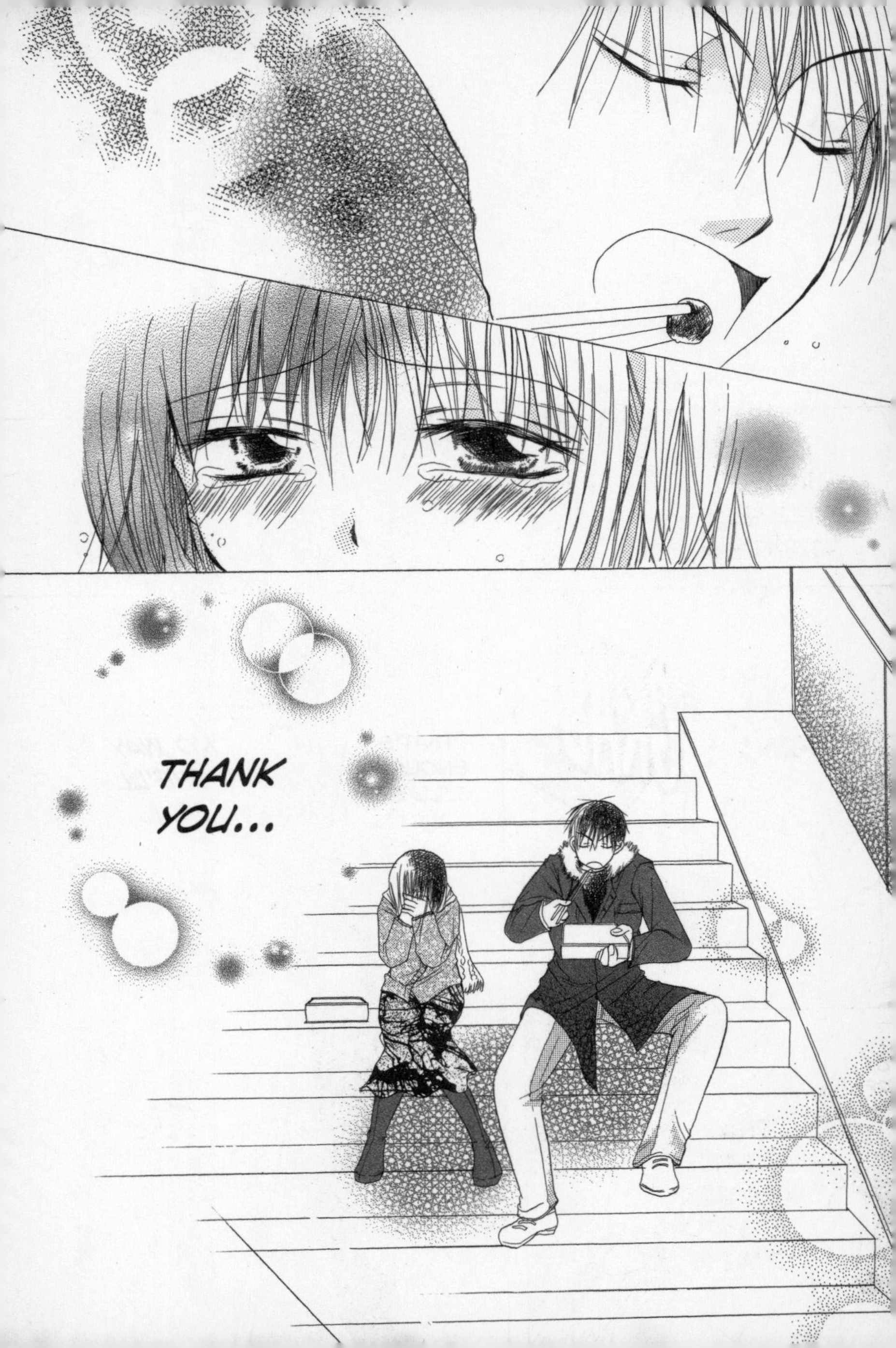
THANK YOU...

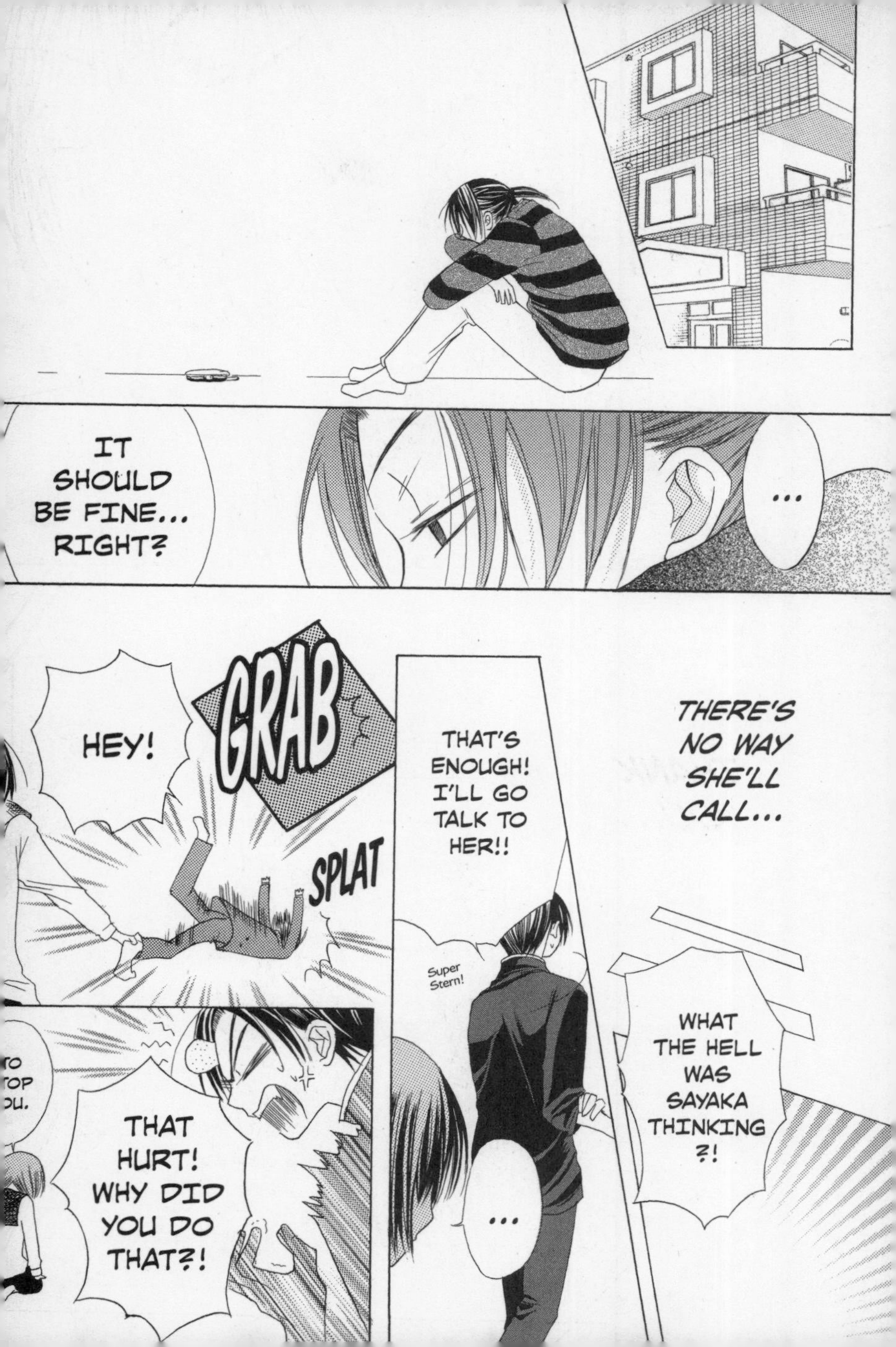
...
IT SHOULD BE FINE... RIGHT?
THERE'S NO WAY SHE'LL CALL...
WHAT THE HELL WAS SAYAKA THINKING?!
THAT'S ENOUGH! I'LL GO TALK TO HER!!
Super Stern!
...
HEY!
GRAB
SPLAT
THAT HURT! WHY DID YOU DO THAT?!

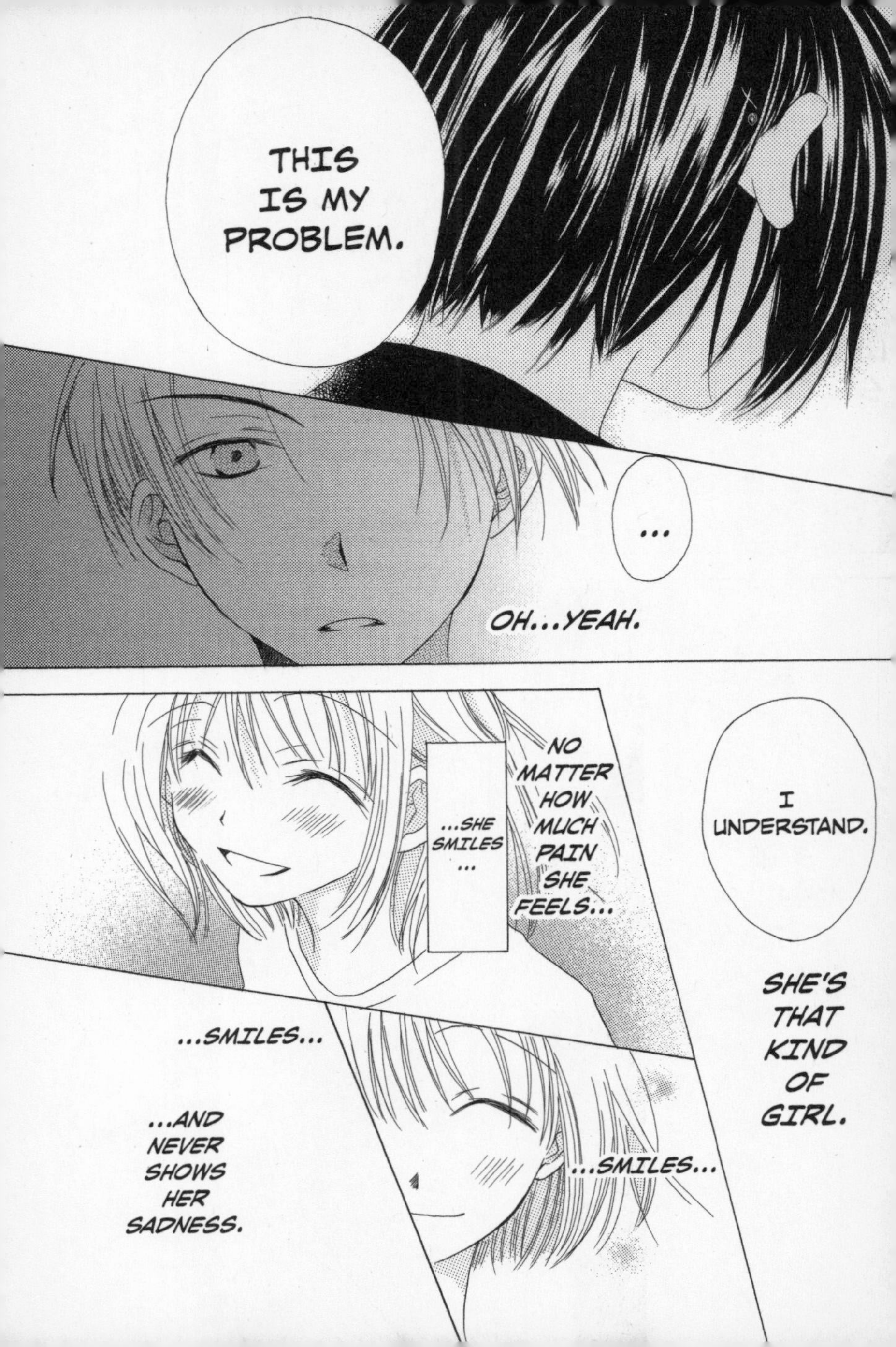

THIS IS MY PROBLEM.
...
OH...YEAH.
I UNDERSTAND.
NO MATTER HOW MUCH PAIN SHE FEELS...
...SHE SMILES...
SHE'S THAT KIND OF GIRL.
...SMILES...
...SMILES...
...AND NEVER SHOWS HER SADNESS.

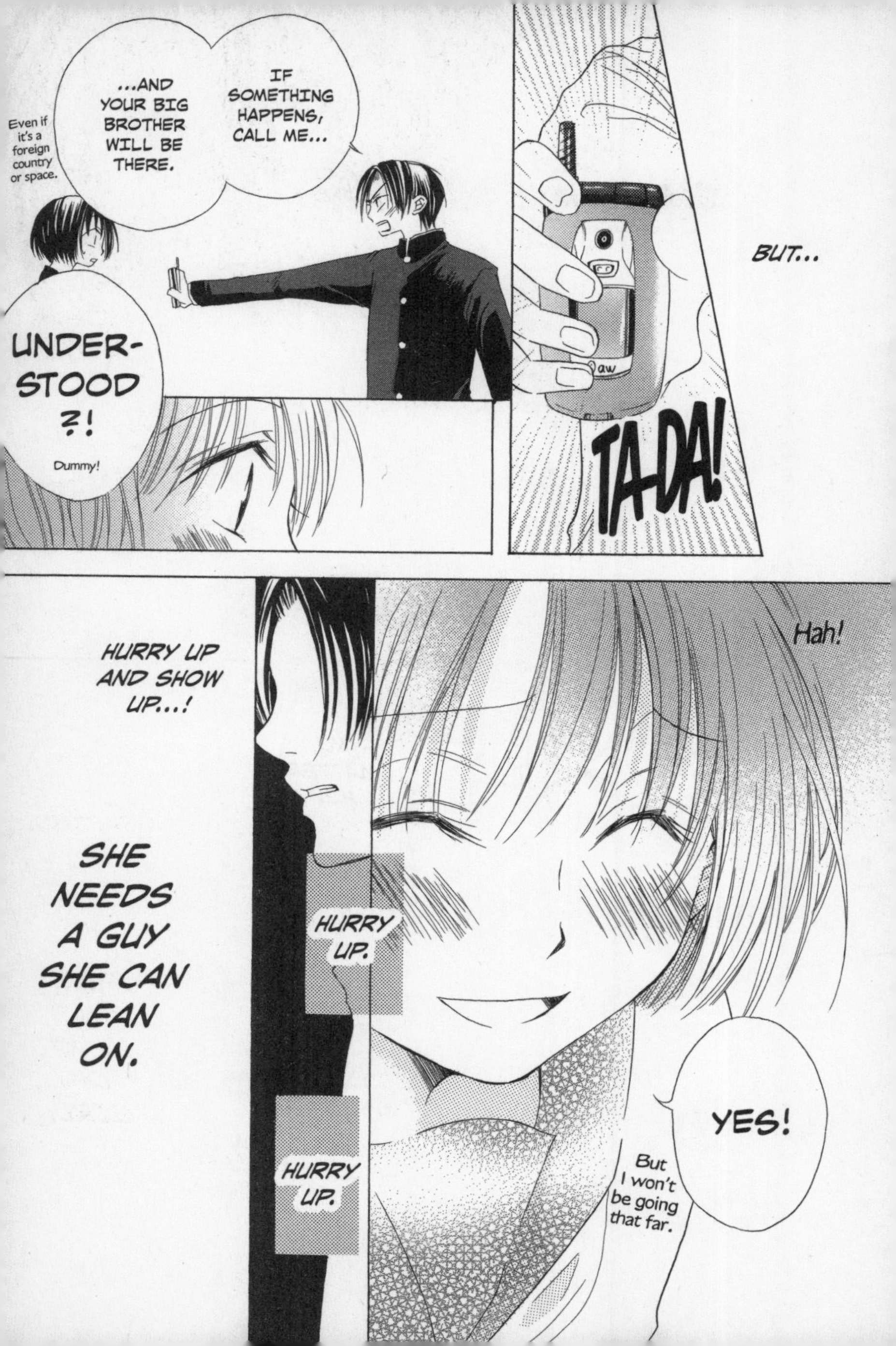
BUT...
TA-DA!
IF SOMETHING HAPPENS, CALL ME...
...AND YOUR BIG BROTHER WILL BE THERE.
Even if it's a foreign country or space.
UNDER-STOOD ?!
Dummy!
Hah!
YES!
But I won't be going that far.
HURRY UP AND SHOW UP...!
SHE NEEDS A GUY SHE CAN LEAN ON.
HURRY UP.
HURRY UP.

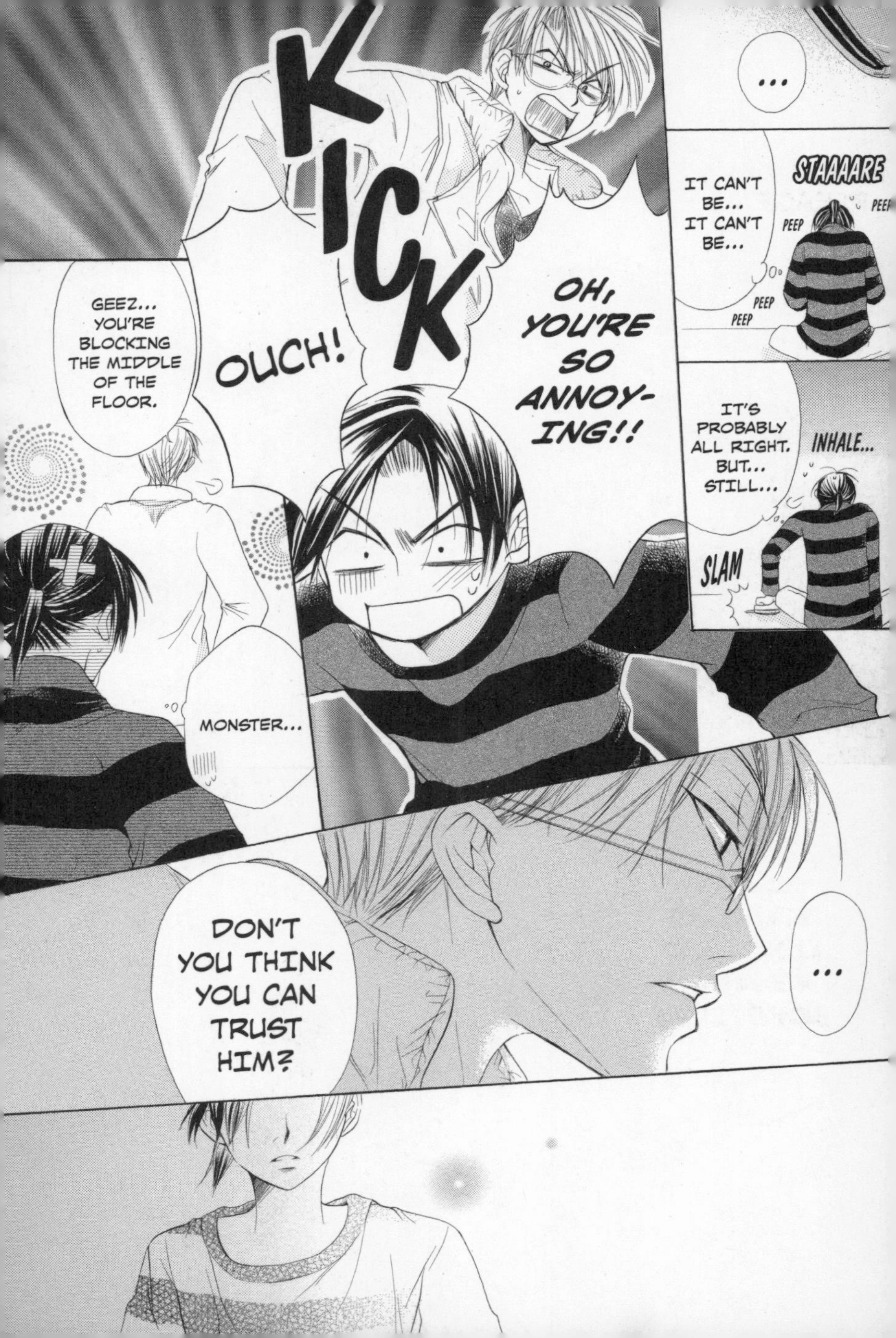
...
STAAAARE
IT CAN'T BE... IT CAN'T BE...
PEEP
PEEP
PEEP
PEEP
INHALE...
IT'S PROBABLY ALL RIGHT. BUT... STILL...
SLAM
KICK
OH, YOU'RE SO ANNOY-ING!!
OUCH!
GEEZ... YOU'RE BLOCKING THE MIDDLE OF THE FLOOR.
MONSTER...
...
DON'T YOU THINK YOU CAN TRUST HIM?

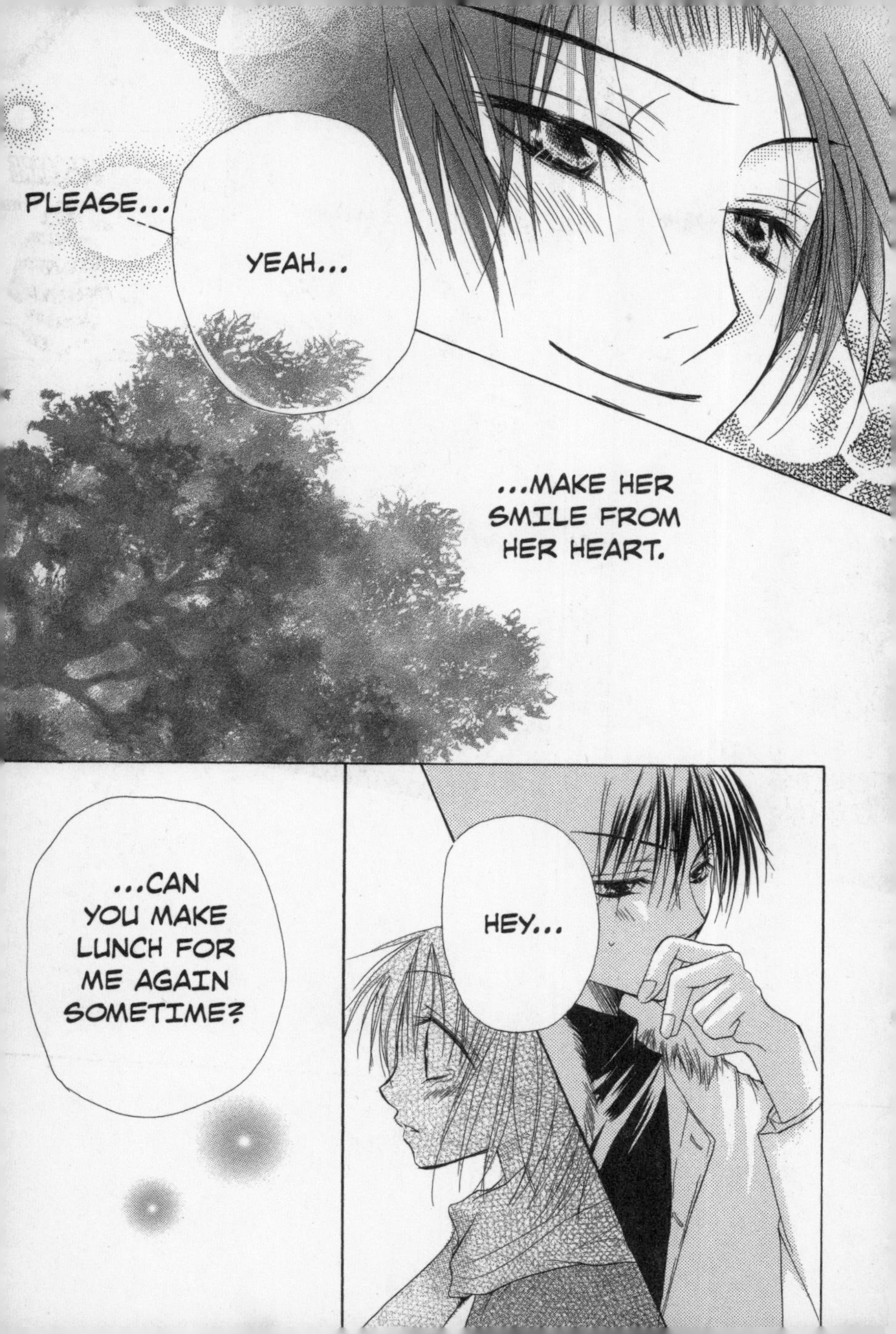
PLEASE...
YEAH...
...MAKE HER SMILE FROM HER HEART.
HEY...
...CAN YOU MAKE LUNCH FOR ME AGAIN SOMETIME?

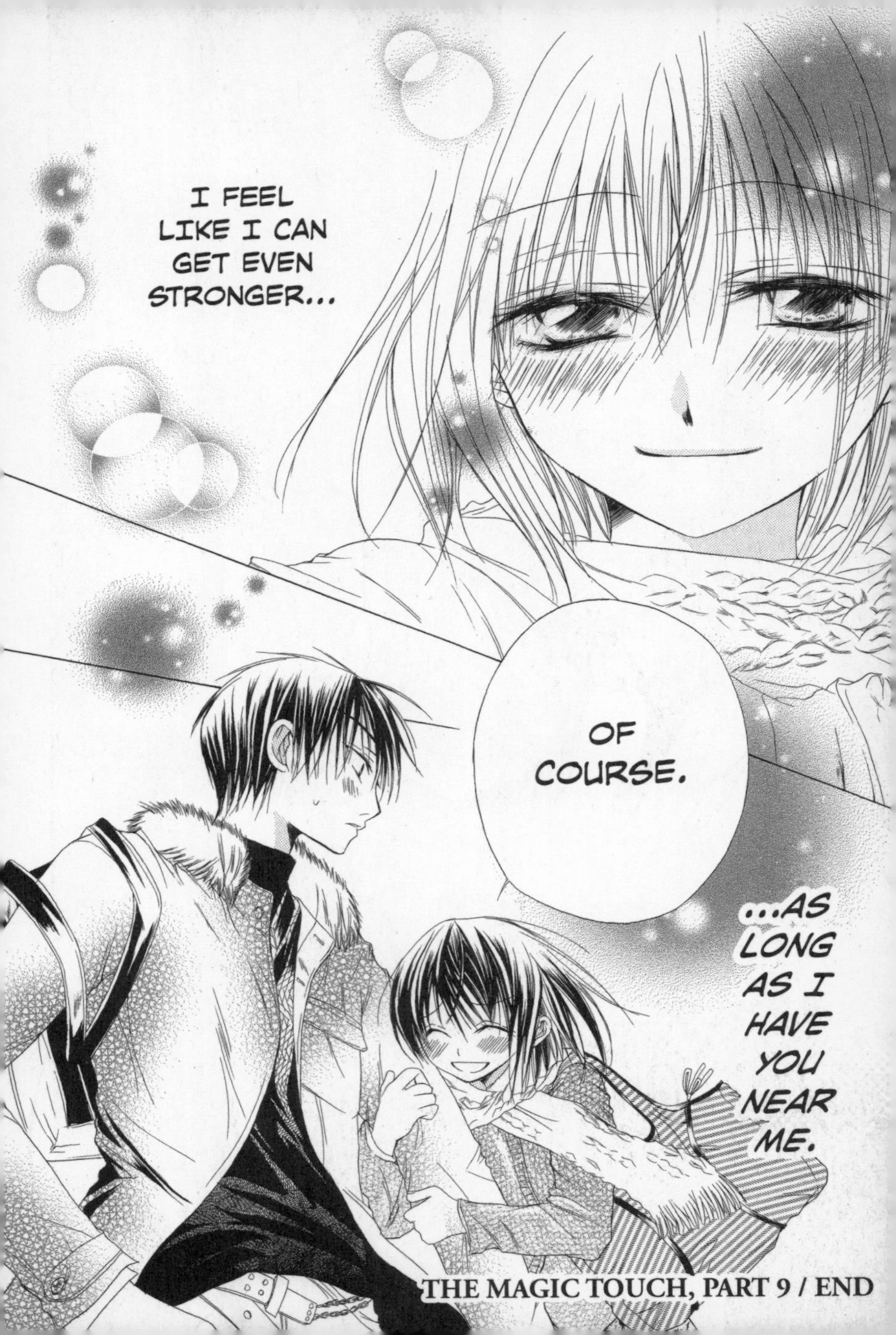
I FEEL LIKE I CAN GET EVEN STRONGER...
OF COURSE.
...AS LONG AS I HAVE YOU NEAR ME.

THE MAGIC TOUCH, PART 9 / END

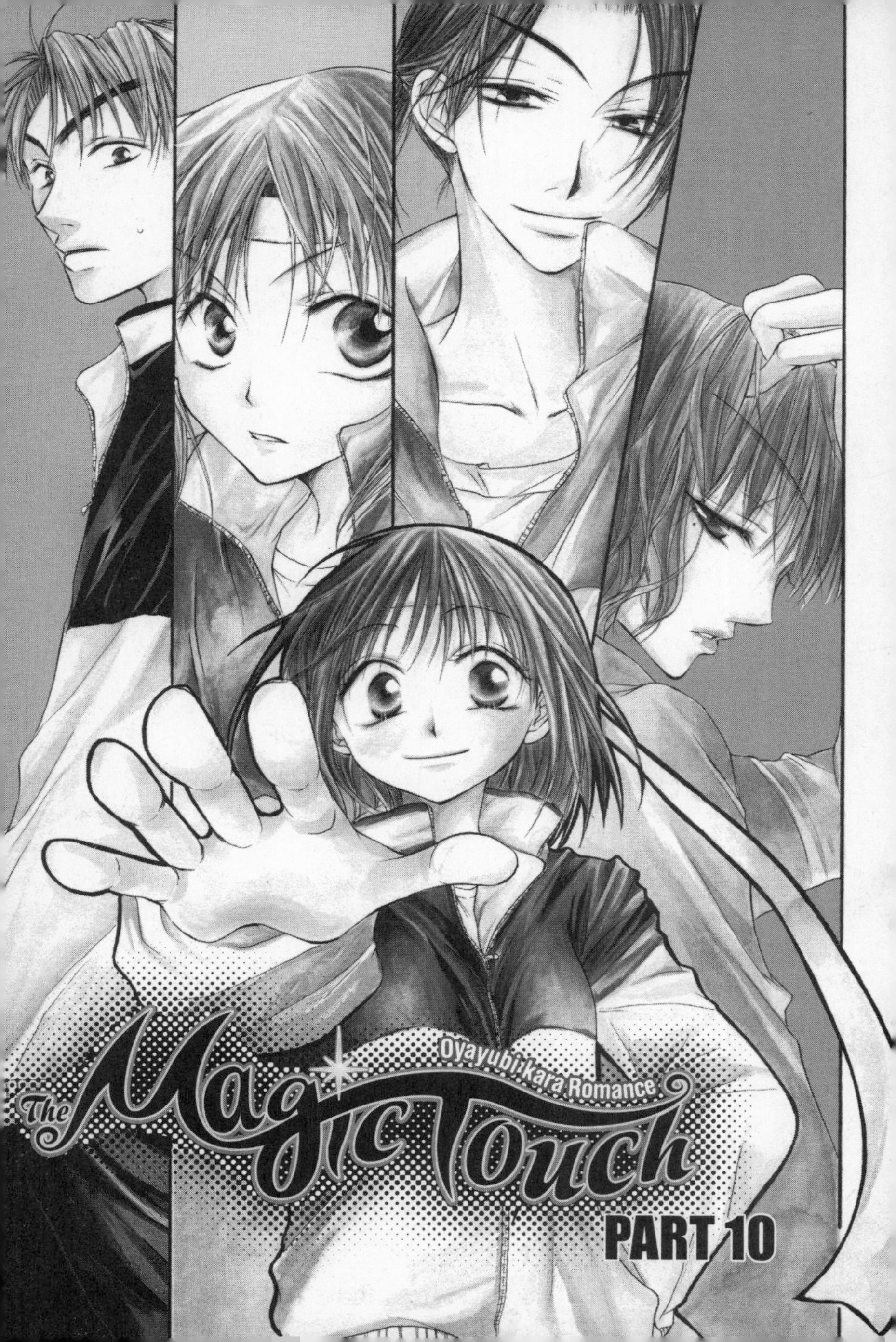
The Magic Touch
Oyayubi Kara Romance
PART 10

GIVING A PRESENT, PART ONE

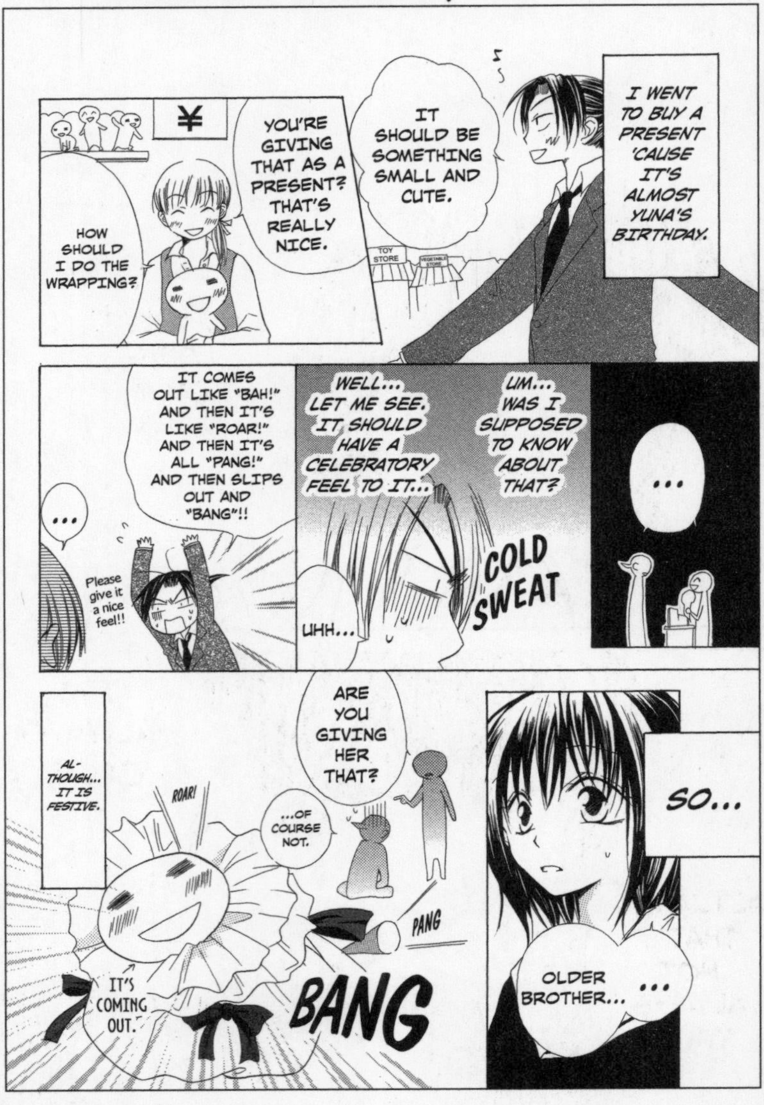
I WENT TO BUY A PRESENT 'CAUSE IT'S ALMOST YUNA'S BIRTHDAY.
IT SHOULD BE SOMETHING SMALL AND CUTE.
TOY STORE
VEGETABLE STORE
¥
YOU'RE GIVING THAT AS A PRESENT? THAT'S REALLY NICE.
HOW SHOULD I DO THE WRAPPING?
...
UM... WAS I SUPPOSED TO KNOW ABOUT THAT?
WELL... LET ME SEE. IT SHOULD HAVE A CELEBRATORY FEEL TO IT...
COLD SWEAT
UHH...
IT COMES OUT LIKE "BAH!" AND THEN IT'S LIKE "ROAR!" AND THEN IT'S ALL "PANG!" AND THEN SLIPS OUT AND "BANG"!!
...
Please give it a nice feel!!
SO...
OLDER BROTHER... ...
ARE YOU GIVING HER THAT?
...OF COURSE NOT.
AL-THOUGH... IT IS FESTIVE.
ROAR!
PANG
BANG
IT'S COMING OUT.

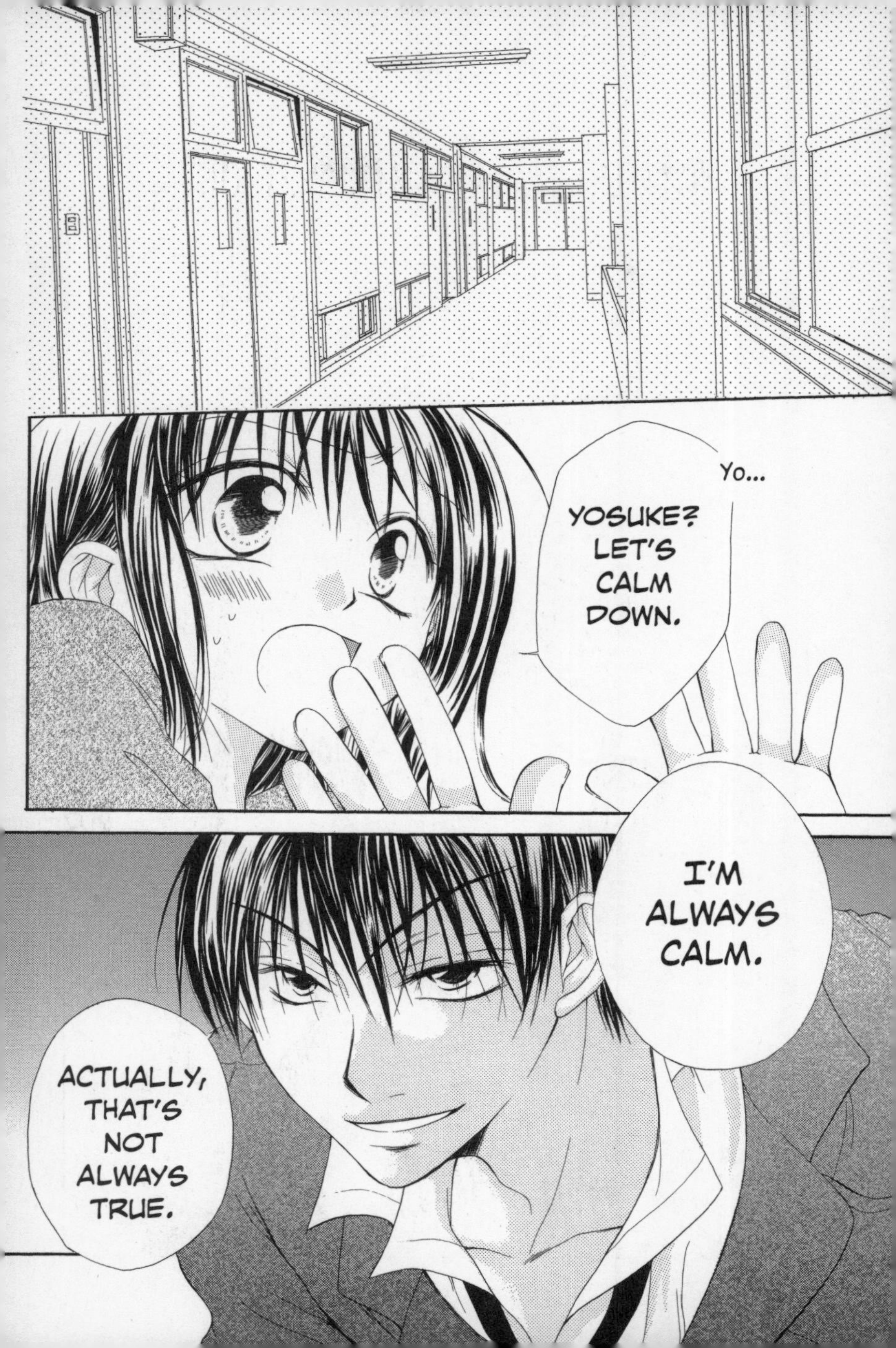
Yo... YOSUKE? LET'S CALM DOWN.
I'M ALWAYS CALM.
ACTUALLY, THAT'S NOT ALWAYS TRUE.

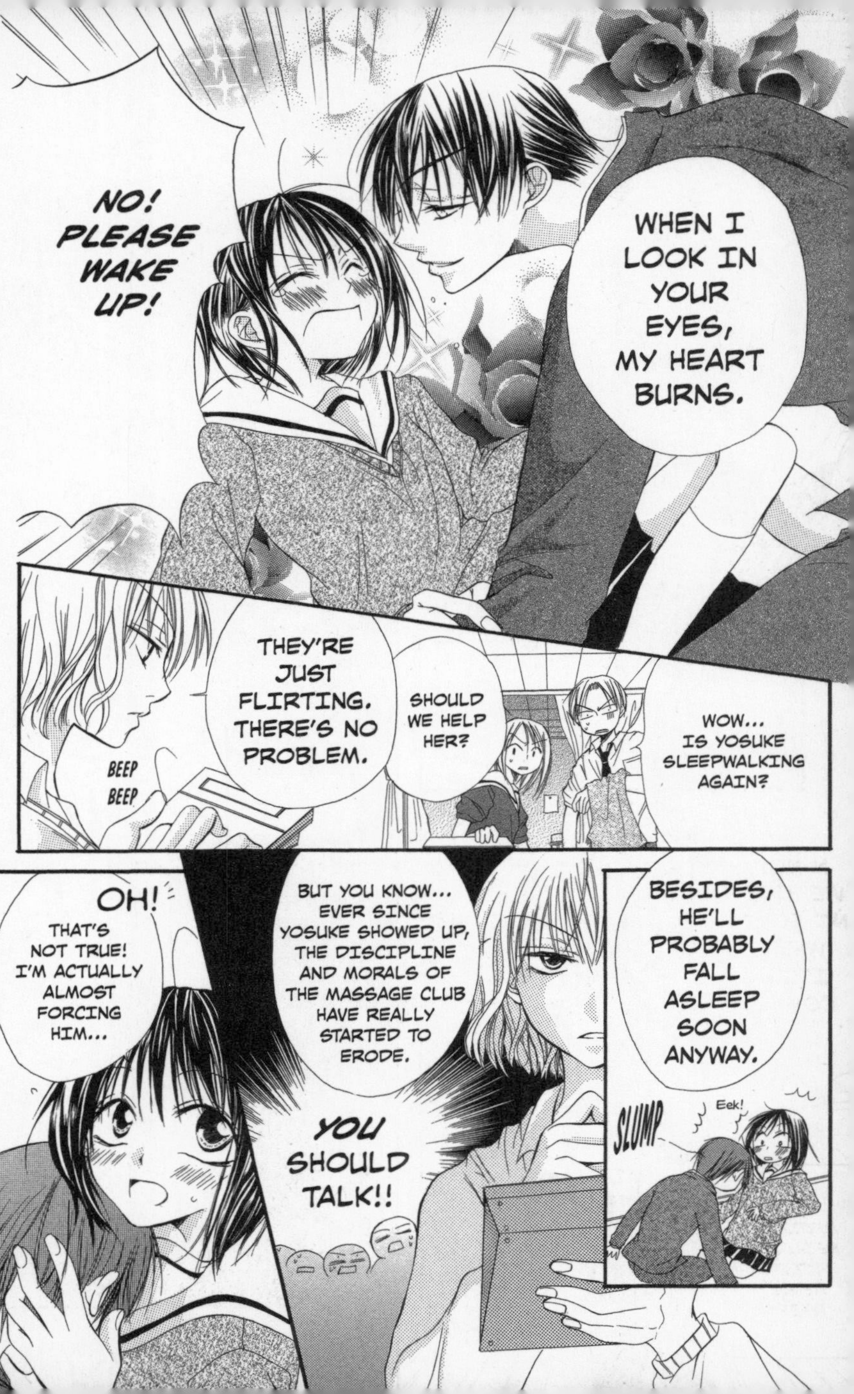
WHEN I LOOK IN YOUR EYES, MY HEART BURNS.
NO! PLEASE WAKE UP!
WOW... IS YOSUKE SLEEPWALKING AGAIN?
SHOULD WE HELP HER?
THEY'RE JUST FLIRTING. THERE'S NO PROBLEM.
BEEP BEEP
BESIDES, HE'LL PROBABLY FALL ASLEEP SOON ANYWAY.
Eek!
SLUMP
BUT YOU KNOW... EVER SINCE YOSUKE SHOWED UP, THE DISCIPLINE AND MORALS OF THE MASSAGE CLUB HAVE REALLY STARTED TO ERODE.
OH!
THAT'S NOT TRUE! I'M ACTUALLY ALMOST FORCING HIM...
YOU SHOULD TALK!!

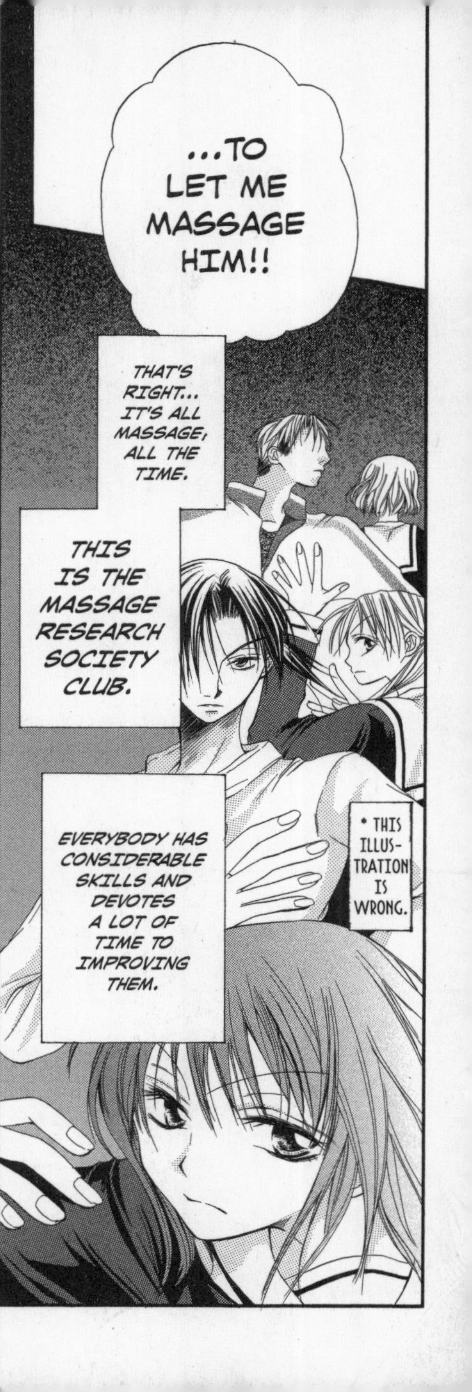
...TO LET ME MASSAGE HIM!!
THAT'S RIGHT... IT'S ALL MASSAGE, ALL THE TIME.
THIS IS THE MASSAGE RESEARCH SOCIETY CLUB.
* THIS ILLUS-TRATION IS WRONG.
EVERYBODY HAS CONSIDERABLE SKILLS AND DEVOTES A LOT OF TIME TO IMPROVING THEM.
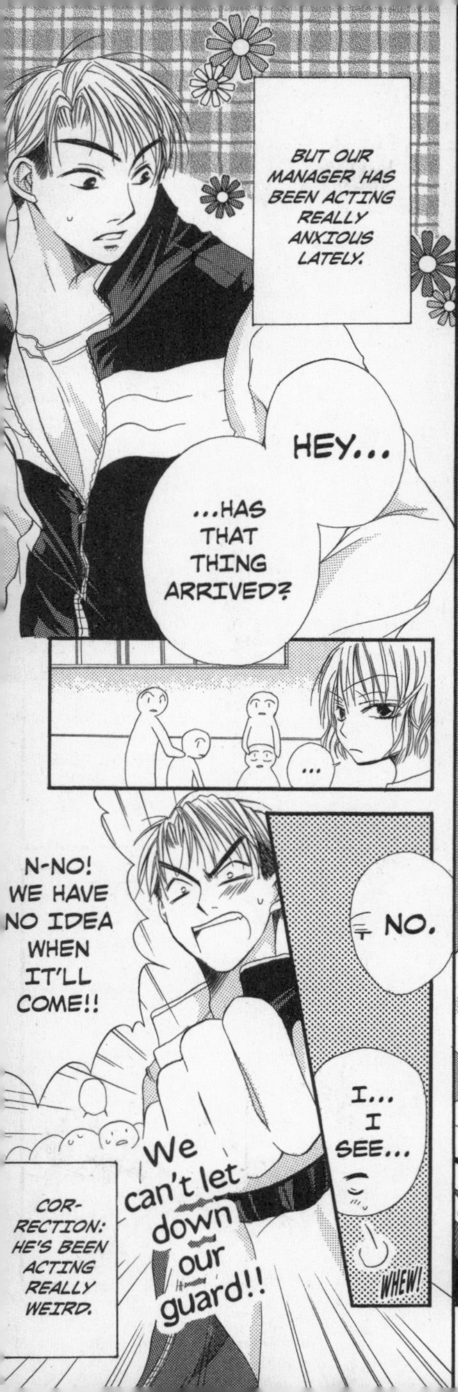
BUT OUR MANAGER HAS BEEN ACTING REALLY ANXIOUS LATELY.
HEY...
...HAS THAT THING ARRIVED?
...
NO.
I... I SEE...
WHEW!
N-NO! WE HAVE NO IDEA WHEN IT'LL COME!!
We can't let down our guard!!
COR-RECTION: HE'S BEEN ACTING REALLY WEIRD.

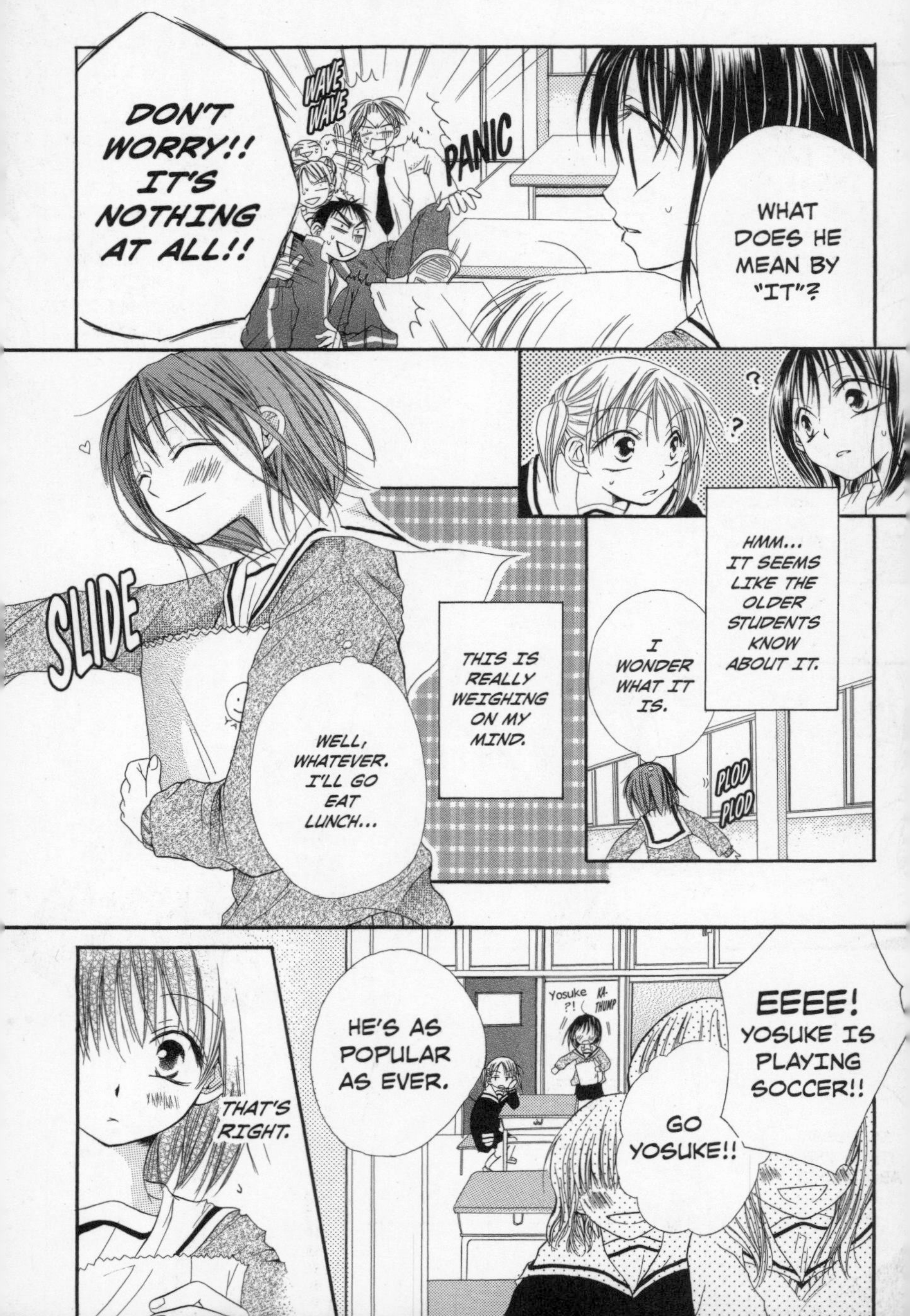
WHAT DOES HE MEAN BY "IT"?
PANIC
WAVE WAVE
DON'T WORRY!! IT'S NOTHING AT ALL!!
? ?
HMM... IT SEEMS LIKE THE OLDER STUDENTS KNOW ABOUT IT.
I WONDER WHAT IT IS.
PLOD PLOD
THIS IS REALLY WEIGHING ON MY MIND.
SLIDE
WELL, WHATEVER. I'LL GO EAT LUNCH...
EEEE! YOSUKE IS PLAYING SOCCER!!
GO YOSUKE!!
Yosuke ?!
KA-THUMP
HE'S AS POPULAR AS EVER.
THAT'S RIGHT.

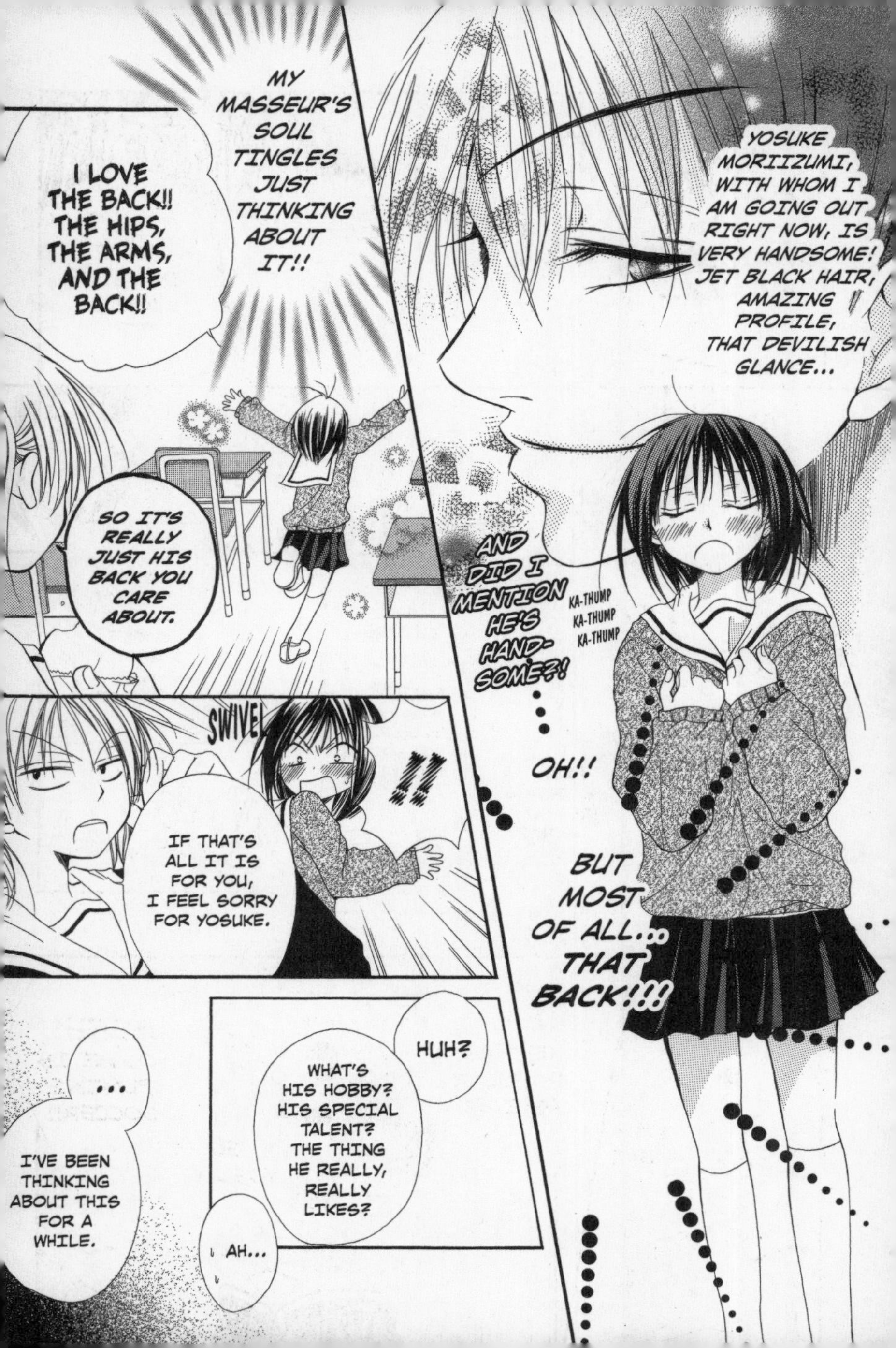
YOSUKE MORIIZUMI, WITH WHOM I AM GOING OUT RIGHT NOW, IS VERY HANDSOME! JET BLACK HAIR, AMAZING PROFILE, THAT DEVILISH GLANCE...
AND DID I MENTION HE'S HAND-SOME?!
KA-THUMP KA-THUMP KA-THUMP
OH!!
BUT MOST OF ALL... THAT BACK!!!
MY MASSEUR'S SOUL TINGLES JUST THINKING ABOUT IT!!
I LOVE THE BACK!! THE HIPS, THE ARMS, AND THE BACK!!
SO IT'S REALLY JUST HIS BACK YOU CARE ABOUT.
SWIVEL
!!
IF THAT'S ALL IT IS FOR YOU, I FEEL SORRY FOR YOSUKE.
HUH?
WHAT'S HIS HOBBY? HIS SPECIAL TALENT? THE THING HE REALLY, REALLY LIKES?
AH...
...
I'VE BEEN THINKING ABOUT THIS FOR A WHILE.

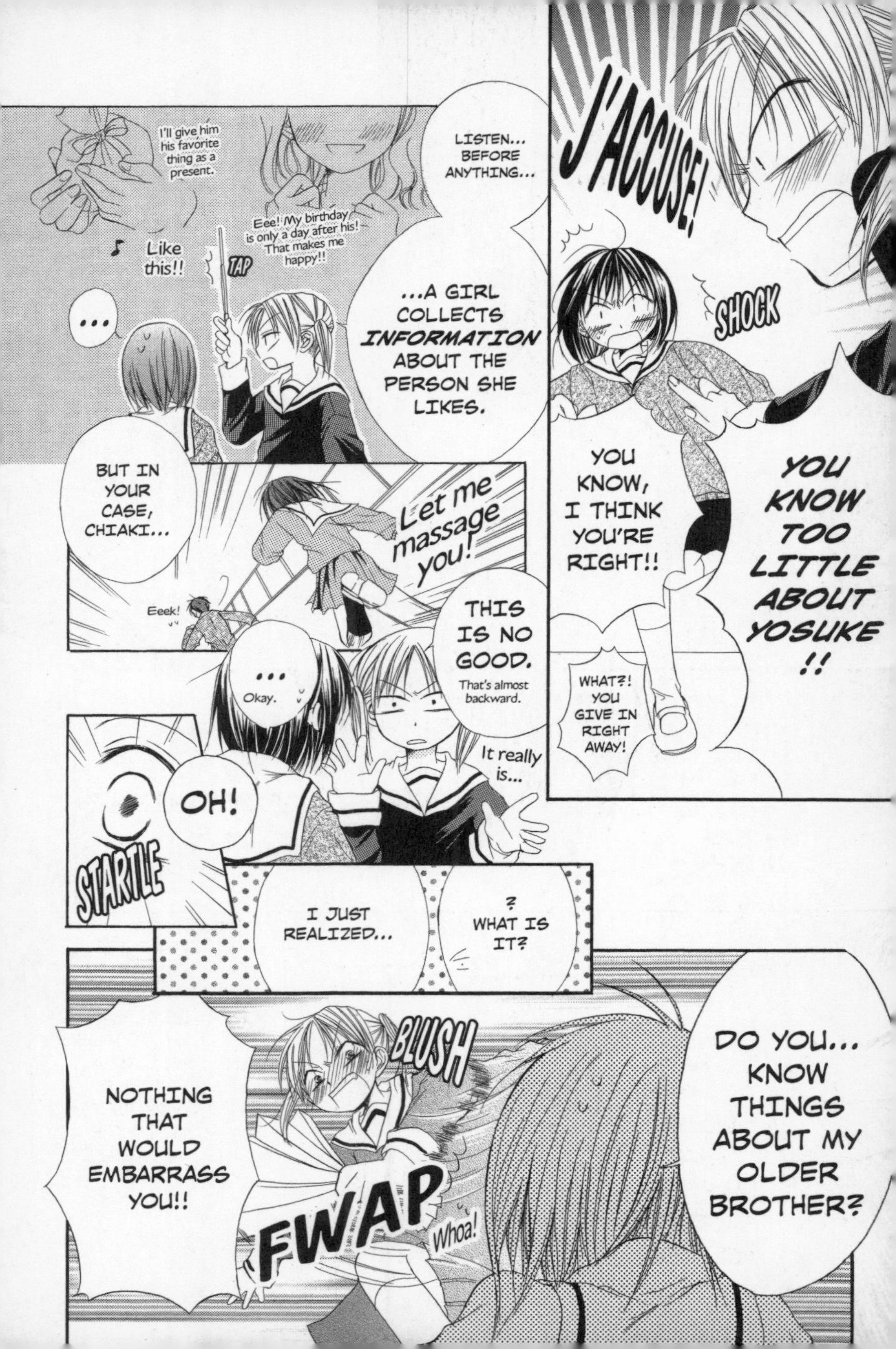
J'ACCUSE!
SHOCK
YOU KNOW TOO LITTLE ABOUT YOSUKE!!
YOU KNOW, I THINK YOU'RE RIGHT!!
WHAT?! YOU GIVE IN RIGHT AWAY!
LISTEN... BEFORE ANYTHING...
...A GIRL COLLECTS INFORMATION ABOUT THE PERSON SHE LIKES.
Eee! My birthday is only a day after his! That makes me happy!!
I'll give him his favorite thing as a present.
Like this!!
TAP
...
BUT IN YOUR CASE, CHIAKI...
Let me massage you!
Eeek!
THIS IS NO GOOD.
That's almost backward.
...
Okay.
It really is...
OH!
STARTLE
? WHAT IS IT?
I JUST REALIZED...
DO YOU... KNOW THINGS ABOUT MY OLDER BROTHER?
BLUSH
NOTHING THAT WOULD EMBARRASS YOU!!
FWAP
Whoa!

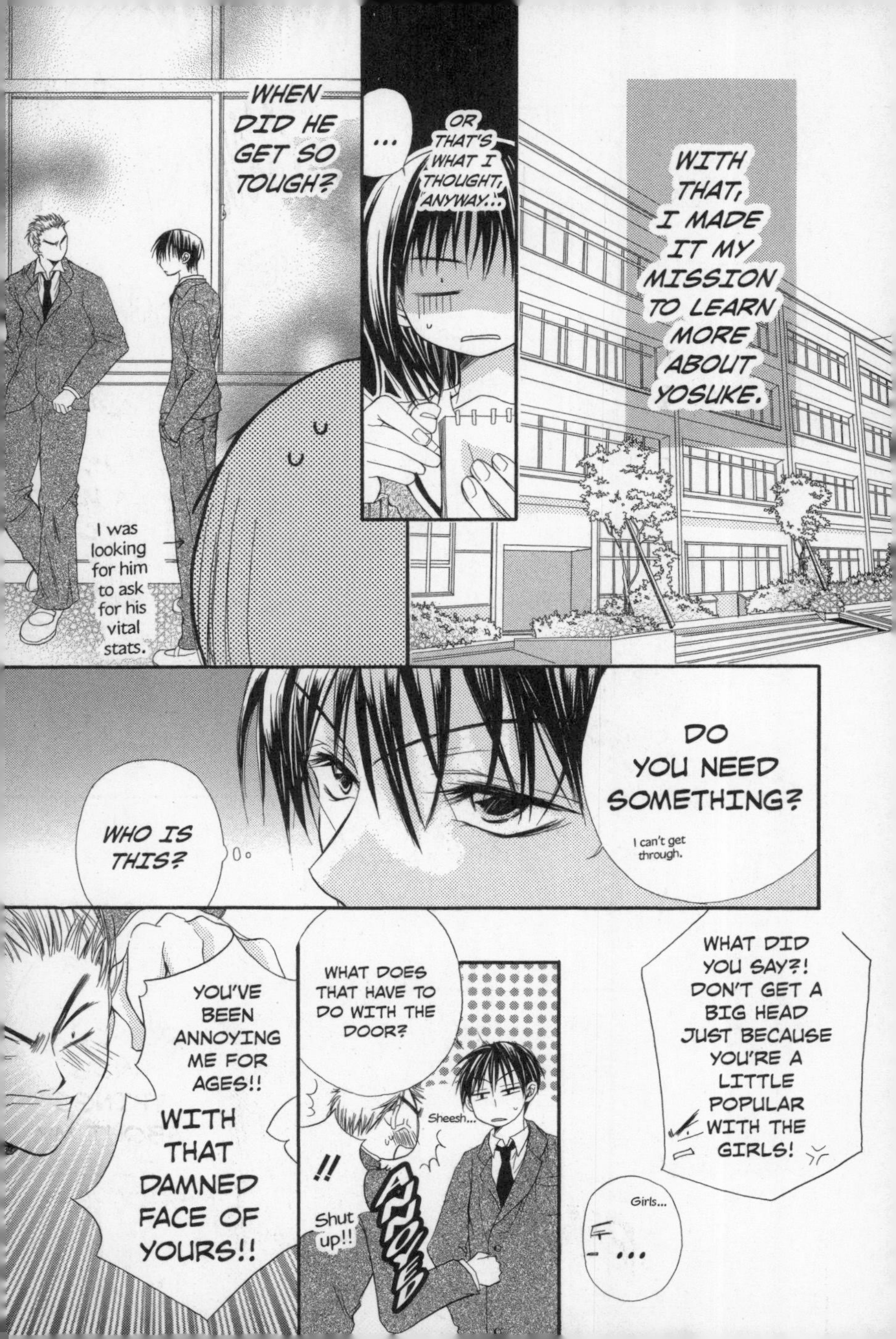
WITH THAT, I MADE IT MY MISSION TO LEARN MORE ABOUT YOSUKE.
OR THAT'S WHAT I THOUGHT, ANYWAY...
...
WHEN DID HE GET SO TOUGH?
I was looking for him to ask for his vital stats.
DO YOU NEED SOMETHING?
I can't get through.
WHO IS THIS?
WHAT DID YOU SAY?! DON'T GET A BIG HEAD JUST BECAUSE YOU'RE A LITTLE POPULAR WITH THE GIRLS!
Girls...
...
WHAT DOES THAT HAVE TO DO WITH THE DOOR?
Sheesh...
!!
Shut up!!
YOU'VE BEEN ANNOYING ME FOR AGES!!
WITH THAT DAMNED FACE OF YOURS!!

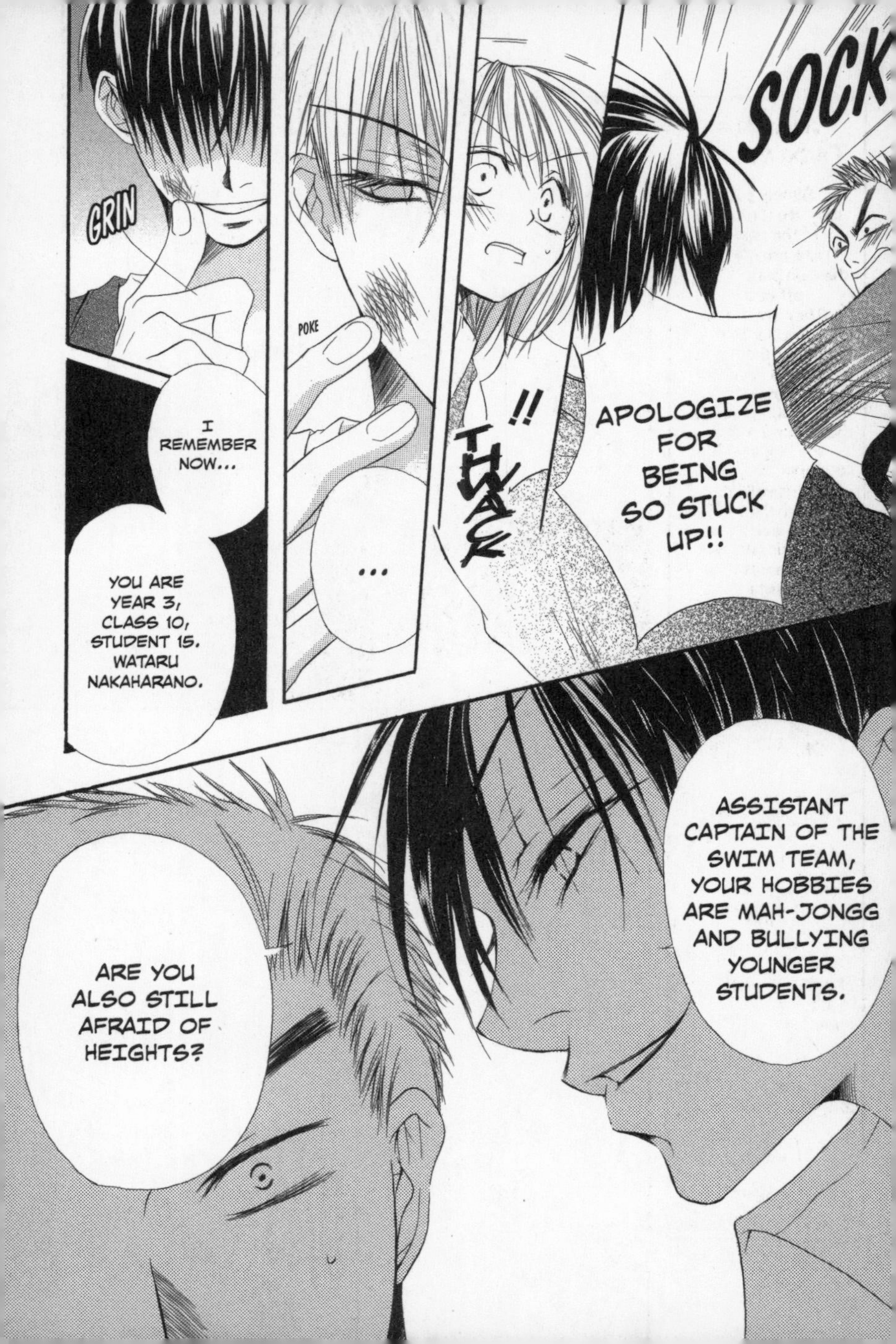
SOCK
APOLOGIZE FOR BEING SO STUCK UP!!
!!
THWACK
POKE
...
GRIN
I REMEMBER NOW...
YOU ARE YEAR 3, CLASS 10, STUDENT 15. WATARU NAKAHARANO.
ASSISTANT CAPTAIN OF THE SWIM TEAM, YOUR HOBBIES ARE MAH-JONGG AND BULLYING YOUNGER STUDENTS.
ARE YOU ALSO STILL AFRAID OF HEIGHTS?

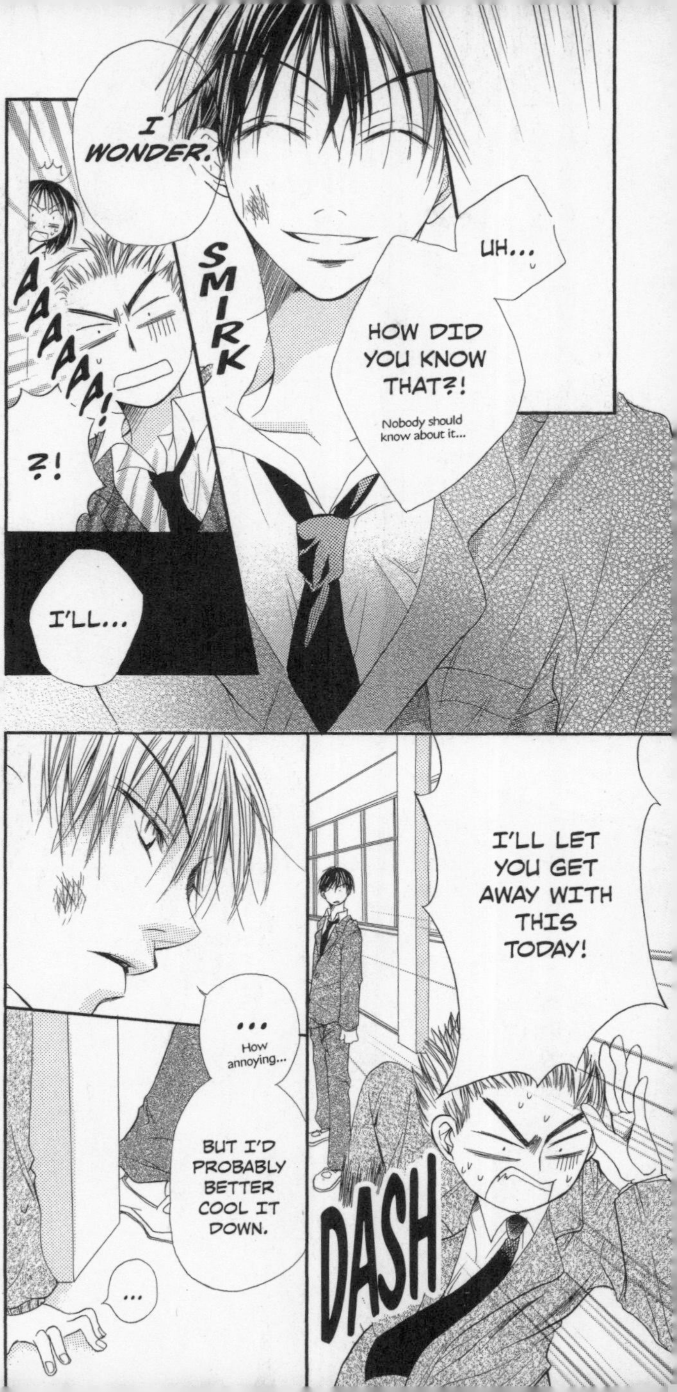
I WONDER.
SMIRK
UH...
HOW DID YOU KNOW THAT?!
Nobody should know about it...
AAAAAA!
?!
I'LL...
I'LL LET YOU GET AWAY WITH THIS TODAY!
DASH
...
How annoying...
BUT I'D PROBABLY BETTER COOL IT DOWN.
...

What Are Tsubo Spirits?

Simply put, they are the spirits of the tsubo. There are many of them on people with stiff backs. They are of no particular size; some of them are small and some are large. Generally speaking, the stiffer a muscle is, the bigger the corresponding tsubo's spirit will be. And all the tsubo compete every day to get their stiffness fixed as soon as possible! (Just kidding.)

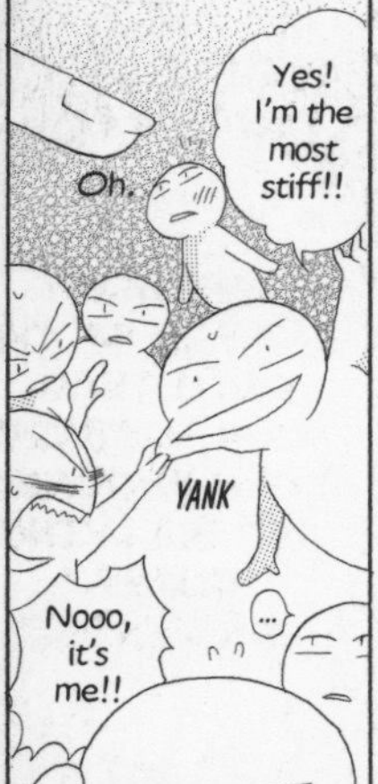
Yes! I'm the most stiff!!
Oh.
YANK
Nooo, it's me!!
...
SHY
WAIGUAN
I get picked pretty often myself.

FIGURE 1

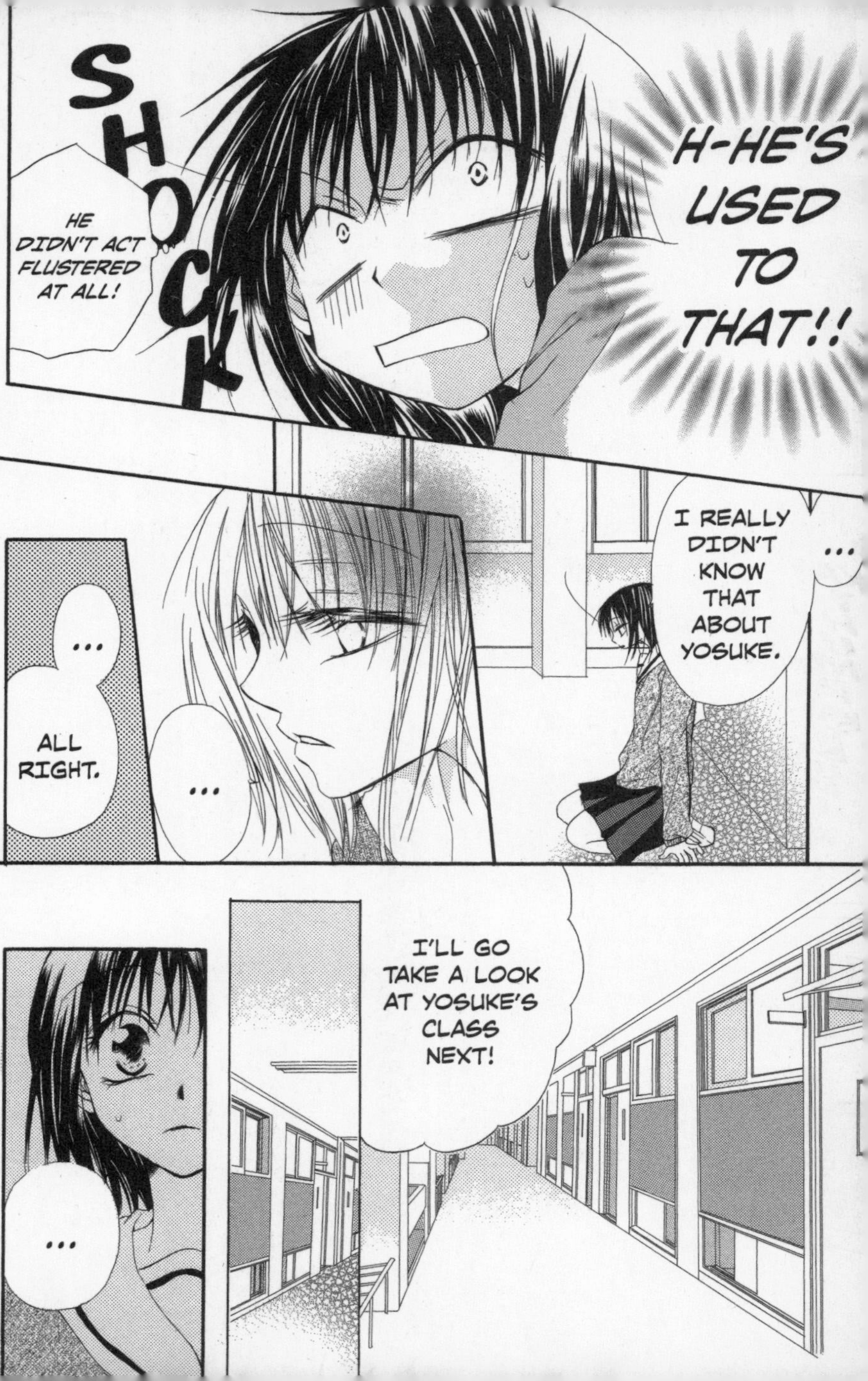
H-HE'S USED TO THAT!!
SHOCK
HE DIDN'T ACT FLUSTERED AT ALL!
...
I REALLY DIDN'T KNOW THAT ABOUT YOSUKE.
...
ALL RIGHT.
...
I'LL GO TAKE A LOOK AT YOSUKE'S CLASS NEXT!
...

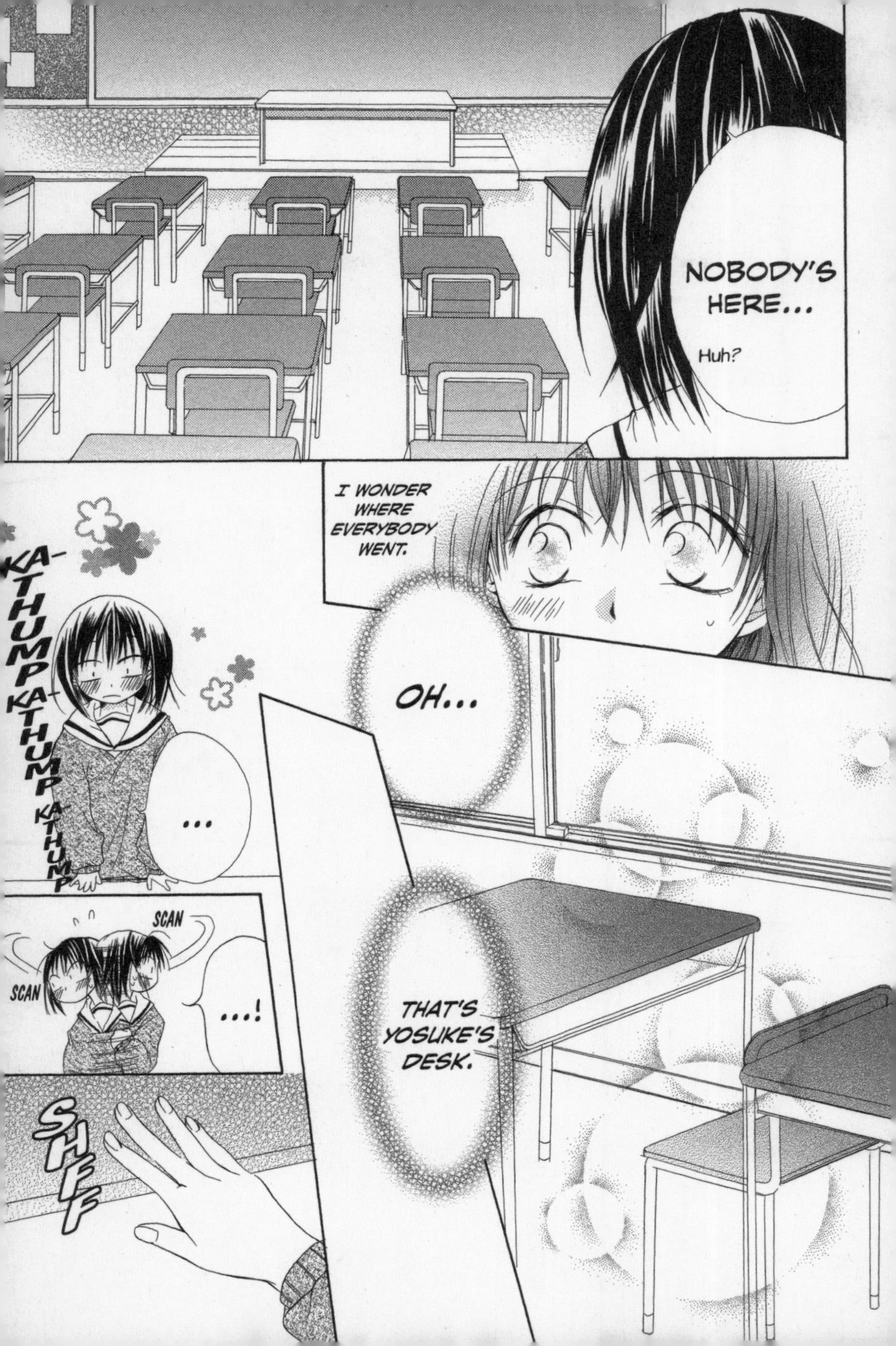

NOBODY'S HERE...
Huh?
I WONDER WHERE EVERYBODY WENT.
OH...
THAT'S YOSUKE'S DESK.
KA-THUMP KA-THUMP KA-THUMP KA-THUMP
...
SCAN
SCAN
...!
SHFF

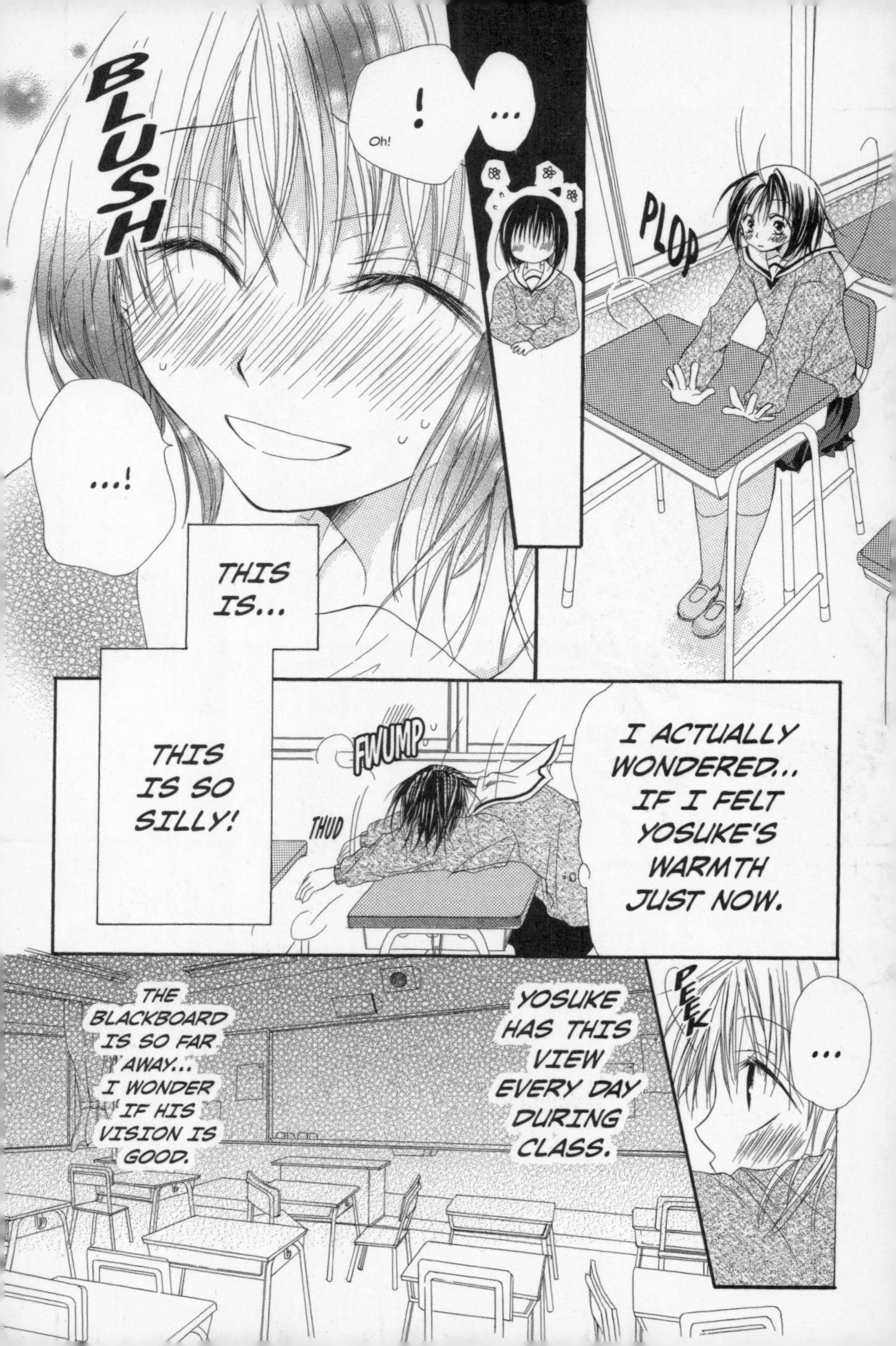
PLOP
...
!
Oh!
BLUSH
...!
THIS IS...
I ACTUALLY WONDERED... IF I FELT YOSUKE'S WARMTH JUST NOW.
FWUMP
THUD
THIS IS SO SILLY!
PEEK
...
YOSUKE HAS THIS VIEW EVERY DAY DURING CLASS.
THE BLACKBOARD IS SO FAR AWAY... I WONDER IF HIS VISION IS GOOD.

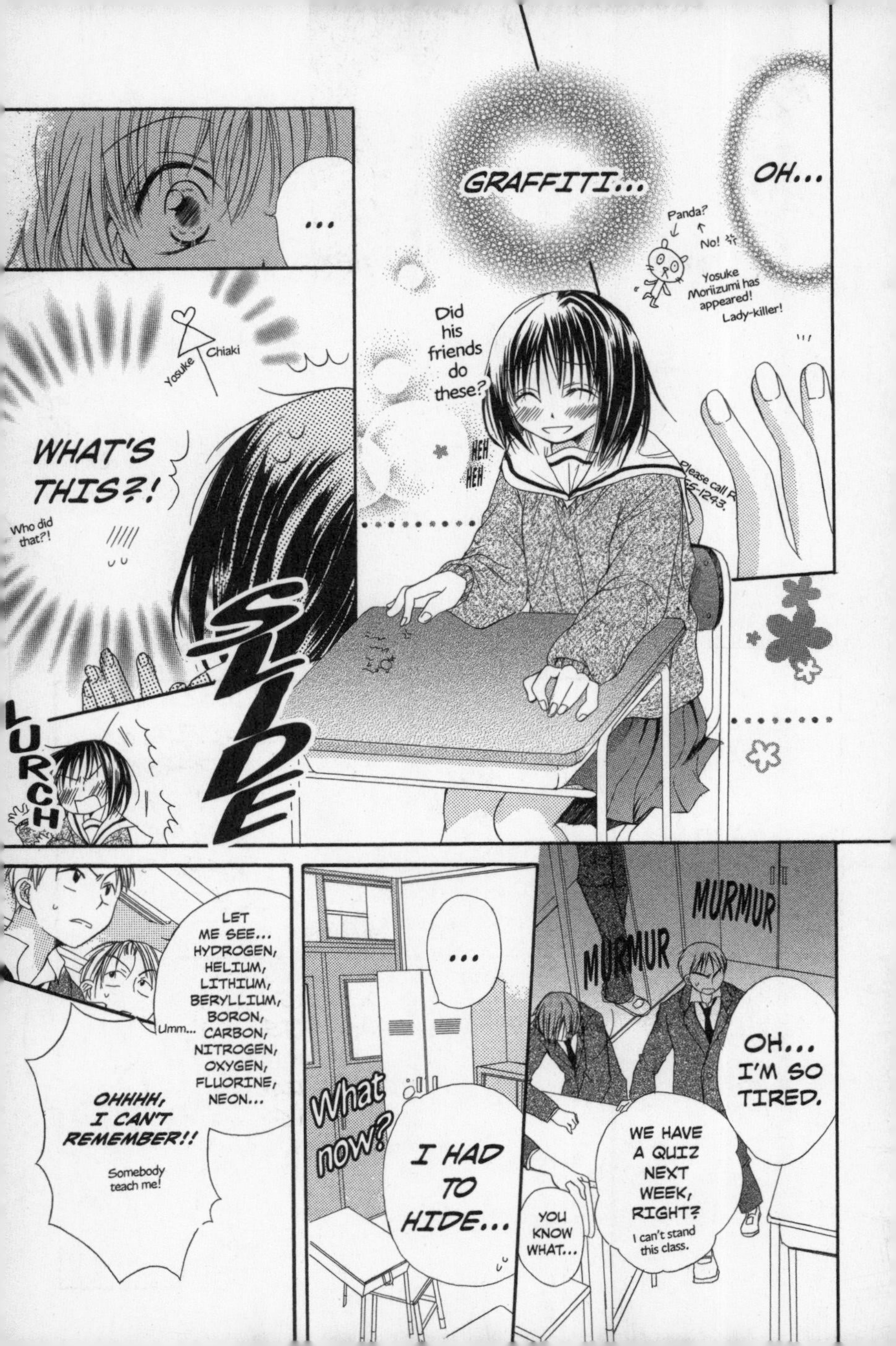

OH...
GRAFFITI...
Panda?
No!
Yosuke Moriizumi has appeared!
Lady-killer!
Did his friends do these?
HEH HEH
Please call R
5-1243.
...
Yosuke Chiaki
WHAT'S THIS?!
Who did that?!
SLIDE
LURCH
MURMUR
MURMUR
OH... I'M SO TIRED.
WE HAVE A QUIZ NEXT WEEK, RIGHT?
I can't stand this class.
YOU KNOW WHAT...
...
What now?
I HAD TO HIDE...
LET ME SEE... HYDROGEN, HELIUM, LITHIUM, BERYLLIUM, BORON, CARBON, NITROGEN, OXYGEN, FLUORINE, NEON...
Umm...
OHHHH, I CAN'T REMEMBER!!
Somebody teach me!

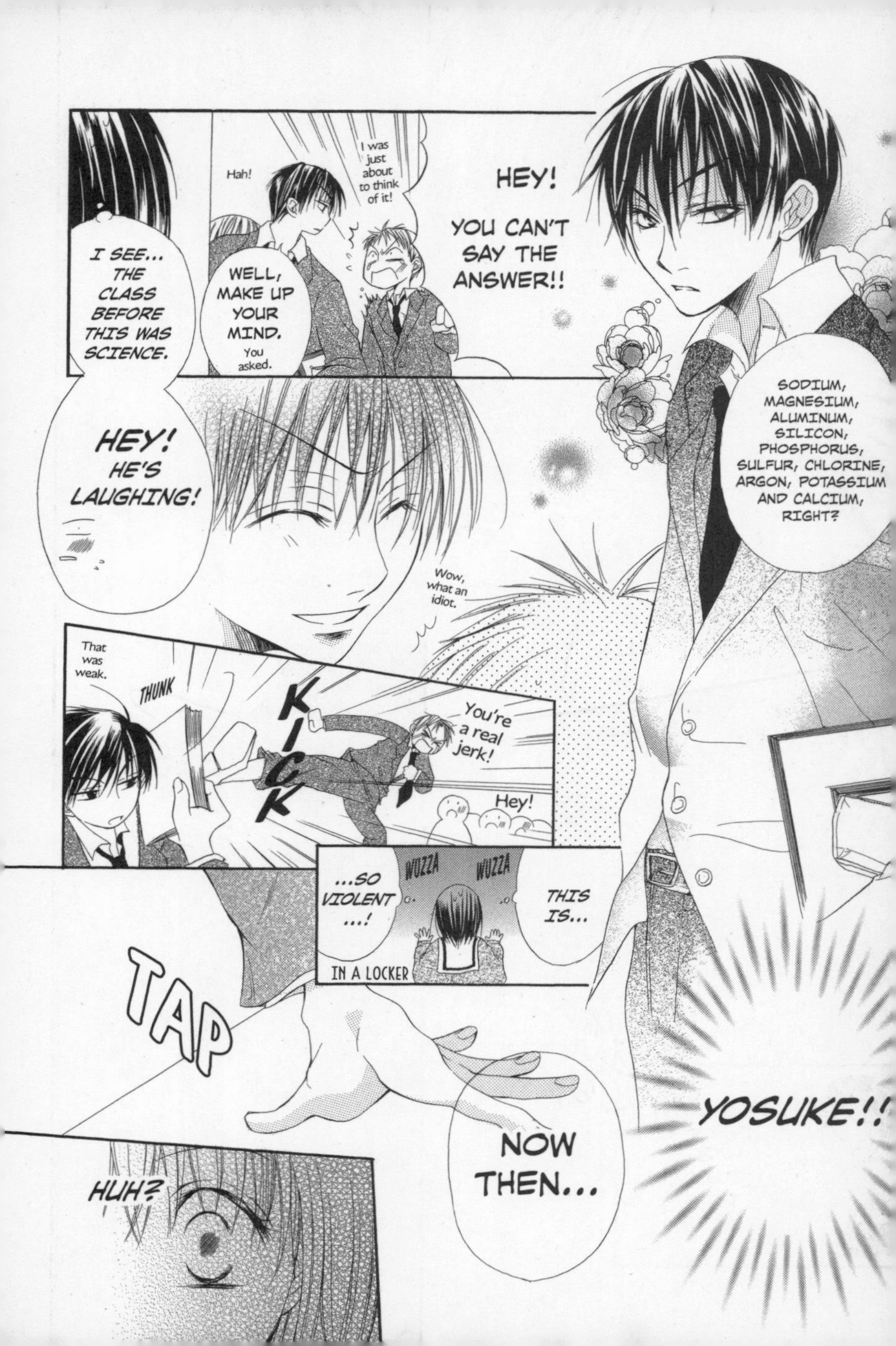
SODIUM, MAGNESIUM, ALUMINUM, SILICON, PHOSPHORUS, SULFUR, CHLORINE, ARGON, POTASSIUM AND CALCIUM, RIGHT?
HEY!
YOU CAN'T SAY THE ANSWER!!
I was just about to think of it!
WELL, MAKE UP YOUR MIND.
You asked.
Hah!
I SEE... THE CLASS BEFORE THIS WAS SCIENCE.
Wow, what an idiot.
HEY! HE'S LAUGHING!
You're a real jerk!
KICK
Hey!
THUNK
That was weak.
THIS IS...
WUZZA
WUZZA
...SO VIOLENT ...!
IN A LOCKER
YOSUKE!!
NOW THEN...
TAP
HUH?

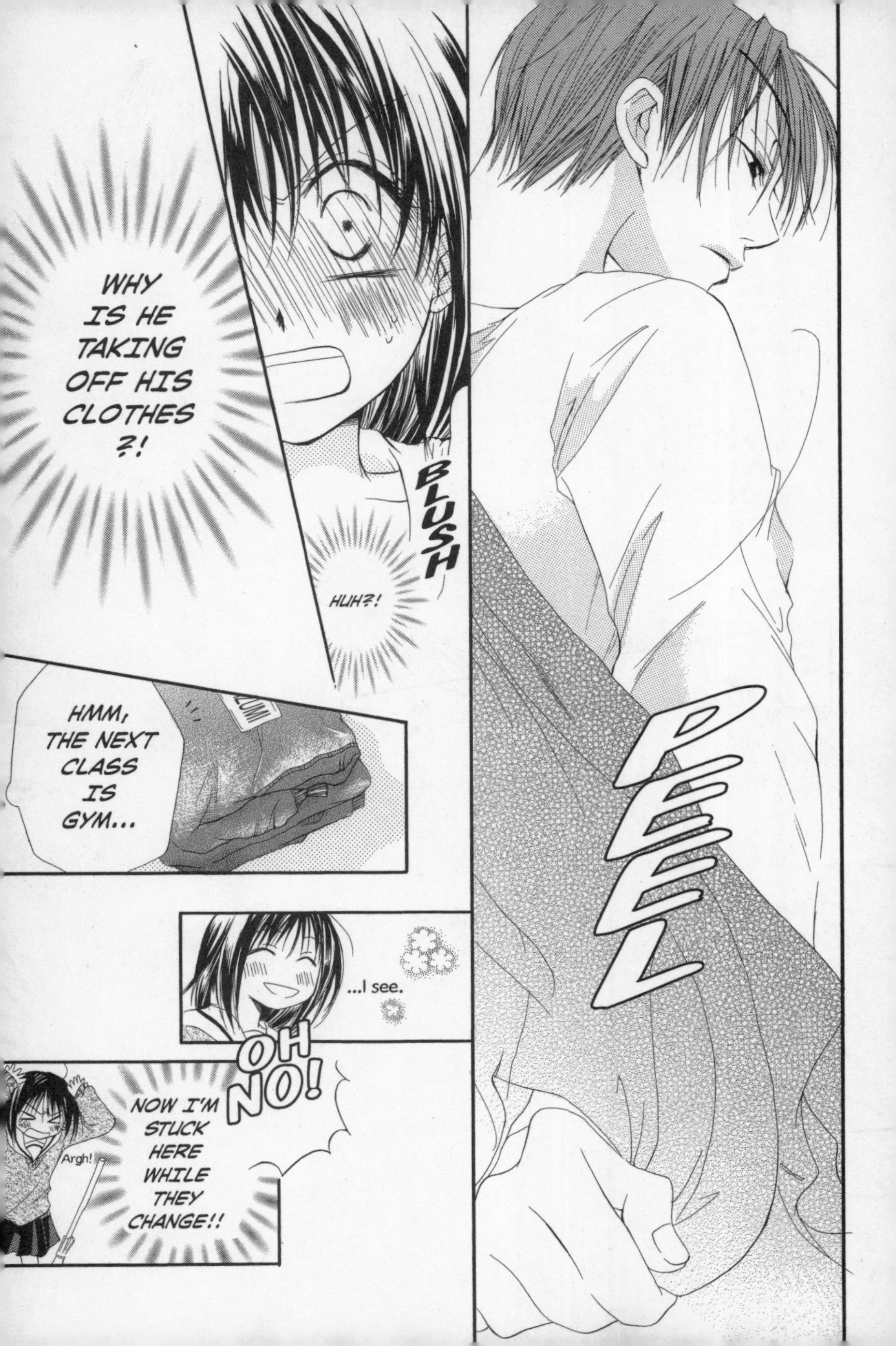
PEEL
BLUSH
HUH?!
WHY IS HE TAKING OFF HIS CLOTHES?!
HMM, THE NEXT CLASS IS GYM...
...I see.
OH NO!
NOW I'M STUCK HERE WHILE THEY CHANGE!!
Argh!

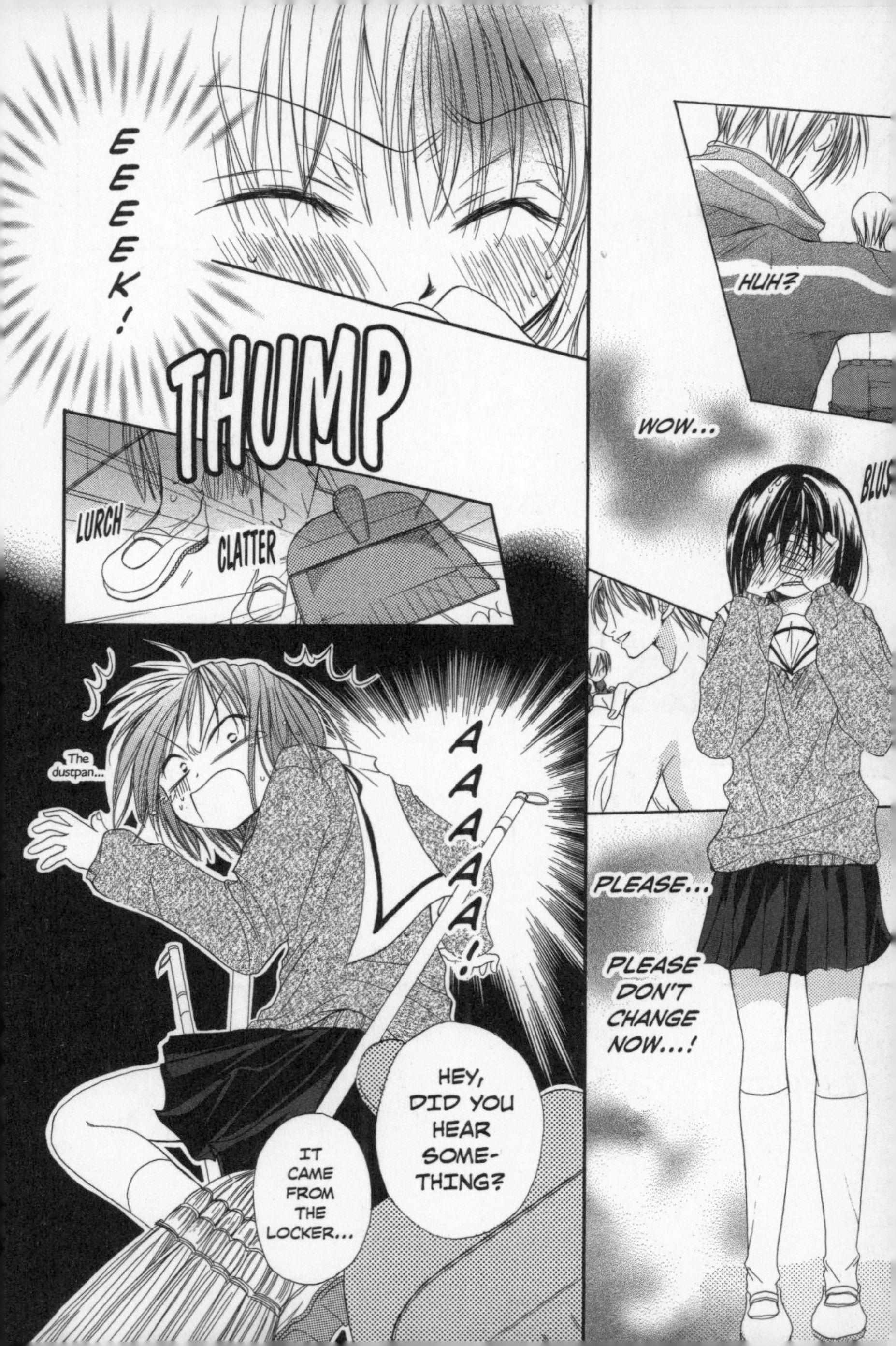
HUH?
WOW...
BLUS
PLEASE...
PLEASE DON'T CHANGE NOW...!
EEEEK!
THUMP
LURCH
CLATTER
AAAAAA!
The dustpan...
HEY, DID YOU HEAR SOME-THING?
IT CAME FROM THE LOCKER...

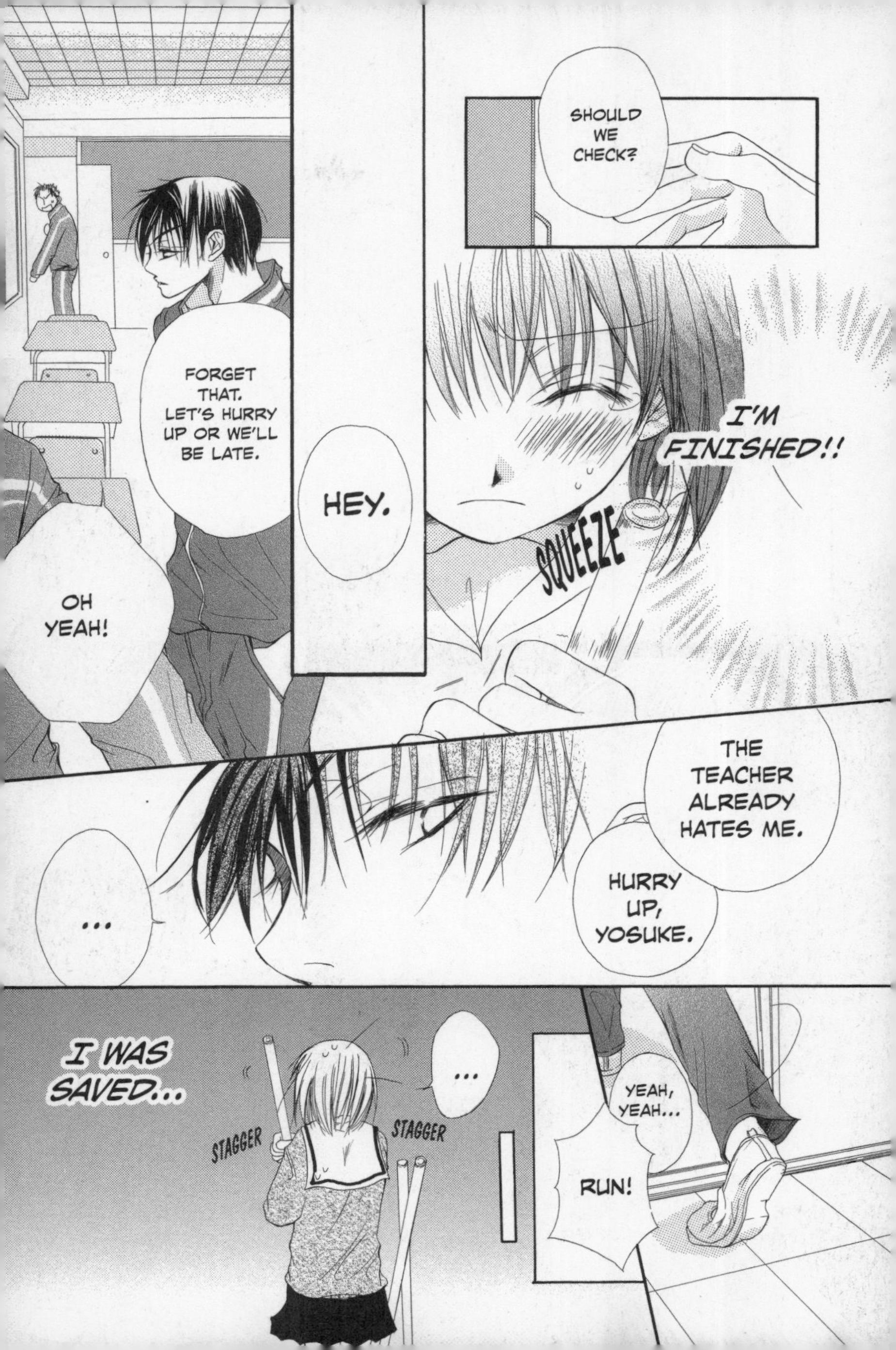
SHOULD WE CHECK?
I'M FINISHED!!
SQUEEZE
HEY.
FORGET THAT. LET'S HURRY UP OR WE'LL BE LATE.
OH YEAH!
THE TEACHER ALREADY HATES ME.
HURRY UP, YOSUKE.
...
YEAH, YEAH...
RUN!
...
I WAS SAVED...
STAGGER
STAGGER

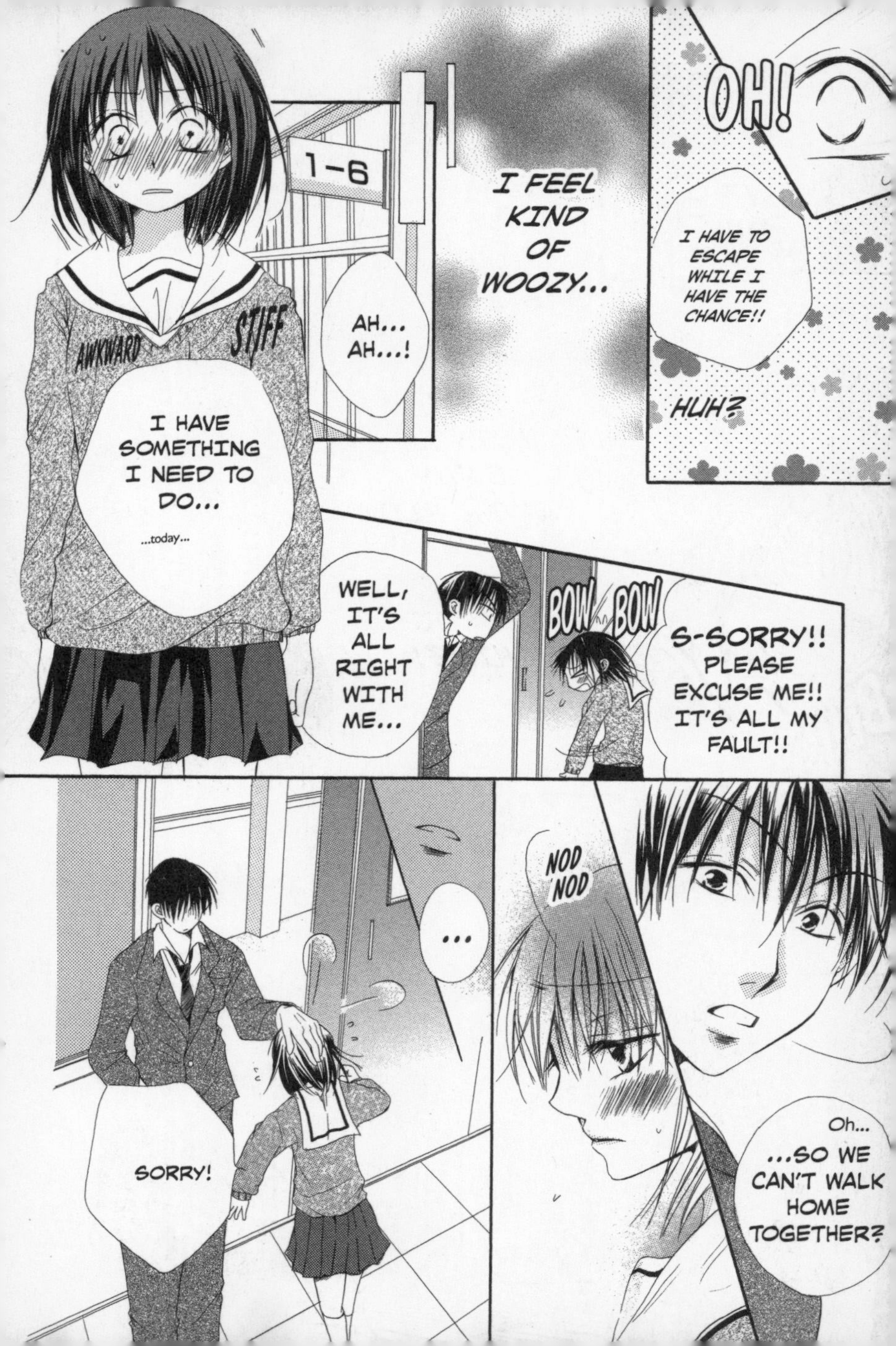
OH!
I HAVE TO ESCAPE WHILE I HAVE THE CHANCE!!
HUH?
I FEEL KIND OF WOOZY...
AH... AH...!
S-SORRY!! PLEASE EXCUSE ME!! IT'S ALL MY FAULT!!
BOW BOW
WELL, IT'S ALL RIGHT WITH ME...
AWKWARD
STIFF
I HAVE SOMETHING I NEED TO DO...
...today...
Oh...
...SO WE CAN'T WALK HOME TOGETHER?
NOD NOD
...
SORRY!

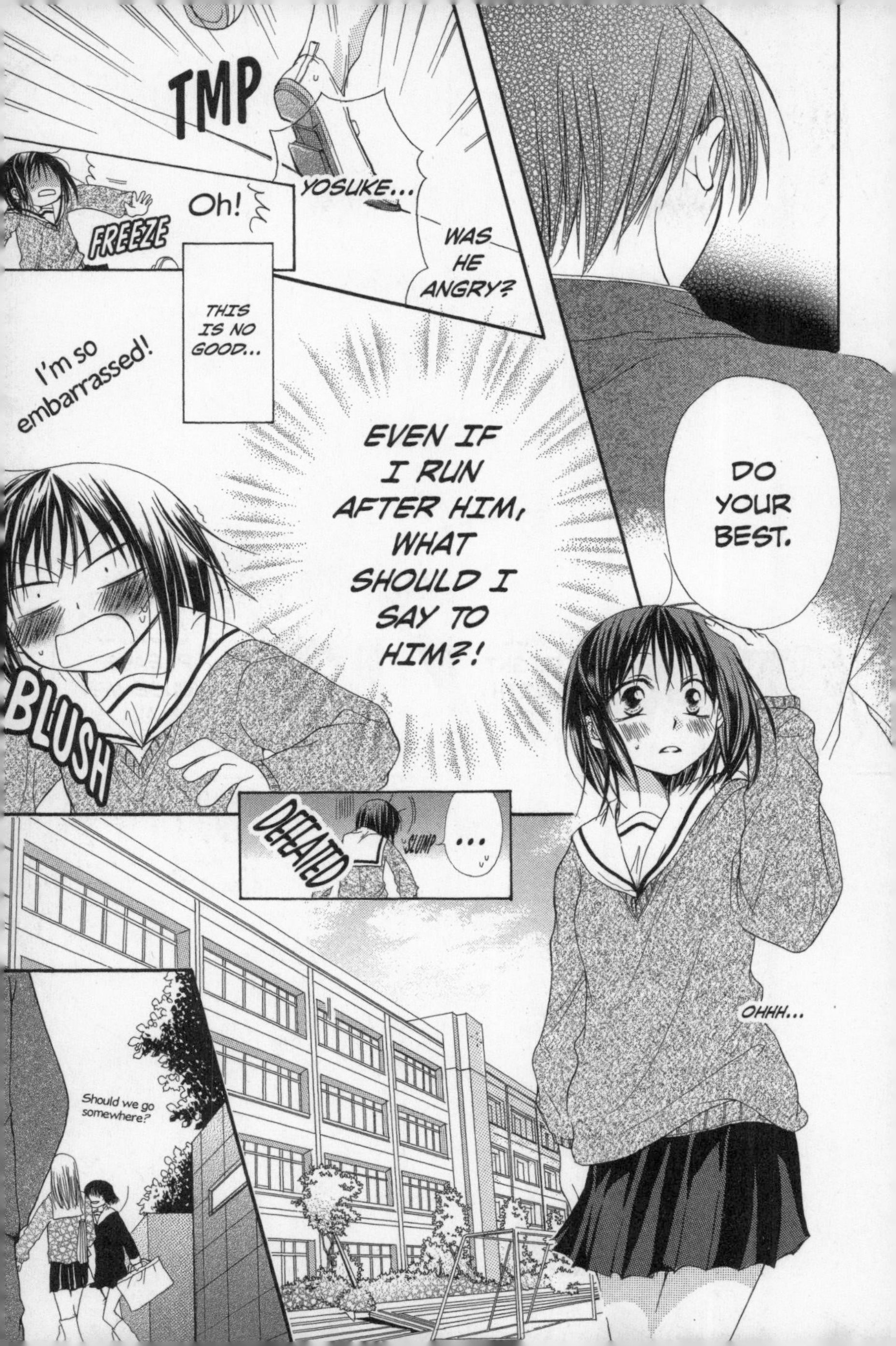
DO YOUR BEST.
OHHH...
TMP
YOSUKE...
WAS HE ANGRY?
Oh!
FREEZE
THIS IS NO GOOD...
EVEN IF I RUN AFTER HIM, WHAT SHOULD I SAY TO HIM?!
I'm so embarrassed!
BLUSH
DEFEATED
SLUMP
...
Should we go somewhere?

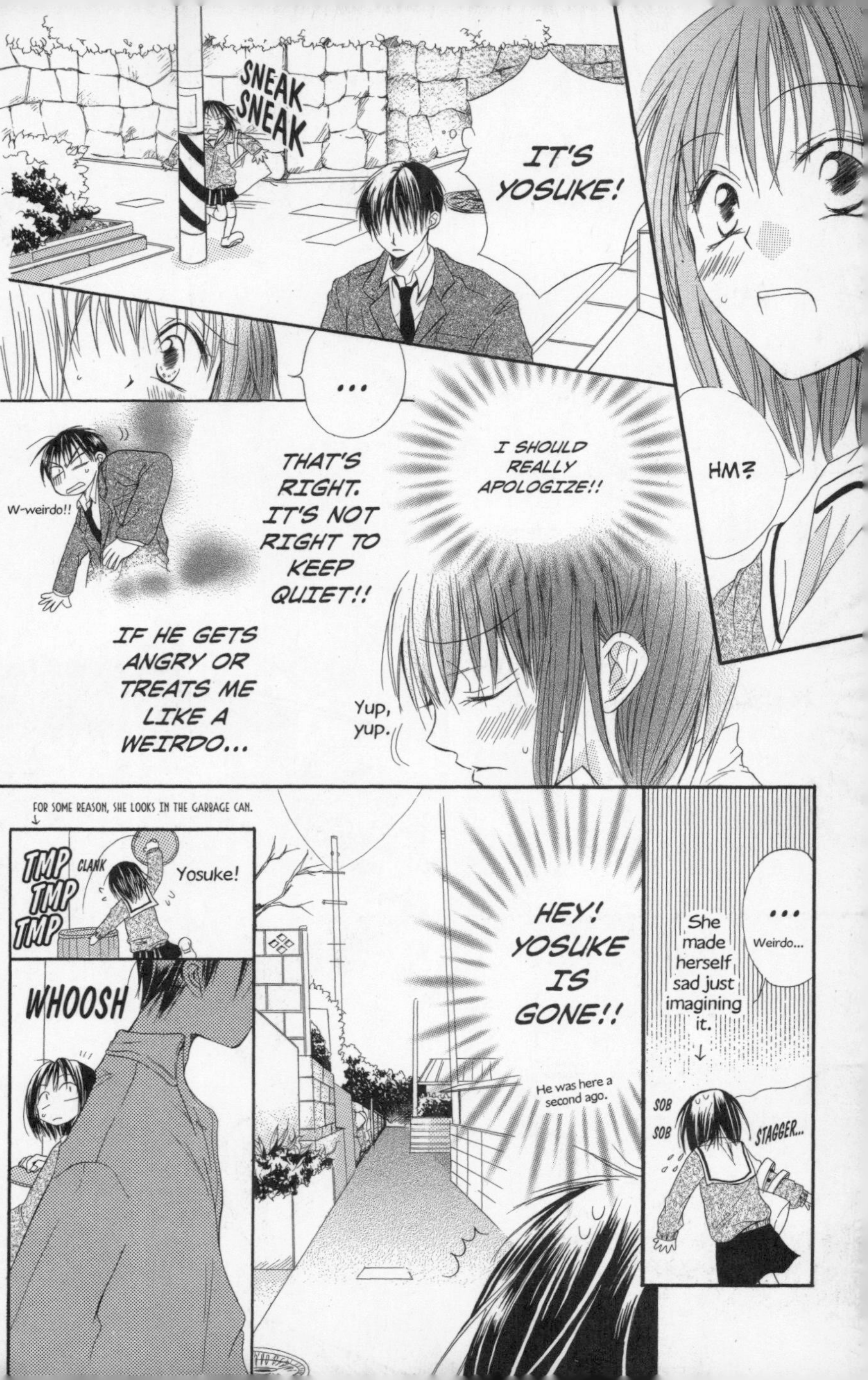
IT'S YOSUKE!
HM?
SNEAK SNEAK
...
I SHOULD REALLY APOLOGIZE!!
THAT'S RIGHT. IT'S NOT RIGHT TO KEEP QUIET!!
W-weirdo!!
IF HE GETS ANGRY OR TREATS ME LIKE A WEIRDO...
Yup, yup.
...
Weirdo...
She made herself sad just imagining it.
SOB SOB
STAGGER...
HEY! YOSUKE IS GONE!!
He was here a second ago.
FOR SOME REASON, SHE LOOKS IN THE GARBAGE CAN.
TMP TMP TMP
CLANK
Yosuke!
WHOOSH

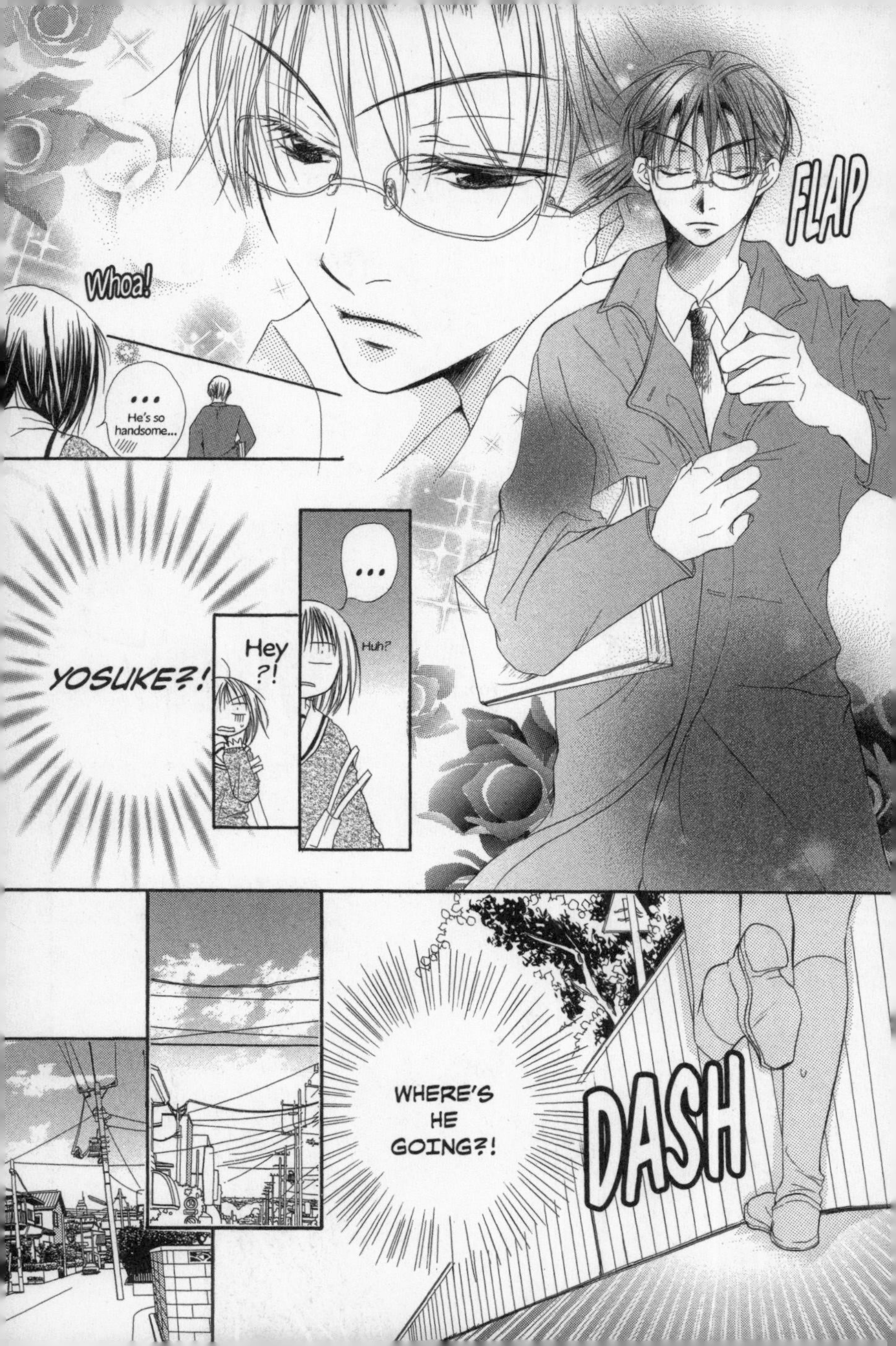
FLAP
Whoa!
...
He's so handsome...
...
Huh?
Hey ?!
YOSUKE?!
DASH
WHERE'S HE GOING?!

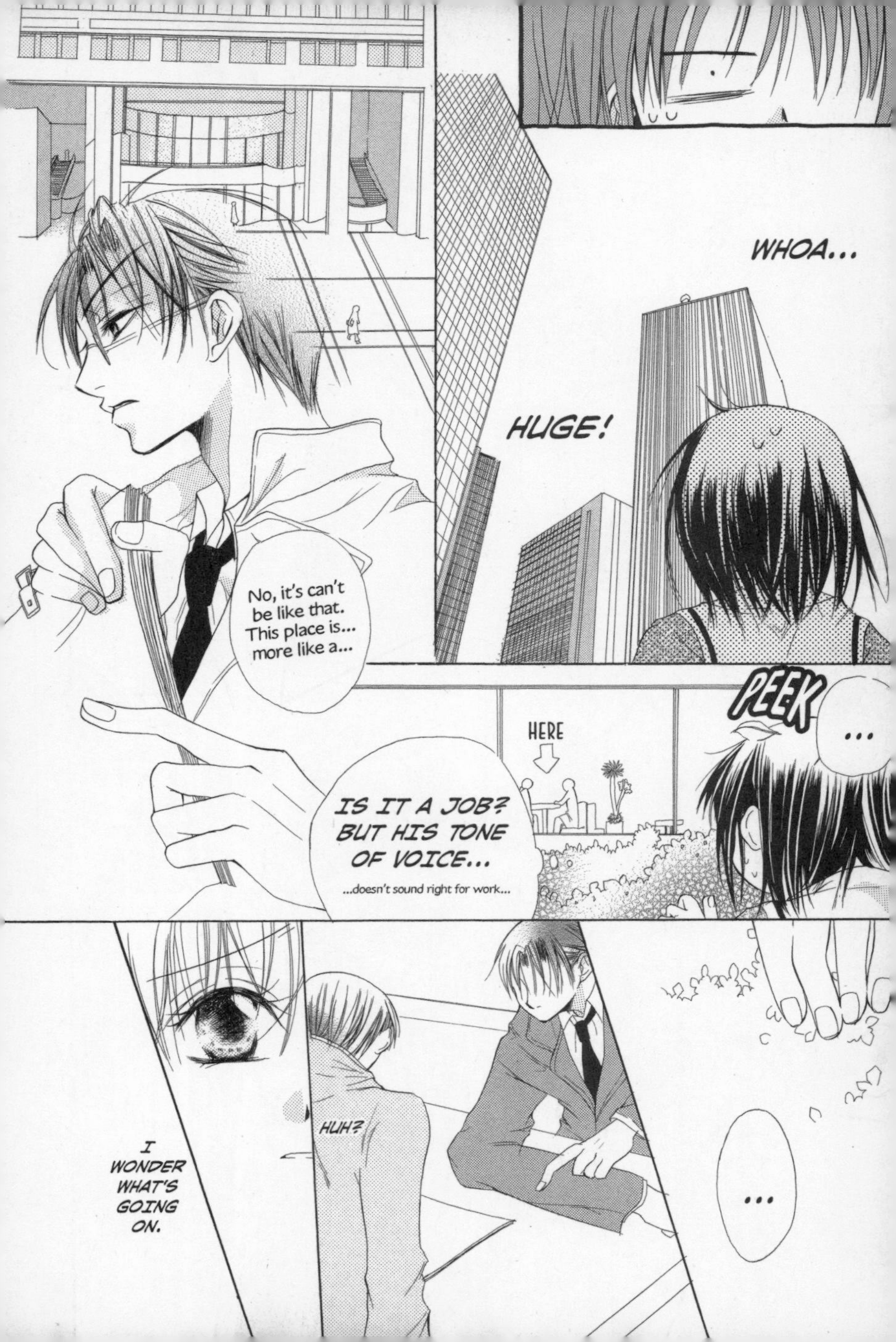
WHOA...
HUGE!
No, it's can't be like that. This place is... more like a...
PEEK
...
HERE
IS IT A JOB? BUT HIS TONE OF VOICE...
...doesn't sound right for work...
...
HUH?
I WONDER WHAT'S GOING ON.

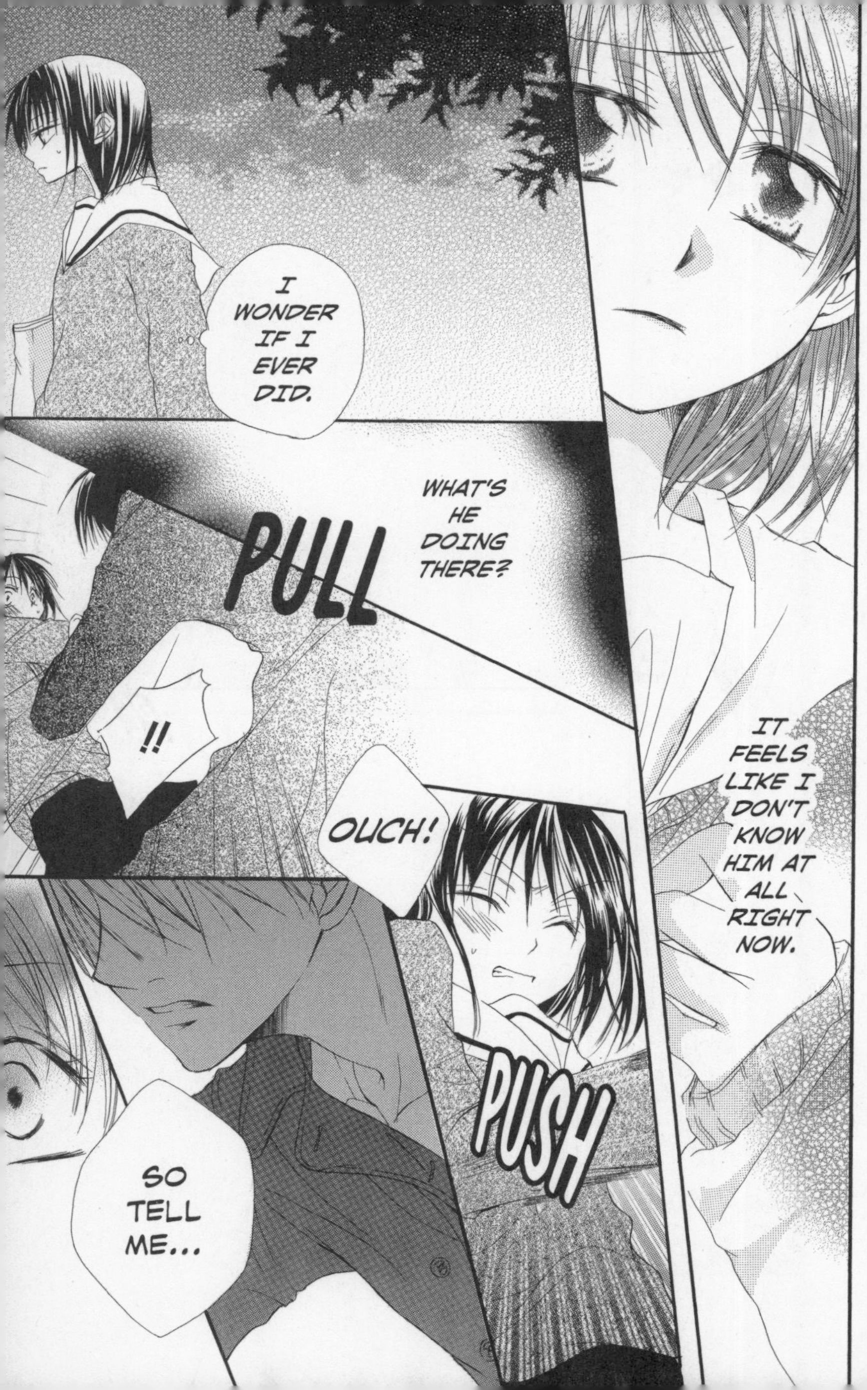
IT FEELS LIKE I DON'T KNOW HIM AT ALL RIGHT NOW.
I WONDER IF I EVER DID.
WHAT'S HE DOING THERE?
PULL
!!
OUCH!
PUSH
SO TELL ME...

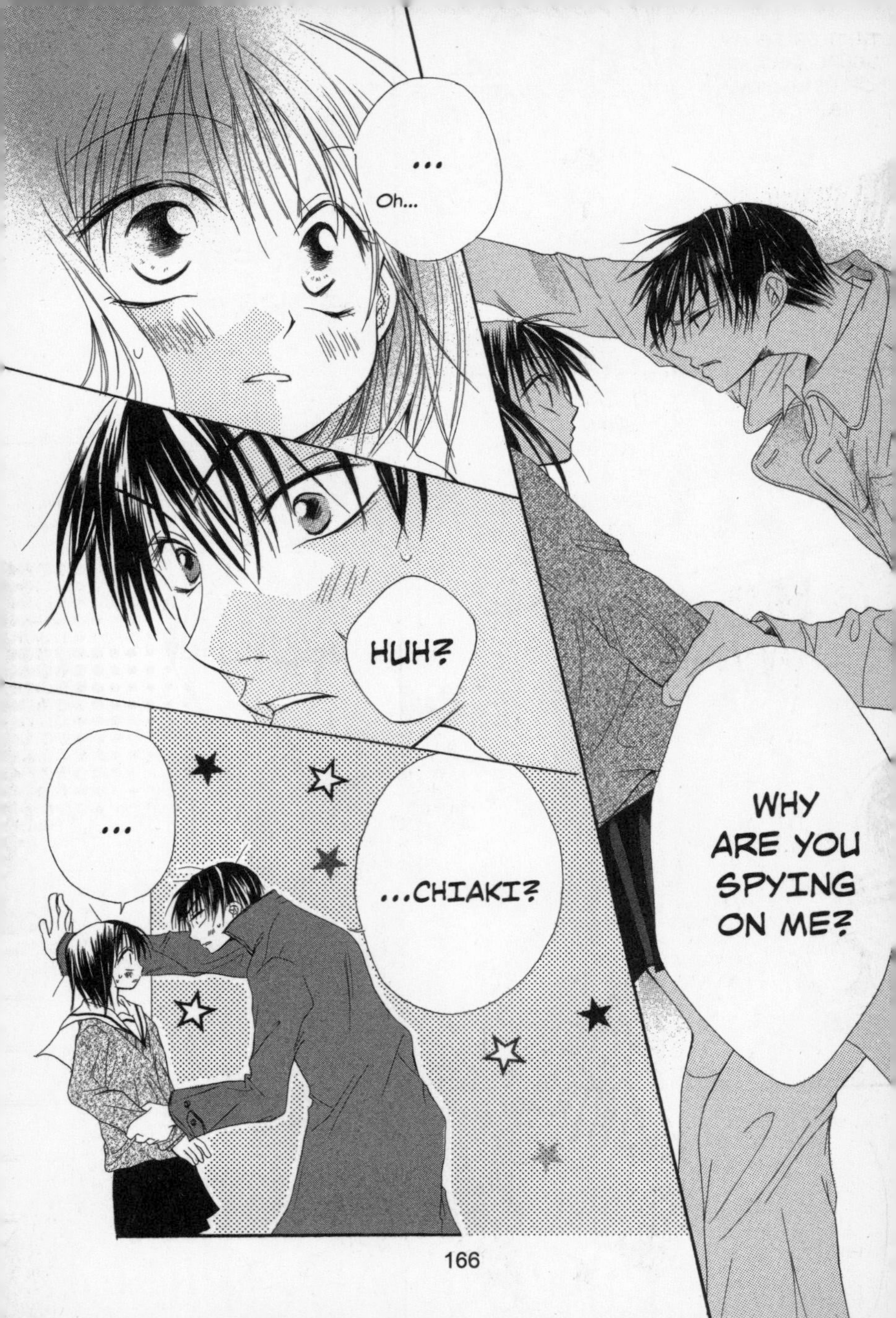
WHY ARE YOU SPYING ON ME?
...
Oh...
HUH?
...CHIAKI?
...

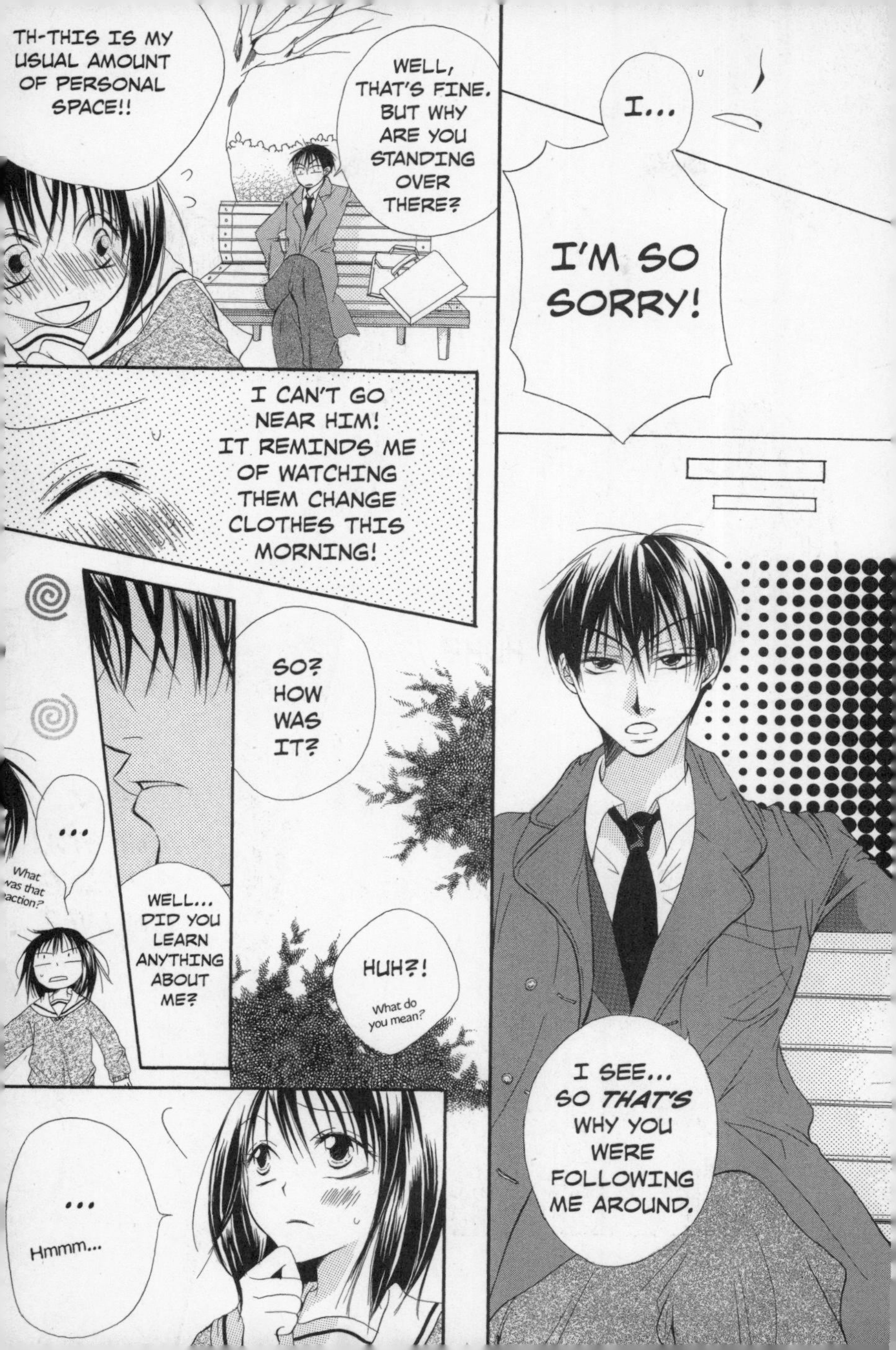
I...
I'M SO SORRY!
I SEE... SO *THAT'S* WHY YOU WERE FOLLOWING ME AROUND.
TH-THIS IS MY USUAL AMOUNT OF PERSONAL SPACE!!
WELL, THAT'S FINE. BUT WHY ARE YOU STANDING OVER THERE?
I CAN'T GO NEAR HIM! IT REMINDS ME OF WATCHING THEM CHANGE CLOTHES THIS MORNING!
SO? HOW WAS IT?
...
What was that reaction?
WELL... DID YOU LEARN ANYTHING ABOUT ME?
HUH?!
What do you mean?
...
Hmmm...

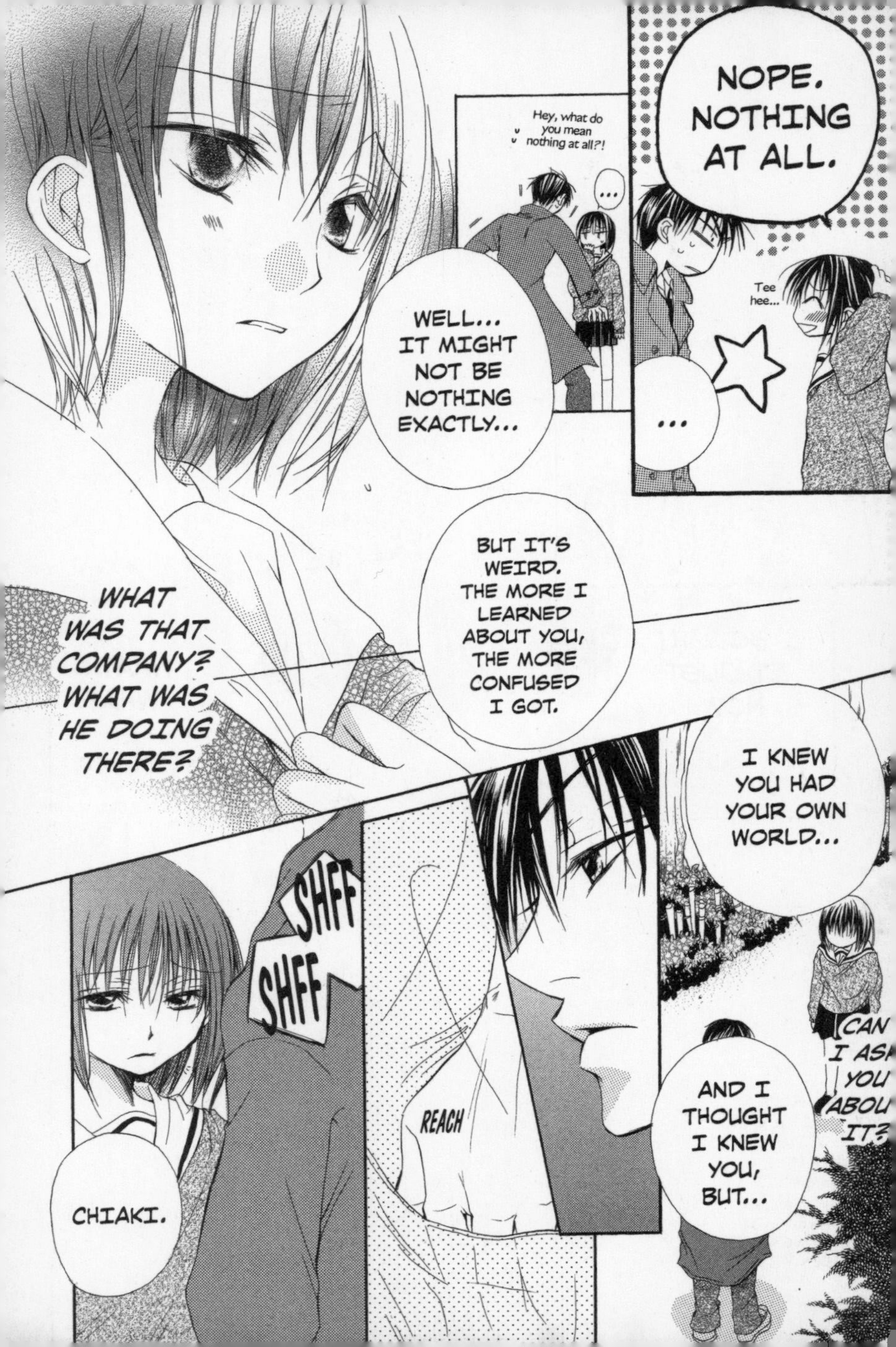
NOPE. NOTHING AT ALL.
Tee hee...
...
Hey, what do you mean nothing at all?!
...
WELL... IT MIGHT NOT BE NOTHING EXACTLY...
BUT IT'S WEIRD. THE MORE I LEARNED ABOUT YOU, THE MORE CONFUSED I GOT.
WHAT WAS THAT COMPANY? WHAT WAS HE DOING THERE?
I KNEW YOU HAD YOUR OWN WORLD...
CAN I AS YOU ABOU IT?
AND I THOUGHT I KNEW YOU, BUT...
REACH
SHFF
SHFF
CHIAKI.

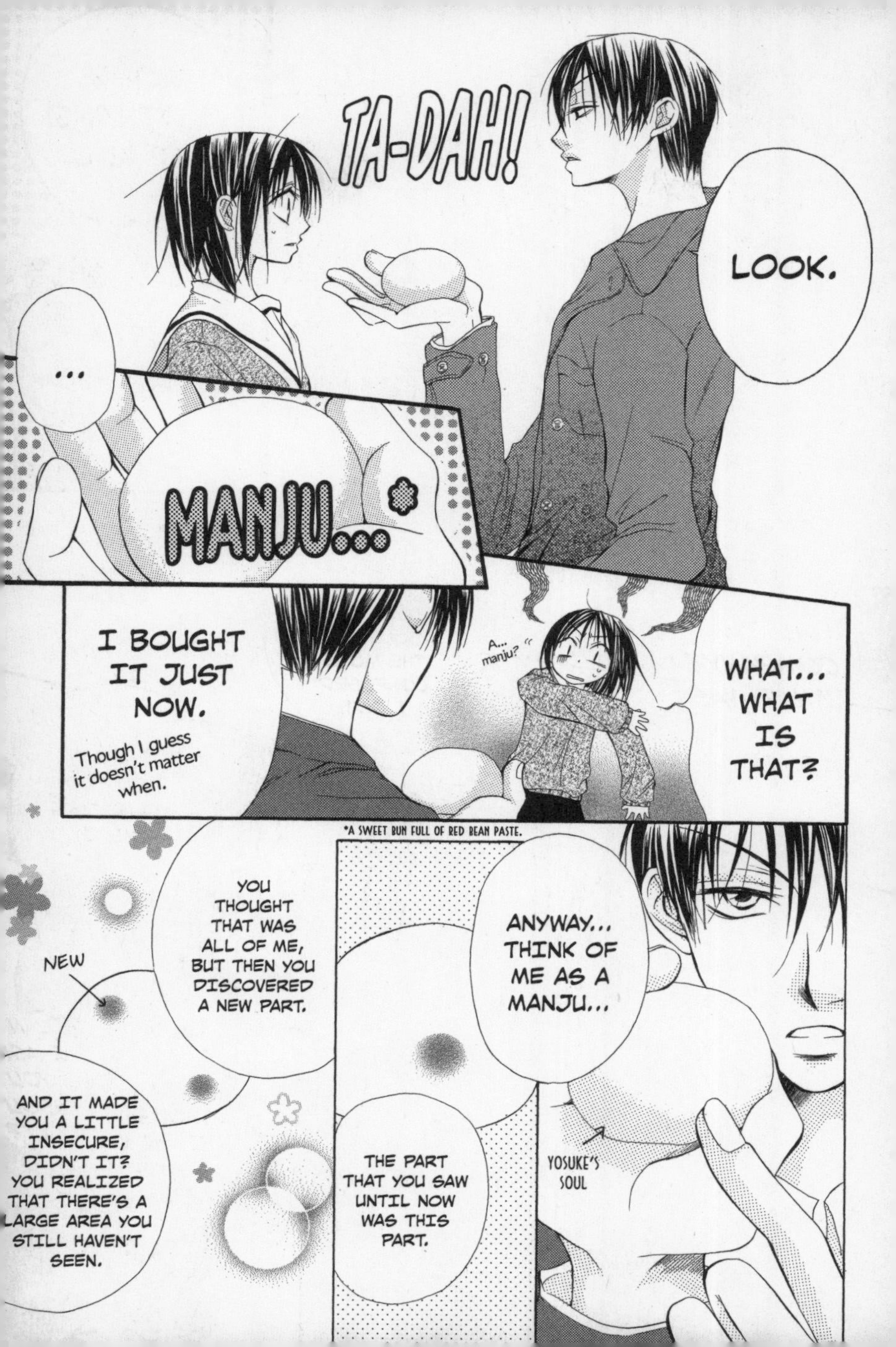
TA-DAH!
LOOK.
...
MANJU... *
WHAT... WHAT IS THAT?
A... manju?
I BOUGHT IT JUST NOW.
Though I guess it doesn't matter when.
ANYWAY... THINK OF ME AS A MANJU...
YOSUKE'S SOUL
THE PART THAT YOU SAW UNTIL NOW WAS THIS PART.
YOU THOUGHT THAT WAS ALL OF ME, BUT THEN YOU DISCOVERED A NEW PART.
NEW
AND IT MADE YOU A LITTLE INSECURE, DIDN'T IT? YOU REALIZED THAT THERE'S A LARGE AREA YOU STILL HAVEN'T SEEN.
*A SWEET BUN FULL OF RED BEAN PASTE.

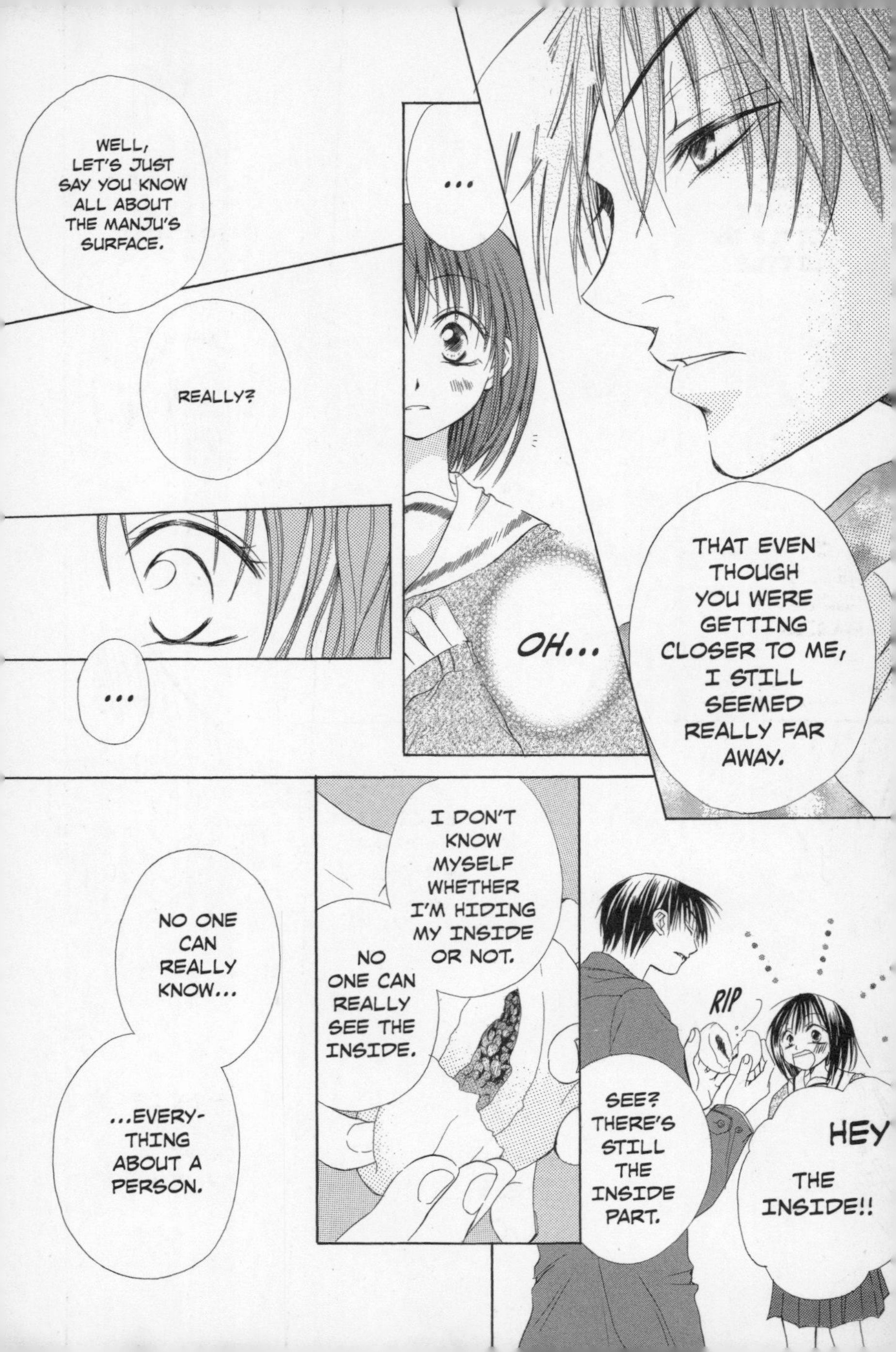
...
THAT EVEN THOUGH YOU WERE GETTING CLOSER TO ME, I STILL SEEMED REALLY FAR AWAY.
OH...
WELL, LET'S JUST SAY YOU KNOW ALL ABOUT THE MANJU'S SURFACE.
REALLY?
...
HEY
THE INSIDE!!
RIP
SEE? THERE'S STILL THE INSIDE PART.
I DON'T KNOW MYSELF WHETHER I'M HIDING MY INSIDE OR NOT.
NO ONE CAN REALLY SEE THE INSIDE.
NO ONE CAN REALLY KNOW...
...EVERY-THING ABOUT A PERSON.

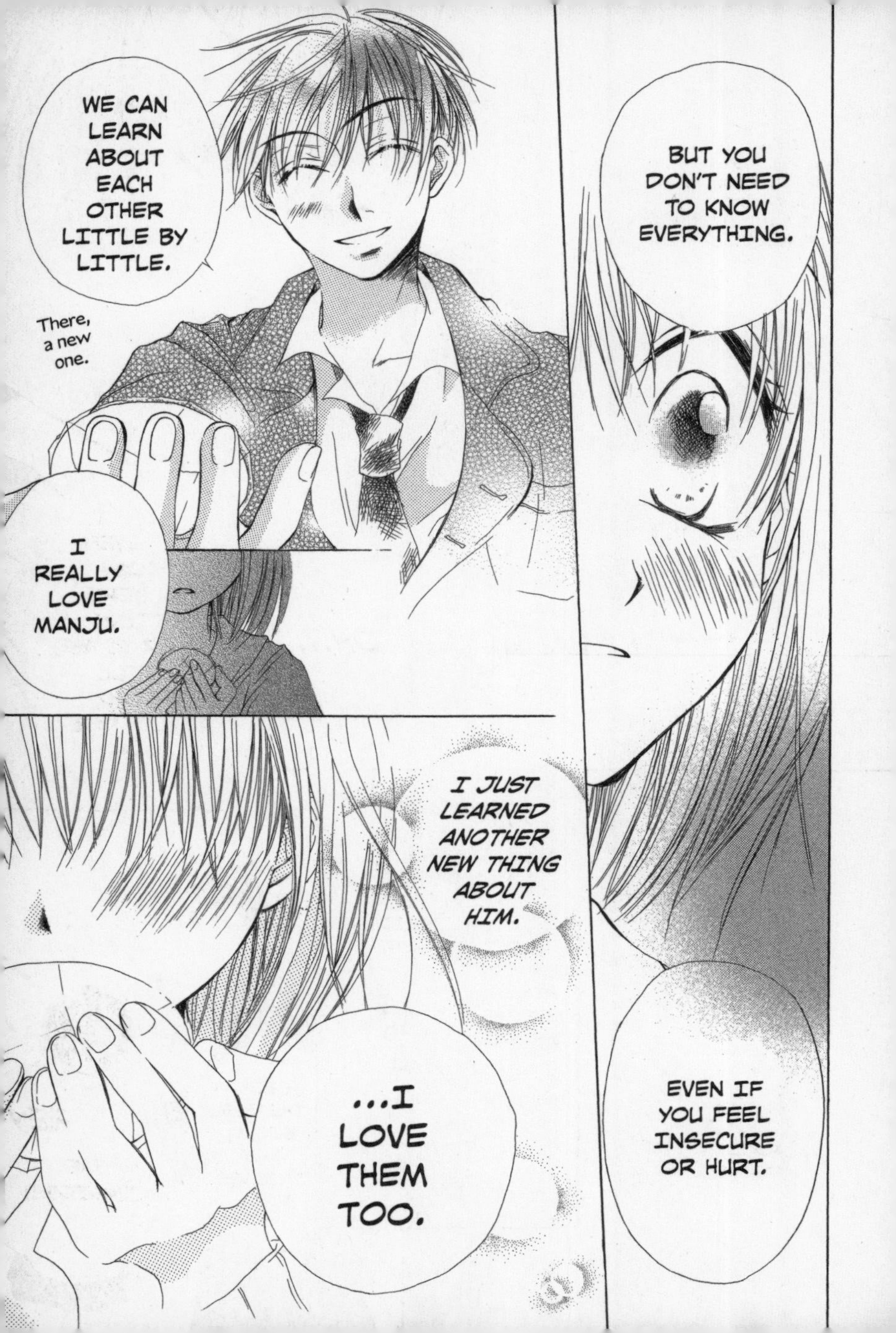
BUT YOU DON'T NEED TO KNOW EVERYTHING.
EVEN IF YOU FEEL INSECURE OR HURT.
WE CAN LEARN ABOUT EACH OTHER LITTLE BY LITTLE.
There, a new one.
I REALLY LOVE MANJU.
I JUST LEARNED ANOTHER NEW THING ABOUT HIM.
...I LOVE THEM TOO.

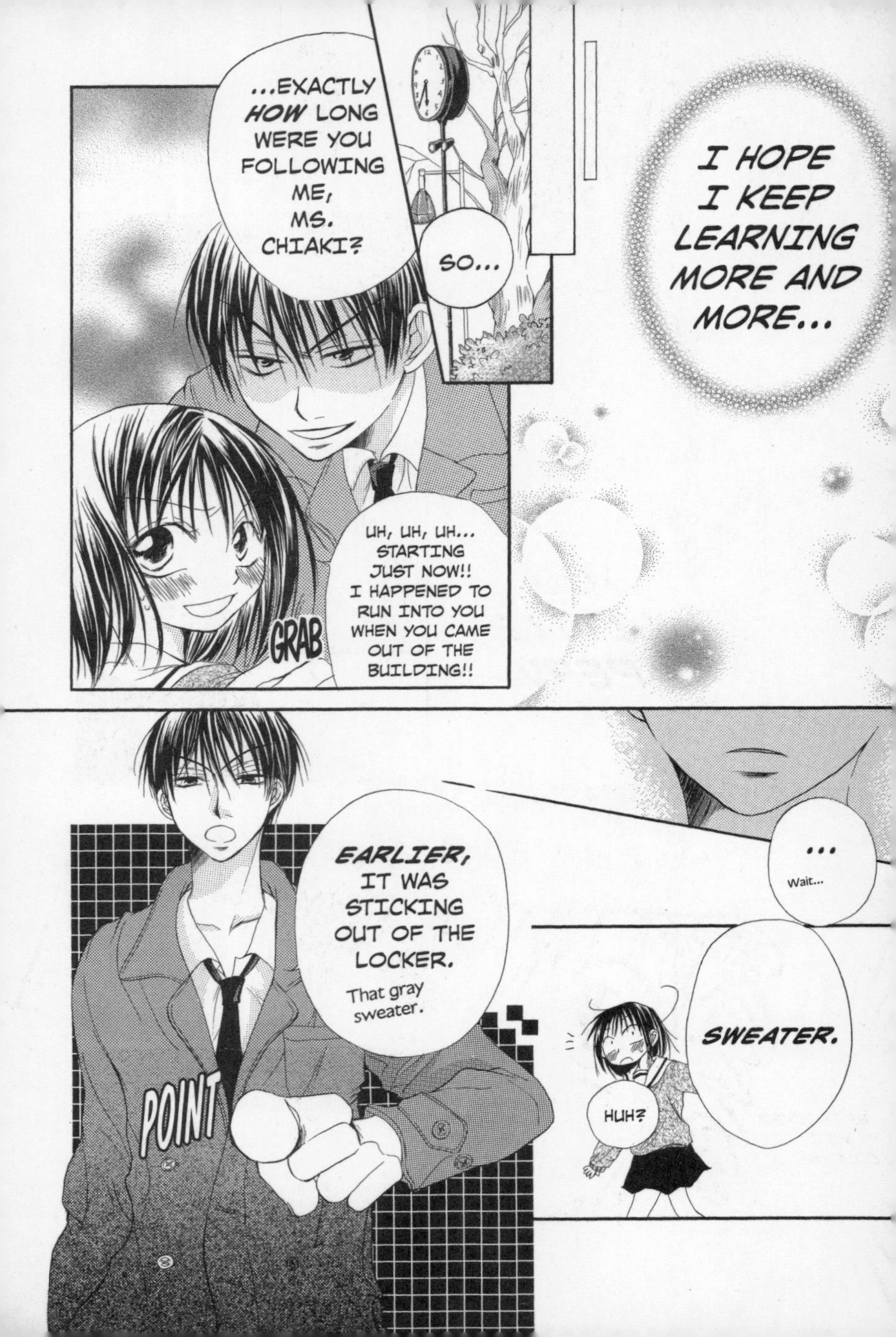
I HOPE I KEEP LEARNING MORE AND MORE...
SO...
...EXACTLY HOW LONG WERE YOU FOLLOWING ME, MS. CHIAKI?
UH, UH, UH... STARTING JUST NOW!! I HAPPENED TO RUN INTO YOU WHEN YOU CAME OUT OF THE BUILDING!!
GRAB
...
Wait...
SWEATER.
HUH?
EARLIER, IT WAS STICKING OUT OF THE LOCKER.
That gray sweater.
POINT

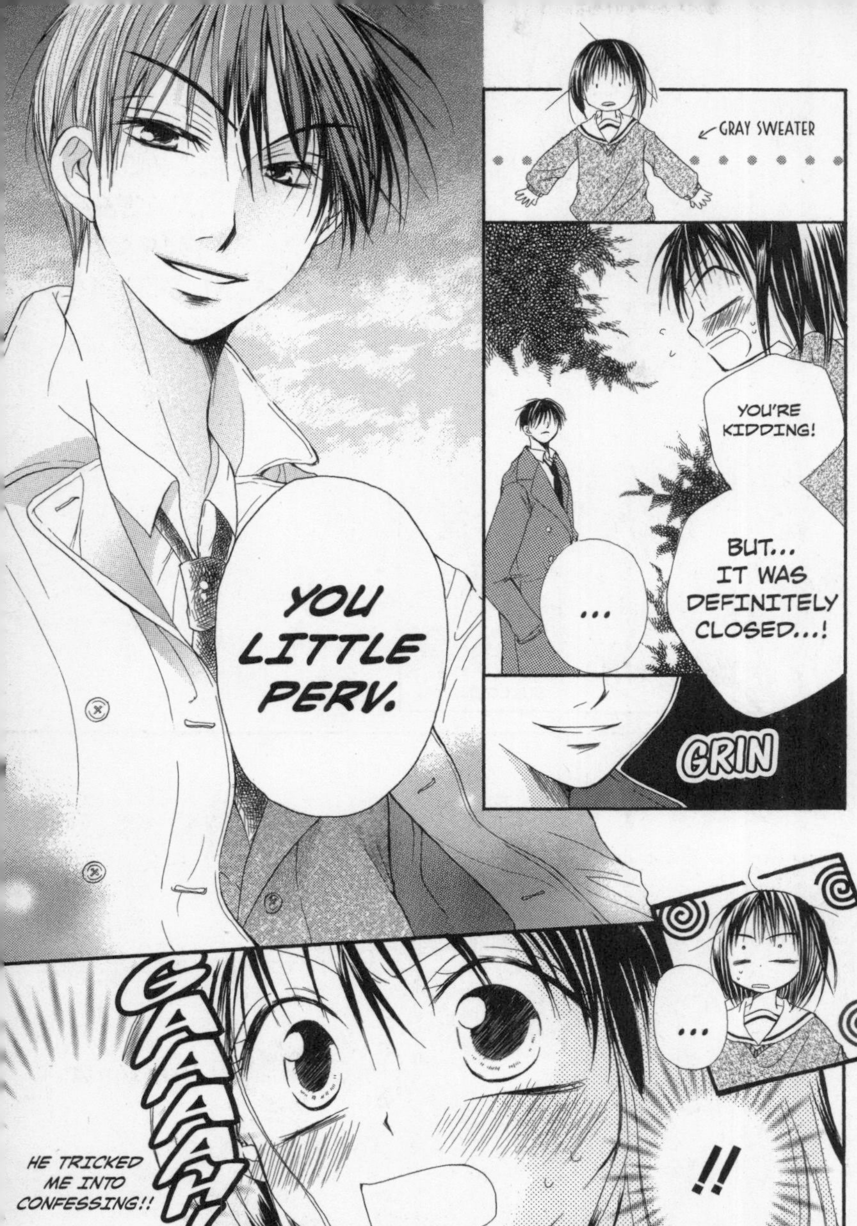
GRAY SWEATER
YOU'RE KIDDING!
BUT... IT WAS DEFINITELY CLOSED...!
...
GRIN
YOU LITTLE PERV.
...
!!
GAAAAH!
HE TRICKED ME INTO CONFESSING!!

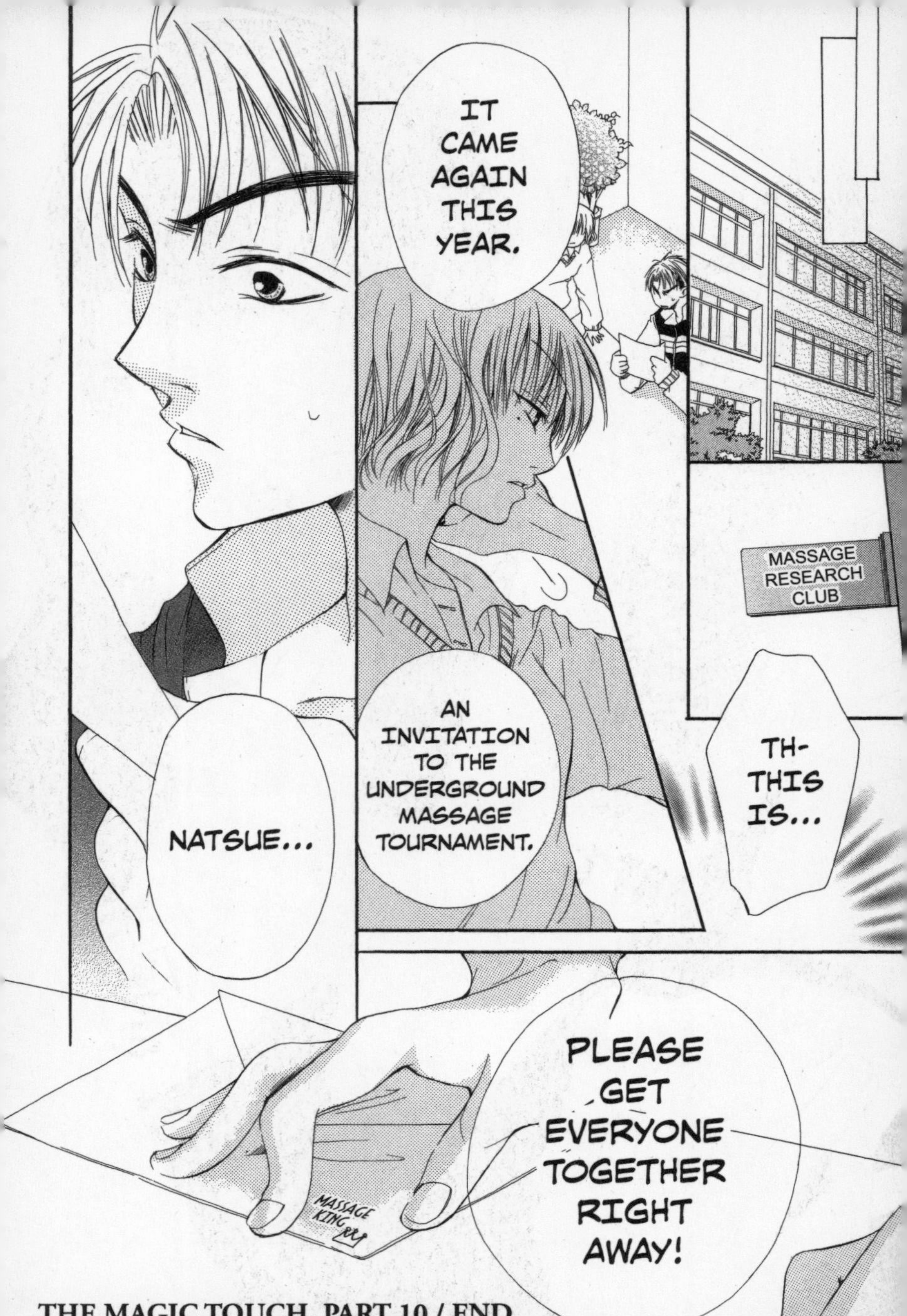
MASSAGE RESEARCH CLUB
TH-THIS IS...
IT CAME AGAIN THIS YEAR.
AN INVITATION TO THE UNDERGROUND MASSAGE TOURNAMENT.
NATSUE...
PLEASE GET EVERYONE TOGETHER RIGHT AWAY!
MASSAGE KING

THE MAGIC TOUCH, PART 10 / END

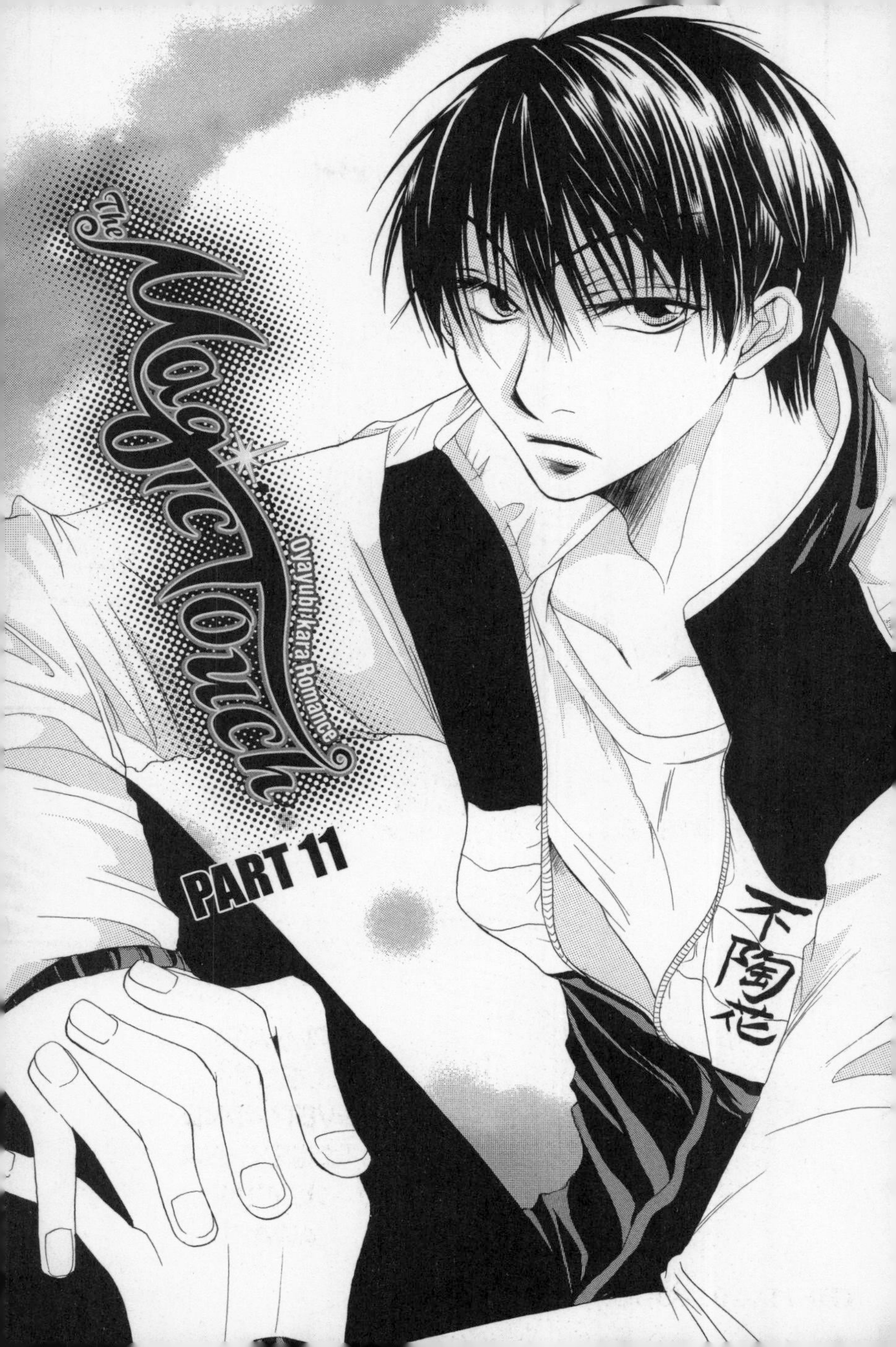
The Magic Touch
Oyayubi kara Romance
PART 11
不陶花

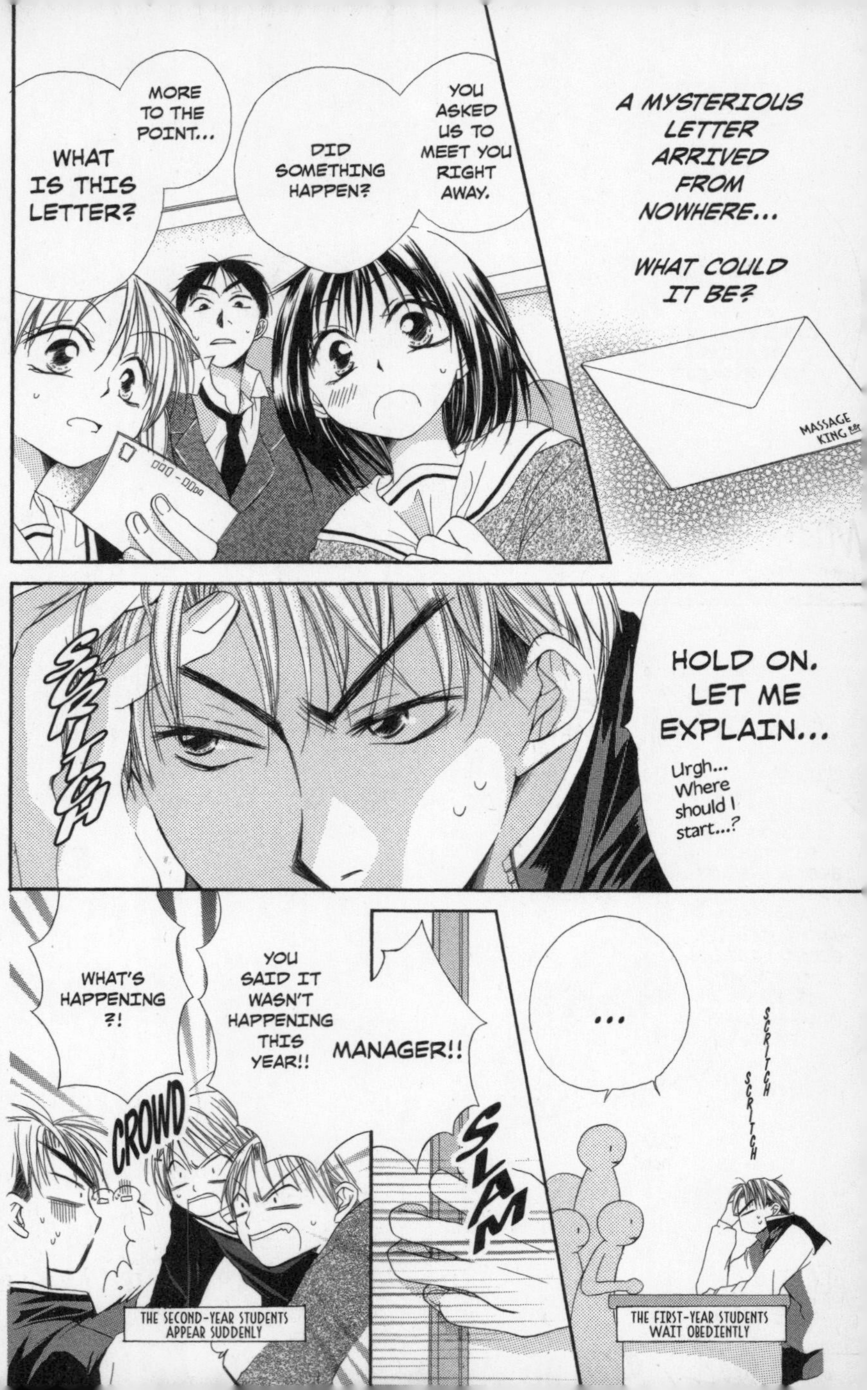
A MYSTERIOUS LETTER ARRIVED FROM NOWHERE...
WHAT COULD IT BE?
MASSAGE KING
YOU ASKED US TO MEET YOU RIGHT AWAY.
DID SOMETHING HAPPEN?
MORE TO THE POINT...
WHAT IS THIS LETTER?
HOLD ON. LET ME EXPLAIN...
Urgh... Where should I start...?
SCRITCH
...
SCRITCH SCRITCH
THE FIRST-YEAR STUDENTS WAIT OBEDIENTLY
MANAGER!!
SLAM
YOU SAID IT WASN'T HAPPENING THIS YEAR!!
WHAT'S HAPPENING?!
CROWD
THE SECOND-YEAR STUDENTS APPEAR SUDDENLY

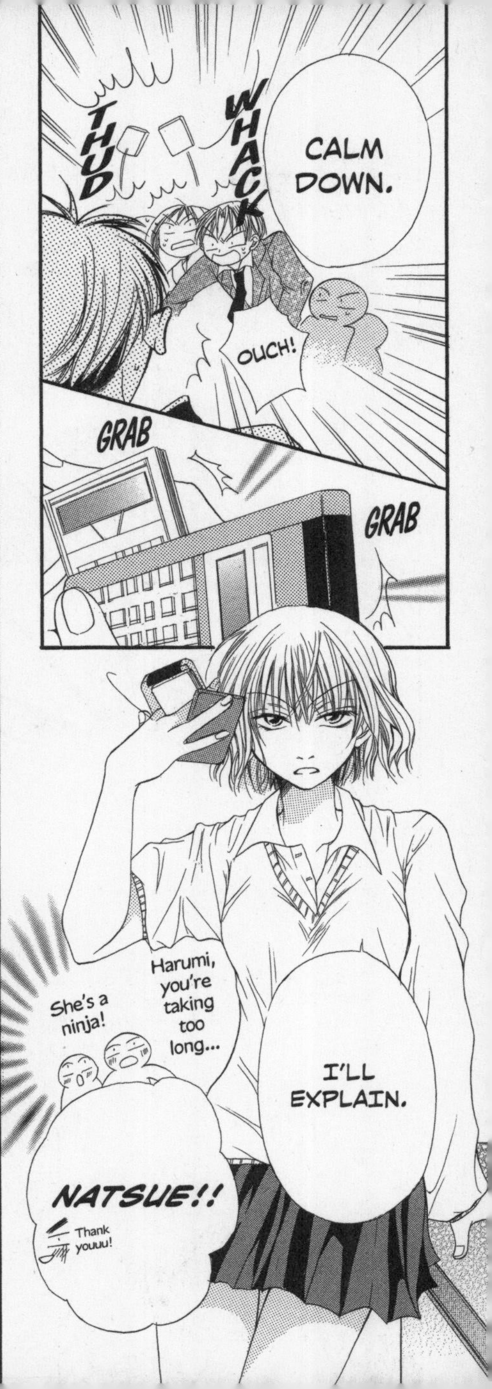
CALM DOWN.
WHACK
THUD
OUCH!
GRAB
GRAB
I'LL EXPLAIN.
Harumi, you're taking too long...
She's a ninja!
NATSUE!!
Thank youuu!

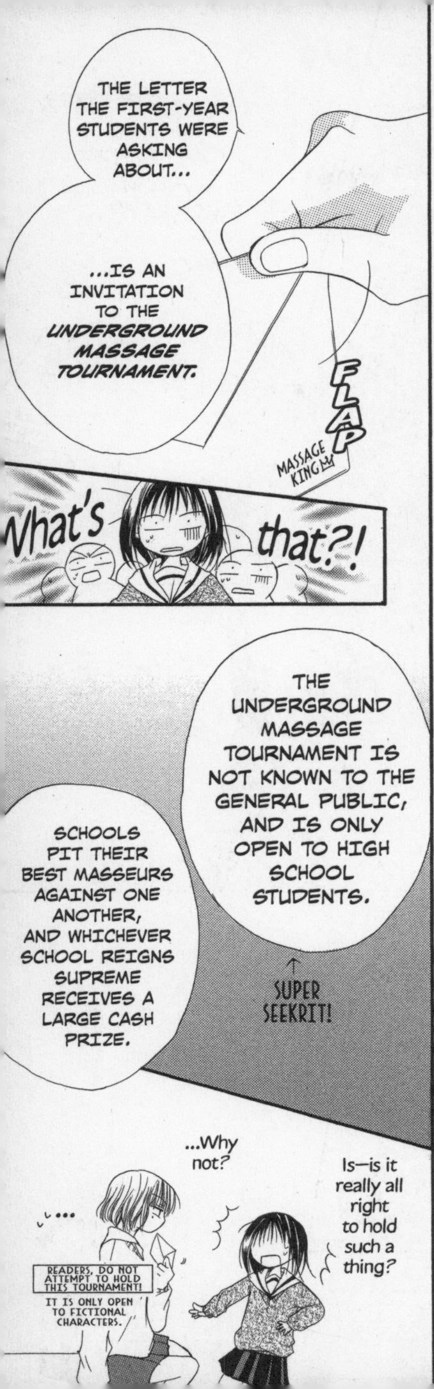
THE LETTER THE FIRST-YEAR STUDENTS WERE ASKING ABOUT...
...IS AN INVITATION TO THE *UNDERGROUND MASSAGE TOURNAMENT.*
FLAP
MASSAGE KING
What's that?!
THE UNDERGROUND MASSAGE TOURNAMENT IS NOT KNOWN TO THE GENERAL PUBLIC, AND IS ONLY OPEN TO HIGH SCHOOL STUDENTS.
SCHOOLS PIT THEIR BEST MASSEURS AGAINST ONE ANOTHER, AND WHICHEVER SCHOOL REIGNS SUPREME RECEIVES A LARGE CASH PRIZE.
↑ SUPER SEEKRIT!
Is—is it really all right to hold such a thing?
...Why not?
...
READERS, DO NOT ATTEMPT TO HOLD THIS TOURNAMENT!
IT IS ONLY OPEN TO FICTIONAL CHARACTERS.

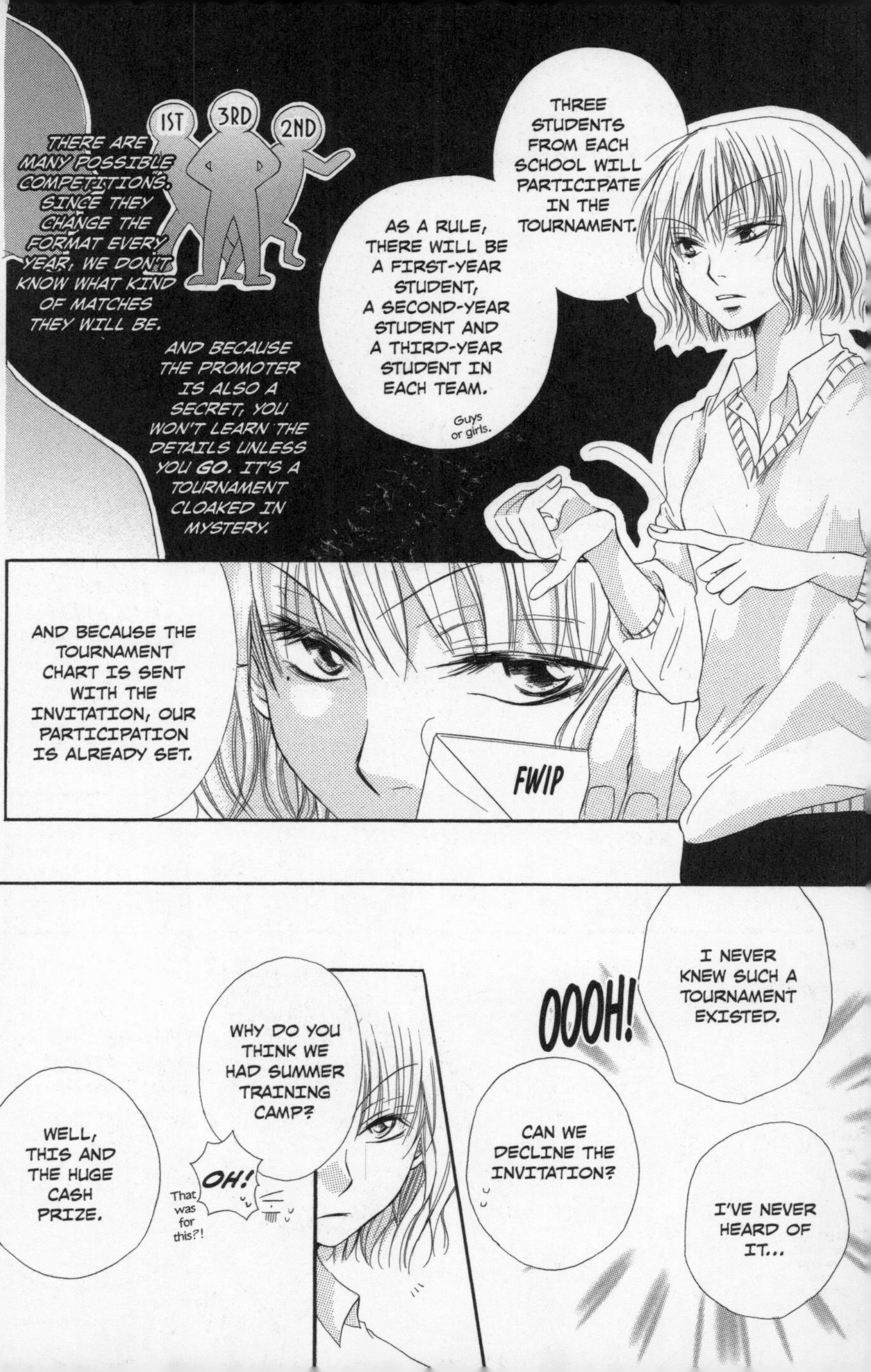
THREE STUDENTS FROM EACH SCHOOL WILL PARTICIPATE IN THE TOURNAMENT.
AS A RULE, THERE WILL BE A FIRST-YEAR STUDENT, A SECOND-YEAR STUDENT AND A THIRD-YEAR STUDENT IN EACH TEAM.
Guys or girls.
1ST
3RD
2ND
THERE ARE MANY POSSIBLE COMPETITIONS. SINCE THEY CHANGE THE FORMAT EVERY YEAR, WE DON'T KNOW WHAT KIND OF MATCHES THEY WILL BE.
AND BECAUSE THE PROMOTER IS ALSO A SECRET, YOU WON'T LEARN THE DETAILS UNLESS YOU GO. IT'S A TOURNAMENT CLOAKED IN MYSTERY.
AND BECAUSE THE TOURNAMENT CHART IS SENT WITH THE INVITATION, OUR PARTICIPATION IS ALREADY SET.
FWIP
I NEVER KNEW SUCH A TOURNAMENT EXISTED.
OOOH!
I'VE NEVER HEARD OF IT...
CAN WE DECLINE THE INVITATION?
WHY DO YOU THINK WE HAD SUMMER TRAINING CAMP?
OH!
That was for this?!
WELL, THIS AND THE HUGE CASH PRIZE.

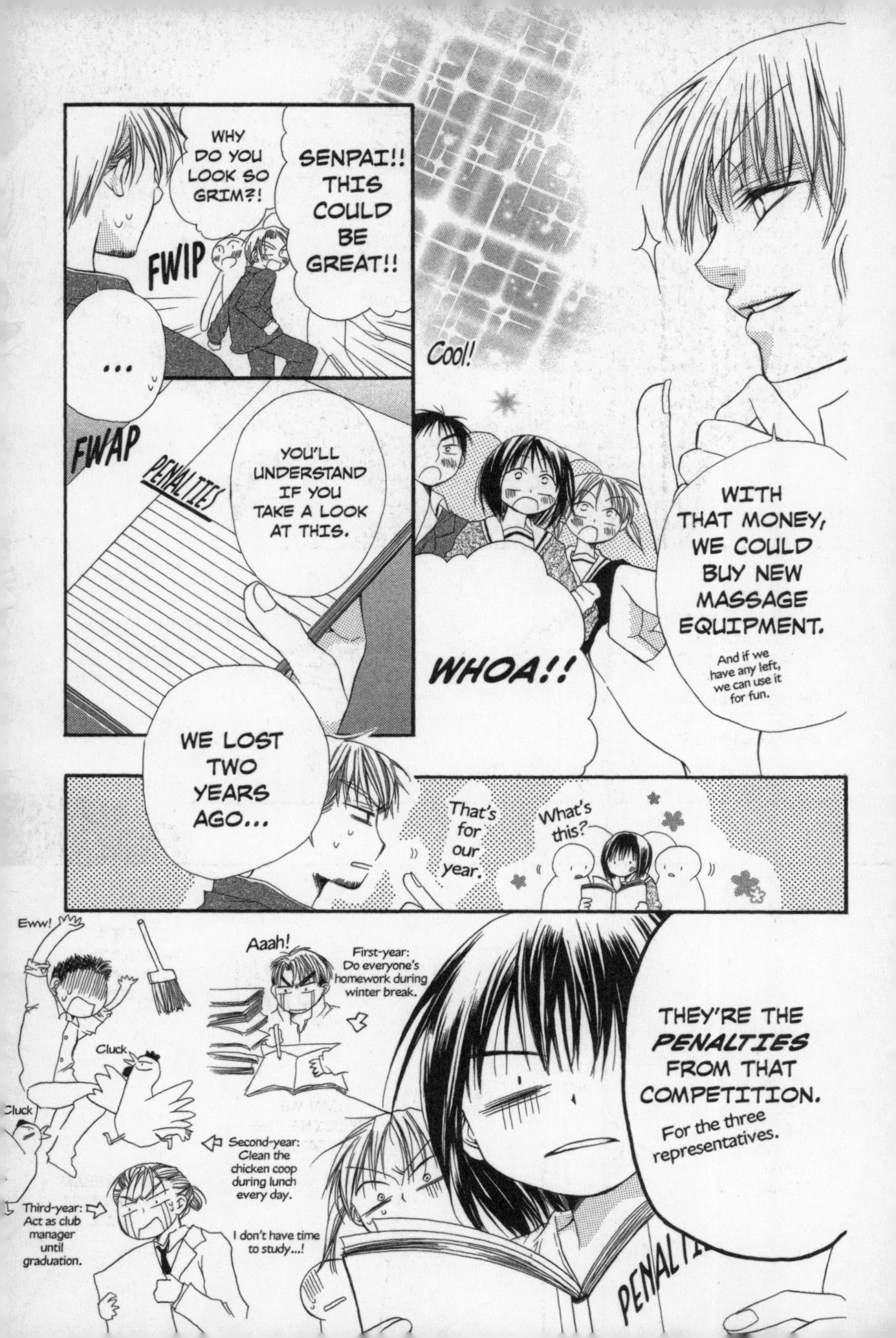
Cool!
WITH THAT MONEY, WE COULD BUY NEW MASSAGE EQUIPMENT.
And if we have any left, we can use it for fun.
WHOA!!
SENPAI!! THIS COULD BE GREAT!!
WHY DO YOU LOOK SO GRIM?!
FWIP
...
FWAP
PENALTIES
YOU'LL UNDERSTAND IF YOU TAKE A LOOK AT THIS.
WE LOST TWO YEARS AGO...
What's this?
That's for our year.
THEY'RE THE PENALTIES FROM THAT COMPETITION.
For the three representatives.
PENALTIES
First-year: Do everyone's homework during winter break.
Aaah!
Second-year: Clean the chicken coop during lunch every day.
Eww!
Cluck
Cluck
Third-year: Act as club manager until graduation.
I don't have time to study...!

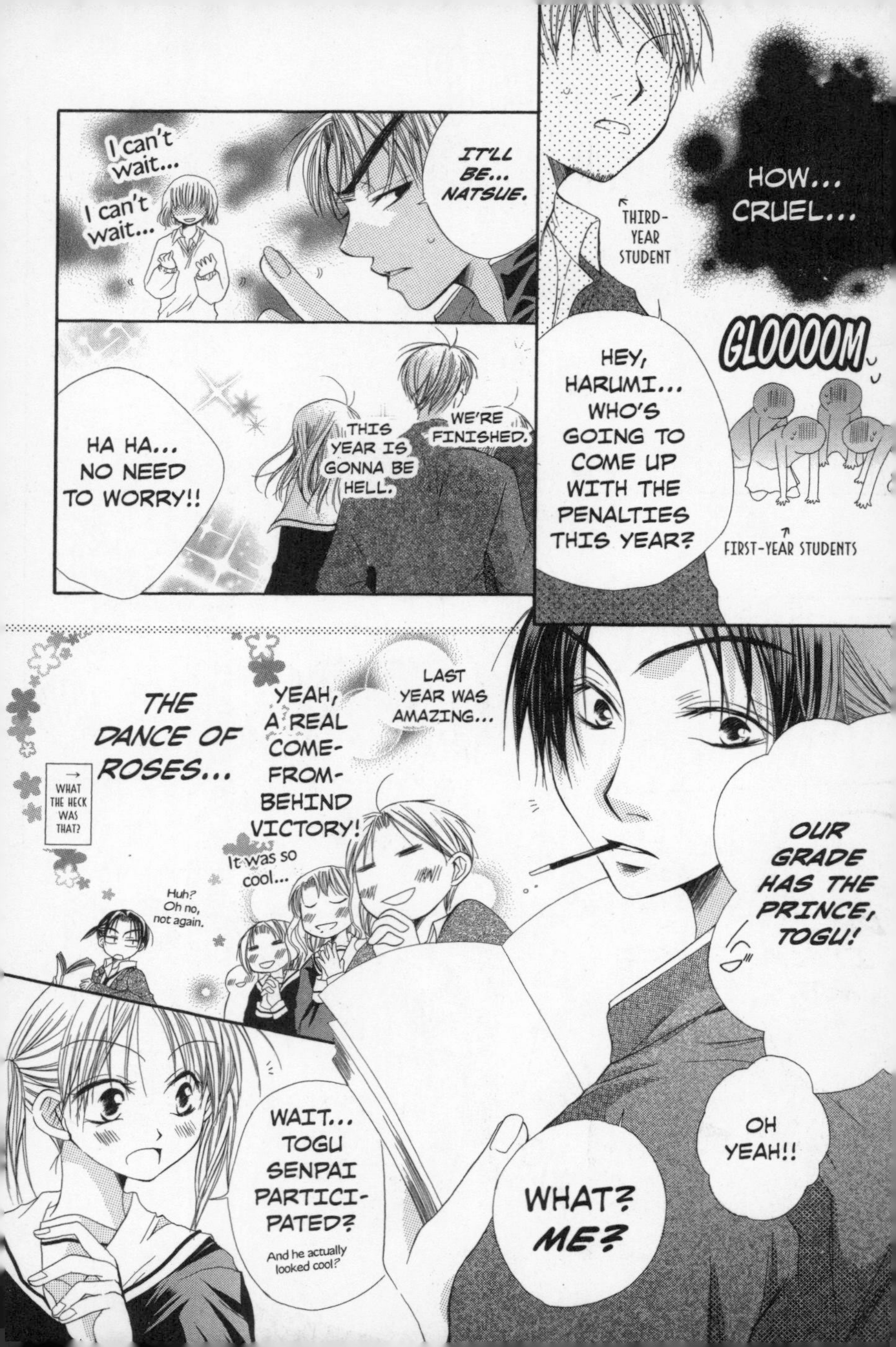
HOW... CRUEL...
THIRD-YEAR STUDENT
GLOOOM
HEY, HARUMI... WHO'S GOING TO COME UP WITH THE PENALTIES THIS YEAR?
FIRST-YEAR STUDENTS
IT'LL BE... NATSUE.
I can't wait...
I can't wait...
WE'RE FINISHED.
THIS YEAR IS GONNA BE HELL.
HA HA... NO NEED TO WORRY!!
OUR GRADE HAS THE PRINCE, TOGU!
LAST YEAR WAS AMAZING...
YEAH, A REAL COME-FROM-BEHIND VICTORY!
THE DANCE OF ROSES...
WHAT THE HECK WAS THAT?
It was so cool...
Huh? Oh no, not again.
OH YEAH!!
WHAT? ME?
WAIT... TOGU SENPAI PARTICIPATED?
And he actually looked cool?

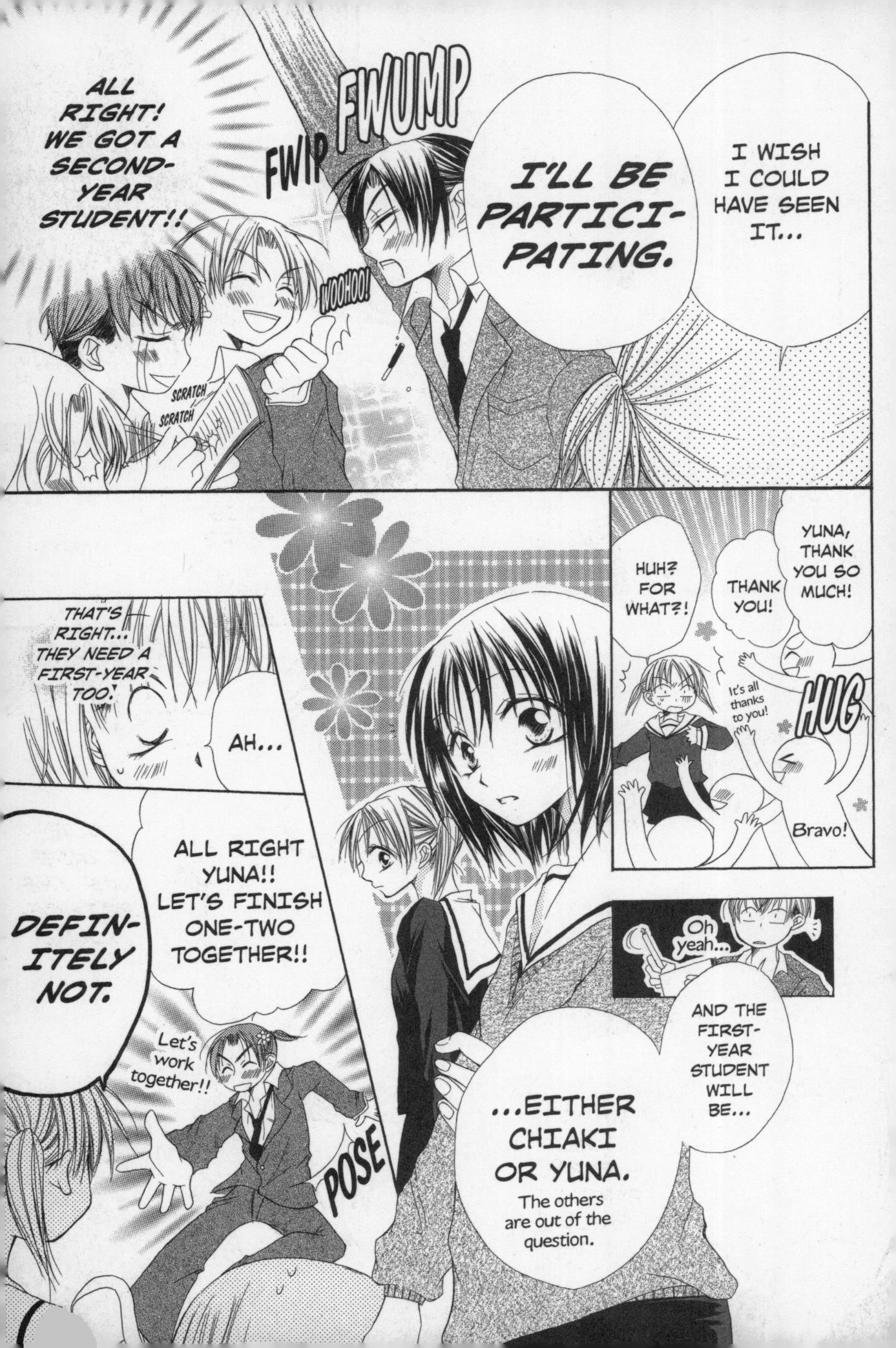
I WISH I COULD HAVE SEEN IT...
I'LL BE PARTICIPATING.
FWUMP
FWIP
WOOHOO!
ALL RIGHT! WE GOT A SECOND-YEAR STUDENT!!
SCRATCH SCRATCH
YUNA, THANK YOU SO MUCH!
THANK YOU!
HUH? FOR WHAT?!
HUG
It's all thanks to you!
Bravo!
Oh yeah...
AND THE FIRST-YEAR STUDENT WILL BE...
...EITHER CHIAKI OR YUNA.
The others are out of the question.
THAT'S RIGHT... THEY NEED A FIRST-YEAR TOO.
AH...
ALL RIGHT YUNA!! LET'S FINISH ONE-TWO TOGETHER!!
DEFINITELY NOT.
Let's work together!!
POSE

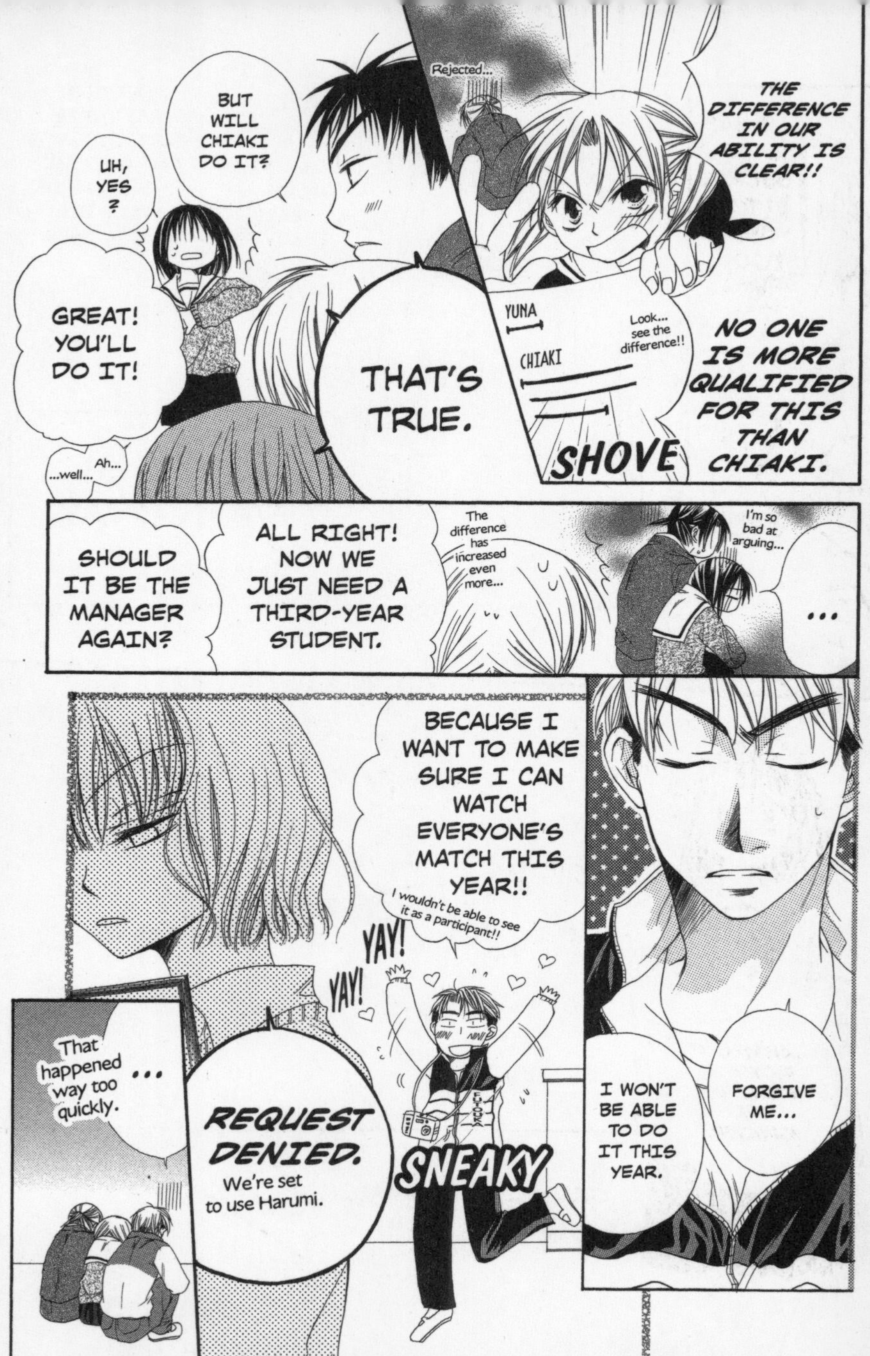
Rejected...
THE DIFFERENCE IN OUR ABILITY IS CLEAR!!
YUNA
CHIAKI
Look... see the difference!!
NO ONE IS MORE QUALIFIED FOR THIS THAN CHIAKI.
SHOVE
BUT WILL CHIAKI DO IT?
UH, YES?
THAT'S TRUE.
GREAT! YOU'LL DO IT!
Ah... ...well...
I'm so bad at arguing...
...
The difference has increased even more...
ALL RIGHT! NOW WE JUST NEED A THIRD-YEAR STUDENT.
SHOULD IT BE THE MANAGER AGAIN?
FORGIVE ME...
I WON'T BE ABLE TO DO IT THIS YEAR.
BECAUSE I WANT TO MAKE SURE I CAN WATCH EVERYONE'S MATCH THIS YEAR!!
I wouldn't be able to see it as a participant!!
YAY!
YAY!
SNEAKY
REQUEST DENIED.
We're set to use Harumi.
...
That happened way too quickly.

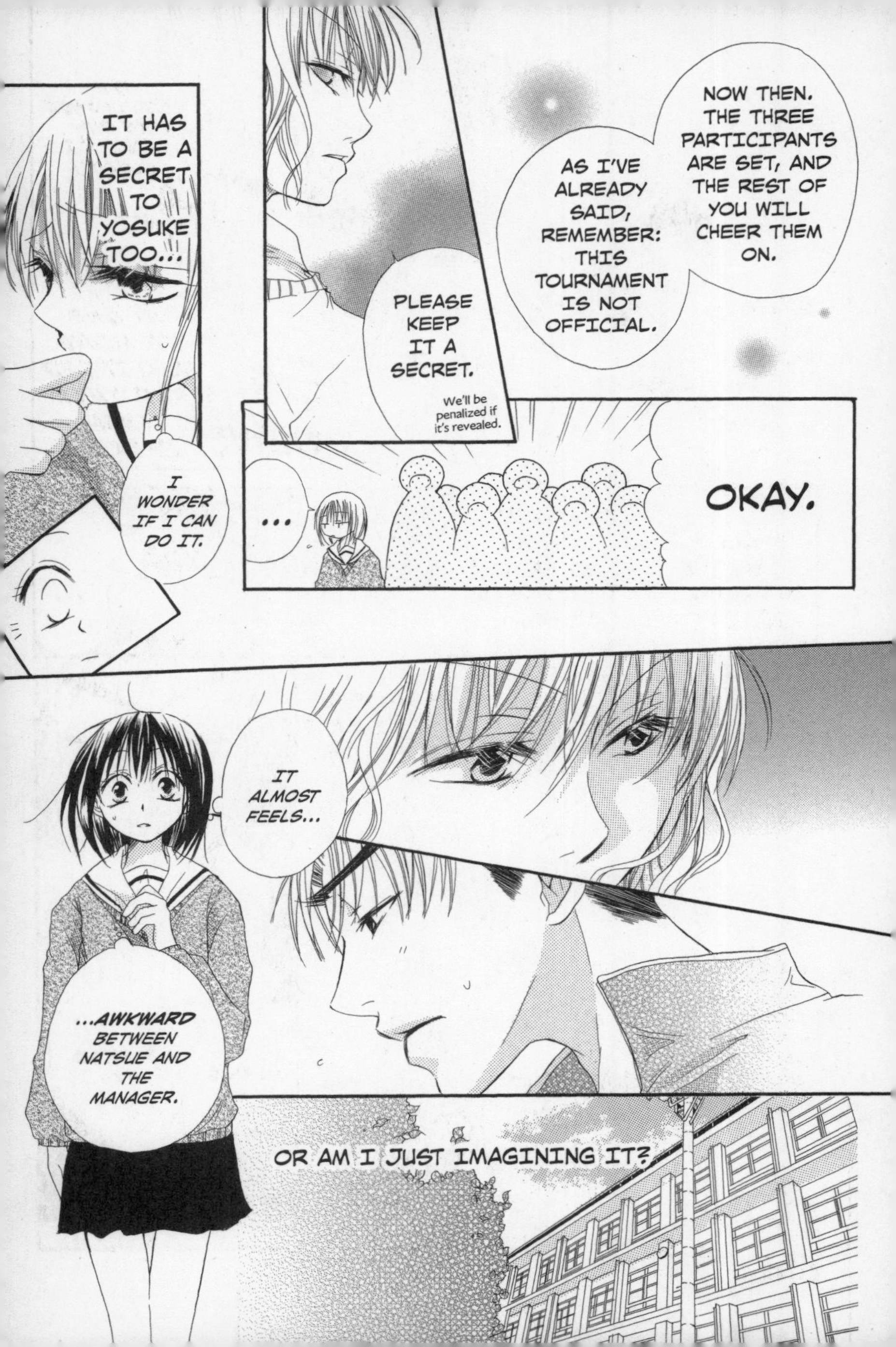
NOW THEN. THE THREE PARTICIPANTS ARE SET, AND THE REST OF YOU WILL CHEER THEM ON.
AS I'VE ALREADY SAID, REMEMBER: THIS TOURNAMENT IS NOT OFFICIAL.
PLEASE KEEP IT A SECRET.
We'll be penalized if it's revealed.
IT HAS TO BE A SECRET TO YOSUKE TOO...
OKAY.
...
I WONDER IF I CAN DO IT.
IT ALMOST FEELS...
...AWKWARD BETWEEN NATSUE AND THE MANAGER.
OR AM I JUST IMAGINING IT?

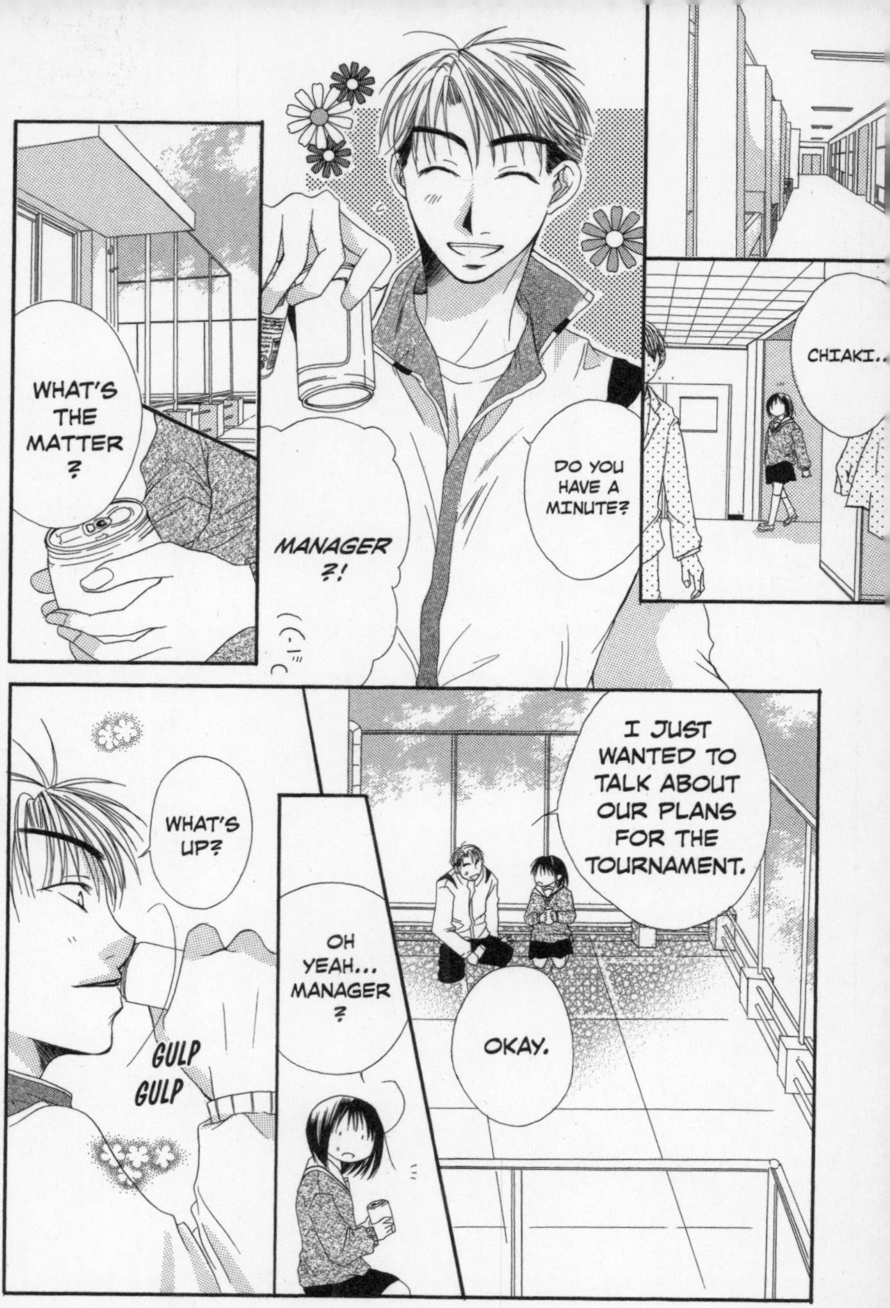
CHIAKI...
DO YOU HAVE A MINUTE?
MANAGER ?!
WHAT'S THE MATTER ?
I JUST WANTED TO TALK ABOUT OUR PLANS FOR THE TOURNAMENT.
OKAY.
OH YEAH... MANAGER ?
WHAT'S UP?
GULP GULP

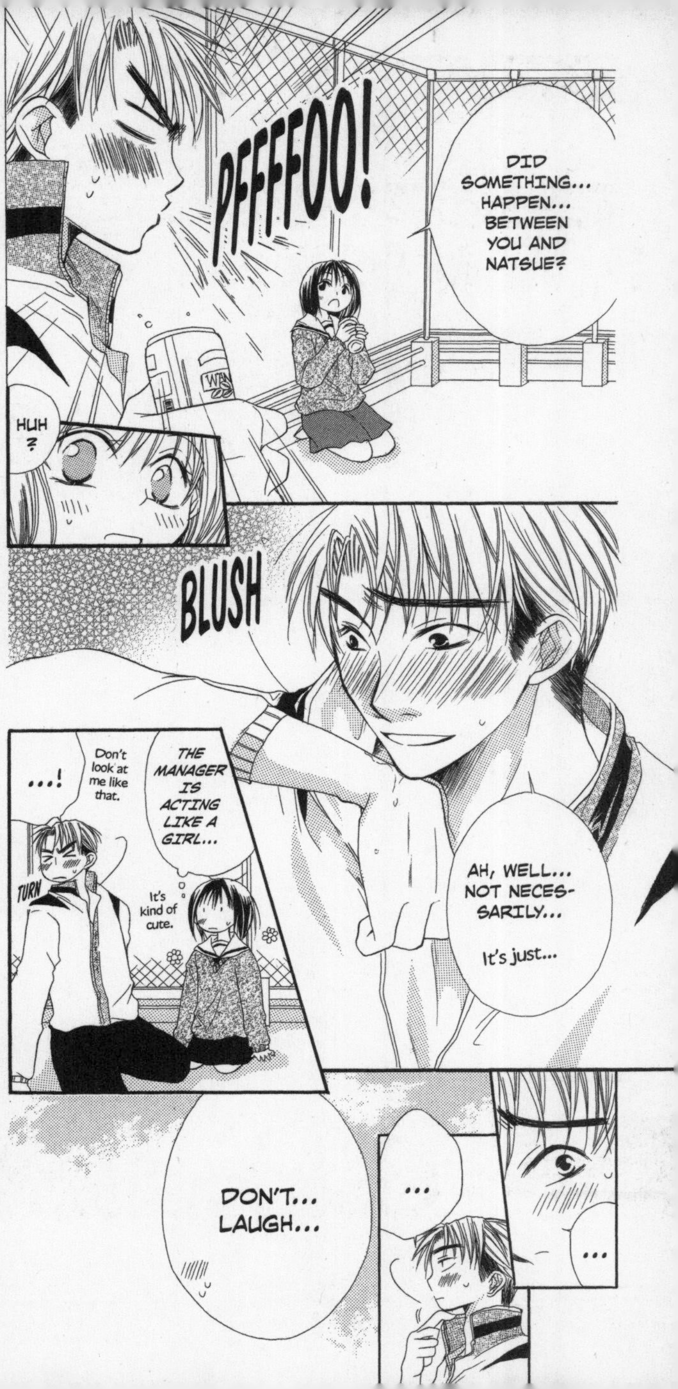
DID SOMETHING... HAPPEN... BETWEEN YOU AND NATSUE?
PFFFFOO!
HUH?
BLUSH
AH, WELL... NOT NECES-SARILY...
It's just...
THE MANAGER IS ACTING LIKE A GIRL...
Don't look at me like that.
...!
It's kind of cute.
TURN
...
...
DON'T... LAUGH...

Togu, Collector of Weird T-Shirts!

I don't have that many chances to draw normal clothes, but I love weird T-shirts, so I was happy when someone noticed the T-shirts in the summer training camp episode. <laugh> Lately I've been into shirts that say "Samurai," "Professional" and "Single Strike." Sometimes they're sold at gift shops... though no one in their right mind would ever be seen in one.

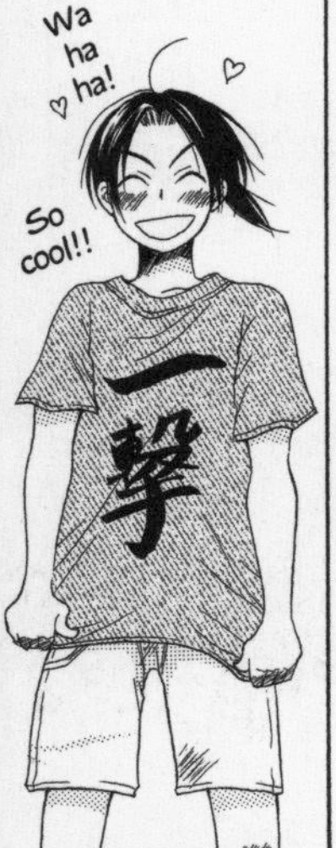
Wa ha ha!
So cool!!
一撃

SINGLE STRIKE

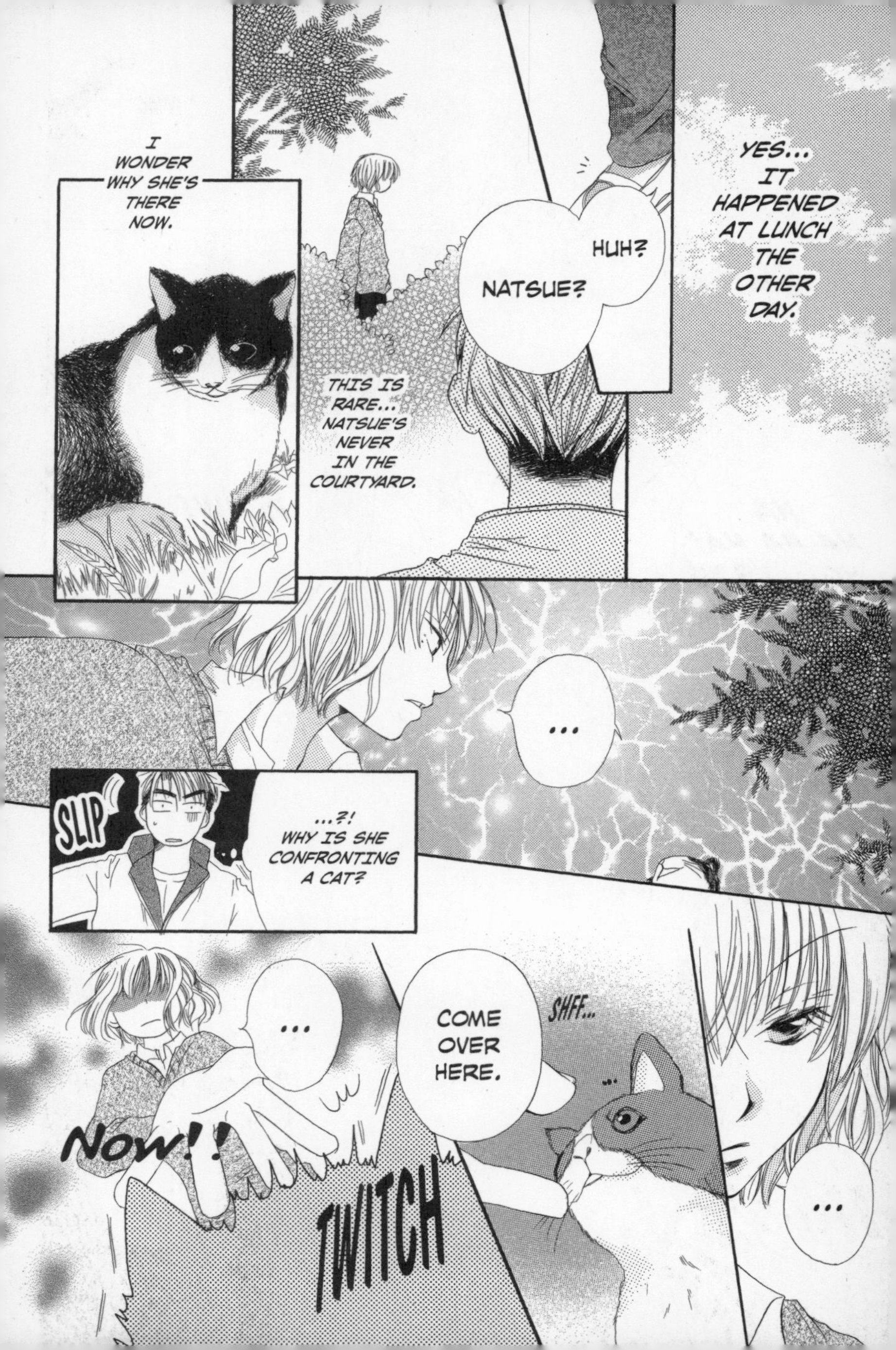
YES... IT HAPPENED AT LUNCH THE OTHER DAY.
HUH?
NATSUE?
THIS IS RARE... NATSUE'S NEVER IN THE COURTYARD.
I WONDER WHY SHE'S THERE NOW.
...
...?! WHY IS SHE CONFRONTING A CAT?
SLIP
...
SHFF...
COME OVER HERE.
...
TWITCH
Now!!

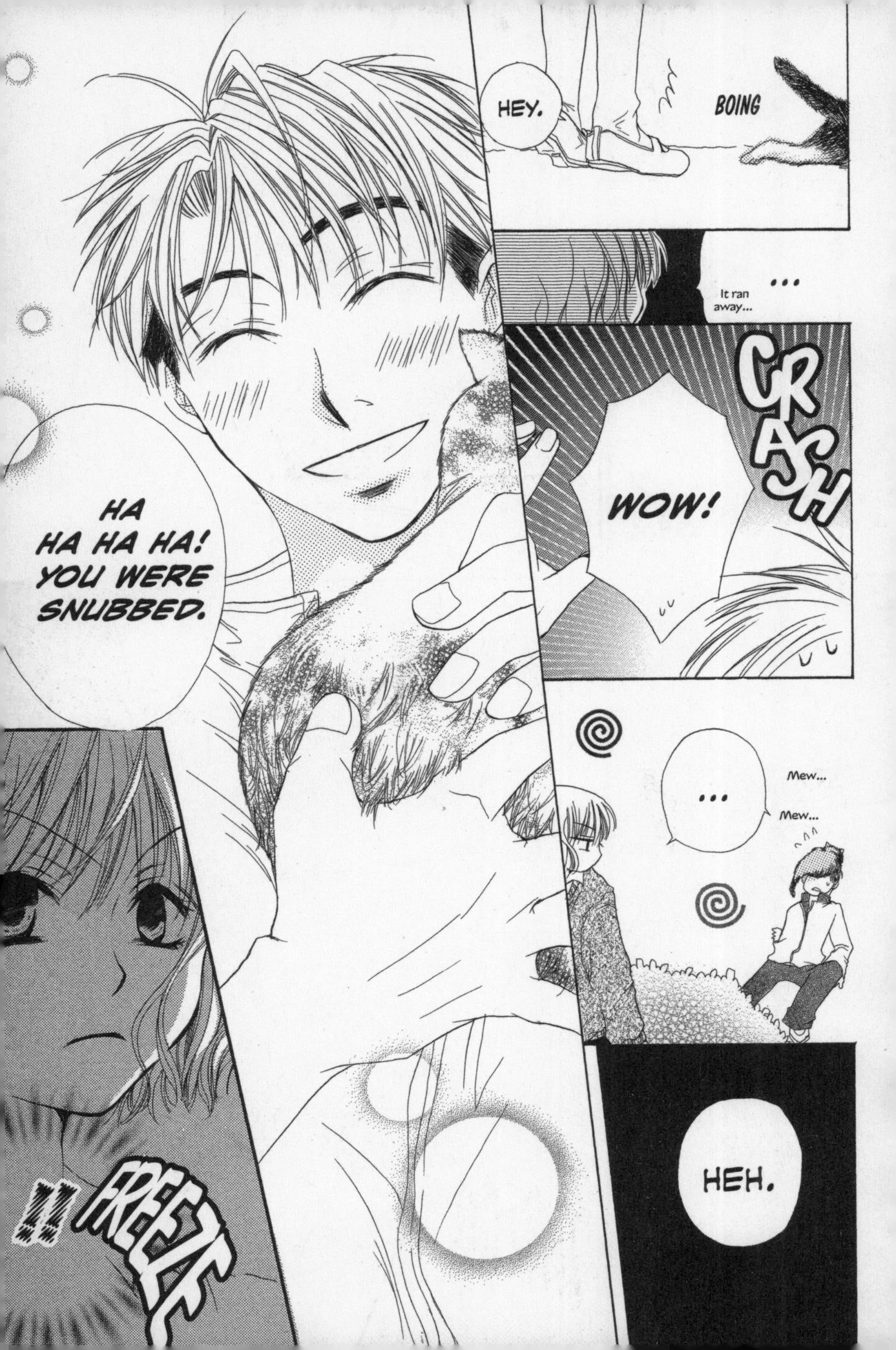

HEY.
BOING
...
It ran away...
CRASH
WOW!
...
Mew...
Mew...
HEH.
HA HA HA HA HA! YOU WERE SNUBBED.
FREEZE!!

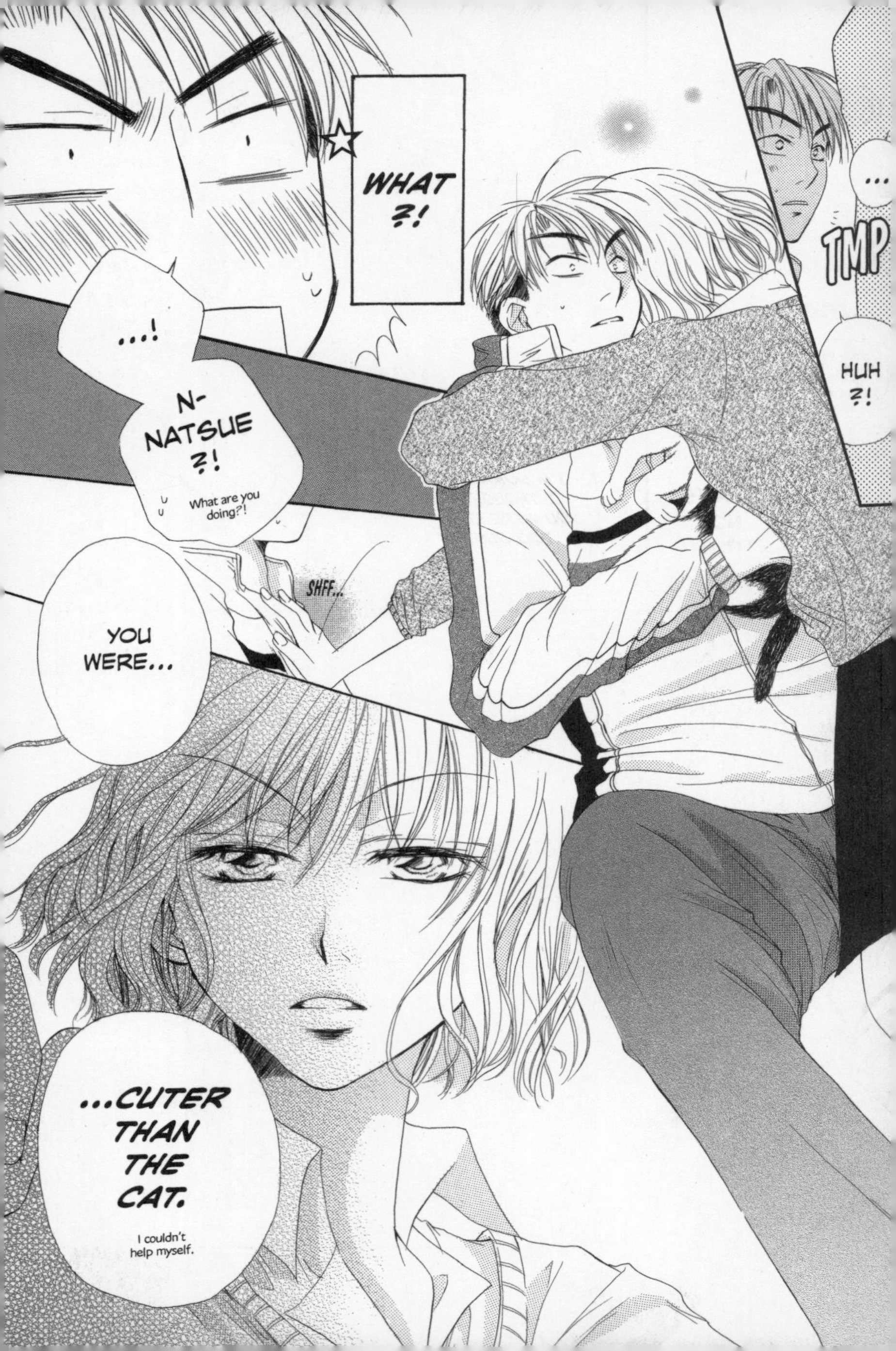
...
TMP
HUH ?!
WHAT ?!
...!
N-NATSUE ?!
What are you doing?!
SHFF...
YOU WERE...
...CUTER THAN THE CAT.
I couldn't help myself.

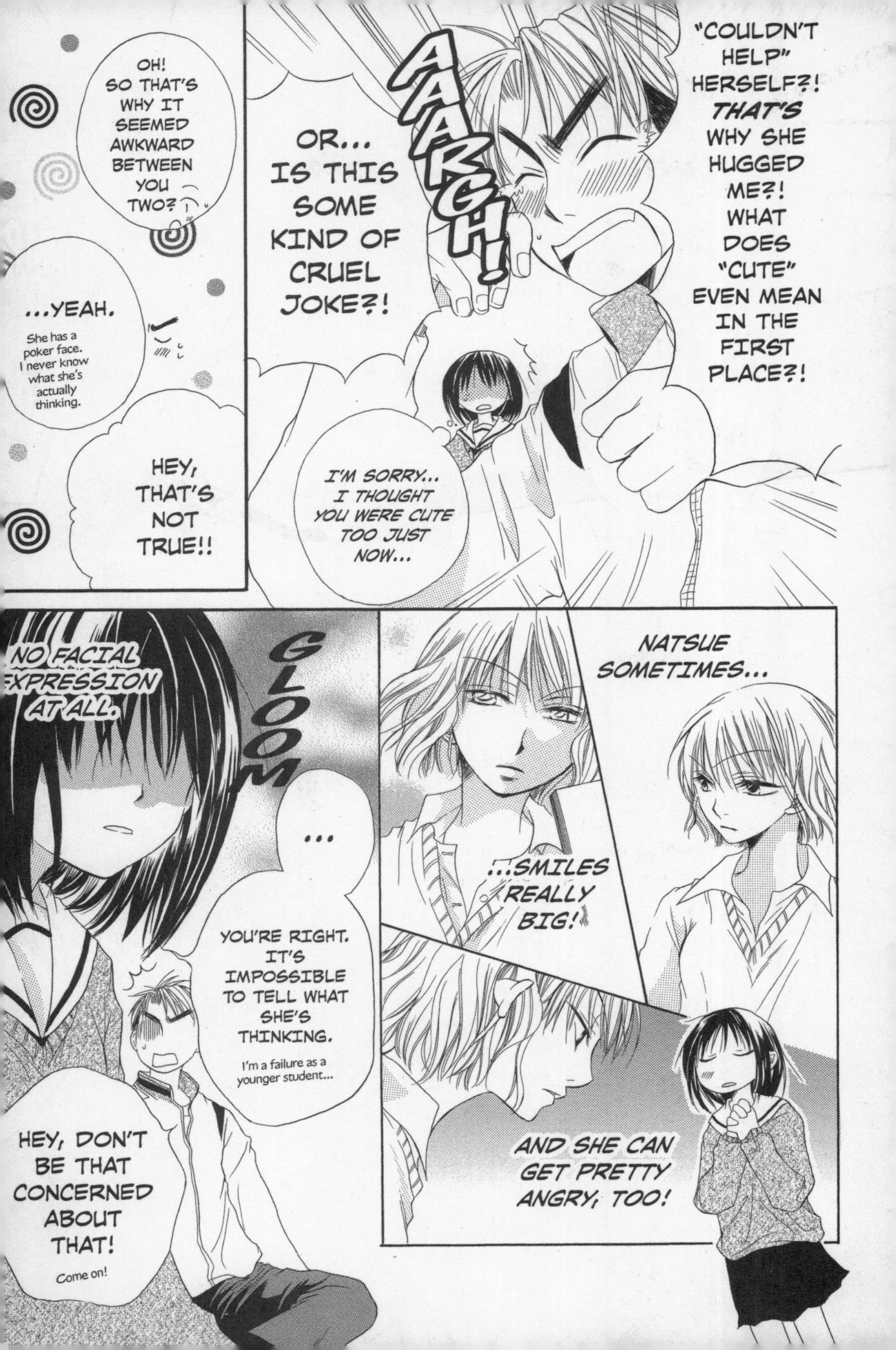
"COULDN'T HELP" HERSELF?! THAT'S WHY SHE HUGGED ME?! WHAT DOES "CUTE" EVEN MEAN IN THE FIRST PLACE?!
AAARGH!
OR... IS THIS SOME KIND OF CRUEL JOKE?!
I'M SORRY... I THOUGHT YOU WERE CUTE TOO JUST NOW...
OH! SO THAT'S WHY IT SEEMED AWKWARD BETWEEN YOU TWO?
...YEAH.
She has a poker face. I never know what she's actually thinking.
HEY, THAT'S NOT TRUE!!
NATSUE SOMETIMES...
...SMILES REALLY BIG!
AND SHE CAN GET PRETTY ANGRY, TOO!
NO FACIAL EXPRESSION AT ALL.
GLOOM
...
YOU'RE RIGHT. IT'S IMPOSSIBLE TO TELL WHAT SHE'S THINKING.
I'm a failure as a younger student...
HEY, DON'T BE THAT CONCERNED ABOUT THAT!
Come on!

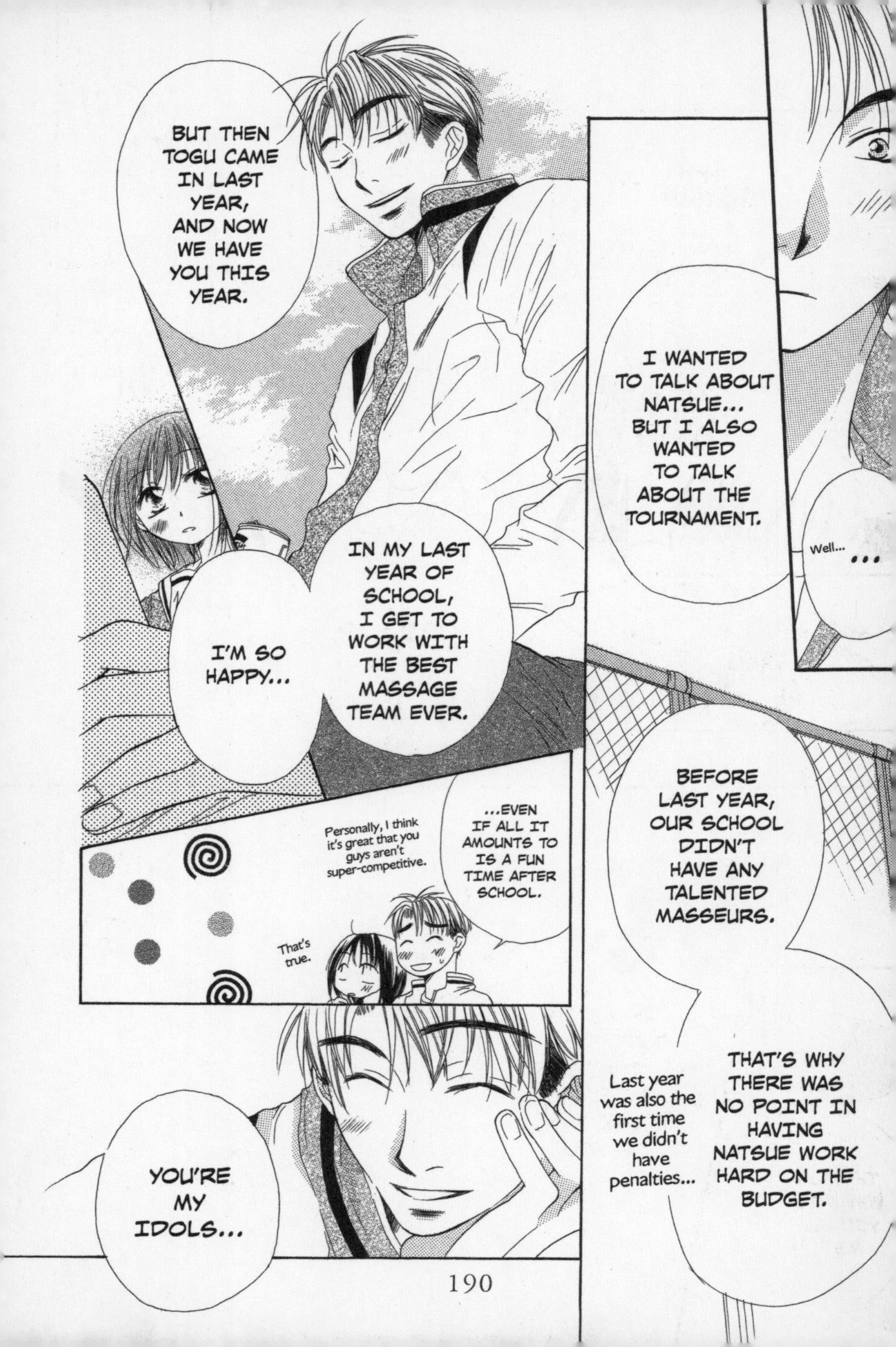
Well... ...
I WANTED TO TALK ABOUT NATSUE... BUT I ALSO WANTED TO TALK ABOUT THE TOURNAMENT.
BEFORE LAST YEAR, OUR SCHOOL DIDN'T HAVE ANY TALENTED MASSEURS.
THAT'S WHY THERE WAS NO POINT IN HAVING NATSUE WORK HARD ON THE BUDGET.
Last year was also the first time we didn't have penalties...
BUT THEN TOGU CAME IN LAST YEAR, AND NOW WE HAVE YOU THIS YEAR.
IN MY LAST YEAR OF SCHOOL, I GET TO WORK WITH THE BEST MASSAGE TEAM EVER.
I'M SO HAPPY...
...EVEN IF ALL IT AMOUNTS TO IS A FUN TIME AFTER SCHOOL.
Personally, I think it's great that you guys aren't super-competitive.
That's true.
YOU'RE MY IDOLS...

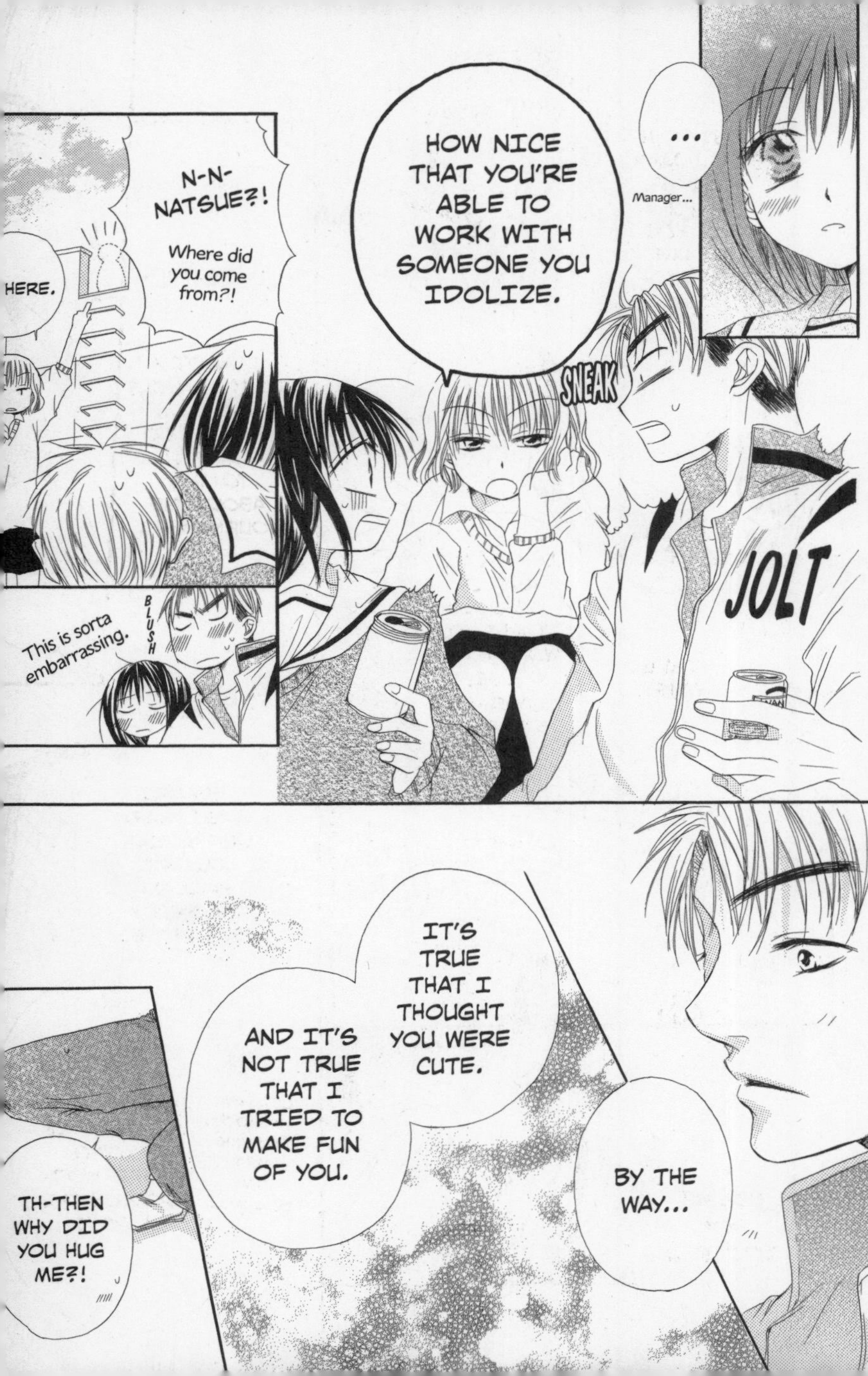
...
Manager...
HOW NICE THAT YOU'RE ABLE TO WORK WITH SOMEONE YOU IDOLIZE.
SNEAK
JOLT
N-N-NATSUE?!
Where did you come from?!
HERE.
BLUSH
This is sorta embarrassing.
BY THE WAY...
IT'S TRUE THAT I THOUGHT YOU WERE CUTE.
AND IT'S NOT TRUE THAT I TRIED TO MAKE FUN OF YOU.
TH-THEN WHY DID YOU HUG ME?!

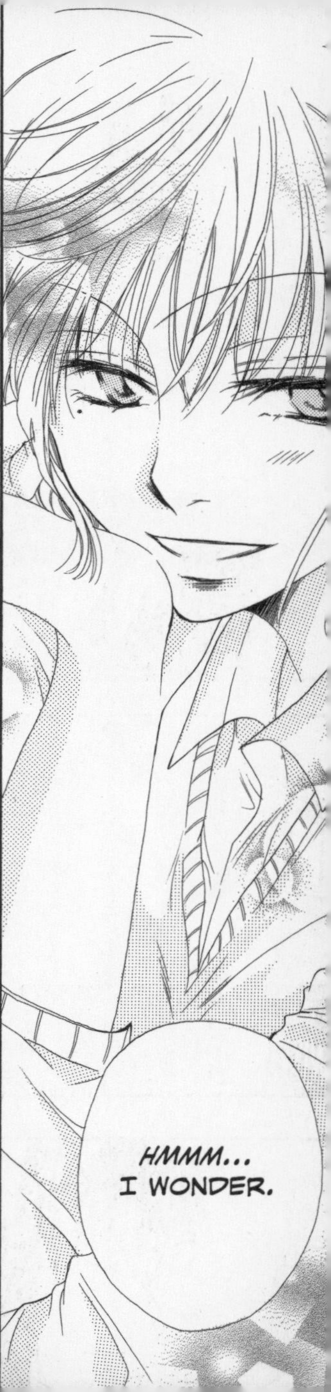
HMMM...
I WONDER.

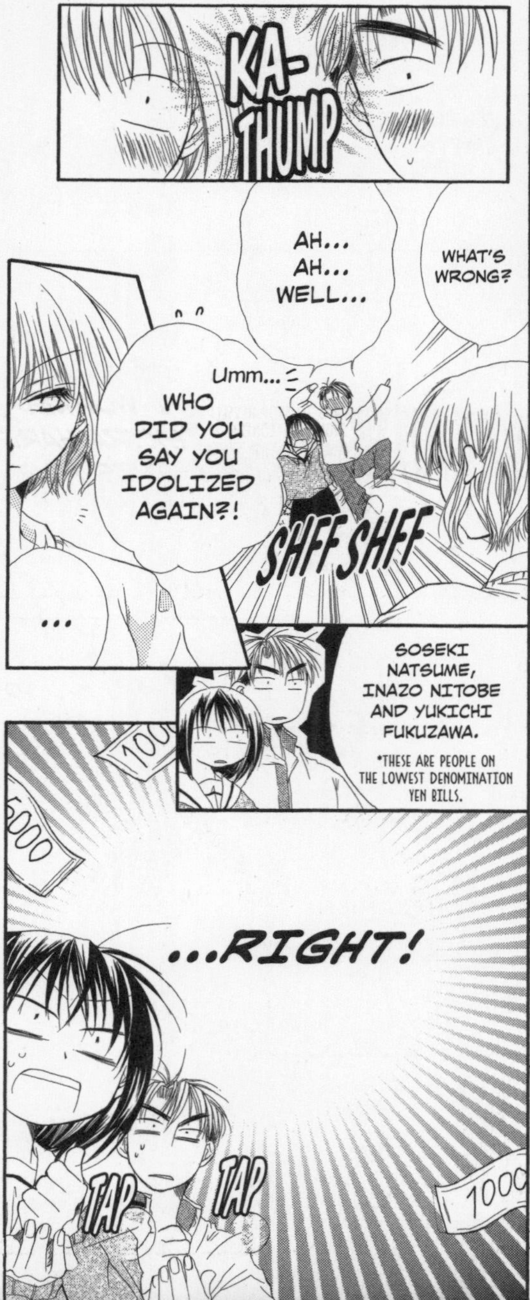
KA-THUMP
WHAT'S WRONG?
AH... AH... WELL...
Umm...
WHO DID YOU SAY YOU IDOLIZED AGAIN?!
SHFF SHFF
...
SOSEKI NATSUME, INAZO NITOBE AND YUKICHI FUKUZAWA.
*THESE ARE PEOPLE ON THE LOWEST DENOMINATION YEN BILLS.
1000
5000
...RIGHT!
TAP
TAP
1000

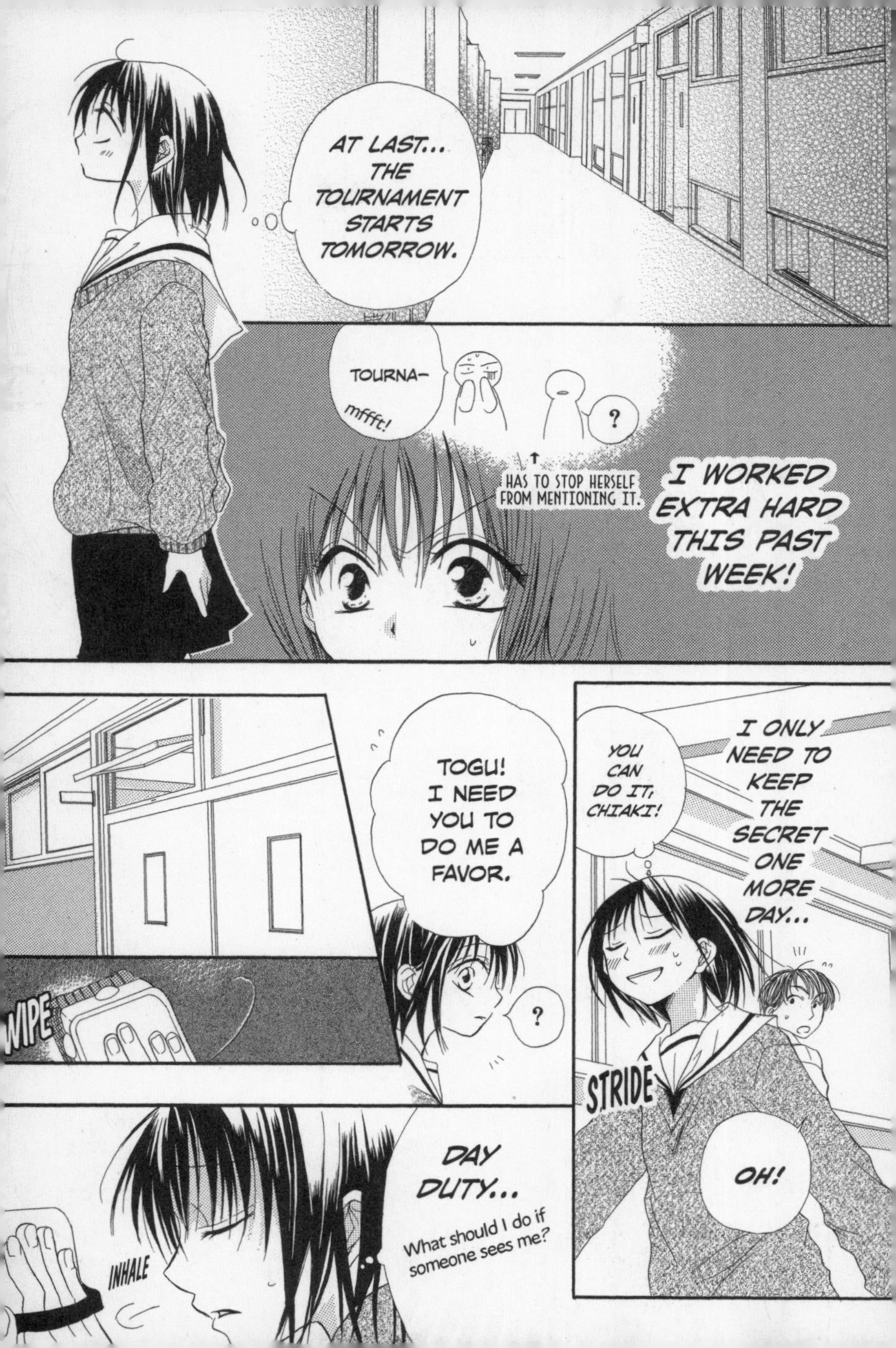
AT LAST... THE TOURNAMENT STARTS TOMORROW.
TOURNA-
mffft!
?
HAS TO STOP HERSELF FROM MENTIONING IT.
I WORKED EXTRA HARD THIS PAST WEEK!
I ONLY NEED TO KEEP THE SECRET ONE MORE DAY...
YOU CAN DO IT, CHIAKI!
STRIDE
OH!
TOGU! I NEED YOU TO DO ME A FAVOR.
?
WIPE
DAY DUTY...
What should I do if someone sees me?
INHALE

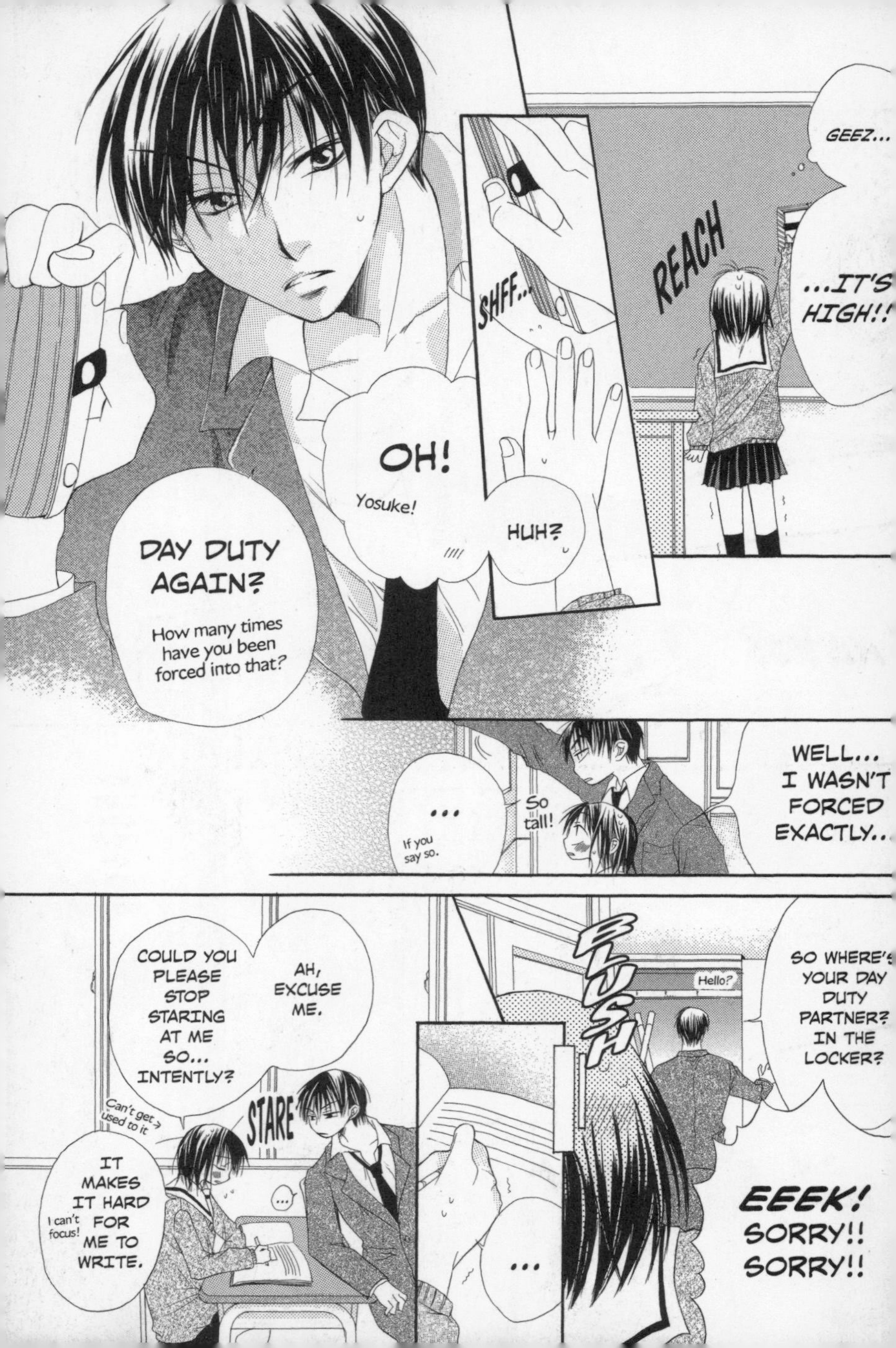
GEEZ...
REACH
...IT'S HIGH!!
SHFF...
HUH?
OH!
Yosuke!
DAY DUTY AGAIN?
How many times have you been forced into that?
WELL... I WASN'T FORCED EXACTLY...
So tall!
...
If you say so.
SO WHERE'S YOUR DAY DUTY PARTNER? IN THE LOCKER?
Hello?
BLUSH
EEEK! SORRY!! SORRY!!
...
COULD YOU PLEASE STOP STARING AT ME SO... INTENTLY?
AH, EXCUSE ME.
STARE
Can't get used to it
...
IT MAKES IT HARD FOR ME TO WRITE.
I can't focus!

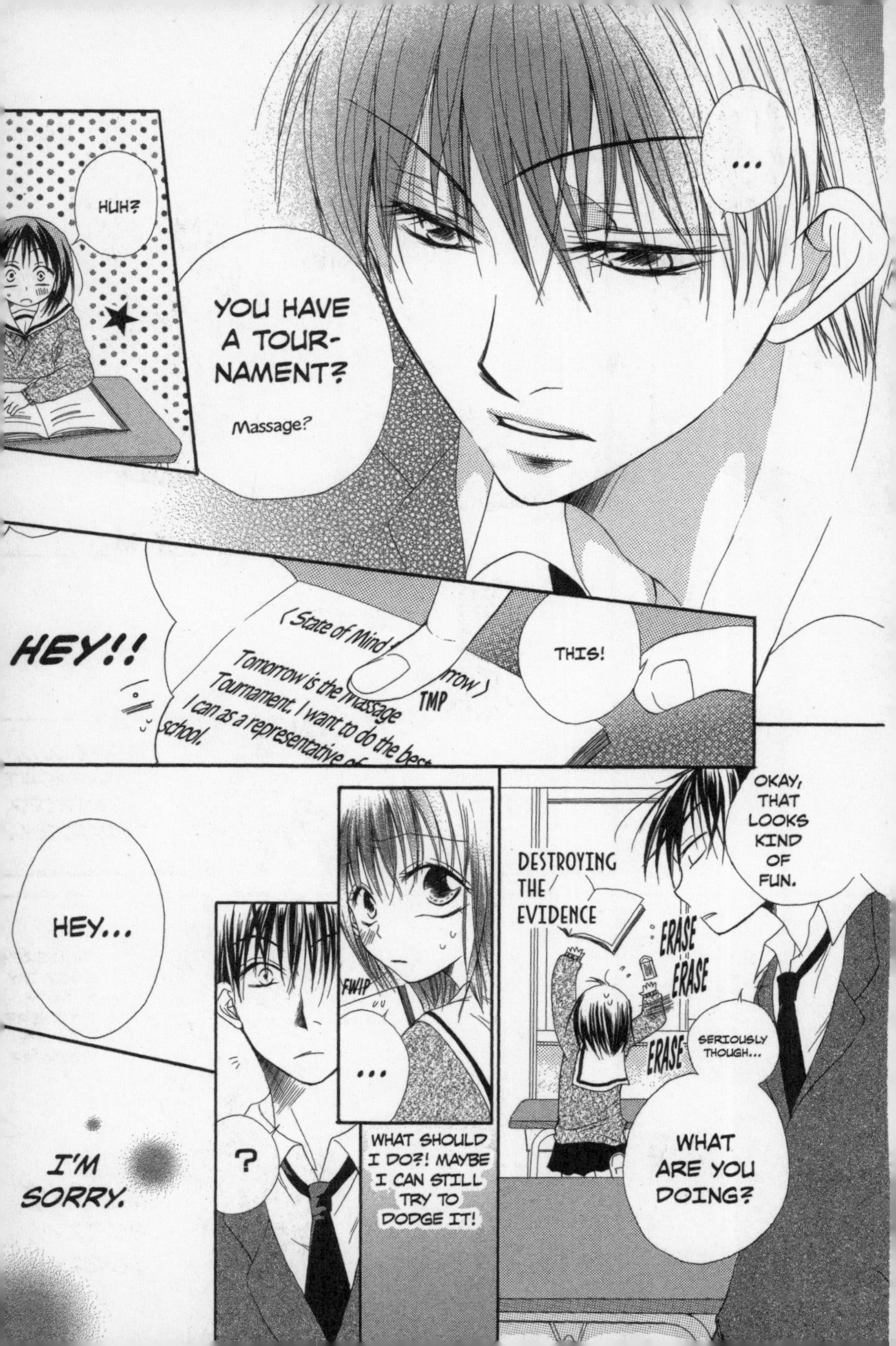
...
YOU HAVE A TOUR-NAMENT?
Massage?
HUH?
THIS!
〈State of Mind f rrow〉
Tomorrow is the Massage Tournament. I want to do the best I can as a representative of school.
TMP
HEY!!
OKAY, THAT LOOKS KIND OF FUN.
DESTROYING THE EVIDENCE
ERASE
ERASE
ERASE
SERIOUSLY THOUGH...
WHAT ARE YOU DOING?
FWIP
...
WHAT SHOULD I DO?! MAYBE I CAN STILL TRY TO DODGE IT!
?
HEY...
I'M SORRY.

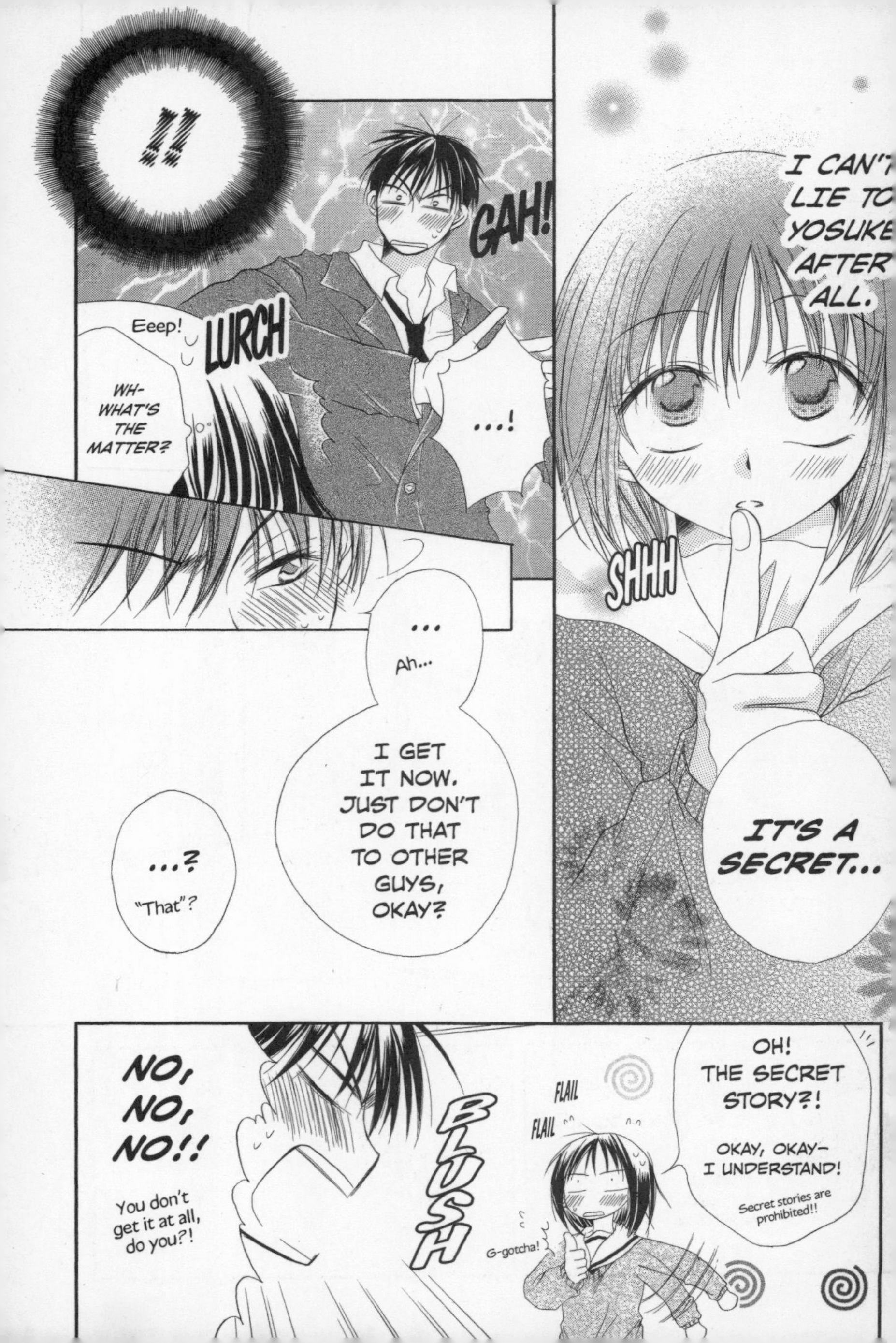
I CAN'T LIE TO YOSUKE AFTER ALL.
SHHH
IT'S A SECRET...
!!
GAH!
Eeep!
LURCH
WH- WHAT'S THE MATTER?
...!
...
Ah...
I GET IT NOW. JUST DON'T DO THAT TO OTHER GUYS, OKAY?
...?
"That"?
OH! THE SECRET STORY?!
OKAY, OKAY— I UNDERSTAND!
Secret stories are prohibited!!
FLAIL
FLAIL
G-gotcha!
BLUSH
NO, NO, NO!!
You don't get it at all, do you?!

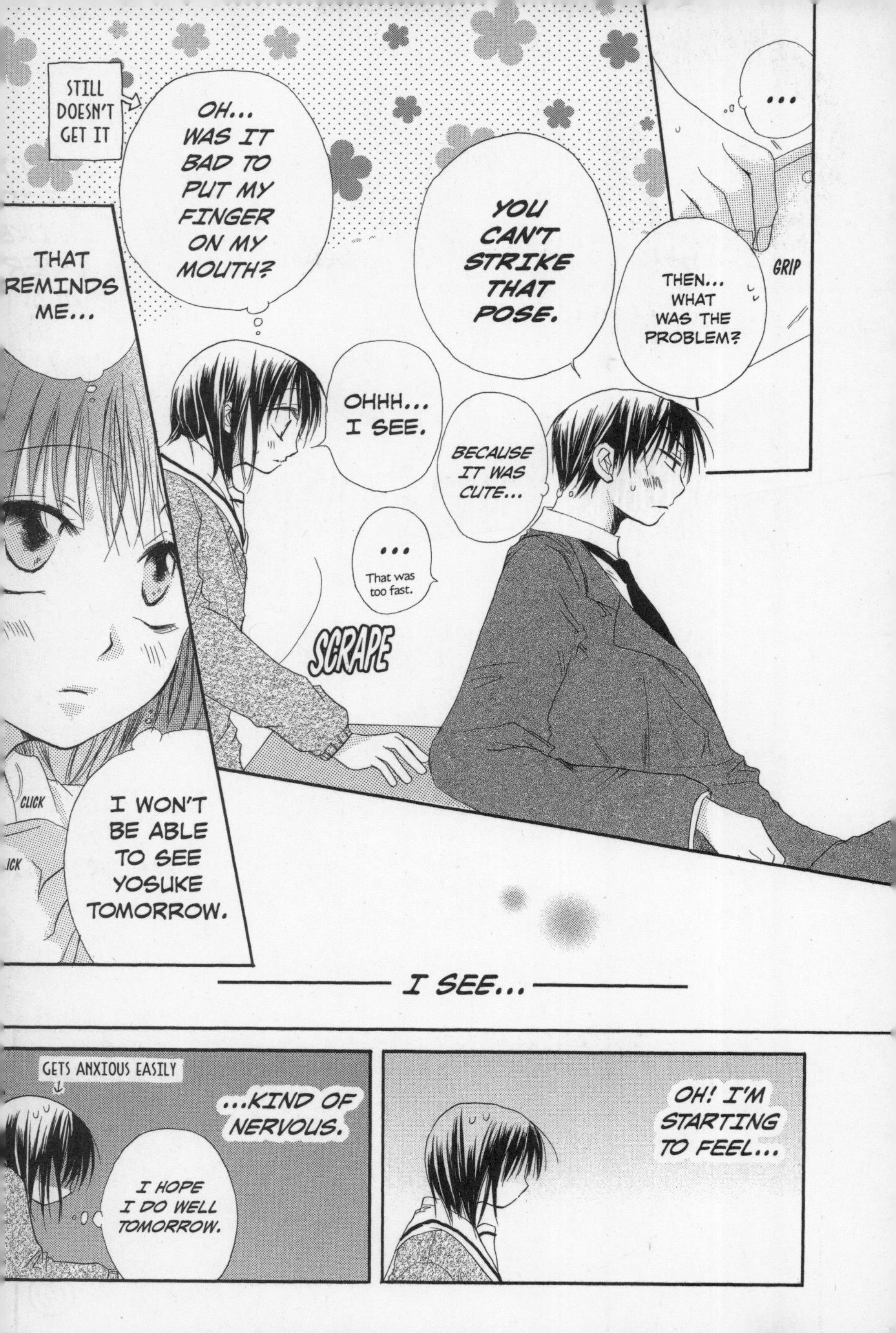
...
GRIP
THEN... WHAT WAS THE PROBLEM?
YOU CAN'T STRIKE THAT POSE.
OH... WAS IT BAD TO PUT MY FINGER ON MY MOUTH?
STILL DOESN'T GET IT
BECAUSE IT WAS CUTE...
OHHH... I SEE.
...
That was too fast.
SCRAPE
THAT REMINDS ME...
CLICK
I WON'T BE ABLE TO SEE YOSUKE TOMORROW.
LICK
I SEE...
OH! I'M STARTING TO FEEL...
...KIND OF NERVOUS.
GETS ANXIOUS EASILY
I HOPE I DO WELL TOMORROW.

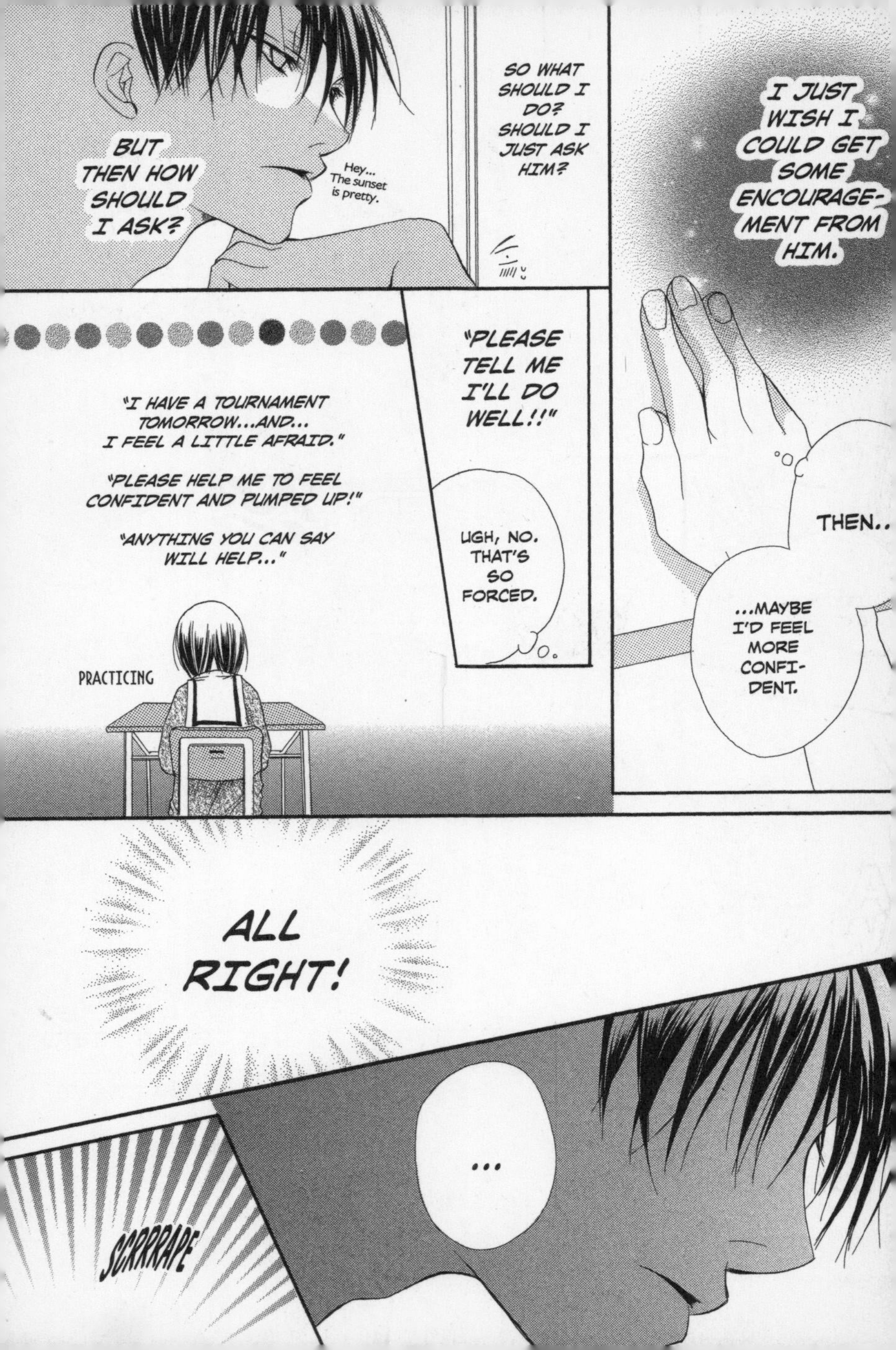
I JUST WISH I COULD GET SOME ENCOURAGE-MENT FROM HIM.
THEN..
...MAYBE I'D FEEL MORE CONFI-DENT.
SO WHAT SHOULD I DO? SHOULD I JUST ASK HIM?
Hey... The sunset is pretty.
BUT THEN HOW SHOULD I ASK?
"PLEASE TELL ME I'LL DO WELL!!"
UGH, NO. THAT'S SO FORCED.
"I HAVE A TOURNAMENT TOMORROW...AND... I FEEL A LITTLE AFRAID."
"PLEASE HELP ME TO FEEL CONFIDENT AND PUMPED UP!"
"ANYTHING YOU CAN SAY WILL HELP..."
PRACTICING
ALL RIGHT!
...
SCRRRAPE

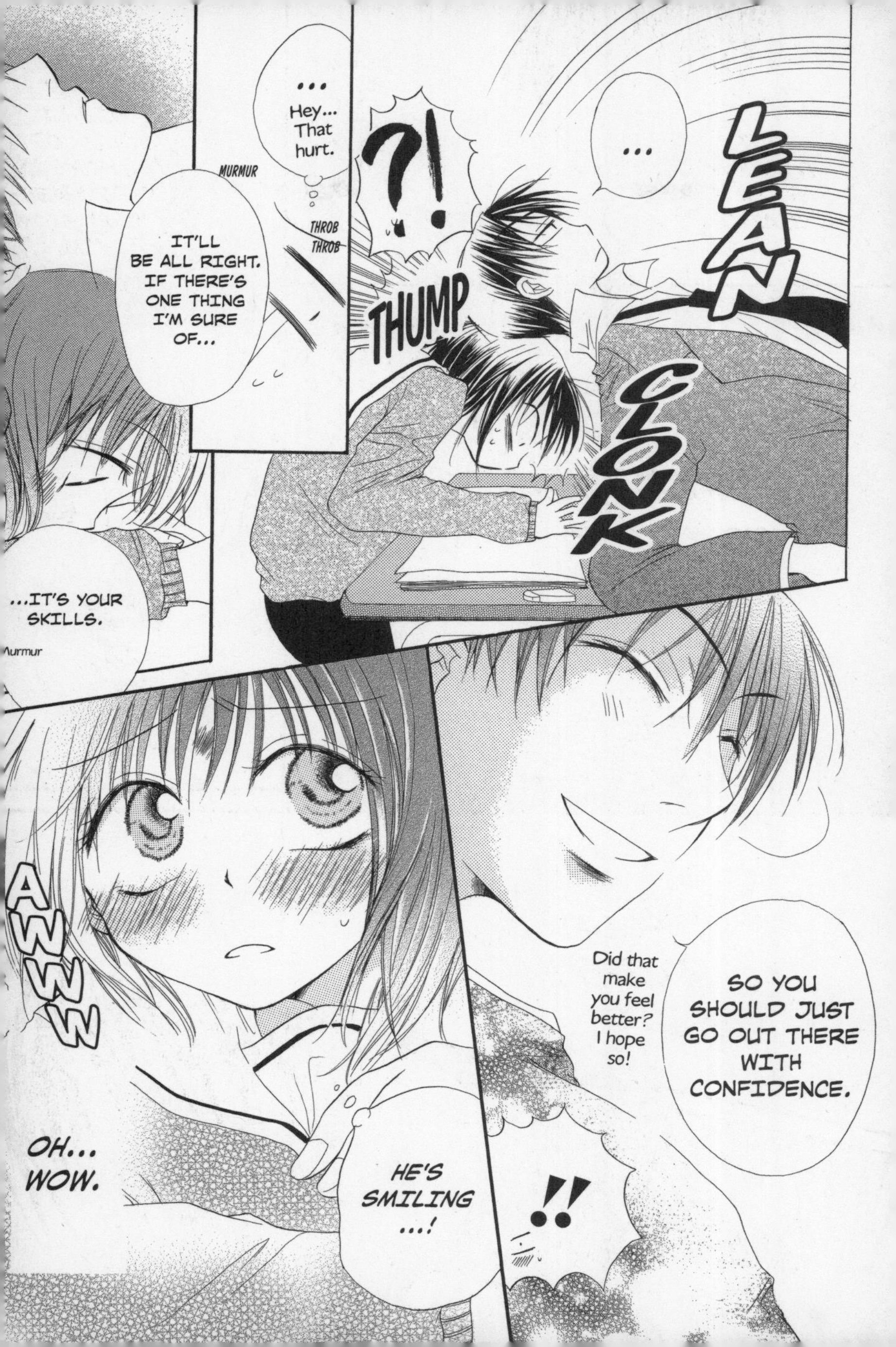
...
LEAN
CLONK
THUMP
?!
...
Hey... That hurt.
THROB THROB
MURMUR
IT'LL BE ALL RIGHT. IF THERE'S ONE THING I'M SURE OF...
...IT'S YOUR SKILLS.
Murmur
SO YOU SHOULD JUST GO OUT THERE WITH CONFIDENCE.
Did that make you feel better? I hope so!
!!
AWWW
OH... WOW.
HE'S SMILING ...!

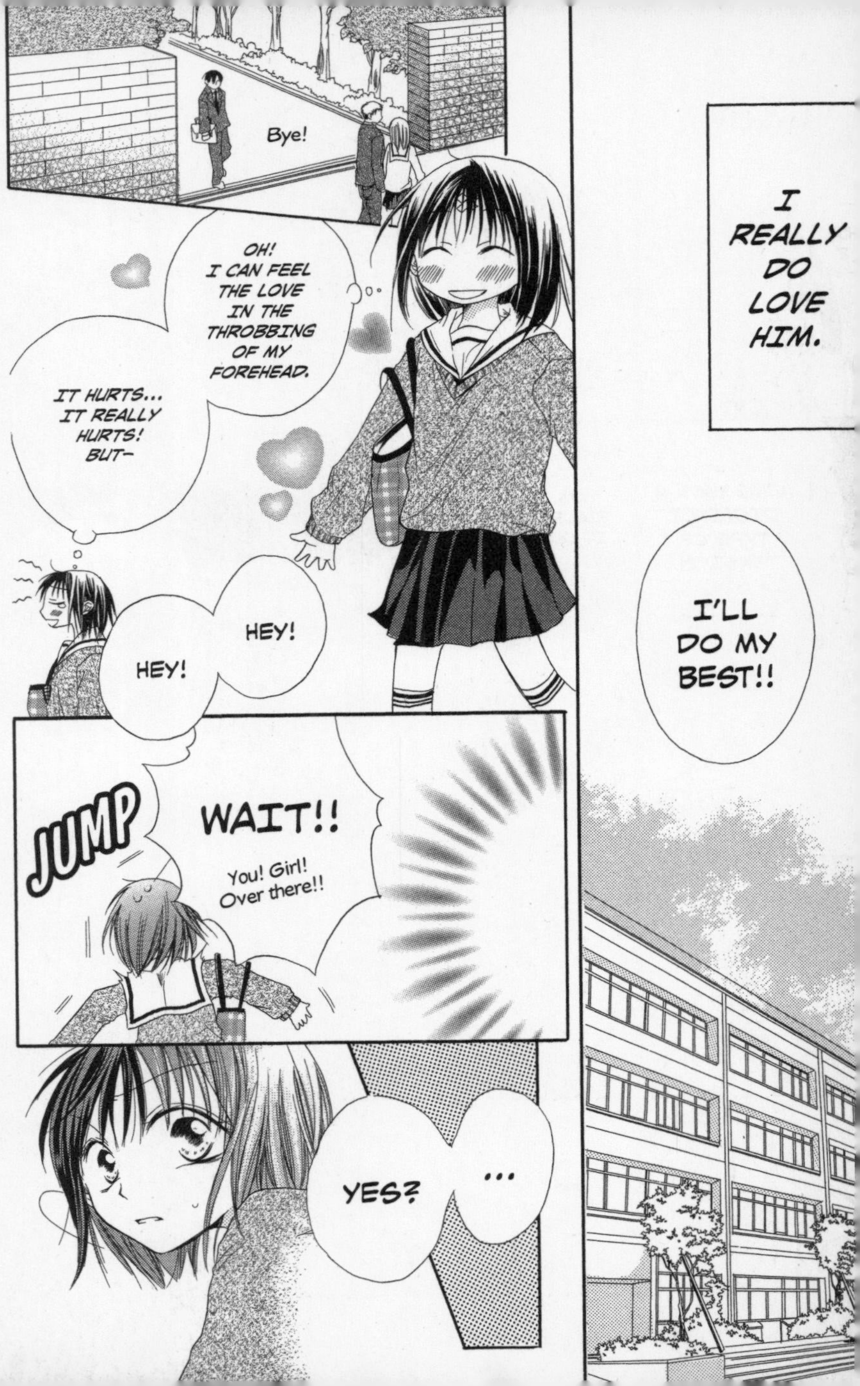

I REALLY DO LOVE HIM.
I'LL DO MY BEST!!
Bye!
OH! I CAN FEEL THE LOVE IN THE THROBBING OF MY FOREHEAD.
IT HURTS... IT REALLY HURTS! BUT-
HEY!
HEY!
WAIT!!
JUMP
You! Girl! Over there!!
...
YES?

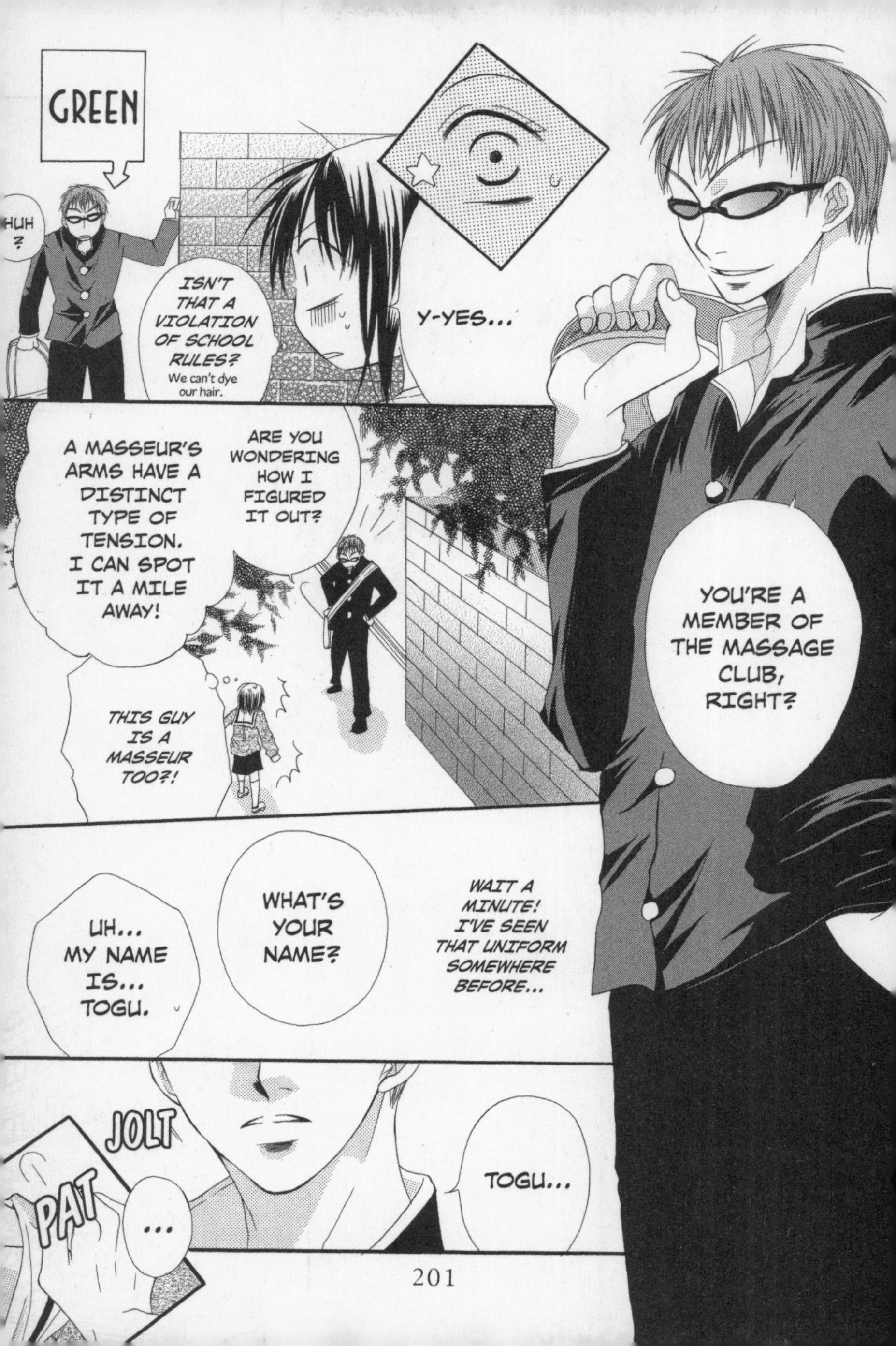
YOU'RE A MEMBER OF THE MASSAGE CLUB, RIGHT?
Y-YES...
ISN'T THAT A VIOLATION OF SCHOOL RULES?
We can't dye our hair.
GREEN
HUH?
ARE YOU WONDERING HOW I FIGURED IT OUT?
A MASSEUR'S ARMS HAVE A DISTINCT TYPE OF TENSION. I CAN SPOT IT A MILE AWAY!
THIS GUY IS A MASSEUR TOO?!
WAIT A MINUTE! I'VE SEEN THAT UNIFORM SOMEWHERE BEFORE...
WHAT'S YOUR NAME?
UH... MY NAME IS... TOGU.
TOGU...
JOLT
...
PAT

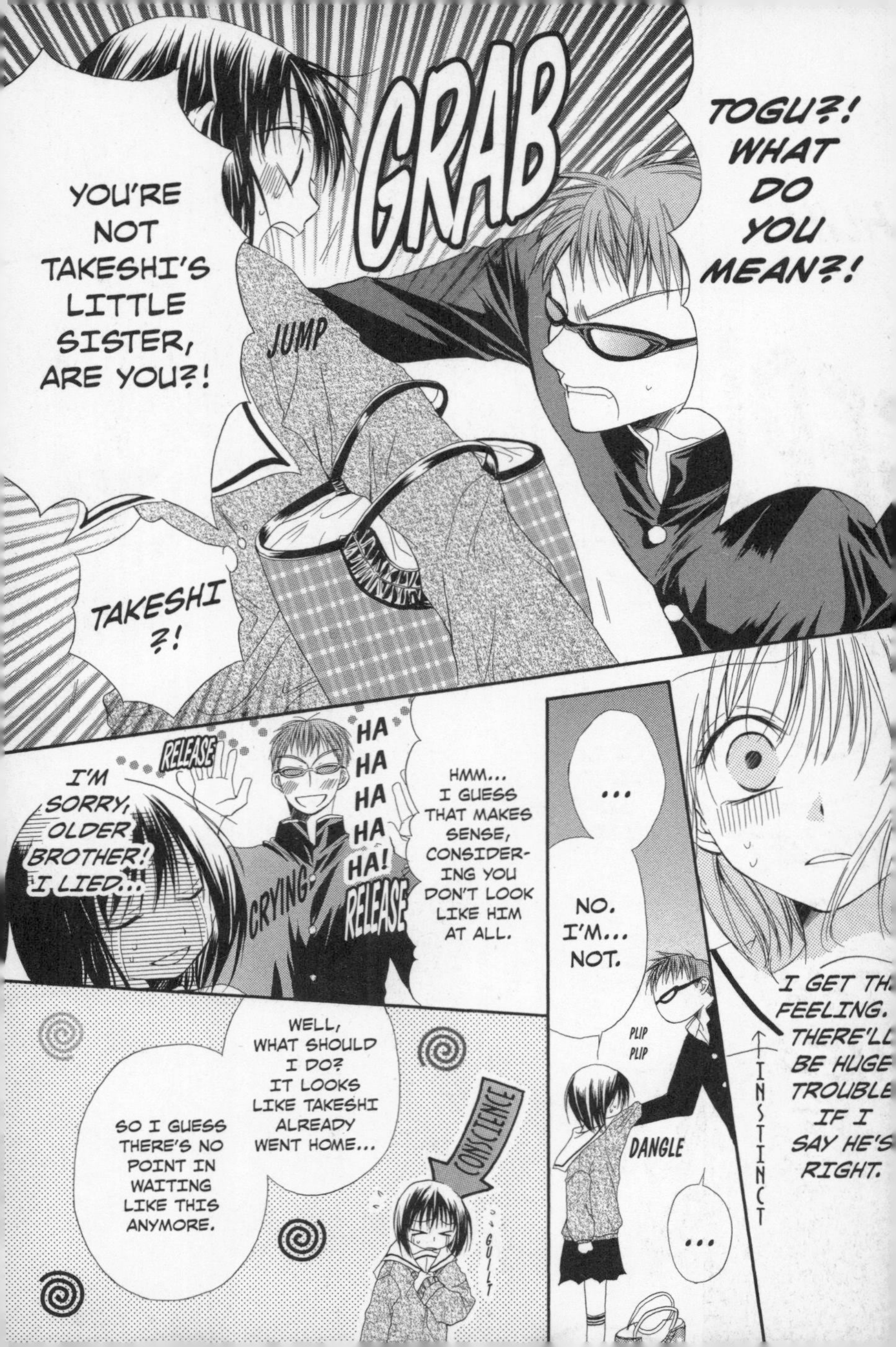
TOGU?! WHAT DO YOU MEAN?!
GRAB
YOU'RE NOT TAKESHI'S LITTLE SISTER, ARE YOU?!
JUMP
TAKESHI ?!
...
NO. I'M... NOT.
I GET TH FEELING. THERE'LL BE HUGE TROUBLE IF I SAY HE'S RIGHT.
INSTINCT
PLIP PLIP
DANGLE
...
HMM... I GUESS THAT MAKES SENSE, CONSIDER-ING YOU DON'T LOOK LIKE HIM AT ALL.
HA HA HA HA HA!
RELEASE
RELEASE
CRYING
I'M SORRY, OLDER BROTHER! I LIED...
WELL, WHAT SHOULD I DO? IT LOOKS LIKE TAKESHI ALREADY WENT HOME...
SO I GUESS THERE'S NO POINT IN WAITING LIKE THIS ANYMORE.
CONSCIENCE
GUILT

...
HEY, CAN I ASK YOU TO DELIVER A MESSAGE TO HIM?
GRIN
GRAB
OH, YES! SURE!
TELL HIM...
I'LL BE WAITING AT THE TOURNAMENT.
HUH?
EEP!
WHAT DOES THAT MEAN?

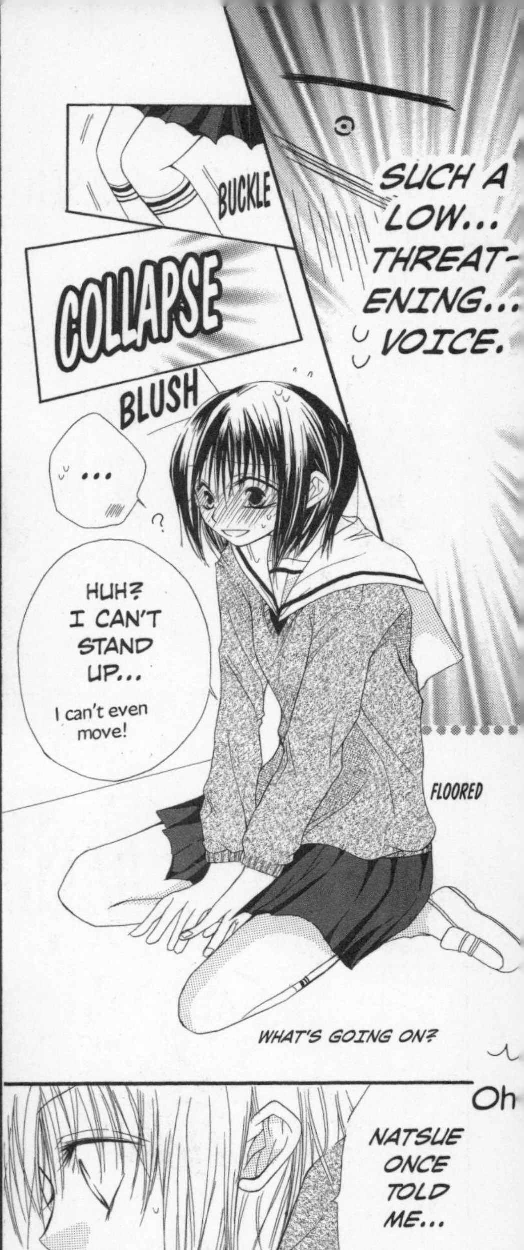
SUCH A LOW... THREAT-ENING... VOICE.
BUCKLE
COLLAPSE
BLUSH
...
HUH? I CAN'T STAND UP...
I can't even move!
FLOORED
WHAT'S GOING ON?
Oh
NATSUE ONCE TOLD ME...

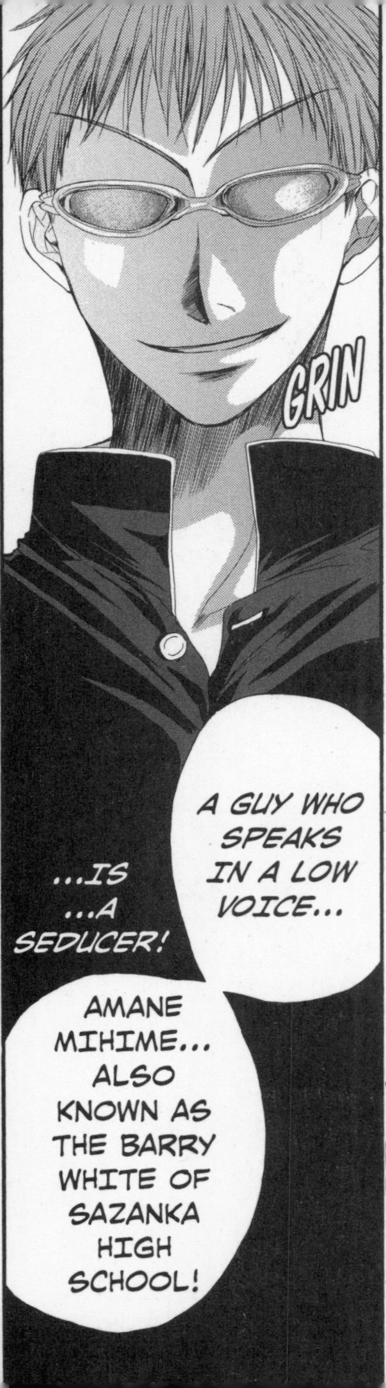
GRIN
A GUY WHO SPEAKS IN A LOW VOICE...
...IS ...A SEDUCER!
AMANE MIHIME... ALSO KNOWN AS THE BARRY WHITE OF SAZANKA HIGH SCHOOL!

THE MAGIC TOUCH, PART 11 / END

GIVING A PRESENT, PART 2

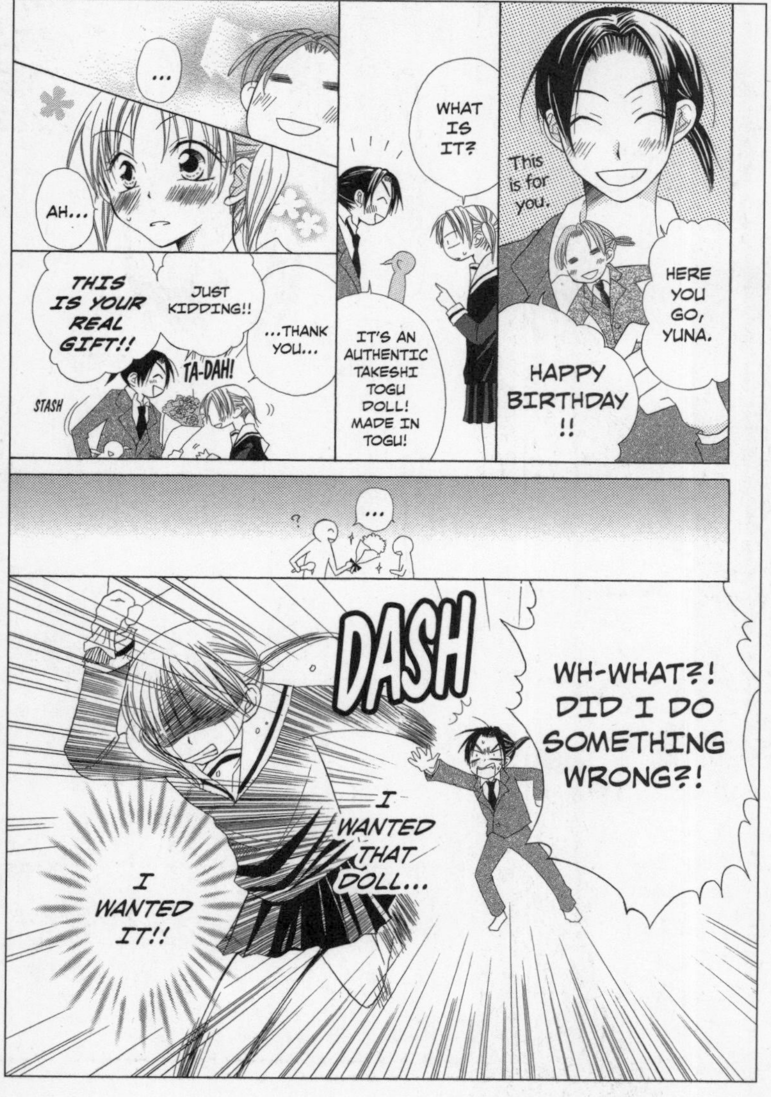
This is for you.
HERE YOU GO, YUNA.
HAPPY BIRTHDAY!!
WHAT IS IT?
IT'S AN AUTHENTIC TAKESHI TOGU DOLL! MADE IN TOGU!
...
AH...
...THANK YOU...
JUST KIDDING!!
THIS IS YOUR REAL GIFT!!
TA-DAH!
STASH
...
WH-WHAT?! DID I DO SOMETHING WRONG?!
DASH
I WANTED THAT DOLL...
I WANTED IT!!

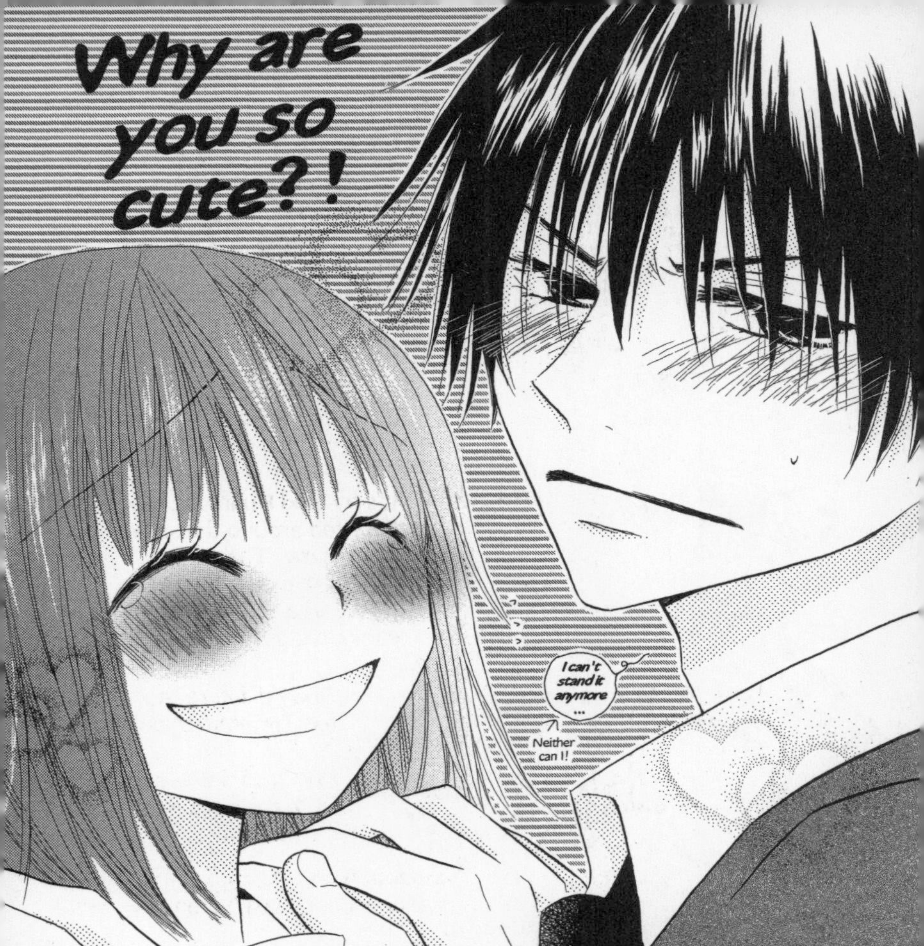
Why are you so cute?!
I can't stand it anymore...
Neither can I!

CONGRATULATIONS ON THE MAGIC TOUCH VOLUME 2!

(I LOVE THESE TWO!)
VERSION TWO:
THE MANAGER AND NATSUE

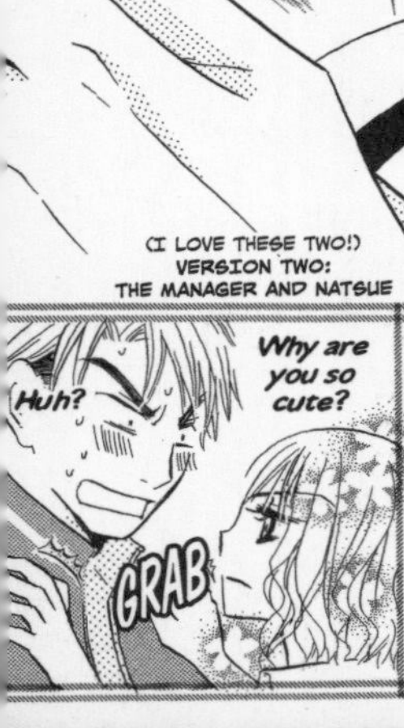
Why are you so cute?
Huh?
GRAB

A massage manga! You can almost feel the knots unravel before you even open the book! And once you ***do*** start reading, Chiaki's cuteness is even ***more*** relaxing than a massage!! I'm completely knocked out. I, Yuki Fujimoto, am in complete support of *The Magic Touch* and its intrepid champion, Miss Tsubaki! Congratulations on Volume 2!! Hey... I'm kind of writing the same thing that Iyo Takarada did in Volume 1. <laughter> Well, thanks for the space!

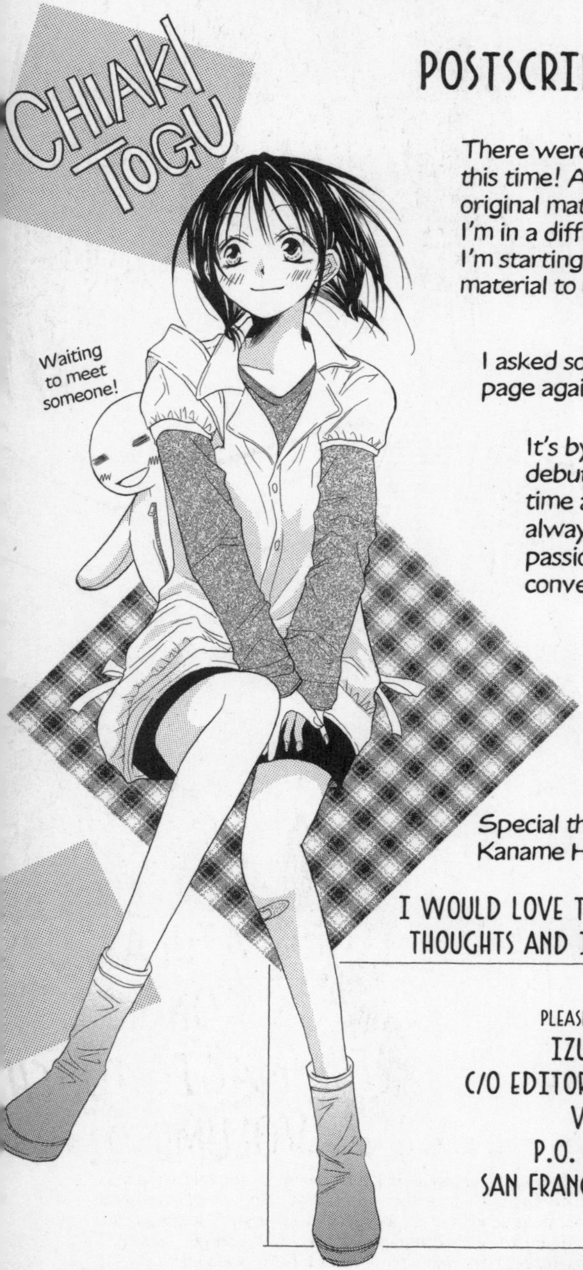
CHIAKI TOGU
Waiting to meet someone!

POSTSCRIPT

There were three bonus manga this time! And a little bit of original material for this volume... I'm in a difficult situation because I'm starting to run out of old material to use. What should I do?

I asked someone to make a guest page again! That's it right there.

It's by Yuki Fujimoto, who debuted around the same time as me. Thanks for always providing me with passionate and interesting conversations. I love you!!

And I'd like to thank you, too, for reading this book.

I want to thank everyone from the bottom of my heart...

Special thanks to Sister, Kaname H., Chiaki N., and my Editor.

I WOULD LOVE TO HEAR YOUR THOUGHTS AND IMPRESSIONS.

PLEASE SEND LETTERS TO:
IZUMI TSUBAKI
C/O EDITOR, THE MAGIC TOUCH
VIZ MEDIA
P.O. BOX 77010
SAN FRANCISCO, CA 94107

Izumi Tsubaki began drawing manga in her first
year of high school. She was soon selected to be
in the top ten of *Hana to Yume*'s HMC (Hana to
Yume Mangaka Course), and subsequently won
Hana to Yume's Big Challenge contest. Her debut
title, *Chijimete Distance* (Shrink the Distance),
ran in 2002 in *Hana to Yume* magazine, issue 17.
In addition to *The Magic Touch* (originally published in Japan as *Oyayubi kara Romance*, or
"Romance from the Thumbs"), she is also currently
working on the manga series *Oresama Teacher*
(I'm the Teacher).

Tsubaki-sensei hails from Saitama Prefecture, her
birthday is December 11, and she confesses that
she enjoys receiving massages more than she
enjoys giving them.

THE MAGIC TOUCH
Vol. 2
The Shojo Beat Manga Edition

STORY AND ART BY
IZUMI TSUBAKI

English Adaptation/Lorelei Laird
Translation/Nori Minami
Touch-up Art & Lettering/James Gaubatz
Design/Sean Lee
Editor/Carol Fox

Editor in Chief, Books/Alvin Lu
Editor in Chief, Magazines/Marc Weidenbaum
VP, Publishing Licensing/Rika Inouye
VP, Sales & Product Marketing/Gonzalo Ferreyra
VP, Creative/Linda Espinosa
Publisher/Hyoe Narita

Oyayubi kara Romance by Izumi Tsubaki
© Izumi Tsubaki 2003
All rights reserved.
First published in Japan in 2004 by HAKUSENSHA, Inc., Tokyo.
English language translation rights arranged with HAKUSENSHA, Inc., Tokyo.
The stories, characters and incidents mentioned in this publication are entirely fictional.

No portion of this book may be reproduced or transmitted in any form or by any means
without written permission from the copyright holders.

Printed in Canada

Published by VIZ Media, LLC
P.O. Box 77010
San Francisco, CA 94107

Shojo Beat Manga Edition
10 9 8 7 6 5 4 3 2 1
First printing, June 2009

PARENTAL ADVISORY
THE MAGIC TOUCH is rated T+ for
Older Teen and is recommended
for ages 13 and up.
ratings.viz.com

www.viz.com

store.viz.com

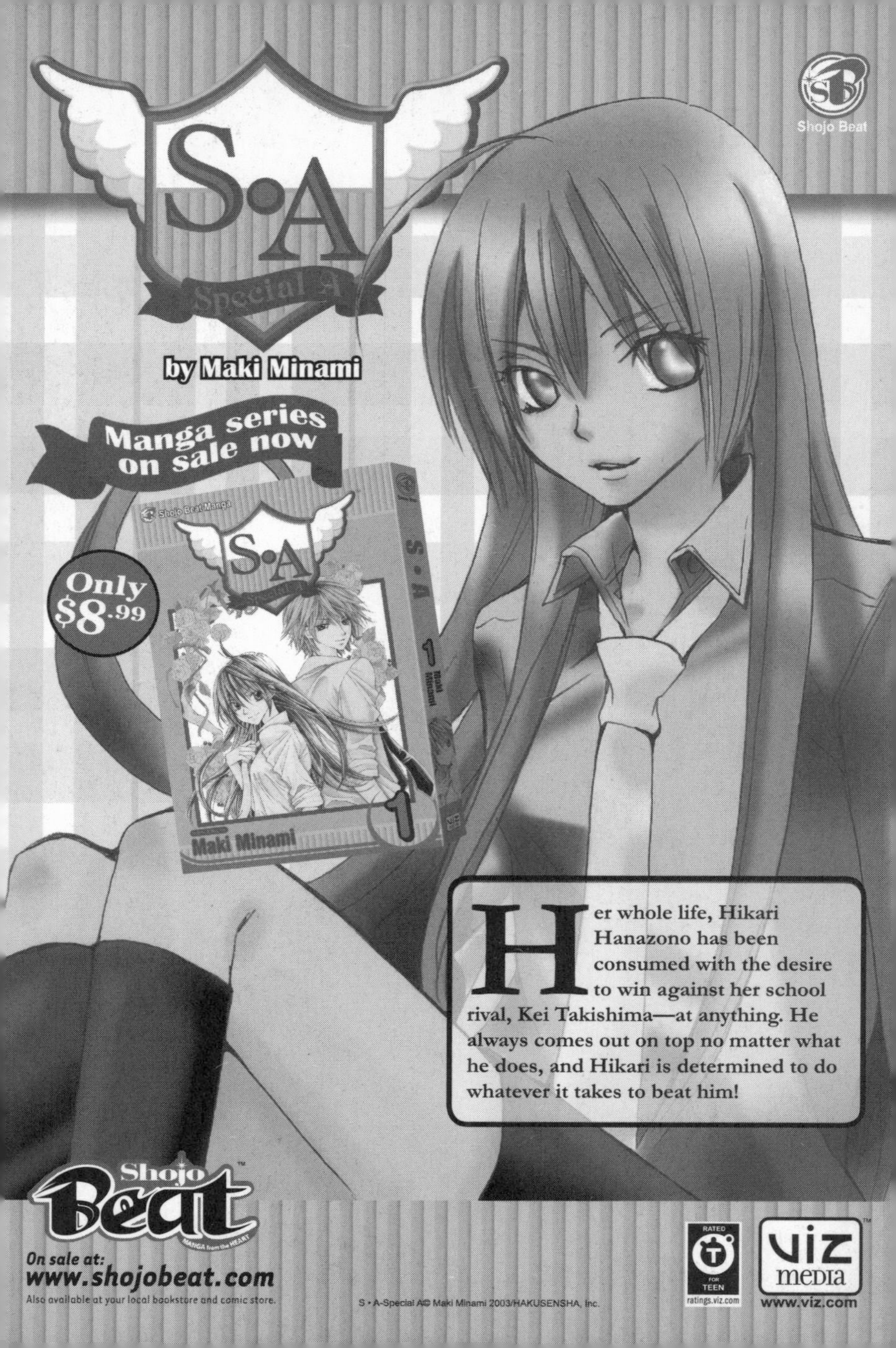

S•A
Special A
by Maki Minami
Shojo Beat
Manga series on sale now
Only $8.99
Shojo Beat Manga
Maki Minami
Her whole life, Hikari Hanazono has been consumed with the desire to win against her school rival, Kei Takishima—at anything. He always comes out on top no matter what he does, and Hikari is determined to do whatever it takes to beat him!
Shojo Beat
MANGA from the HEART
On sale at:
www.shojobeat.com
Also available at your local bookstore and comic store.
S • A-Special A© Maki Minami 2003/HAKUSENSHA, Inc.
RATED T FOR TEEN
ratings.viz.com
VIZ media
www.viz.com

Compelled to Serve
Captive Hearts

Megumi lives a carefree life of luxury
until he inexplicably finds himself
kneeling at the feet of a girl he's never
met. How did he go from being happily
served to being the humiliated servant?

Find out in *Captive Hearts*—
manga series on sale now!

Also known as *Toraware no Minoue*

On sale at
www.shojobeat.com
Also available at your
local bookstore and
comic store.

By Matsuri Hino,
creator of
Vampire Knight
and *MeruPuri*

Toraware no Minoue © Matsuri Hino
1998/HAKUSENSHA, Inc.

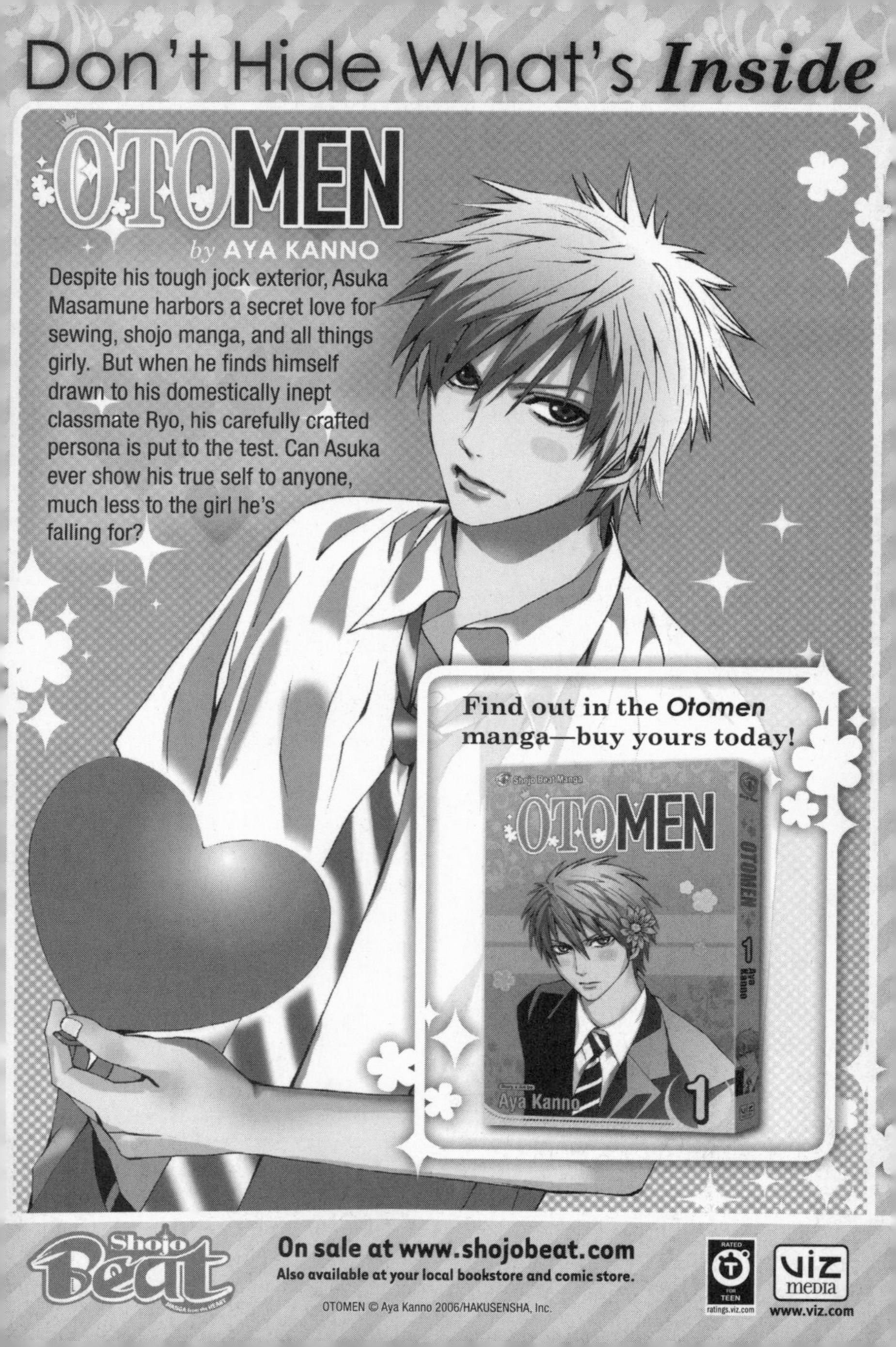
Don't Hide What's *Inside*
OTOMEN
by AYA KANNO
Despite his tough jock exterior, Asuka Masamune harbors a secret love for sewing, shojo manga, and all things girly. But when he finds himself drawn to his domestically inept classmate Ryo, his carefully crafted persona is put to the test. Can Asuka ever show his true self to anyone, much less to the girl he's falling for?
Find out in the *Otomen* manga—buy yours today!
Shojo Beat Manga
OTOMEN
1
Aya Kanno
Shojo Beat
On sale at www.shojobeat.com
Also available at your local bookstore and comic store.
OTOMEN © Aya Kanno 2006/HAKUSENSHA, Inc.
RATED T FOR TEEN
ratings.viz.com
VIZ media
www.viz.com

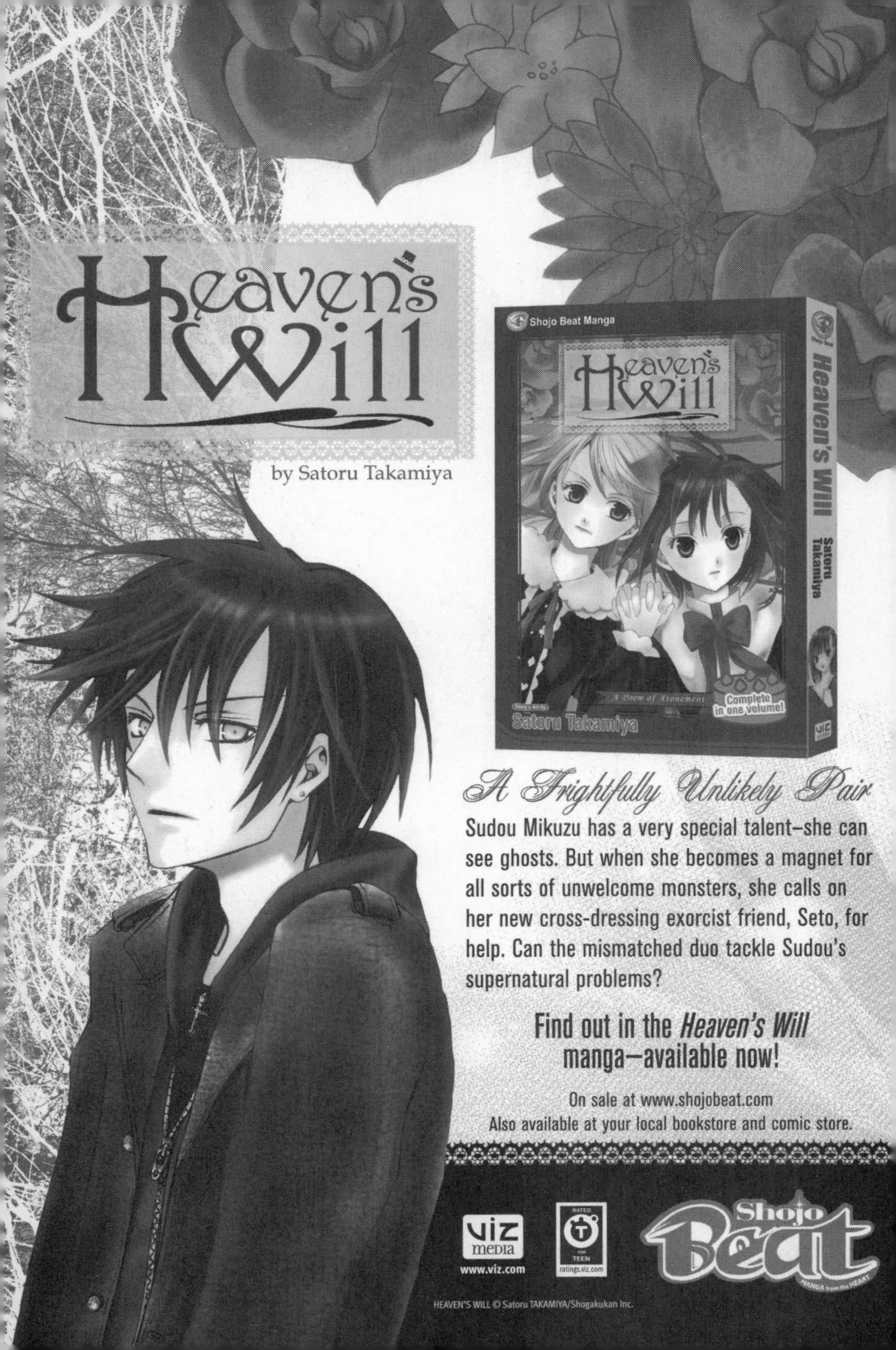
Heaven's Will
by Satoru Takamiya
Shojo Beat Manga
Heaven's Will
A Poem of Atonement
Satoru Takamiya
Complete in one volume!
A Frightfully Unlikely Pair
Sudou Mikuzu has a very special talent–she can see ghosts. But when she becomes a magnet for all sorts of unwelcome monsters, she calls on her new cross-dressing exorcist friend, Seto, for help. Can the mismatched duo tackle Sudou's supernatural problems?
Find out in the *Heaven's Will* manga—available now!
On sale at www.shojobeat.com
Also available at your local bookstore and comic store.
VIZ media
www.viz.com
RATED T FOR TEEN
ratings.viz.com
Shojo Beat
MANGA from the HEART
HEAVEN'S WILL © Satoru TAKAMIYA/Shogakukan Inc.

Tell us what you think about Shojo Beat Manga!

Our survey is now available online. Go to:

shojobeat.com/mangasurvey

Help us make our product offerings better!

THE REAL DRAMA BEGINS IN...

VIZ media

Shojo Beat

FULL MOON WO SAGASHITE © 2001 by Arina Tanemura/SHUEISHA Inc.
Fushigi Yûgi: Genbu Kaiden © 2004 Yuu WATASE/Shogakukan Inc.
Ouran Koko Host Club © Bisco Hatori 2002/HAKUSENSHA, Inc.